Jin쌤's
DIGITAL
SAT
PRACTICE
TESTS

Jin 쌤's
DIGITAL SAT PRACTICE TESTS

발 행   2024년 11월 15일 초판 1쇄

저 자   배진오
발행인   최영민
발행처   피앤피북
주 소   경기도 파주시 신촌로 16
전 화   031 – 8071 – 0088
팩 스   031 – 942 – 8688
전자우편   hermonh@naver.com
출판등록   2015년 3월 27일
등록번호   제406 – 2015 – 31호

ISBN   979 – 11 – 94085 – 21 – 8 (53410)

✥ 저자직강 인터넷 강의는 SAT, AP No.1 인터넷 강의 사이트인
  마스터프랩 (www.masterprep.net) 에서 보실 수 있습니다.

Jin쌤's
DIGITAL
SAT
PRACTICE
TESTS

4 Full-length Reading and Writing Tests

Jin Bae 지음

HERMONHOUSE

A Personal Message from Jin 쌤

Hey there,

I am SO glad you're here!

Let's get right to it.

My mission is simple: I want to help you miss fewer than five questions consistently in the Evidence-Based Reading and Writing (ERW) section of the SAT.

I know how challenging the SAT can be, especially for those of you who didn't grow up speaking English. However, I also know that with the right mindset and approach, you can achieve scores beyond what you believed was possible.

How do I know this?

Well, for the past 14 years, I taught in Seoul's 대치동 and 압구정 neighborhoods-two of the most academically competitive districts in the world. During that time, I had the privilege of working with over 7,000 students, many of whom have gone on to score in the top percentiles in standardized tests like the SAT, TOEFL, and ACT. In fact, a whopping 80% of my students scored in at least the 90th percentile, and countless achieved scores in the 99th percentile.

These are statistics I am truly proud of and quite humbled by-not because they provide any type of validation of me, but because they are a testament to the incredible potential in each of you.

This practice test book is just one way I can help you brush up against your potential.

This book was designed to offer quality practice tests to students who are frustrated by the lack of quality test questions; however, this book was not created as a standalone resource to achieve top 1% scores. In fact, many of you will likely not score in the 99th percentile solely with this book. Most of you need foundational knowledge about reading, writing, and problem-solving. And ideally, you need an expert you can interact with and receive feedback from regularly.

As such, I have taken the following steps to increase the likelihood of your success:

https://www.youtube.com/@JinTeaches...: I'll be sharing my best and most practical test-taking tips and strategies, teaching foundational knowledge lessons, and training you to become a more confident test taker on my YouTube channel. I'll also be hosting live classes and Q&A sessions for those who want to connect with me in real time.

https://www.masterprep.net: I've partnered with South Korea's #1 online education platform for students studying abroad to create several online courses for the Digital SAT Reading and Writing sections. This platform is great for students who are looking for a more structured, traditional approach to learning.

 https://mocks.roadmaptestprep.com: As founder of Roadmap Test Prep, it is my joy and privilege to offer you a FREE full-length Digital SAT diagnostic exam on a platform that looks and functions just like the actual test. You'll especially love the detailed score report and review system in helping you organize your performance and improve your scores. Simply email me at jin@roadmaptestprep.com and I'll reply with a magic link that you can use to access the test.

Your test prep journey does not have to be a lonely one-there are people in this world who are committed to supporting you each step of the way.

Here's to Your Success,

Table of Contents

Practice Test

1

Reading and Writing

27 Questions, 32 Minutes

The new interns quickly became valued team members due to their _____ ability to learn and adapt. Within just a few days, they were handling complex tasks that usually require weeks of training. The supervisor noted that such quick mastery is rare and highly commendable.

1

Which choice completes the text with the most logical and precise word or phrase?

A) mediocre

B) remarkable

C) indifferent

D) predictable

CONTINUE

Online shopping has become a popular convenience for many people, offering the ability to purchase items from the comfort of home. However, the environmental cost of shipping products across the globe can be _____. Environmental experts warn that increased shipping contributes significantly to carbon emissions and other environmental impacts.

Which choice completes the text with the most logical and precise word or phrase?

A) beneficial
B) negligible
C) substantial
D) symbolic

Despite the _____ nature of the new policy, it quickly gained traction among the employees, who appreciated its emphasis on flexibility and work-life balance. Initially, there were concerns about how the changes would diminish productivity, but these were soon overshadowed by positive feedback.

Which choice completes the text with the most logical and precise word or phrase?

A) controversial
B) tentative
C) restrictive
D) innovative

CONTINUE

The following text is adapted from Mary Shelley's 1818 novel Frankenstein. Victor *Frankenstein* reflects on his scientific endeavors.

The labors I endured were severe; I felt the bitterness of disappointment and trembled with passion when I thought of the failures that had dashed my hopes. But I could not rest; a thousand conflicting emotions rendered repose impossible, and I toiled with a zeal that might have been termed madness.

4

As used in the text, what does the word "toiled" most nearly mean?

A) Struggled
B) Rested
C) Slacked
D) Escaped

The Amazon rainforest, often referred to as the "lungs of the Earth," plays a crucial role in regulating the planet's climate. It absorbs large amounts of carbon dioxide and releases oxygen, helping to stabilize global temperatures. However, deforestation poses a significant threat to this vital ecosystem. Efforts to protect the Amazon are essential not only for preserving biodiversity but also for combating climate change.

5

Which choice best states the main purpose of the text?

A) To highlight the biodiversity of the Amazon rainforest and its impact on global ecology
B) To explain the process of deforestation and the challenges of reforestation efforts in the Amazon
C) To discuss the importance of the Amazon rainforest in climate regulation and the dangers it faces
D) To argue that the protection of the Amazon from deforestation is the most critical factor in fighting global climate change

CONTINUE ➡

The development of the electric vehicle (EV) has been marked by significant technological advancements. Recent studies by automotive engineers have shown that battery efficiency can be dramatically improved through the use of solid-state technology. This improvement was not only observed in lab tests: <u>drivers reported a 25% increase in range and a 30% reduction in charging time when using solid-state batteries in everyday conditions</u>. These findings have led to widespread optimism about the future of electric vehicles, especially in terms of their potential to reduce carbon emissions.

6

Which choice best describes the function of the underlined portion in the text as a whole?

A) It presents a theoretical benefit of solid-state technology that the study later aims to confirm.

B) It provides real-world evidence to substantiate the claim that solid-state technology improves battery efficiency.

C) It introduces a potential complication of solid-state technology that the study intends to address.

D) It establishes a relationship between lab test results and real-world applications of solid-state technology.

CONTINUE

The Smithsonian Institution, founded in 1846, is a group of museums and research institutions administered by the United States government. It has grown to include 19 museums, 21 libraries, nine research centers, and a zoo. Another significant cultural institution is the Getty Center in Los Angeles, which opened in 1997. It is known for its architecture, gardens, and views overlooking the city, as well as its extensive art collection.

7

Which choice best describes the overall structure of the text?

A) It details the history of one institution, then introduces the educational programs of another.

B) It explains the evolution and expansion of one institution, then compares it with the structure and features of another.

C) It discusses one long-established cultural institution, then highlights the significance and key attractions of a newer one.

D) It describes the mission of one institution, then contrasts it with that of another.

CONTINUE

The following text is adapted from Jane Austen's 1814 novel *Mansfield Park.* The text describes an interaction between two characters.

Every time they met, she would bring up her grand plans for the future, full of ambition and determination, and he would listen, nodding politely but with a growing sense of unease. Her words, passionate and fiery, seemed to ignite the room, yet he couldn't shake the feeling that they were merely shadows of her true desires, cloaked in the expectations of society. As they parted ways, her enthusiasm seemed to linger, while his uncertainty deepened.

8

Which choice best describes the function of the underlined portion in the text as a whole?

A) To emphasize the characters' shared commitment to achieving their goals.

B) To convey the man's sense that the woman's expressed ambitions are insincere.

C) To reveal the man's physical discomfort with the predicament he is in.

D) To draw attention to the man's admiration for the woman's passionate and fiery words.

CONTINUE

The following text is adapted from Louisa May Alcott's 1868 novel *Little Women*.

Jo was the only one who remained calm. Beth, the quiet one, burst into tears as soon as the letter was read. Meg tried to comfort her, but her own voice was broken with sobs. Amy, who was the youngest, hid her face in Jo's skirts and cried silently. Jo, however, set her lips together, gave herself a little shake, and said, "Now, don't cry, Bethy! Don't cry, girls. We must be brave and make Father proud."

9

According to the text, what is true about Jo?

A) She comforts Amy by crying with her.

B) She hides her face in her skirts and cries silently.

C) She bursts into tears after reading the letter.

D) She remains composed and encourages her sisters.

CONTINUE

The following text is adapted from Robert Frost's 1920 poem "The Road Not Taken."

In the poem, Frost suggests that the choices we make have a significant impact on our lives, writing, _____

10

Which quotation from "The Road Not Taken" most effectively illustrates the claim?

A) "Two roads diverged in a yellow wood, / And sorry I could not travel both / And be one traveler, long I stood / And looked down one as far as I could / To where it bent in the undergrowth;"

B) "Then took the other, as just as fair, / And having perhaps the better claim, / Because it was grassy and wanted wear; / Though as for that the passing there / Had worn them really about the same,"

C) "I shall be telling this with a sigh / Somewhere ages and ages hence: / Two roads diverged in a wood, and I— / I took the one less traveled by, / And that has made all the difference."

D) "And both that morning equally lay / In leaves no step had trodden black. / Oh, I kept the first for another day! / Yet knowing how way leads on to way, / I doubted if I should ever come back."

CONTINUE

The cause of the Great Fire of Rome remains a topic of debate among historians. Early historian Tacitus claims that Nero started the fire to clear space for his new palace, the Domus Aurea. According to Tacitus, Nero watched the city burn from his palace roof, playing his lyre and singing about the destruction of Troy. However, recent historian Anthony Barrett argues that the fire was likely an accident caused by the cramped and flammable conditions of Rome's wooden structures, emphasizing the lack of concrete evidence against Nero.

11

Which finding, if true, would most directly support Barrett's claim?

A) Evidence showing that Tacitus often exaggerated events in his historical accounts to criticize Roman emperors

B) Contemporary letters from Roman citizens praising Nero's quick response to the fire and his efforts to aid the victims

C) Contemporary letters from Roman citizens reporting that they saw Nero's men setting fire to buildings in strategic locations

D) Archaeological studies indicating that fires were a common hazard in ancient Rome due to the dense and wooden nature of the city's buildings

CONTINUE ➡

In the remote forests of New Guinea, the male Vogelkop Superb Bird-of-Paradise exhibits a rare and seemingly contradictory display behavior. Despite its vibrant plumage and elaborate dance meant to attract females, the bird often chooses dimly lit forest floors as its stage. Researchers Ed Scholes and Tim Laman analyzed over 100 hours of footage and discovered that the bird's dark surroundings enhance the visibility of its striking colors and intricate movements. They hypothesize that this behavior maximizes the visual impact of the display, increasing the likelihood of attracting a mate.

12

Which finding, if true, would most directly support the researchers' hypothesis?

A) Other species of birds perform their displays in well-lit areas but have less vibrant plumage compared to the Vogelkop Superb Bird-of-Paradise.

B) Female Vogelkop Superb Birds-of-Paradise are more likely to respond to displays performed in darker environments compared to those in brighter settings.

C) The Vogelkop Superb Bird-of-Paradise's dance involves rapid movements that are difficult to see in well-lit environments.

D) Observations indicate that the Vogelkop Superb Bird-of-Paradise spends most of its time in dark forest floors, regardless of its display behavior.

CONTINUE →

Memory Test Performance
by Sleep Duration

Groups	Sleep Duration	Average Correct Answers on Memory Test
Group 1	8 hours	89
Group 2	5 hours	65
Group 3	4 hours	60
Group 4	7 hours	78
Group 5	6 hours	70

A recent study on the effects of sleep on cognitive performance revealed that individuals who slept for eight hours, considered the optimal sleep duration, performed significantly better on memory tests compared to those who slept for six or fewer hours. The study measured the number of correct answers on a standardized memory test among different sleep groups. The test consisted of 100 questions. The researchers concluded that optimal sleep duration significantly enhances memory retention, as evidenced by the fact that _____

13

Which choice most effectively uses data from the table to complete the statement?

A) reducing sleep to five hours decreases memory performance more significantly than reducing it to six hours.

B) sleeping seven hours is almost as beneficial for memory as sleeping eight hours, given the minimal difference in average scores.

C) individuals in Group 1 have a substantially higher number of correct answers compared to those who had fewer than 6 hours of sleep.

D) the difference in memory test performance between those in Group 3 and those in Group 1 is negligible.

CONTINUE

Average Lifespan and Reproductive Rates of Mammal Species

Mammal Species	Average Lifespan (years)	Average Reproductive Rate (offspring per year)
Elephant	70	0.2
Rabbit	10	50
Dog	13	5
Dolphin	40	0.5
Bat	20	1

A team of biologists working across various continents studied numerous mammal species to understand the relationship between their average lifespans and their reproductive rates. They found that reproductive strategies are influenced by a complex interplay of factors—environmental pressures, predation, and resource availability—rather than lifespan alone. Thus, they claim that species with vastly different lifespans can have similar reproductive strategies in terms of the number of offspring they produce annually.

14

Which choice best describes data from the table that support the researchers' claim?

A) Elephants and Dolphins have the longest lifespans but the lowest reproductive rates, indicating a complex interplay of factors at work.

B) Bats and Rabbits show a significant difference in reproductive rates, despite differences in their lifespans.

C) Elephants and Rabbits have the biggest difference in both lifespan and reproductive rate.

D) Both Elephants and Dolphins, despite having a 30-year difference in lifespan, have low reproductive rates.

CONTINUE ➡

A recent study on consumer behavior revealed a surprising finding: when given a choice between products labeled as "limited edition" and _____ without such labels, even if the items are identical, consumers overwhelmingly chose the "limited edition" version; this suggests that perceived scarcity significantly influences purchasing decisions, tapping into a psychological desire for exclusivity and uniqueness.

15

Which choice completes the text so that it conforms to the conventions of Standard English?

A) them

B) products

C) it

D) they're

Albert Einstein believed that imagination was more important than knowledge, as he famously stated that while knowledge is _____ encircles the world. He also held a deep conviction in the interconnectedness of the universe, viewing scientific discovery as a way to glimpse the underlying harmony of nature and the cosmos.

16

Which choice completes the text so that it conforms to the conventions of Standard English?

A) limited; imagination

B) limited. Imagination

C) limited: imagination

D) limited, imagination

CONTINUE

Oscar-nominated African-American _____ is renowned for her commanding presence and emotional depth, bringing complex characters to life with unparalleled authenticity. In her role as Rose Maxson in Fences, she masterfully portrays a woman grappling with love, betrayal, and resilience, delivering a performance that is both heartrending and fiercely powerful.

17

Which choice completes the text so that it conforms to the conventions of Standard English?

A) actress Viola Davis
B) actress, Viola Davis,
C) actress, Viola Davis
D) actress Viola Davis,

In the late 1990s, the value of internet-based companies surged dramatically, with the stocks of even unprofitable start-ups trading at astronomical prices. Many economists contend that this "dot-com bubble" was a quintessential example of speculative frenzy, in which investors' fervor for technological innovation _____ valuations far beyond what the underlying business models could sustain.

18

Which choice completes the text so that it conforms to the conventions of Standard English?

A) fueling
B) having fueled
C) fueled
D) to fuel

CONTINUE

Physicists investigating quantum entanglement—a phenomenon wherein particles become interconnected, such that the state of one instantaneously influences the state of another, regardless of distance—have uncovered an intriguing _____ in certain high-energy environments, entangled particles exhibit nonlocal correlations that defy classical explanations, suggesting the presence of an underlying, yet-to-be-understood force that transcends conventional physical laws.

19

Which choice completes the text so that it conforms to the conventions of Standard English?

A) anomaly

B) anomaly,

C) anomaly:

D) anomaly while

Spiders, engaging in a remarkable behavior known as ballooning, propel themselves into the air by releasing silk threads that catch the wind. Ballooning allows spiders to travel vast distances, sometimes hundreds of miles, across land and sea; this astonishing ability, which even enables them to colonize new territories, relies on the spiders' instinctive use of atmospheric electricity to lift _____ into the sky.

20

Which choice completes the text so that it conforms to the conventions of Standard English?

A) themselves

B) itself

C) them

D) it

CONTINUE

The ancient Greek game of *petteia*—believed to have been played with small stones or counters on a grid, similar to a modern-day board game-was governed by rules that, though not entirely documented, likely _____ strategic placement and capture, as players sought to outmaneuver their opponents. *Petteia* was a test of both skill and intellect, reflecting the competitive spirit of Greek society.

Driven by an insatiable curiosity about the human mind, _____

21

Which choice completes the text so that it conforms to the conventions of Standard English?

A) involves
B) was involved in
C) has involved
D) involved

22

Which choice completes the text so that it conforms to the conventions of Standard English?

A) studies on memories reveal that they are far more malleable than researchers previously thought.
B) memories are far more malleable than researchers previously thought.
C) researchers' understanding of memories is such that they are far more malleable than previously thought.
D) researchers have discovered that memories are far more malleable than previously thought.

CONTINUE ➔

The human brain, a remarkably intricate organ composed of approximately 86 billion neurons, communicates via an elaborate network of synapses and neurotransmitters; _____ even minor disruptions in these pathways, such as those caused by neurodegenerative diseases, can lead to profound cognitive and motor impairments, underscoring the delicate balance required for optimal brain function.

Which choice completes the text with the most logical transition?

A) for example,

B) consequently,

C) in other words,

D) similarly,

Characterized by short-term contracts and freelance work, the gig economy has dramatically altered the traditional employment landscape, creating opportunities for people where none existed previously. This shift, _____ while providing flexibility for workers, has also led to concerns about job security and the lack of benefits typically associated with full-time employment.

Which choice completes the text with the most logical transition?

A) however,

B) for instance,

C) moreover,

D) in fact,

CONTINUE →

Cognitive behavioral therapy (CBT), widely regarded as an effective treatment for anxiety and depression, focuses on identifying and changing negative thought patterns that contribute to mental health issues. _____ patients who engage in CBT often experience significant improvements in their symptoms, as they learn to reframe their thinking and develop healthier coping mechanisms.

25

Which choice completes the text with the most logical transition?

A) In contrast,

B) Eventually,

C) Nevertheless,

D) To this end,

CONTINUE

While researching a topic, a student has taken the following notes:

- Microplastics are increasingly being detected in marine organisms worldwide.
- Ecologist Dr. Nalini Ramaswamy was concerned over the potential impact of microplastics on marine ecosystems and human health.
- In a 2017 study, she analyzed the stomach contents of fish from different coastal regions to assess the prevalence of microplastics.
- Her research revealed that a significant proportion of the sampled fish—around 60%—had ingested microplastics.
- Her findings suggest that microplastic pollution is a widespread issue.
- She sent her findings to policy makers to advocate for stricter regulations on plastic waste.

26

The student wants to explain the purpose of Dr. Ramaswamy's study. Which choice most effectively uses relevant information from the notes to accomplish this goal?

A) Her study revealed that microplastics were present in a significant proportion of the fish sampled, suggesting the widespread nature of this pollution.

B) She analyzed the stomach contents of fish and uncovered the prevalence of microplastics in marine organisms.

C) She wanted to determine whether microplastics were, in fact, increasingly being detected in marine organisms worldwide.

D) She was worried about the possible consequences of microplastics on marine life and human health.

CONTINUE →

While researching a topic, a student has taken the following notes:

- Solar panels convert sunlight into electricity and provide a clean and renewable energy source that reduces dependence on fossil fuels.
- Wind turbines harness the power of wind to generate electricity and are often installed in large wind farms.
- Solar panels are most effective in sunny climates but require large amounts of space for installation.
- Wind turbines can be installed both onshore and offshore but have been criticized for their impact on bird populations.
- Both solar and wind energy are key components in reducing carbon emissions and combating climate change.

27

The student wants to compare the drawbacks of solar panels and wind turbines as renewable energy sources. Which choice most effectively uses relevant information from the notes to accomplish this goal?

A) Solar panels are a renewable energy source that reduces dependence on fossil fuels, while wind turbines are often installed in large wind farms to generate electricity.

B) Solar panels and wind turbines both have disadvantages. For example, large amounts of space are needed to install solar panels.

C) Both solar panels and wind turbines contribute to reducing carbon emissions and combating climate change, but there are also drawbacks of each.

D) Solar panels require significant space for installation, whereas wind turbines can negatively impact bird populations.

If you finish before the time is called, you may check your work on this module only.
On Test Day, you will only be able to move to the next module when time expires.

 **Answer Key**

Question Number	Correct Answer	Level of Difficulty	Question Type
1	B	Easy	**Craft and Structure:** *Words in Context*
2	C	Medium	**Craft and Structure:** *Words in Context*
3	A	Medium	**Craft and Structure:** *Words in Context*
4	A	Medium	**Craft and Structure:** *Interpreting Words in Context*
5	C	Easy	**Craft and Structure:** *Main Purpose*
6	B	Medium	**Craft and Structure:** *Function of Underlined Portion*
7	C	Medium	**Craft and Structure:** *Overall Structure of the Text*
8	B	Medium	**Craft and Structure:** *Function of Underlined Portion*
9	D	Easy	**Information and Ideas:** *Detail*
10	C	Hard	**Information and Ideas:** *Citing Text as Evidence*
11	D	Hard	**Information and Ideas:** *Supporting a Claim*
12	B	Medium	**Information and Ideas:** *Supporting a Claim*
13	C	Easy	**Information and Ideas:** *Citing Text as Evidence (Infographic)*

Question Number	Correct Answer	Level of Difficulty	Question Type
14	D	Hard	**Information and Ideas:** *Supporting a Claim (Infographic)*
15	B	Easy	**Standard English Conventions:** *Pronouns*
16	D	Medium	**Standard English Conventions:** *Punctuation and Sentence Structure*
17	A	Medium	**Standard English Conventions:** *Commas*
18	C	Easy	**Standard English Conventions:** *Verbs*
19	C	Hard	**Standard English Conventions:** *Sentence Structure*
20	A	Medium	**Standard English Conventions:** *Pronouns*
21	D	Hard	**Standard English Conventions:** *Verbs*
22	D	Easy	**Standard English Conventions:** *Modifiers*
23	B	Medium	**Expressions of Writing:** *Transitions*
24	A	Easy	**Expressions of Writing:** *Transitions*
25	D	Medium	**Expressions of Writing:** *Transitions*
26	D	Easy	**Expressions of Writing:** *Rhetorical Synthesis*
27	D	Easy	**Expressions of Writing:** *Rhetorical Synthesis*

Instructions

Count the number of questions you got correct in Module 1.

Enter your score here: _____.

If your score is **18 or higher**, move on to the **HARD version** of Module 2.

If your score is **below 18**, proceed to the **EASY version** of Module 2.

 **Explanations**

1. Words in Context: Easy

Answer: B) remarkable

Step-by-Step Explanation:

1. Let's look at what the passage is saying. It praises the intern for learning quickly and handling complex tasks in just a few days.
2. Notice the phrase "Within just a few days." This sequence of time expression emphasizes the speed at which the intern learned and adapted, which is key to understanding their exceptional ability.
3. The words "rare and highly commendable" tell us that the intern's performance is exceptional.
4. Ask yourself, what word describes something impressive or worthy of attention? "Remarkable" fits perfectly because it means something is impressive or noteworthy.

Explanation of Incorrect Options:

A) mediocre: This is incorrect because it implies average performance, which contradicts the description of the intern's abilities as "rare and highly commendable."

C) indifferent: This is incorrect because it suggests a lack of interest or concern, which does not match the context of being praised for quick mastery.

D) predictable: This is incorrect because it implies something expected, which contradicts the idea that the intern's performance is "rare."

2. Words in Context: Medium

Answer: C) substantial

Step-by-Step Explanation:

1. Let's read the passage together. It starts by saying that online shopping is convenient. Notice the word "However" at the beginning of the second sentence. This transition word indicates a contrast, meaning the next part will show a downside or negative aspect.
2. The phrase "environmental cost" and the clause "increased shipping contributes significantly to carbon emissions" tell us that the impact is quite serious.
3. Now, we need a word that means a serious or significant impact.
4. Ask yourself, what word would best describe a large negative effect on the environment? "Substantial" means large or significant, which fits perfectly here. So, the correct answer is "substantial."

Explanation of Incorrect Options:

A) beneficial: This is incorrect because it implies a positive impact, which contradicts the negative environmental cost discussed in the passage.

B) negligible: This is incorrect because it means very small or unimportant, which contradicts the phrase "significantly contributes."

D) symbolic: This is incorrect because it suggests something representational rather than real, which isn't consistent with the context of significant environmental costs.

3. Words in Context: Medium

Answer: A) controversial

Step-by-Step Explanation:

1. Let's understand the passage. It mentions that the new policy was initially met with concerns, but the concerns were quickly overshadowed by positive feedback.
2. Notice the word "Despite" at the beginning of the first sentence. This contrasting word indicates that what follows in this phrase is unexpected given the initial concerns.
3. The independent clause in the first sentence indicates that the new policy gained traction because employees appreciated its benefits.
4. Therefore, the type of word we need in the underlined blank is a negative word that reflects the initial concerns or resistance to the new policy.
5. Ask yourself, what word describes something that might initially cause concern or resistance? "Controversial" fits perfectly because it means causing public disagreement or debate, which aligns with the initial concerns mentioned in the passage.

Explanation of Incorrect Options:

B) tentative: This is incorrect because it implies uncertainty, which does not fit the context of causing debate and then gaining acceptance.

C) obscure: This is incorrect because it suggests being unclear or hard to understand, which does not match the context of a debated policy.

D) innovative: This is incorrect because it implies being new or creative, which does not convey the idea of causing concerns.

4. Interpreting Words in Context: Medium

Answer: A) Struggled

Context Clues:

- The phrases "labors I endured were severe" and "a zeal that might have been termed madness" indicate that Victor was working very hard and intensely.
- The word "toiled" is used in a context that suggests continuous, strenuous effort.

Step-by-Step Explanation:

1. Let's understand the passage. It describes Victor's intense and tireless work on his experiments.
2. The phrase "labors I endured were severe" suggests that the work was hard and demanding.
3. Ask yourself, what word fits best with the idea of working very hard and continuously? "Struggled" fits perfectly because it means making a strenuous effort.

Explanation of Incorrect Options:

B) Rested: This is incorrect because it implies taking a break, which contradicts the context of continuous and intense work.

C) Slacked: This is incorrect because it implies being lazy or reducing effort, which does not match the context of severe labor and zeal.

D) Escaped: This is incorrect because it implies getting away from something, which does not fit the context of working hard and enduring severe labors.

5. Main Purpose: Easy

Answer: C) To discuss the importance of the Amazon rainforest in climate regulation and the dangers it faces

Logical Breakdown and Explanation:

To determine the main purpose of the text, we need to focus on the overarching message that the passage is trying to convey. The passage discusses the crucial role of the Amazon rainforest in regulating the planet's climate and highlights the threats posed by deforestation. It emphasizes that protecting the Amazon is essential not only for preserving biodiversity but also for combating climate change.

Option C is correct because it accurately reflects the main purpose of the passage: discussing the importance of the Amazon rainforest in climate regulation and the dangers it faces due to deforestation. This option captures the big picture and aligns with the passage's focus on both the significance of the rainforest and the threats it encounters.

Option A is incorrect because it focuses on the biodiversity of the Amazon and its impact on global ecology. While biodiversity is mentioned, the passage primarily emphasizes climate regulation, making biodiversity a secondary detail rather than the main purpose.

Option B is incorrect because it suggests the passage explains the process of deforestation and the challenges of reforestation. The passage mentions deforestation as a threat but does not go into the specific processes or challenges of reforestation, making this option off-topic.

Option D is incorrect because it implies the passage argues that protecting the Amazon from deforestation is the most critical factor in fighting global climate change. While the passage highlights the importance of protection, it does not make such a strong argument or present it as the single most critical factor, making this option too extreme.

6. Function of the Underlined Portion: Medium

Answer: B) It provides real-world evidence to substantiate the claim that solid-state technology improves battery efficiency.

Logical Breakdown and Explanation:

To determine the function of the underlined portion in the passage, we need to focus on what role this specific detail plays in the broader context. The passage discusses advancements in electric vehicle (EV) technology, particularly highlighting the improvements in battery efficiency through solid-state technology. The underlined portion—"drivers reported a 25% increase in range and a 30% reduction in charging time when using solid-state batteries in everyday conditions"—provides a concrete example that supports the broader claim that solid-state technology significantly enhances battery performance.

Option B correctly states that the underlined portion provides real-world evidence to substantiate the claim that solid-state technology improves battery efficiency. The passage begins by highlighting the potential benefits of this technology, and the underlined portion moves beyond theoretical lab results to show that these benefits are actually realized by drivers in everyday scenarios. This real-world data—a 25% increase in range and a 30% reduction in charging time—directly supports the broader argument that solid-state technology is effective, not just in controlled environments but in practical, everyday use.

Option A is incorrect because it suggests the underlined portion presents a theoretical benefit, but the underlined text reports actual results from drivers, not a theory.

Option C is incorrect because it implies the underlined portion introduces a complication, but the passage focuses on positive outcomes, not problems.

Option D is incorrect because it suggests the underlined portion compares lab tests to real-world applications, but the underlined text only provides real-world results without drawing such a comparison.

7. Overall Structure of the Text: Medium

Answer: C) It discusses one long-established cultural institution, then highlights the significance and key attractions of a newer one.

Logical Breakdown and Explanation:

To determine which choice best describes the overall structure of the text, we need to examine how the passage organizes and presents information about the two institutions. The passage first introduces the Smithsonian Institution, providing details about its founding, growth, and the range of museums, libraries, and research centers it includes. It then shifts to the Getty Center, focusing on its more recent establishment, notable architecture, and art collection.

Option C is correct because it accurately describes the overall structure of the text: the passage first discusses a long-established cultural institution, the Smithsonian, and then highlights the significance and key attractions of a newer institution, the Getty Center. This structure is evident as the passage moves from one institution to another, focusing on their respective characteristics.

Option A is incorrect because it misrepresents the structure by suggesting the passage transitions from detailing the history of one institution to introducing the educational programs of another. The passage doesn't focus on educational programs, so this option does not accurately capture the passage's structure.

Option B is incorrect because it refers to "comparing" the two institutions. The passage doesn't actually compare the Smithsonian and the Getty Center; it describes them individually without drawing a direct comparison.

Option D is incorrect because it suggests a "contrast" between the two institutions' missions. The passage doesn't discuss or contrast the missions of these institutions, making this part of the answer choice wrong.

8. Function of the Underlined Portion: Medium

Answer: B) To convey the man's sense that the woman's expressed ambitions are insincere.

Logical Breakdown and Explanation:

To determine the function of the underlined portion in the text, we need to focus on what the underlined portion is "doing" and how it contributes to the overall narrative and interaction between the characters. The underlined portion—"he couldn't shake the feeling that they were merely shadows of her true desires, cloaked in the expectations of society"—gives us insight into the man's perception of the woman's ambitions. He feels that her expressed ambitions may not be genuine and are instead influenced by societal expectations.

Option B is correct because it directly addresses the man's growing suspicion that the woman's ambitions are not genuine. The underlined portion specifically mentions that he feels her words are "merely shadows of her true desires," suggesting he believes her expressed ambitions are influenced by societal expectations rather than her true feelings. This aligns with the idea that he perceives her ambitions as insincere.

Option A is incorrect because it emphasizes "shared commitment," which is not supported by the passage. The text actually highlights a growing sense of unease and uncertainty in the man, not a mutual commitment to goals.

Option C is incorrect because it focuses on "physical discomfort," but the text discusses the man's internal emotional unease rather than any physical discomfort.

Option D is incorrect because it suggests that the underlined portion draws attention to the man's "admiration" for the woman's words. However, the passage does not indicate admiration; instead, it emphasizes his growing doubt about the sincerity of her ambitions.

9. Detail: Easy

Answer: D) She remains composed and encourages her sisters.

Logical Breakdown and Explanation:

To determine what is true about Jo according to the text, we need to focus on her actions and behavior as described in the passage. The text highlights that while the other sisters are emotional and crying, Jo is the only one who remains calm. She sets her lips together, shakes herself, and encourages her sisters to be brave, telling them not to cry.

Option D is correct because it accurately reflects Jo's behavior as described in the text. The passage describes Jo as the only one who "remained calm" while her sisters were emotional. She "remains composed" by setting her lips together and giving herself a shake, and then she takes on a leadership role by encouraging her sisters to "be brave" and not cry, showing her strength and determination.

Option A is incorrect because it suggests that Jo comforts Amy by crying with her. However, the text specifically states that Jo remains calm and does not cry.

Option B is incorrect because it describes actions that Amy, not Jo, takes. The text states that Amy hides her face in Jo's skirts and cries silently, not Jo.

Option C is incorrect because it suggests that Jo bursts into tears after reading the letter, but the text clearly indicates that Jo remains composed and does not cry, unlike her sisters.

10. Citing Text as Evidence: Hard

Answer: C) "I shall be telling this with a sigh / Somewhere ages and ages hence: / Two roads diverged in a wood, and I— / I took the one less traveled by, / And that has made all the difference."

Logical Breakdown and Explanation:

To determine which quotation from "The Road Not Taken" most effectively illustrates the claim that the choices we make have a significant impact on our lives, we need to focus on the lines that highlight the lasting effects of a decision. The poem reflects on the importance of choice, suggesting that decisions shape our paths in life.

Option C is correct because it directly supports the claim that the choices we make significantly impact our lives. The lines "I took the one less traveled by, / And that has made all the difference" clearly express the idea that the speaker's choice of path—representing a life decision—has profoundly affected his life, reinforcing the significance of the choices we make.

Option A is incorrect because it describes the speaker's contemplation at the moment of choice, "Two roads diverged in a yellow wood," but it doesn't illustrate the impact of that choice on the speaker's life. The focus here is on the decision-making process, not the consequences.

Option B is incorrect because it focuses on the speaker making a choice between two roads and the reasons for that choice, "Then took the other, as just as fair, / Because it was grassy and wanted wear." However, it does not discuss how this decision ultimately impacted the speaker's life. The emphasis is on the reasoning behind the choice, not on the consequences of that choice.

Option D is incorrect because it explores the possibility of revisiting the other road, "I doubted if I should ever come back," rather than focusing on the impact of the choice that was actually made. It reflects on the uncertainty of choices rather than their consequences.

11. Supporting a Claim: Hard

Answer: D) Archaeological studies indicating that fires were a common hazard in ancient Rome due to the dense and wooden nature of the city's buildings

Logical Breakdown and Explanation:

To determine which finding would most directly support Barrett's claim that the Great Fire of Rome was likely an accident caused by the city's flammable conditions rather than being deliberately started by Nero, we need to look for evidence that aligns with the idea that the fire was an accidental consequence of Rome's structural vulnerabilities.

Option D is correct because it directly supports Barrett's claim by providing archaeological evidence that fires were a common hazard in ancient Rome due to the dense and wooden nature of the city's buildings. This finding makes Barrett's claim more believable, as it adds strength to the idea that the fire was likely an accident rather than a deliberate act by Nero.

Option A is incorrect because, while it suggests that Tacitus may have exaggerated events, it does not provide direct evidence that supports Barrett's claim about the fire being an accident. It focuses more on discrediting Tacitus than on confirming the accidental nature of the fire.

Option B is incorrect because it highlights Nero's response to the fire, not the cause of the fire itself. Praising Nero's efforts after the fire shifts the focus to his actions during the aftermath, which might improve his image but does nothing to support or validate the claim that the fire was accidental. Instead, it redirects attention away from the core issue of how the fire started, leaving Barrett's argument about the fire's accidental nature unaddressed.

Option C is incorrect because it suggests that Nero's men were seen setting fires, which would directly contradict Barrett's claim that the fire was an accident. This option would actually undermine Barrett's argument rather than support it.

12. Supporting a Claim: Medium

Answer: B) Female Vogelkop Superb Birds-of-Paradise are more likely to respond to displays performed in darker environments compared to those in brighter settings.

Logical Breakdown and Explanation:

To determine which finding would most directly support the researchers' hypothesis that the Vogelkop Superb Bird-of-Paradise chooses dimly lit forest floors to maximize the visual impact of its display, we need to look for evidence that directly links the dark environment to the effectiveness of the display in attracting a mate.

Option B is correct because it directly strengthens the researchers' hypothesis by providing evidence that female Vogelkop Superb Birds-of-Paradise are more likely to respond to displays in darker environments. This directly supports the claim in the passage that the bird's choice of dimly lit forest floors enhances the visual impact of its display and the likelihood of attracting a mate. By showing that females are more attracted to these displays in darker settings, the finding makes the hypothesis more believable and increases the likelihood that the researchers' hypothesis is true.

Option A is incorrect because it introduces a comparison to other species of birds that perform in well-lit areas and have less vibrant plumage. However, the passage doesn't mention other species at all, making this comparison irrelevant to the hypothesis about why the Vogelkop Superb Bird-of-Paradise specifically chooses dimly lit environments for its display.

Option C is incorrect because it suggests that the bird's rapid movements are difficult to see in well-lit environments. While this highlights a challenge in bright settings, it doesn't address the core issue of how dimly lit environments enhance the visual impact of the bird's display for mating purposes. The focus here is misplaced, as it doesn't directly relate to the bird's strategic choice of setting.

Option D is incorrect because it notes that the Vogelkop Superb Bird-of-Paradise spends most of its time on dark forest floors regardless of its display behavior. This detail about the bird's general habitat preference doesn't connect to the hypothesis that the bird intentionally selects darker areas to maximize the impact of its display, making it irrelevant to the claim.

13. Citing Text as Evidence (Infographic): Easy

Answer: C) individuals in Group 1 have a substantially higher number of correct answers compared to those who had fewer than 6 hours of sleep.

Logical Breakdown and Explanation:

To determine which choice most effectively uses data from the table to complete the statement, we need to focus on the key finding from the study: that optimal sleep duration (8 hours) significantly enhances memory retention compared to sleeping fewer than 6 hours. The data provided in the table shows that as sleep duration decreases, so does performance on the memory test.

Option C is correct because it accurately reflects the data from the table. Group 1, which slept 8 hours, had an average of 89 correct answers, while Groups 2 and 3, which slept 5 and 4 hours, had significantly lower scores of 65 and 60, respectively. This provides evidence of the researchers' conclusion that optimal sleep duration (8 hours) enhances memory retention.

Option A is incorrect because it focuses on the comparison between sleeping five hours and six hours, which is not relevant to the key point of the passage. The passage aims to provide evidence that optimal sleep duration (8 hours) significantly enhances memory retention. Focusing on the slight difference between five and six hours of sleep misses the point of the question, which is to demonstrate the substantial improvement in memory performance with 8 hours of sleep.

Option B is incorrect because the statement it makes is **not true**. It suggests that sleeping seven hours is almost as beneficial for memory as sleeping eight hours, implying a minimal difference in scores. However, the table shows a significant difference between the scores of those who slept 7 hours (78) and those who slept 8 hours (89). This difference is not minimal, making the statement inaccurate according to the data provided.

Option D is incorrect because the statement it makes is **not true**. It claims that the difference in memory test performance between Group 3 (4 hours of sleep) and Group 1 (8 hours of sleep) is negligible. The table clearly shows a large gap in performance (60 correct answers for Group 3 vs. 89 correct answers for Group 1), so the difference is substantial, not negligible. This directly contradicts the data in the table.

14. Support a Claim (Infographic): Hard

Answer: D) Both Elephants and Dolphins, despite having a 30-year difference in lifespan, have low reproductive rates.

Logical Breakdown and Explanation:

To determine which choice best describes data from the table that support the researchers' claim, we need to identify data that illustrate the idea that mammal species with vastly different lifespans can have similar reproductive strategies in terms of the number of offspring they produce annually. The table provides information on both average lifespans and reproductive rates, allowing us to evaluate the connections between these factors.

Option D is correct because it highlights that both Elephants and Dolphins, despite having a significant 30-year difference in lifespan (70 years for Elephants and 40 years for Dolphins), have similarly low reproductive rates (0.2 and 0.5 offspring per year, respectively). This supports the researchers' claim that reproductive strategies are not solely determined by lifespan, as these two species with very different lifespans exhibit similar reproductive behaviors.

Option A is incorrect because, although it correctly notes that Elephants and Dolphins have long lifespans and low reproductive rates, it does not directly address the idea that species with different lifespans can have similar reproductive strategies. Instead, it focuses on the interplay of factors influencing reproductive rates, which, while relevant, does not directly support the specific claim about lifespan and reproductive strategies.

Option B is incorrect because the statement it makes is **not true**. Bats and Rabbits do show a significant difference in reproductive rates (1 offspring per year for Bats and 50 offspring per year for Rabbits), but they also have a significant difference in lifespan (20 years for Bats and 10 years for Rabbits). This does not support the claim that species with different lifespans can have similar reproductive strategies; instead, it shows the opposite—differences in lifespan are accompanied by differences in reproductive rates.

Option C is incorrect because, although it accurately describes that Elephants and Rabbits have the biggest difference in both lifespan and reproductive rate, this does not support the researchers' claim. The claim is about species with different lifespans having similar reproductive strategies, not about species with the most significant differences in both lifespan and reproductive rate.

15. Pronouns: Easy

Answer: B) products

Logical Breakdown and Explanation:

Option B is correct because "products" directly matches and parallels the earlier mention of "products" in the sentence. The sentence compares products labeled as "limited edition" with those without such labels. Using "products" keeps this comparison clear and grammatically correct. Using a noun is often the most straightforward way to ensure clarity and grammatical correctness. By plugging "products" into the passage, it makes perfect sense and keeps the meaning logical and coherent.

Option A is incorrect because "them" is grammatically incorrect in this context. You cannot attach a modifier like "without labels" directly to the object pronoun "them." Only determiners (such as "those") can be correctly attached to modifiers. Therefore, "them without labels" is not a grammatically valid phrase.

Option C is incorrect because "it" is a singular pronoun, which doesn't match the plural noun "products" mentioned earlier in the sentence. This creates a grammatical error, as the pronoun must agree in number with its antecedent.

Option D is incorrect because "they're" is a contraction for "they are," which doesn't logically or grammatically fit within the sentence. This choice disrupts the intended comparison between the two types of products and makes the sentence awkward and unclear.

16. Punctuation and Sentence Structure: Medium

Answer: D) limited, imagination

Logical Breakdown and Explanation:

To determine the correct answer, we need to focus on the correct punctuation to connect the two parts of the sentence in a way that maintains grammatical accuracy and clarity.

Option D is correct because the comma correctly links the dependent clause "while knowledge is limited" with the independent clause "imagination encircles the world." This punctuation maintains the intended flow of the sentence, effectively contrasting the limited nature of knowledge with the expansive nature of imagination.

Option A is incorrect because the semicolon is used to separate two independent clauses, but the phrase "while knowledge is limited" is not independent and cannot stand alone as a complete sentence. Therefore, the semicolon is not appropriate in this context.

Option B is incorrect because a period is used to separate two independent clauses. However, "while knowledge is limited" is not an independent clause and cannot stand alone as a complete sentence. Since the phrase before the period does not meet the requirement of being an independent clause, using a period here violates the rule that periods should only separate complete sentences.

Option C is incorrect because a colon should follow an independent clause, but "while knowledge is limited" is not a complete sentence on its own. Using a colon here violates the punctuation rule that requires the preceding clause to be independent.

17. Commas: Medium

Answer: A) actress Viola Davis

Logical Breakdown and Explanation:

To determine the correct answer, we need to identify whether the appositive is essential or nonessential based on the first noun phrase.

Option A is correct because "actress Viola Davis" is an essential appositive. The first noun phrase, "Oscar-nominated African-American actress," can refer to more than one person, so "Viola Davis" is needed to specify who is being discussed. Since this information is essential to the sentence, no commas should be used.

Option B is incorrect because it places commas around "Viola Davis," treating it as a nonessential appositive. However, since "Oscar-nominated African-American actress" could refer to more than one person, "Viola Davis" is essential to clarify which actress is being mentioned. The unnecessary commas create a punctuation error.

Option C is incorrect because it places a single comma before "Viola Davis." This disrupts the flow and violates the comma rule that you should never have just one comma between a subject and a verb. The appositive is essential, so no commas should be used.

Option D is incorrect because it places a single comma after "Viola Davis." This creates a similar issue as in Option C, where a single comma appears between the subject and verb, which is grammatically incorrect. Again, since "Viola Davis" is essential, no commas should be used.

18. Verbs: Easy

Answer: C) fueled

Logical Breakdown and Explanation:

To determine the correct answer, we need to focus on the correct verb form and ensure that it appropriately functions as a verb within the sentence structure.

Option C is correct because "fueled" is a simple past tense verb that creates a proper sentence structure. In this context, the phrase "in which investors' fervor for technological innovation fueled valuations" is a dependent clause, and dependent clauses must always contain a functioning verb. "Fueled" serves as the actual verb in the clause, correctly describing the action that took place during the dot-com bubble, ensuring the sentence is grammatically complete.

Option A is incorrect because "fueling" is a present participle, which by itself cannot function as a main verb in this context. Participles require an auxiliary verb to form a complete verb phrase (e.g., "was fueling"). Without that, the sentence is left with an incomplete verb, making the structure incorrect.

Option B is incorrect because "having fueled" is a perfect participle, which also cannot function as a main verb without an auxiliary verb. The phrase "having fueled" would need a preceding auxiliary verb (e.g., "was having") to correctly function in the sentence, but here it stands alone, making the sentence incomplete and grammatically incorrect.

Option D is incorrect because "to fuel" is an infinitive, and infinitives also cannot serve as the main verb of a sentence without an auxiliary verb. In this sentence, "to fuel" doesn't function as an actual verb and leaves the dependent clause without a verb, thus creating a sentence structure error.

19. Sentence Structure: Hard

Answer: C) anomaly:

Logical Breakdown and Explanation:

To determine which choice is grammatical, we need to focus on sentence structure and ensure that the punctuation rules are followed.

Option C is correct because the colon is appropriately used after "anomaly" to introduce an explanation of the anomaly. The clause before the colon, "Physicists have uncovered an intriguing anomaly," is an independent clause, which is required before a colon. The information that follows the colon—"in certain high-energy environments, entangled particles exhibit nonlocal correlations that defy classical explanations"—expands on and explains the nature of the "intriguing anomaly," making the sentence both grammatically correct and logically coherent.

Option A is incorrect because it creates a run-on sentence by not providing any punctuation between two independent clauses. The two independent clauses are "Physicists have uncovered an intriguing anomaly" and "entangled particles exhibit nonlocal correlations that defy classical explanations." Without punctuation to separate these clauses, the sentence structure is incorrect.

Option B is incorrect because using a comma after "anomaly" also creates a run-on sentence. The comma incorrectly attempts to link the same two independent clauses: "Physicists have uncovered an intriguing anomaly" and "entangled particles exhibit nonlocal correlations that defy classical explanations." Since these clauses are independent, the comma alone is insufficient and leads to a grammatically incorrect sentence structure.

Option D is incorrect because the word "while" introduces a subordinate clause that suggests a contrast or simultaneous action, but it doesn't logically connect to the idea presented in the first part of the sentence. The initial part of the sentence states that physicists have uncovered "an intriguing anomaly," which sets up an expectation for further explanation or elaboration on this anomaly. However, "while" typically introduces a contrasting or simultaneous idea rather than an explanation, which disrupts the flow and meaning of the sentence. This results in a nonsensical structure, where the sentence becomes disjointed and fails to make logical sense.

20. Pronouns: Medium

Answer: A) themselves

Logical Breakdown and Explanation:

Option A is correct because "themselves" is a reflexive pronoun that clearly and logically refers back to "spiders." The sentence discusses how spiders use atmospheric electricity to lift themselves into the sky, so "themselves" correctly matches the plural subject "spiders" and maintains the clarity and grammatical sense of the sentence.

Option B is incorrect because "itself" is a singular reflexive pronoun, which does not match the plural antecedent "spiders." Using "itself" creates a pronoun-antecedent agreement error, as it refers to something singular, while "spiders" is plural.

Option C is incorrect because "them" is a plural pronoun but not reflexive, which is required in this context. The sentence needs to indicate that the spiders are performing the action on themselves, so "them" lacks the necessary reflexive form and creates an illogical meaning, indicating that the spiders are performing the action to lift something else ("them") and not the spiders themselves.

Option D is incorrect because "it" is a singular pronoun, which does not match the plural noun "spiders." Like **Option B**, this creates a pronoun-antecedent agreement error, making the sentence grammatically incorrect.

21. Verbs: Hard

Answer: D) involved

Logical Breakdown and Explanation:

To determine which choice completes the text so that it conforms to the conventions of Standard English, we need to focus on subject-verb agreement, particularly in the dependent clause. The subject of the verb in this clause is "rules," which is plural.

Option D is correct because "involved" is the only verb that correctly agrees with the plural subject "rules." The sentence reads, "rules that… involved strategic placement and capture," which is grammatically correct.

Option A is incorrect because "involves" is a singular verb form, which does not agree with the plural subject "rules."

Option B is incorrect because "was involved in" incorrectly suggests a singular subject, which does not match the plural "rules."

Option C is incorrect because "has involved" is a singular verb form and also doesn't agree with the plural subject "rules."

To identify the subject, ask yourself "what involved something?" After you reread the sentence with this focus, you'll know that the answer is "rules," which is the subject of the dependent clause. This focus on subject-verb agreement immediately eliminates Options A, B, and C, leaving Option D as the correct choice.

22. Modifiers: Easy

Answer: D) researchers have discovered that memories are far more malleable than previously thought.

Logical Breakdown and Explanation:

To determine which choice completes the text so that it conforms to the conventions of Standard English, we need to focus on how the modifying phrase at the beginning of the sentence is logically connected to the noun it modifies.

Option D is correct because the modifying phrase "Driven by an insatiable curiosity about the human mind" logically describes "researchers." The sentence makes sense because researchers, driven by curiosity, would be the ones discovering new insights about memory. The noun "researchers" is correctly and logically connected to the modifying phrase because the noun appears at the beginning of the independent clause.

Option A is incorrect because the subject "studies" does not logically match the modifying phrase. The phrase "Driven by an insatiable curiosity about the human mind" should describe a person or group of people, not "studies." Therefore, this creates a grammatical error called a 'dangling modifier.'

Option B is incorrect because the subject "memories" does not logically match the modifying phrase. Memories cannot be driven by curiosity, so the sentence structure is illogical.

Option C is incorrect because "researchers'" with an apostrophe is a possessive form, which means it's not functioning as the main noun of the sentence but rather as an adjective modifying the noun "understanding." The modifying phrase "Driven by an insatiable curiosity about the human mind" is intended to describe the noun that appears at the beginning of the independent clause, which, in this case, is "understanding." It doesn't make any logical sense to say that it was "understanding" that was driven by curiosity.

23. Transitions: Medium

Answer: B) consequently,

Logical Breakdown and Explanation:

IC 1: The human brain is a complex organ that communicates via synapses and neurotransmitters.

IC 2: Even minor disruptions in these pathways can cause significant cognitive and motor impairments, underscoring the delicate balance required for optimal brain function.

Relationship: The relationship between IC 1 and IC 2 is one of cause and effect. IC 1 discusses the intricate nature of the brain's communication network, while IC 2 explains the consequences of disruptions to this network.

Option B ("consequently,") is correct because it clearly indicates the effect that follows from the cause mentioned in IC 1. The disruptions in the brain's pathways lead to the impairments described in IC 2, making "consequently" the most logical transition.

Option A ("for example,") is incorrect because IC 2 is not giving an example of the complex nature of the brain; it's explaining the result of disruptions in that complexity.

Option C ("in other words,") is incorrect because it suggests rephrasing IC 1, but IC 2 is actually elaborating on the effect, not simply rephrasing the earlier idea.

Option D ("similarly,") is incorrect because it implies a comparison, which isn't the intended relationship between IC 1 and IC 2.

24. Transitions: Easy

Answer: A) however,

Logical Breakdown and Explanation:

IC 1: The gig economy has altered traditional employment by creating new opportunities.
IC 2: This shift, while providing flexibility, has also raised concerns about job security and the lack of benefits.

Relationship: The relationship between IC 1 and IC 2 is one of contrast. IC 1 highlights the positive impact of the gig economy, while IC 2 introduces the negative consequences that accompany this shift.

Option A ("however,") is correct because it signals a contrast between the positive effects mentioned in IC 1 and the concerns outlined in IC 2. "However" appropriately marks the shift from the opportunities to the downsides.

Option B ("for instance,") is incorrect because IC 2 isn't providing an example of the opportunities discussed in IC 1; it's presenting a contrasting idea.

Option C ("moreover,") is incorrect because it implies that IC 2 is adding to the positive aspects of IC 1, rather than contrasting with them.

Option D ("in fact,") is incorrect because it suggests emphasis or confirmation, which doesn't align with the contrast between IC 1 and IC 2.

25. Transitions: Medium

Answer: D) To this end,

Logical Breakdown and Explanation:

IC 1: Cognitive behavioral therapy (CBT) is effective in treating anxiety and depression by changing negative thought patterns.
IC 2: Patients who engage in CBT often experience significant improvements in their symptoms.

Relationship: The relationship between IC 1 and IC 2 is one of purpose and result. IC 1 describes the goal of CBT, and IC 2 explains the outcome that typically results from this therapeutic approach.

Option D ("To this end,") is correct because it introduces the result of the purpose described in IC 1. The phrase "To this end" logically connects the goal of CBT with the improvements in symptoms that patients experience, making it the most appropriate transition.

Option A ("In contrast,") is incorrect because it implies a contrast, which doesn't fit the context of connecting the purpose of CBT with its outcomes.

Option B ("Eventually,") is incorrect because it introduces a sequence of time, suggesting that the improvements happen as a result of a process over time. However, the sentence is not focusing on the timing of the improvements but rather on the direct result of engaging in CBT. "Eventually" implies a gradual progression, which doesn't align with the topic of the passage. The passage doesn't focus on the progression of time; rather, it focuses on the relationship described between the purpose of CBT and the improvements it leads to.

Option C ("Nevertheless,") is incorrect because it suggests an exception or contradiction, which isn't appropriate here as IC 2 supports the effectiveness of CBT described in IC 1.

26. Rhetorical Synthesis: Easy

Answer: D) She was worried about the possible consequences of microplastics on marine life and human health.

Logical Breakdown and Explanation:

Restated Goal: The student wants to explain the purpose of Dr. Ramaswamy's study. The objective is to choose the answer that most directly relates to why Dr. Ramaswamy conducted her research, focusing on the reason behind the study.

Option D is correct because it directly addresses the underlying reason for Dr. Ramaswamy's study. The notes state that Dr. Ramaswamy was concerned about the potential impact of microplastics on marine life and human health, which motivated her to conduct the research. This option clearly connects her concerns to the purpose of the study, making it the most relevant choice to explain why she undertook the research.

Option A is incorrect because it focuses on the findings of the study rather than its purpose. While revealing that a significant proportion of fish had ingested microplastics is important, it does not explain why Dr. Ramaswamy conducted the study.

Option B is incorrect because it describes the method and findings of the study without clearly indicating the purpose behind Dr. Ramaswamy's research. It doesn't fully address the reason for the study.

Option C is incorrect because it presents the detection of microplastics as a fact, not as the aim of the study. The notes do not suggest that determining whether microplastics were detected was the goal of her research, but rather that this was an established fact she investigated further.

27. Rhetorical Synthesis: Easy

Answer: D) Solar panels require significant space for installation, whereas wind turbines can negatively impact bird populations.

Logical Breakdown and Explanation:

Restated Goal: The student wants to compare the drawbacks of solar panels and wind turbines as renewable energy sources. The objective is to choose the answer that most directly addresses the disadvantages of both solar panels and wind turbines, based on the notes.

Option D is correct because it directly compares the specific drawbacks of solar panels and wind turbines. The notes indicate that solar panels require significant space for installation, while wind turbines can negatively impact bird populations. This option effectively uses the relevant information to make a clear comparison of the disadvantages of each energy source.

Option A is incorrect because it does not address the drawbacks of either solar panels or wind turbines. Instead, it focuses on general information about their use and benefits, which does not fulfill the goal of comparing their disadvantages.

Option B is incorrect because, while it mentions that large amounts of space are needed to install solar panels, it fails to address the drawbacks of wind turbines, making the comparison incomplete and less effective.

Option C is incorrect because it acknowledges that there are drawbacks to both solar panels and wind turbines but does not specify what those drawbacks are. It does not provide a direct comparison based on the specific disadvantages mentioned in the notes.

Page Intentionally Left Blank

EASY: Reading and Writing

27 Questions, 32 Minutes

The recent _____ in tourism in Kyoto, Japan, has positively impacted local businesses, with many reporting significant increases in revenue. This influx of visitors has also led to improvements in infrastructure and services throughout the city.

1

Which choice completes the text with the most logical and precise word or phrase?

A) decline

B) plateau

C) surge

D) tradition

CONTINUE ▶

During the Renaissance period, Leonardo da Vinci was not only known for his paintings but also for his inventions and scientific observations. His sketchbooks, filled with detailed drawings and notes, demonstrated his _____. Unlike many of his contemporaries, Leonardo approached both art and science with a deep sense of curiosity and analytical thinking.

Which choice completes the text with the most logical and precise word or phrase?

A) indifference
B) mediocrity
C) precision
D) popularity

In 1969, Neil Armstrong and Buzz Aldrin became the first humans to walk on the moon. This historic event was broadcast live, and millions of people around the world watched in awe. Armstrong's famous words, "That's one small step for man, one giant leap for mankind," echoed the _____ of the moment, highlighting the monumental achievement in human exploration.

Which choice completes the text with the most logical and precise word or phrase?

A) insignificance
B) excitement
C) complexity
D) gravity

CONTINUE

Without groundbreaking developments in paleontology, our knowledge of the behaviors and ecosystems of dinosaurs will remain _____. The fossil record, while extensive, provides only a fragmented glimpse into the ancient past.

4

Which choice completes the text with the most logical and precise word or phrase?

A) comprehensive

B) limited

C) definitive

D) inaccurate

The Great Rift Valley, which stretches from Lebanon to Mozambique, is one of the most significant geological features on Earth. This vast trench system was formed by tectonic plate movements and is home to numerous unique ecosystems. The valley's diverse landscapes have been _____ in the study of plate tectonics and evolutionary biology: they offer critical insights into the Earth's geological history and the development of species.

5

Which choice completes the text with the most logical and precise word or phrase?

A) instrumental

B) incidental

C) insignificant

D) implicit

CONTINUE

The Green Revolution, initiated by Norman Borlaug in the 1960s, introduced high-yielding varieties of staple crops such as wheat and rice. While it significantly increased food production in developing countries, the movement also drew skepticism from various quarters. Critics contended that the heavy reliance on chemical fertilizers and pesticides not only led to environmental degradation but also inflicted harm on small-scale farmers. Additionally, the Green Revolution was seen as favoring wealthier farmers who could afford the new technologies, thereby increasing social and economic inequalities.

6

Which choice best states the main purpose of the text?

A) To challenge the environmental and agricultural benefits of the Green Revolution in developing countries

B) To explain the agricultural techniques used in the Green Revolution

C) To compare the movement's impact to that of other revolutions

D) To enumerate the consequences of Borlaug's initiative

CONTINUE

With a diameter of 1.4 billion kilometers, the massive star Betelgeuse is one of the largest stars visible to the naked eye. Ever since ancient astronomers first documented Betelgeuse's fluctuating brightness, scientists have been intrigued by its unpredictable nature. After observing the star using modern telescopes and collecting data on its light emissions, astronomers Emily Levesque and Philip Massey have proposed that Betelgeuse's irregular brightness may be due to large convective cells on its surface, causing the star to pulsate in a complex pattern.

7

Which choice best describes the overall structure of the text?

A) It presents a historical perspective on an astronomical object and then introduces a modern scientific hypothesis to explain observed phenomena.

B) It introduces an opinion astronomers have about a star's characteristics and then describes a new theory that combines elements of previous ones.

C) It compares the light emissions of different stars and then identifies which star has the most erratic behavior.

D) It highlights the discovery of a new telescope and then discusses its role in advancing our understanding of stellar activity.

CONTINUE

Contrary to popular belief, prioritizing one's own interests doesn't necessarily lead to greater happiness. A staggering 70% of individuals assume that self-serving actions will boost their personal satisfaction, yet evidence suggests otherwise. Studies by Jennifer Crocker and her team reveal that well-being stems from a blend of factors such as strong social ties, acts of altruism, and genuine internal motivations. While personal achievements can bring joy, the essence of true happiness is deeply rooted in our social interactions and selfless deeds.

8

Which choice best describes the function of the underlined portion in the text as a whole?

A) It introduces the primary sources of self-serving behavior.

B) It questions the significance of personal achievements in overall happiness.

C) It provides evidence that contradicts the prevailing belief.

D) It identifies key elements that researchers encourage people to undertake.

CONTINUE ➡

Born in 1985 to a Tamil-speaking family in the rural regions of Sri Lanka, Priya Ramanathan is quickly gaining recognition as a significant voice in contemporary literature. In a review, literary critic Sandra Lee claims that Ramanathan's novels have profound cultural significance-through her narratives, Ramanathan adeptly explores the intricacies of Sri Lankan society, portraying her characters with depth and nuance; they often face personal struggles that are intricately tied to their cultural heritage.

9

Which finding, if true, would most directly support the critic's claim?

A) Ramanathan's novels are being translated into several languages, including French and German, making her work accessible to a wider audience.

B) Critics have noted that Ramanathan's writing style is heavily influenced by Western literary traditions, blending Eastern themes with Western techniques.

C) In her novel *The Merchant's Legacy*, Ramanathan features wealthy landowners who act as antagonists, creating conflict and tension within the story.

D) In her novel *The Serpent's Daughter*, Ramanathan portrays Anjali grappling with the loss of her parents while uncovering ancient stories of the Naga people that help her to cope.

CONTINUE

A symbiotic relationship-a close, long-term interaction between two different species that benefits both parties-is essential for the survival of many organisms. One such relationship exists between the acacia tree and the ant. The acacia provides the ants with food and shelter within its hollow thorns, while the ants protect the tree from herbivores and harmful insects. Given the critical importance of this relationship, if either the acacia or the ant were to disappear, _____

Which choice most logically completes the text?

A) both species would likely struggle to survive due to their interdependence, highlighting the fragile balance of their mutualistic relationship.

B) the acacia tree would still flourish, unaffected by the loss of the ants.

C) the ants would most likely adapt by finding another plant that offers the same level of food and shelter as the acacia tree.

D) herbivores would become more prevalent, causing greater damage to the acacia trees and potentially disrupting the ecosystem balance.

CONTINUE ➔

The following text is from Emily Dickinson's poem "Hope is the thing with feathers."

Hope is the thing with feathers
That perches in the soul,
And sings the tune without the words,
And never stops at all,

And sweetest in the gale is heard;
And sore must be the storm
That could abash the little bird
That kept so many warm.

I've heard it in the chillest land,
And on the strangest sea;
Yet, never, in extremity,
It asked a crumb of me.

11

What is the main idea of the text?

A) Hope is a delicate feeling that can easily be destroyed by difficult circumstances.

B) Hope is a persistent and comforting presence that remains even in the harshest conditions.

C) Hope is a fleeting emotion that requires constant nurturing to survive.

D) Hope is a selfish emotion that demands something in return from those it comforts.

CONTINUE

The following text is adapted from Rudolfo Anaya's novel *Bless Me, Ultima*. Antonio and Ultima share a deep but complicated relationship that shapes Antonio's coming of age.

Antonio stood by the river, watching the golden carp swim gracefully in the clear water. Ultima had shown him the sacred fish and told him stories of its magical powers. He felt a deep connection to Ultima, who guided him with wisdom and love. Yet, he was also conflicted by the rumors whispered in the village, accusing Ultima of being a bruja. The duality of her nature, both healer and suspected witch, left Antonio torn between admiration and fear. He could not reconcile the loving guardian he knew with the dark figure others portrayed her to be. Moreover, Antonio wondered how aligning himself with Ultima would affect his standing in the village and his understanding of good and evil.

12

Based on the text, how does Antonio's relationship with Ultima complicate his understanding of morality?

A) Antonio starts to see morality as a rigid concept, with clear distinctions between good and evil, influenced by Ultima's teachings.

B) Antonio struggles to balance his personal loyalty to Ultima with the villagers' negative perception, leading him to question the nature of morality.

C) Antonio views morality through the lens of societal approval, prioritizing the villagers' opinions over his bond with Ultima.

D) Antonio becomes indifferent to the concepts of good and evil, believing they are irrelevant to his personal experiences with Ultima.

CONTINUE →

Factors Contributing to Business Success

Business	Product Quality	CSR	Brand Strength	Adver-tising Spend	Customer Satisfaction
Business A	9	5	9	10%	9
Business B	8	8	6	20%	8
Business C	6	9	5	35%	6
Business D	7	7	7	10%	7

According to a Harvard Business Review study titled "The Elements of Value" by Eric Almquist, John Senior, and Nicolas Bloch, product quality and personal brand are critical factors influencing customer satisfaction and loyalty. The researchers evaluated various businesses and rated their success based on several factors, each rated on a scale from 1 to 10, with 10 being the highest. The factors included product quality, corporate social responsibility (CSR), brand strength, and advertising spend (measured as a percentage of revenue). The study concluded that businesses with high product quality and strong brand strength tend to have higher customer satisfaction.

13

Which choice best describes data from the table that support the researchers' conclusion?

A) Business A has the highest product quality and brand strength scores, resulting in the highest customer satisfaction.

B) Business C has the highest CSR score, yet it has the lowest product quality and brand strength scores.

C) Business B has the highest advertising spend percentage, but it has a lower customer satisfaction compared to Business A.

D) Business D has balanced scores across all factors, yet it has lower customer satisfaction than Business A.

CONTINUE

Electric Vehicle Adoption and Investment by Country in 2023

Country/ Region	Number of Electric Vehicles (2023)	Investment in EVs (2023)
China	14.1 million	$15 billion
United States	1.4 million	$5 billion
European Union	3.2 million	$10 billion
Japan	0.2 million	$2 billion
India	0.08 million	$1 billion
France	0.3 million	$2.5 billion

Electric vehicles (EVs) are becoming increasingly popular worldwide as countries push for cleaner alternatives to traditional fossil fuel-powered cars. This surge in popularity is largely driven by substantial investments and government incentives aimed at reducing carbon emissions. China leads the world with approximately 14.1 million EVs, supported by a $15 billion investment. In comparison, _____

14

Which choice most effectively uses data from the graph to complete the text?

A) the European Union has invested ten times less in EVs compared to China but produced 3.2 million cars.

B) Japan invested twice as much as India in EVs but only has one-fourth the number of EVs as India.

C) the United States has invested one-third of what China has in EVs and about one-tenth of the number of vehicles.

D) India has manufactured the fewest number of electric vehicles but invested more than France.

CONTINUE

Igor Stravinsky's *Le Sacre du Printemps*, a revolutionary ballet that premiered in 1913, incited a riot at Paris's Théâtre des Champs-Élysées. Its discordant, polytonal score, combined with Vaslav Nijinsky's avant-garde choreography, _____ scandalous, yet it irrevocably altered the course of 20th-century music.

Amidst the tumultuous landscape of contemporary geopolitics, Xi Jinping—General Secretary of the Communist Party of _____ as a pivotal figure; his policies, often met with both admiration and skepticism, have reshaped China's role on the global stage, challenging the traditional hegemony of Western powers.

15

Which choice completes the text so that it conforms to the conventions of Standard English?

A) was deemed

B) were deemed

C) are deemed

D) is deemed

16

Which choice completes the text so that it conforms to the conventions of Standard English?

A) China emerges

B) China—emerges

C) China—emerging

D) China, emerges

CONTINUE

The Keynesian multiplier effect, a fundamental concept in macroeconomic theory, suggests that government spending can lead to an increase in overall economic activity greater than the initial expenditure itself. This phenomenon is predicated on the marginal propensity to _____ determines how much of additional income will be spent by consumers.

17

Which choice completes the text so that it conforms to the conventions of Standard English?

A) consume, (MPC), which

B) consume (MPC), it

C) consume (MPC), which

D) consume (MPC) which

The intricate preparation of *paella*, a quintessential Valencian dish, demands a delicate balance of _____ saffron-infused rice, succulent seafood (such as mussels and prawns), tender rabbit, and a medley of fresh vegetables. Originating in the Albufera lagoon region, it reflects the rich agricultural heritage of Spain's eastern coast.

18

Which choice completes the text so that it conforms to the conventions of Standard English?

A) ingredients

B) ingredients,

C) ingredients;

D) ingredients:

CONTINUE

When faced with ethical dilemmas in artificial intelligence, we often ask the following question: who should bear the responsibility for the decisions made by machines? The algorithms, after all, are written by human hands, yet the outcomes they produce can sometimes stray far from their creators' intent. Many experts in the field of ethics and philosophy wonder _____

19

Which choice completes the text so that it conforms to the conventions of Standard English?

A) can we ever truly program morality into a machine?

B) can we ever truly program morality into a machine.

C) whether we can ever truly program morality into a machine?

D) whether we can ever truly program morality into a machine.

Decades from now, historians _____ back on the current era as a pivotal moment in climate policy. As the effects of global warming become increasingly undeniable, governments around the world are grappling with the complexities of balancing economic growth with environmental sustainability—a challenge that will define the next century.

20

Which choice completes the text so that it conforms to the conventions of Standard English?

A) looked

B) are looking

C) will look

D) look

CONTINUE

The microwave oven, a compact device that utilizes electromagnetic radiation to heat and cook food quickly, has become a staple in modern kitchens. Introduced in the mid-20th century and marketed as a tool to save time and money, _____. Its convenience has not only transformed how we cook but also influenced our eating habits, paving the way for the popularity of ready-to-eat and frozen meals.

Which choice completes the text so that it conforms to the conventions of Standard English?

A) this appliance revolutionized meal preparation by significantly reducing cooking time and making reheating leftovers effortless

B) the microwave's revolutionary meal preparation features significantly reduced cooking time and made reheating leftovers effortless

C) cooking time was reduced, and reheating leftovers was made effortless by this revolutionary meal preparation appliance

D) meal preparation was revolutionized by the microwave, significantly reducing cooking time and making reheating leftovers effortless

CONTINUE

The painting, a vivid portrayal of the Dutch countryside, is renowned for its use of light. Van Gogh's brushwork, with _____ thick, expressive strokes, captures the essence of the region's fields and skies. Visitors often remark on the painting's serene beauty; it's a favorite among art lovers.

22

Which choice completes the text so that it conforms to the conventions of Standard English?

A) it's

B) its

C) their

D) its'

Sourdough bread, with its characteristic tangy flavor and chewy texture, has a history that dates back thousands of years, long before the advent of commercial yeast. The process involves a wild yeast starter, a mixture of flour and water left to ferment over several days, which gives the bread its unique taste and texture. This fermentation not only enhances the bread's flavor but also makes it more digestible. Recently, sourdough has seen a resurgence in popularity, particularly among home _____ appreciate the artisanal quality and health benefits of this ancient bread.

23

Which choice completes the text so that it conforms to the conventions of Standard English?

A) bakers, who

B) bakers that

C) bakers who

D) bakers, that

CONTINUE

The Mars Rover, Perseverance, is equipped with cutting-edge technology to explore the Martian surface. This includes a variety of scientific instruments designed to analyze rock samples, detect organic compounds, and search for signs of ancient life. _____ the rover has a sophisticated navigation system that allows it to traverse the rugged terrain of Mars with minimal human intervention.

24

Which choice completes the text with the most logical transition?

A) Furthermore,

B) However,

C) Subsequently,

D) For example,

In the annals of medical history, there is the curious case of "Stone Man Syndrome," a rare genetic disorder that causes soft tissues to gradually turn into bone, effectively imprisoning the individual in an ossified skeleton. Known formally as Fibrodysplasia Ossificans Progressiva (FOP), this condition has no known cure and leaves those affected with severely limited mobility. Research into potential treatments, _____ continues, offering a glimmer of hope to those diagnosed with this debilitating disorder.

25

Which choice completes the text with the most logical transition?

A) therefore,

B) additionally,

C) eventually,

D) nevertheless,

CONTINUE

The "Baigong pipes," discovered in a remote area of China's Qinghai Province, are a set of ancient, rusted metal pipes embedded in rock formations near a desolate mountain. What makes these pipes particularly puzzling is their age-estimated to be over 150,000 years old-and their unexplained origin, as they appear to be man-made but predate known human metalworking. Some speculate that the pipes might be evidence of an advanced ancient civilization; _____ others suggest extraterrestrial visitors.

Which choice completes the text with the most logical transition?

A) similarly,

B) on the other hand,

C) thus,

D) then,

CONTINUE

While researching a topic, a student has taken the following notes:

- The Cambrian Explosion occurred around 540 million years ago.
- Soon after, most major animal phyla appeared in the fossil record.
- This period saw a rapid increase in the diversity of life forms.
- Fossils from this period are found worldwide.
- Possible causes include rising oxygen levels, changes in ocean chemistry, and evolutionary innovations.
- Some scientists debate whether the Cambrian Explosion was truly a sudden event or a more gradual process.

27

The student wants to explain the significance of the Cambrian Explosion in the history of life on Earth. Which choice most effectively uses relevant information from the notes to accomplish this goal?

A) The Cambrian Explosion is known for the rapid increase in biodiversity and the appearance of most major animal phyla in the fossil record globally.

B) Scientific debates continue about whether the Cambrian Explosion was a sudden event or a gradual process over millions of years.

C) The Cambrian Explosion was potentially triggered by factors such as rising oxygen levels, changes in ocean chemistry, and evolutionary innovations.

D) The Cambrian Explosion took place over 500 million years ago and led to many changes in the world, but an aspect of its explosion is still debated.

If you finish before the time is called, you may check your work on this module only.
On Test Day, you will only be able to move to the next module when time expires.

 **Answer Key**

Question Number	Correct Answer	Level of Difficulty	Question Type
1	C	Easy	**Craft and Structure:** *Words in Context*
2	C	Easy	**Craft and Structure:** *Words in Context*
3	D	Medium	**Craft and Structure:** *Words in Context*
4	B	Easy	**Craft and Structure:** *Words in Context*
5	A	Easy	**Craft and Structure:** *Words in Context*
6	D	Medium	**Craft and Structure:** *Main Purpose*
7	A	Hard	**Craft and Structure:** *Overall Structure*
8	C	Medium	**Craft and Structure:** *Function of the Underlined Portion*
9	D	Medium	**Ideas and Information:** *Supporting a Claim*
10	A	Medium	**Ideas and Information:** *Inference*
11	B	Hard	**Ideas and Information:** *Main Idea*
12	B	Hard	**Ideas and Information:** *Detail*
13	A	Medium	**Ideas and Information:** *Supporting a Claim (Infographic)*

Question Number	Correct Answer	Level of Difficulty	Question Type
14	C	Easy	**Ideas and Information:** *Inference (Infographic)*
15	A	Medium	**Standard English Conventions:** *Verbs*
16	B	Hard	**Standard English Conventions:** *Punctuation and Sentence Structure*
17	C	Medium	**Standard English Conventions:** *Punctuation and Sentence Structure*
18	D	Easy	**Standard English Conventions:** *Punctuation and Sentence Structure*
19	D	Easy	**Standard English Conventions:** *Punctuation*
20	C	Medium	**Standard English Conventions:** *Verbs*
21	A	Medium	**Standard English Conventions:** *Modifiers*
22	B	Easy	**Standard English Conventions:** *Pronouns*
23	C	Medium	**Standard English Conventions:** *Pronouns and Punctuation*
24	A	Medium	**Expressions of Writing:** *Transitions*
25	D	Hard	**Expressions of Writing:** *Transitions*
26	B	Medium	**Expressions of Writing:** *Transitions*
27	A	Easy	**Expressions of Writing:** *Rhetorical Synthesis*

Raw Score Conversion Table

Raw Score (# of Correct Answers)	Reading and Writing Section Score	Raw Score (# of Correct Answers)	Reading and Writing Section Score
54	N/A	30	470
53	N/A	29	470
52	N/A	28	450
51	N/A	27	450
50	N/A	26	440
49	N/A	25	430
48	N/A	24	430
47	N/A	23	410
46	N/A	22	410
45	N/A	21	400
44	600	20	390
43	590	19	390
42	580	18	380
41	570	17	360
40	560	16	350
39	550	15	330
38	540	14	300
37	530	13	300
36	530	12	270
35	520	11	260
34	510	10	250
33	500	9	240
32	490	8	220
31	480	7	210

 **Explanations**

1. Words in Context: Easy

Answer: C) surge

Step-by-Step Explanation:

1. Let's look at what the passage is saying. It describes how some recent activity in tourism has positively affected local businesses in Kyoto, Japan, with many reporting significant revenue growth.
2. Notice the word "positively impacted" and the phrase "significant increases in revenue." These details indicate that tourism has increased, leading to positive outcomes for local businesses.
3. The phrase "this influx of visitors" further supports the idea that there has been a noticeable rise in the number of tourists and thus, an increase in tourism itself.
4. Ask yourself, what word describes a sudden or significant increase? "Surge" fits perfectly because it means a rapid or large increase, which aligns with the context of growing tourism.

Explanation of Incorrect Options:

A) decline: This is incorrect because it means a decrease, which contradicts the positive impact and increase in revenue mentioned in the passage.

B) plateau: This is incorrect because it suggests a leveling off or no change, which does not match the idea of a significant increase in tourism.

D) tradition: This is incorrect because it refers to a long-established custom, which does not logically fit the context of a recent increase in tourism.

2. Words in Context: Easy

Answer: C) precision

Step-by-Step Explanation:

1. Let's understand the passage together. It highlights Leonardo da Vinci's reputation for his detailed drawings and notes, which showcase his skill in both art and science.
2. Notice the phrase "detailed drawings and notes" and the reference to his "deep sense of curiosity and analytical thinking." These details suggest that Leonardo approached his work with great care and attention to detail.
3. The word we need should describe Leonardo's careful and meticulous approach to both his art and scientific observations.
4. Ask yourself, what word best describes the careful accuracy and attention to detail that Leonardo demonstrated? "Precision" fits perfectly because it means being exact and accurate, which aligns with the context of his detailed work.

Explanation of Incorrect Options:

A) indifference: This is incorrect because it means a lack of interest or concern, which contradicts the passage's description of Leonardo's curiosity and analytical thinking.

B) mediocrity: This is incorrect because it implies average or below-average quality, which does not match Leonardo's renowned skill and attention to detail.

D) popularity: This is incorrect because it refers to being well-liked or famous, which does not logically fit the context of his meticulous work as described in the passage.

3. Words in Context: Medium

Answer: D) gravity

Step-by-Step Explanation:

1. Let's look at what the passage is saying. It describes the historic event of the first moon landing and emphasizes the importance of Armstrong's famous words during this monumental moment in human history.
2. Notice the phrase "highlighting the monumental achievement in human exploration." This indicates that the moment was of great importance. Moreover, the phrase "one giant leap for mankind" reflects the vast significance of this event for all of humanity, symbolizing a major advancement in human exploration and achievement.
3. The word we need should reflect the seriousness and importance of the event and Armstrong's statement.
4. Ask yourself, what word best captures the serious and significant nature of the moon landing? "Gravity" fits perfectly because it means the seriousness or importance of a situation, which aligns with the context of this historic event.

Explanation of Incorrect Options:

A) insignificance: This is incorrect because it means lack of importance, which directly contradicts the passage's description of the event as monumental.

B) excitement: This is incorrect because while excitement was certainly present, the passage focuses more on the importance and seriousness of the moment rather than the emotions it provoked.

C) complexity: This is incorrect because it refers to something being complicated or intricate, which doesn't align with the context, which emphasizes the importance or seriousness of the achievement.

4. Words in Context: Easy

Answer: B) limited

Step-by-Step Explanation:

1. Let's understand the passage together. It discusses how our understanding of dinosaurs' behaviors and ecosystems is constrained by the incomplete nature of the fossil record.
2. Notice the phrase "The fossil record, while extensive, provides only a fragmented glimpse into the ancient past." This indicates that our current knowledge is incomplete and lacks full detail.
3. The word we need should reflect the idea that our understanding is restricted or not fully developed due to the limitations of the fossil record.
4. Ask yourself, what word best describes something that is not complete or fully developed? "Limited" fits perfectly because it suggests that our knowledge is restricted and not comprehensive, which aligns with the context of the passage.

Explanation of Incorrect Options:

A) comprehensive: This is incorrect because it implies that our knowledge is complete and thorough, which contradicts the passage's description of the fossil record as fragmented and incomplete.

C) definitive: This is incorrect because it suggests that our knowledge is conclusive or final, which does not match the idea that our understanding is still incomplete and dependent on further developments.

D) inaccurate: This is incorrect because the passage does not indicate nor imply that our knowledge is incorrect, but rather that it is incomplete or insufficient.

5. Words in Context: Easy

Answer: A) instrumental

Step-by-Step Explanation:

1. Let's look at what the passage is saying. It describes the Great Rift Valley as a significant geological feature that provides critical insights into Earth's geological history and species development.
2. Notice the phrases "they offer critical insights" and "the study of plate tectonics and evolutionary biology." These indicate that the valley plays an essential role in these fields of study. The information after the colon—"they offer critical insights into the Earth's geological history and the development of species"—is crucial because it directly explains how the Great Rift Valley contributes to scientific understanding, clarifying the valley's instrumental role in advancing these areas of research.
3. The word we need should convey the idea that the Great Rift Valley is crucial or key to understanding these scientific areas.
4. Ask yourself, what word best describes something that is essential or plays a significant role? "Instrumental" fits perfectly because it means serving as a crucial or necessary means, which aligns with the context of the valley's importance in scientific research.

Explanation of Incorrect Options:

B) incidental: This is incorrect because it implies something that is secondary or not essential, which contradicts the passage's emphasis on the valley's critical role in scientific studies.

C) insignificant: This is incorrect because it suggests that the valley is unimportant, which contradicts the passage's description of its importance in understanding geological and biological developments.

D) implicit: This is incorrect because it means something that is implied or understood without being stated directly, which does not fit the context of the valley's active and explicit role in scientific research.

6. Main Purpose: Medium

Answer: D) To enumerate the consequences of Borlaug's initiative

Logical Breakdown and Explanation:

To determine the main purpose of the text, we need to focus on what the text as a whole is "doing" and how it presents its key ideas. The text discusses the Green Revolution, highlighting both its benefits in increasing food production and the criticisms it faced regarding environmental damage and social inequality. The passage provides an overview of the initiative and its impacts, both positive and negative.

Option D is correct because it accurately reflects the main purpose of the text: to enumerate the consequences of Borlaug's initiative, including both the positive outcome of increased food production and the negative criticisms related to environmental harm and social inequality.

Option A is incorrect because to "challenge" an idea means to actively argue against or dispute it. The text does not take an oppositional stance against the Green Revolution's benefits. While it acknowledges some criticisms, it also discusses its success in increasing food production. This balance of pros and cons does not align with the notion of challenging the Green Revolution. Additionally, the passage doesn't discuss "developing countries" at all; thus, this answer is off topic.

Option B is incorrect because it suggests that the text's purpose is to explain the agricultural techniques used in the Green Revolution. To "explain techniques" would require the passage to focus on the specific methods or practices, such as the use of high-yielding crop varieties, fertilizers, or pesticides, in detail. However, the passage only briefly mentions these techniques, which should be looked at as minor details without a focus on the big and major ideas of the text.

Option C is incorrect because it implies that the passage compares the Green Revolution's impact to that of other revolutions. The key idea here is "compare," which means the text would need to draw parallels or contrasts between the Green Revolution and other similar movements. However, the passage does not mention any other revolutions. Its focus is solely on the Green Revolution and its specific outcomes, making this option off topic.

7. Overall Structure: Hard

Answer: A) It presents a historical perspective on an astronomical object and then introduces a modern scientific hypothesis to explain observed phenomena.

Logical Breakdown and Explanation:

To determine the overall structure of the text, we need to analyze how the information is organized and presented. The passage begins with a brief *historical* perspective on Betelgeuse, noting its fluctuating brightness as observed by *ancient* astronomers. It then shifts to a *modern* scientific hypothesis proposed by astronomers Levesque and Massey to explain this phenomenon, focusing on the idea that large convective cells on the star's surface may be responsible for its irregular brightness.

Option A is correct because the passage's structure precisely aligns with this description. It begins by presenting *ancient* observations of Betelgeuse's fluctuating brightness, providing a historical perspective. It then transitions to a contemporary scientific explanation, where *modern* astronomers propose a hypothesis involving convective cells to account for the star's irregular brightness.

Option B is incorrect because the passage does not present an opinion or combine elements of previous theories. Instead, it offers a scientific hypothesis based on new observations.

Option C is incorrect because there is no comparison of different stars' light emissions. The passage focuses exclusively on Betelgeuse.

Option D is incorrect because the passage does not focus on or explain "the discovery of a new telescope."

8. Function of the Underlined Portion: Medium

Answer: C) It provides evidence that contradicts the prevailing belief.

Logical Breakdown and Explanation:

To determine the function of the underlined portion, we need to examine how it fits within the overall argument presented. The passage starts by challenging the common assumption that prioritizing one's own interests leads to greater happiness, introducing a statistic that highlights this widespread belief. However, the text immediately counters this assumption with evidence from studies, suggesting that true happiness is more closely linked to factors like social connections and altruism.

Option C is correct because the underlined portion presents evidence that directly contradicts the prevailing belief that self-serving actions lead to greater happiness. The introduction of the 70% statistic sets up the expectation that self-interest correlates with personal satisfaction, but the passage uses studies by Jennifer Crocker to argue against this belief, emphasizing that happiness is more about social and altruistic behaviors.

Option A is incorrect because it refers to "sources of self-serving behavior." The underlined portion is not about self-serving behaviors, which are actions taken to benefit oneself. Instead, it provides examples of the sources of happiness—an emotional state, not a behavior. The focus is on factors that contribute to well-being, not on the origins of behaviors that serve the self.

Option B is incorrect because it claims the passage "questions the significance of personal achievements in overall happiness." The underlined portion does not address personal achievements; rather, it challenges the assumption that self-serving actions lead to happiness. The underlined portion is more concerned with refuting the effectiveness of self-interest in achieving happiness, not with questioning the importance of personal accomplishments themselves.

Option D is incorrect because the underlined portion discusses factors that contribute to well-being—like strong social ties, acts of altruism, and genuine internal motivations—but it does not frame these as specific actions that researchers are encouraging people to undertake. Instead, these factors are presented as elements that contribute to happiness based on research findings, not as prescribed actions or recommendations from researchers.

9. Supporting a Claim: Medium

Answer: D) In her novel *The Serpent's Daughter*, Ramanathan portrays Anjali grappling with the loss of her parents while uncovering ancient stories of the Naga people, blending her personal struggle with cultural heritage.

Logical Breakdown and Explanation:

To determine which finding most directly supports the critic's claim about the cultural significance of Ramanathan's novels, we need to focus on how each option relates to the critic's claim that the narratives in her novels have profound cultural significance, particularly in how they tie characters' personal struggles to their cultural heritage.

Option D is correct because it directly aligns with the critic's claim. It shows how Ramanathan blends personal struggles with cultural heritage. In *The Serpent's Daughter*, the character Anjali's personal grief (personal struggle) is intertwined with the exploration of ancient stories of the Naga people (cultural heritage), which clearly illustrates how the narrative connects personal and cultural elements. In other words, the example validates the claim, thus making it more believable.

Option A is incorrect because, while the translation of Ramanathan's novels into other languages broadens her audience, this detail is **irrelevant to the claim** about the cultural significance of her work. The critic's claim is focused on how Ramanathan explores the intricacies of Sri Lankan society and her characters' cultural heritage, not on the accessibility of her work to a wider audience. Therefore, this option is off-topic and does not strengthen the critic's argument.

Option B is incorrect because it mentions that Ramanathan's writing style is influenced by Western literary traditions. This detail might be interesting, but it is **off-topic** in the context of supporting the critic's claim about her exploration of Sri Lankan society and cultural heritage. In fact, emphasizing a Western influence could **weaken rather than strengthen** the critic's point about the cultural significance tied specifically to Sri Lankan society.

Option C is incorrect because it describes the presence of wealthy landowners as antagonists in one of Ramanathan's novels. While this plot element may contribute to the story's tension, it is **irrelevant to the claim** about the cultural significance of her work and how her characters' struggles are connected to their cultural heritage. The mere existence of antagonists does not directly support the critic's claim about the personal struggles of characters.

10. Inference: Medium

Answer: A) both species would likely struggle to survive due to their interdependence, highlighting the fragile balance of their mutualistic relationship.

Logical Breakdown and Explanation:

This question asks you to complete a passage that describes a symbiotic relationship between the acacia tree and ants, where each species depends on the other for survival. The passage emphasizes the importance of this mutualistic relationship, suggesting that the survival of both species is interconnected.

Option A is correct because it logically completes the passage by reinforcing the idea that both the acacia tree and the ants would struggle to survive without each other. This choice directly ties into the concept of interdependence discussed in the passage, highlighting the fragile balance of their relationship. The passage sets up the expectation that both species are crucial to each other's survival, making Option A the most logical conclusion.

Option B is incorrect because it contradicts the established information. The passage describes the relationship between the acacia tree and the ants as vital for both species. Suggesting that the acacia tree would flourish without the ants goes against the idea of mutual dependence, making this choice logically inconsistent with the text.

Option C is incorrect because it introduces an idea that is irrelevant to the main focus of the passage. While the passage emphasizes the unique and critical relationship between the acacia tree and the ants, this option implies that the ants could simply find another plant, which downplays the importance of their specific relationship with the acacia tree. This suggestion does not address the potential negative impact on both species if one were to disappear.

Option D is incorrect because it is off topic. While the idea that herbivores would become more prevalent without the ants may be true, it shifts the focus away from the mutualistic relationship between the acacia tree and the ants and towards a broader ecological impact. The passage is centered on the direct interdependence between these two species, not on the effects of their absence on other organisms like herbivores.

11. Main Idea: Hard

Answer: B) Hope is a persistent and comforting presence that remains even in the harshest conditions.

Logical Breakdown and Explanation:

This question asks you to determine the main idea of Emily Dickinson's poem "Hope is the thing with feathers." The poem uses an extended metaphor comparing hope to a bird that resides within the soul, singing its tune persistently, even in the face of harsh conditions. The bird, representing hope, is resilient and requires nothing in return, suggesting that hope is a constant and selfless presence that endures even in the most challenging situations.

Option B is correct because it captures the main idea of the poem: that hope is a persistent and comforting presence that remains even in the harshest conditions. The metaphor of the bird that "never stops" singing and "never" asks for anything in return highlights the enduring and self-sustaining nature of hope, even in difficult circumstances. This option aligns with the overall essence of the poem, reflecting both the resilience and the comforting aspects of hope.

Option A is incorrect because it suggests that hope is a "delicate feeling that can easily be destroyed by difficult circumstances." This is **contradictory** to the poem, which emphasizes the strength and persistence of hope. The poem indicates that hope is not easily destroyed, even in the face of "sore" storms, making this option opposite to the poem's message.

Option C is incorrect because it implies that hope is a "fleeting emotion," which means that it is temporary. This idea is **contradictory** to the poem's description of hope as a constant presence that does not require nurturing. The bird in the poem sings "without the words" and "never stops at all," indicating that hope endures on its own, even in extreme conditions.

Option D is incorrect because it portrays hope as a "selfish emotion that demands something in return from those it comforts." This is **off topic** and **contradictory** to the poem, which clearly states that hope "never, in extremity, asked a crumb of me." The poem presents hope as selfless and giving, requiring nothing in return, making this option not only unsupported by the passage but directly opposed to its message.

12. Detail: Hard

Answer: B) Antonio struggles to balance his personal loyalty to Ultima with the villagers' negative perception, leading him to question the nature of morality.

Logical Breakdown and Explanation:

This question asks how Antonio's relationship with Ultima complicates his understanding of morality, as described in the passage. The correct answer should reflect the internal conflict Antonio feels between his admiration for Ultima and the villagers' negative perception of her, which leads him to question the nature of good and evil.

Option B is correct because it directly addresses Antonio's struggle to balance his personal loyalty to Ultima with the villagers' negative perception of her. The passage explicitly mentions Antonio being "torn between admiration and fear" and his inability to "reconcile the loving guardian he knew with the dark figure others portrayed her to be." This internal conflict causes Antonio to question the nature of morality, as he struggles to balance his loyalty to Ultima with the villagers' negative views, leading him to grapple with what is truly right or wrong.

Option A is incorrect because it suggests that Antonio sees morality as a rigid concept with clear distinctions between good and evil, influenced by Ultima's teachings. This is **not supported by the passage**, which actually describes Antonio's confusion and inability to reconcile the duality in Ultima's nature. The passage emphasizes the ambiguity and complexity of morality, not a rigid understanding.

Option C is incorrect because it implies that Antonio views morality solely through the lens of societal approval, prioritizing the villagers' opinions over his bond with Ultima. This **distorts the information** given in the passage, as Antonio is conflicted and does not simply prioritize the villagers' opinions. He is torn between their views and his personal experiences with Ultima, which complicates his understanding of morality rather than simplifying it to societal approval.

Option D is incorrect because it suggests that Antonio becomes indifferent to the concepts of good and evil, believing they are irrelevant to his personal experiences with Ultima. This **contradicts what the passage says**, as Antonio is deeply conflicted and concerned about the moral implications of his relationship with Ultima.

13. Supporting a Claim (Infographic): Medium

Answer: A) Business A has the highest product quality and brand strength scores, resulting in the highest customer satisfaction.

Logical Breakdown and Explanation:

This question asks you to identify which piece of data from the table best supports the researchers' conclusion that businesses with high product quality and strong brand strength tend to have higher customer satisfaction. The correct answer should directly reflect the relationship between high product quality, strong brand strength, and customer satisfaction, as discussed in the passage.

Option A is correct because it accurately reflects the data from the table and aligns with the researchers' conclusion. Business A has the highest product quality score (9) and the highest brand strength score (9), and it also has the highest customer satisfaction score (9). This directly supports the conclusion that high product quality and strong brand strength are associated with higher customer satisfaction.

Option B is incorrect because, while it accurately states that Business C has the highest CSR score, this information is **irrelevant** to the researchers' conclusion. The passage emphasizes the importance of product quality and brand strength, not CSR, in determining customer satisfaction. Therefore, even though the data might be true, it does not support the specific conclusion of the study.

Option C is incorrect because it introduces the idea that Business B has the highest advertising spend percentage, but this fact is **irrelevant** to the researchers' conclusion. The study focuses on the impact of product quality and brand strength on customer satisfaction, not advertising spend. While the data presented is accurate, it does not relate to the key factors highlighted in the passage.

Option D is incorrect because, although it is true that Business D has balanced scores across all factors, this observation is **off-topic** and does not directly support the conclusion about the relationship between product quality, brand strength, and customer satisfaction. The focus of the passage is on the importance of high scores in product quality and brand strength, not on balanced scores across all factors.

14. Inference (Infographic): Easy

Answer: A) Business A has the highest product quality and brand strength scores, resulting in the highest customer satisfaction.

Logical Breakdown and Explanation:

This question asks you to choose the option that most effectively uses data from the table to complete the text about electric vehicle (EV) adoption and investment by country. The correct answer should accurately reflect the data and be consistent with the ideas discussed in the passage, particularly in comparison to China, which is emphasized as a leader in EV adoption and investment.

Option C is correct because it accurately reflects the data and is consistent with the passage's focus on comparing other countries to China. The United States has invested $5 billion in EVs, which is one-third of China's $15 billion investment, and has approximately 1.4 million EVs, which is about one-tenth of China's 14.1 million EVs. This option uses the data correctly and fits well with the passage's emphasis on China's leadership in the EV market.

Option A is incorrect because it is **not true** according to the data. The European Union has invested $10 billion in EVs, which is not "ten times less" than China's $15 billion investment. Additionally, the statement doesn't accurately compare the production figures or provide a meaningful comparison to China's leading position.

Option B is incorrect because it is **not true** based on the data. Japan has invested $2 billion in EVs, which is indeed twice as much as India's $1 billion investment, but Japan (0.2 million) actually has more EVs than India (.08 million), not "one-fourth the number of EVs as India." This makes the statement inaccurate and inconsistent with the data provided.

Option D is incorrect because it **presents an idea that doesn't fit** with the passage's focus on comparing EV adoption and investment to China's. While it's true that India has manufactured the fewest EVs and invested more than France, this comparison is not relevant to the passage's discussion of China's leadership in EV adoption and investment. The focus should be on comparisons that are consistent with the ideas developed in the passage.

15. Verbs: Medium

Answer: A) was deemed

Logical Breakdown and Explanation:

This question asks you to select the choice that correctly completes the sentence while conforming to the conventions of Standard English. Specifically, you need to ensure that the verb agrees with the subject and that the tense is appropriate for the context.

Option A is correct because it uses the singular verb "was deemed," which correctly agrees with the singular subject "its score" (referring to the discordant, polytonal score of *Le Sacre du Printemps*). An important point to remember is that the subject is never found in nonessential information ("combined with Vaslav Nijinsky's avant-garde choreography"). Also, the sentence describes an event that occurred in the past (the 1913 premiere), so the past tense is appropriate.

Option B is incorrect because it creates a subject-verb disagreement. The subject "its score" is singular, but "*were* deemed" is a plural verb, which does not agree with the singular subject. Identifying this disagreement should be the first step in recognizing why this option is incorrect.

Option C is incorrect because it also creates a subject-verb disagreement. The subject "its score" is singular, but "*are* deemed" is a plural verb, which does not agree with the singular subject. Just like in Option B, the mismatch between the subject and verb is the key reason this option is incorrect.

Option D is incorrect because it also uses the present tense "is deemed," which is **wrong tense** for the context. The sentence discusses how the ballet was perceived at the time of its premiere, so the past tense is necessary.

16. Punctuation and Sentence Structure: Hard

Answer: B) China-emerges

Logical Breakdown and Explanation:

This question asks you to select the choice that correctly completes the sentence while conforming to the conventions of Standard English. Specifically, you need to ensure that the punctuation and sentence structure are correct.

Option B is correct because it correctly uses a pair of dashes to set off the nonessential appositive phrase "General Secretary of the Communist Party of China." The dash before "emerges" serves as the necessary closing dash that corresponds to the opening dash after "Xi Jinping." This use of dashes correctly separates the appositive from the main clause, "Xi Jinping emerges as a pivotal figure," ensuring that the sentence conforms to the conventions of Standard English by maintaining a grammatical sentence structure.

Option A is incorrect because it fails to account for the dash after "Xi Jinping." The dash after his name introduces a nonessential appositive phrase ("General Secretary of the Communist Party of China"), which needs to be closed off properly to maintain sentence balance. Since this sentence has an opening dash, it requires a corresponding closing dash after the appositive. By not including a second dash after "China," Option A disrupts the sentence structure, leaving the sentence improperly punctuated.

Option C is incorrect because it creates a sentence fragment. The word "emerging" is a participle, not a verb, so it cannot stand alone as the main verb of the sentence. This makes the sentence incomplete and grammatically incorrect.

Option D is incorrect because it incorrectly uses a comma after "China" instead of the necessary second dash. The sentence already contains an opening dash after "Xi Jinping" to introduce the nonessential appositive phrase "General Secretary of the Communist Party of China." To properly close off this phrase and maintain sentence balance, a second dash should be used after "China." By using a comma instead of a dash, Option D disrupts the sentence structure and fails to properly set off the appositive, leading to a punctuation error.

17. Punctuation and Sentence Structure: Medium

Answer: C) consume (MPC), which

Logical Breakdown and Explanation:

This question asks you to choose the option that correctly completes the sentence while conforming to the conventions of Standard English, particularly focusing on proper punctuation and sentence structure.

Option C is correct because it uses proper punctuation. Following the parentheses, the relative pronoun "which" is correctly preceded by a comma, as it introduces a nonessential relative clause that provides additional information about the MPC.

Option A is incorrect because it places a comma before the parentheses, which is a **punctuation rule violation**. Commas should never be placed directly before parentheses, making this choice grammatically incorrect.

Option B is incorrect because it creates a **run-on sentence**. The independent clause "it determines how much of additional income will be spent by consumers" follows another independent clause "this phenomenon is predicated on the marginal propensity to consume." However, only a comma separates the two ICs, leading to a run-on sentence.

Option D is incorrect because it omits the necessary comma before "which." The word "which" introduces a nonessential relative clause, so it must be preceded by a comma according to **comma rule conventions**. The absence of this comma makes the sentence grammatically incorrect.

18. Punctuation and Sentence Structure: Easy

Answer: D) ingredients:

Logical Breakdown and Explanation:

This question asks you to choose the option that correctly completes the sentence while following the conventions of Standard English, particularly focusing on the correct use of punctuation when introducing a list.

Option D is correct because it uses a colon, which is the appropriate punctuation mark to introduce a list after a general term. The colon correctly separates the general term "ingredients" from the specific items in the list: "saffron-infused rice, succulent seafood (such as mussels and prawns), tender rabbit, and a medley of fresh vegetables." This choice follows the standard punctuation rules for introducing a list.

Option A is incorrect because it lacks any punctuation after the word "ingredients." According to punctuation rules, a colon or dash is needed to separate the general term "ingredients" from the specific list that follows. Without the proper punctuation, the sentence is incomplete and does not conform to the conventions of Standard English.

Option B is incorrect because it uses a comma after "ingredients." While commas can be used to separate items within a list, they are not appropriate for introducing a list after a general term. The sentence requires a colon or dash to introduce the list, making this option a punctuation rule violation.

Option C s incorrect because it uses a semicolon, which is meant to separate two independent clauses (ICs). However, the information after "ingredients" is not an independent clause (IC); it is a list that specifies the components of the "ingredients." Since the semicolon is used to join two ICs, its use here is incorrect.

19. Punctuation: Easy

Answer: D) whether we can ever truly program morality into a machine.

Logical Breakdown and Explanation:

This question asks you to select the choice that correctly completes the sentence, focusing on whether a direct or indirect question is needed and ensuring proper word order.

Option D is correct because it uses an indirect question structure, which is appropriate given the context of the passage. The sentence that the underlined portion is a part of states, "Many experts in the field of ethics and philosophy wonder," indicating that the sentence is reporting the experts' consideration rather than directly asking a question. An indirect question, like "whether we can ever truly program morality into a machine," ends with a period because it is part of a declarative statement. Also, the sentence correctly follows the structure of an indirect question, with the subject "we" preceding the verb "can," and this structure aligns with the reflective and reporting nature of the passage.

Option A is incorrect because it uses the structure of a direct question ("can we ever truly program morality into a machine?") in a context that requires an indirect question. This leads to a sentence structure error, as the context does not call for a direct question.

Option B is incorrect because it uses the structure of a direct question but ends with a period, creating a punctuation error. Additionally, the context requires an indirect question, making the word order incorrect as well (the verb "can" should follow the subject "we" in an indirect question).

Option C is incorrect because, although it starts correctly with "whether," it uses the wrong punctuation mark—a question mark—at the end of the sentence. Since the sentence is an indirect question, it should end with a period, not a question mark.

20. Verbs: Medium

Answer: C) will look

Logical Breakdown and Explanation:

This question asks you to choose the option that correctly completes the sentence, focusing on selecting the appropriate verb tense that aligns with the time reference given in the passage.

Option C is correct because it uses the future tense "will look," which aligns with the time reference "Decades from now." The passage refers to a future perspective, where historians will reflect on the current era as a pivotal moment in climate policy. The future tense is necessary to match this reference to a time that has not yet occurred, making "will look" the correct choice.

Option A is incorrect because it uses the past tense "looked," which contradicts the time reference "Decades from now." The past tense implies that the action has already happened, which does not fit with the idea of historians looking back in the future.

Option B is incorrect because it uses the present continuous tense "are looking," which also contradicts the future time reference. The present continuous tense suggests an action happening right now, which does not match the future perspective of "Decades from now."

Option D is incorrect because it uses the present tense "look," which, like the present continuous tense, does not align with the future time reference. The present tense implies that the action is happening in the current moment, which is inconsistent with the future-oriented context of the sentence.

21. Modifiers: Medium

Answer: A) this appliance revolutionized meal preparation by significantly reducing cooking time and making reheating leftovers effortless

Logical Breakdown and Explanation:

This question asks you to select the option that correctly completes the sentence, ensuring that the modifier at the beginning of the clause is logically modifying the correct noun.

Option A is correct because it places the correct noun "this appliance" immediately after the modifying phrase "Introduced in the mid-20th century and marketed as a tool to save time and money." The modifying phrase logically describes "this appliance" (the microwave oven), making this sentence clear and grammatically correct. The sentence effectively conveys that the microwave revolutionized meal preparation by reducing cooking time and making reheating leftovers effortless.

Option B is incorrect because it creates a modifier issue. The modifying phrase "Introduced in the mid-20th century and marketed as a tool to save time and money" does not logically modify "the microwave's revolutionary meal preparation *features*." The phrase should modify the microwave itself, not its features, leading to a dangling modifier error.

Option C is incorrect because it also creates a modifier issue. The modifying phrase "Introduced in the mid-20th century and marketed as a tool to save time and money" is left dangling, as the sentence begins with "*cooking time* was reduced," which is not what the phrase logically modifies. This results in an unclear and grammatically incorrect sentence.

Option D is incorrect because it creates a similar modifier issue. The modifying phrase is followed by "*meal preparation* was revolutionized by the microwave," which is not the correct noun for the modifier to logically modify. The phrase should modify the microwave directly, not the process of meal preparation, leading to a dangling modifier error.

22. Pronouns: Easy

Answer: B) its

Logical Breakdown and Explanation:

This question asks you to select the correct pronoun to complete the sentence, focusing on proper usage and agreement with the noun being referred to.

Option B is correct because it uses the correct singular possessive pronoun "its," which refers to the singular noun "brushwork" in the sentence. The pronoun "its" correctly indicates that the thick, expressive strokes belong to Van Gogh's brushwork. Since both the pronoun and the noun are singular, this choice ensures proper pronoun-noun agreement.

Option A is incorrect because "it's" is a contraction for "it is" or "it has," which does not make sense when plugged back into the sentence. If you replace "it's" with "it is" or "it has," the sentence would read "Van Gogh's brushwork, with it is thick, expressive strokes," which is grammatically incorrect.

Option C is incorrect because it uses the plural pronoun "their," which does not agree with the singular noun "brushwork." This creates a **pronoun-noun disagreement** error, as "their" should refer to a plural noun, not a singular one like "brushwork."

Option D is incorrect because *its'* does not exist in the English language. This is a common trick answer that may appear on tests, but it is never correct. The proper possessive form is *its* without an apostrophe.

23. Pronouns and Punctuation: Medium

Answer: C) bakers who

Logical Breakdown and Explanation:

This question asks you to choose the option that correctly completes the sentence, focusing on the correct use of relative pronouns and punctuation, especially distinguishing between essential and nonessential clauses.

Option C is correct because it uses the correct relative pronoun "who" to refer to "bakers," which are people. The clause "who appreciate the artisanal quality and health benefits of this ancient bread" is essential because it specifies which bakers are being discussed. No commas are needed since this clause is essential to the meaning of the sentence.

Option A is incorrect because it incorrectly treats the "who" clause as nonessential by adding a comma before "who." The clause is essential to the meaning of the sentence because it specifies which bakers are being referred to, so no comma should be used.

Option B is incorrect because it uses the relative pronoun "that," which is used to describe things or objects, not people. Since "bakers" refers to people, the correct pronoun is "who," not "that."

Option D is incorrect because it uses "that" instead of "who" and also incorrectly treats the clause as nonessential by adding a comma before "that." This creates both a relative pronoun error and a punctuation error.

24. Transitions: Medium

Answer: A) Furthermore,

Logical Breakdown and Explanation:

This question asks you to choose the transition word that best connects the ideas in the passage logically. The correct transition should smoothly link the description of the Mars Rover's scientific instruments with the subsequent mention of its navigation system.

Option A is correct because "Furthermore," continues the discussion of the Mars Rover's features and functions in a positive, additive manner. The passage first highlights the Rover's scientific instruments, which are designed to analyze rock samples and search for signs of ancient life. "Furthermore," logically extends this discussion by introducing the Rover's sophisticated navigation system, which complements its scientific capabilities by allowing it to traverse the Martian terrain. This transition effectively continues the positive enumeration of the Rover's advanced technology.

Option B is incorrect because "However," introduces a contrast, which is illogical in this context. There is no contrast between the scientific instruments and the navigation system; both are part of the Rover's advanced technology.

Option C is incorrect because "Subsequently," indicates a sequence of events in time, which does not fit logically with the description of the Rover's features. The passage is not discussing events that happen one after another, but rather different aspects of the Rover's technology.

Option D is incorrect because "For example," introduces a specific instance to illustrate a general point. The passage is not providing an example of a previously mentioned generalization but rather adding another feature of the Rover, making this transition illogical.

25. Transitions: Hard

Answer: D) nevertheless,

Logical Breakdown and Explanation:

This question asks you to choose the transition that most logically connects the discussion of "Stone Man Syndrome" and the ongoing research into potential treatments. The correct transition should accurately reflect the relationship between the incurable nature of the condition and the hope provided by ongoing research.

Option D is correct because "nevertheless," effectively captures the contrast between the grim reality of the condition (having no known cure and severely limiting mobility) and the ongoing research that offers hope. The word "nevertheless" indicates that despite the challenges and lack of a cure, research continues, providing a positive outlook for the future.

Option A is incorrect because "therefore" suggests a cause-and-effect relationship that does not fit the context. The continuation of research is not a direct consequence of the previous statement but rather a contrast, making this transition illogical.

Option B is incorrect because "additionally" implies adding information that is similar in nature, which does not capture the contrast between the incurable condition and the hope offered by research. The word "additionally" would not appropriately connect the idea of severe limitation with the continuing effort to find treatments.

Option C is incorrect because "eventually" suggests a sequence of events over time, which does not fit logically with the sentence. The sentence is discussing current ongoing research, not something that will happen later, making this transition imprecise.

26. Transitions: Medium

Answer: B) on the other hand,

Logical Breakdown and Explanation:

This question asks you to choose the transition that best connects the two speculative explanations about the origin of the "Baigong pipes." The correct transition should logically compare or contrast the two different theories presented in the passage.

Option B is correct because "on the other hand" introduces a contrast between the two speculative explanations: one suggests an advanced ancient civilization, and the other suggests extraterrestrial visitors. The phrase "on the other hand" is used to present a different or opposing idea, which fits the context of comparing these two distinct theories.

Option A is incorrect because "similarly" suggests that the following idea is akin to the previous one, which does not accurately reflect the relationship between the two different theories. The transition would imply that the two ideas are alike, which is not the intended contrast.

Option C is incorrect because "thus" indicates a cause-and-effect relationship or a conclusion, which is not appropriate here. The sentence does not imply that the second theory (extraterrestrial visitors) is a consequence of the first theory (advanced ancient civilization), making this transition illogical.

Option D is incorrect because "then" suggests a sequence of events or a progression in time, which does not fit the context of presenting two contrasting theories simultaneously. The sentence is not describing a chronological order but rather two different possibilities, making this transition unsuitable.

27. Rhetorical Synthesis: Easy

Answer: A) The Cambrian Explosion is known for the rapid increase in biodiversity and the appearance of most major animal phyla in the fossil record globally.

Logical Breakdown and Explanation:

This question asks you to choose the option that most effectively uses the relevant information from the student's notes to explain the significance of the Cambrian Explosion in the history of life on Earth. The correct choice should focus on the key aspects of the Cambrian Explosion that highlight its importance.

Option A is correct because it effectively uses relevant information from the notes to explain the significance of the Cambrian Explosion. It highlights the "rapid increase in biodiversity" and the "appearance of most major animal phyla in the fossil record globally," which are key points in understanding the Cambrian Explosion as a significant event in the history of life on Earth. This option provides a clear and comprehensive explanation that directly addresses the student's goal.

Option B is incorrect because, while it mentions the scientific debate about the nature of the Cambrian Explosion, it does not directly explain its significance in the history of life. The focus on the debate does not achieve the intended goal of explaining the event's importance, making it less relevant.

Option C is incorrect because it discusses possible causes of the Cambrian Explosion, which, while interesting, does not directly address its significance in the history of life. The focus on potential triggers is incomplete and misses the main point about the rapid increase in biodiversity and the appearance of major animal phyla.

Option D is incorrect because it mentions the timing of the Cambrian Explosion and alludes to changes in the world, but it is vague and does not provide a clear explanation of the event's significance. Additionally, it mentions the ongoing debate, which is less relevant to explaining the importance of the Cambrian Explosion itself. This makes the answer incomplete and less focused on the student's goal.

HARD: Reading and Writing

27 Questions, 32 Minutes

Scholars often scrutinize the credibility of historical accounts, especially when the sources have apparent biases. While it is essential to consider potential biases, from a strictly logical perspective, the source of a historical claim is _____: it does not inherently determine the validity of the information presented.

1

Which choice completes the text with the most logical and precise word or phrase?

A) irrelevant

B) pivotal

C) detrimental

D) factual

CONTINUE

The following text is from Emily Brontë's 1847 novel *Wuthering Heights*. The narrator, Lockwood, is reflecting on his interactions with the local inhabitants.

I had spent several evenings with the inhabitants of Wuthering Heights, trying to understand their complex relationships and turbulent emotions. Mr. Heathcliff was a man of few words and intense expressions; his demeanor often left me feeling _____. Despite my efforts to engage him in conversation, he remained aloof and cold.

2

Which choice completes the text with the most logical and precise word or phrase?

A) exhausted

B) comforted

C) uneasy

D) enraged

CONTINUE

Whether the scientific contributions of figures like Nikola Tesla or Marie Curie are viewed as revolutionary or, conversely, relatively ____, their impact on modern technology and medicine is undeniable. Understanding their work requires a comprehensive grasp of the scientific principles they discovered and the societal challenges they overcame.

3

Which choice completes the text with the most logical and precise word or phrase?

A) prolific

B) stagnant

C) ingenious

D) inconsequential

In 1854, the pioneering mycologist Elias Magnus Fries published his seminal work on fungi, *Hymenomycetes Europaei*. His detailed descriptions and classifications of various fungal species <u>illuminated</u> the intricate structures and reproductive mechanisms of these organisms. Despite the esoteric nature of his research, Fries' contributions significantly advanced the field of mycology.

4

As used in the text, what does the word "illuminated" most nearly mean?

A) simplified

B) clarified

C) disseminated

D) obscured

CONTINUE

The discovery of the rare deep-sea organism, *Bathypterois grallator* (commonly known as the tripod fish), has intrigued marine biologists for decades. Hypothesizing that the tripod fish uses its elongated fins to detect prey in the pitch-dark environment of the deep sea, Dr. Anika Rao and her team conducted a series of deep-sea dives and remotely operated vehicle (ROV) observations. They found that the fish's fins are highly sensitive to vibrations, allowing it to sense nearby prey. However, they also observed that the tripod fish sometimes used these fins to navigate the seafloor, suggesting a multifunctional use rather than a singular purpose proposed by the researchers.

5

Which choice best describes the overall structure of the text?

A) It introduces a rare marine species, discusses its environmental adaptations, and then explains how these adaptations contribute to its survival.

B) It presents the characteristics of a deep-sea fish, explains a hypothesis about its feeding habits, and then shows how new data disproves the hypothesis.

C) It introduces a controversial hypothesis about a marine creature, describes an experiment to test the hypothesis, and concludes with data that support the hypothesis.

D) It introduces a rare organism, proposes a hypothesis about its unique feature, and then presents findings that both support and challenge the hypothesis.

CONTINUE

The following text is adapted from Algernon Blackwood's 1907 short story "The Willows." Two friends, navigating the remote Danube River by canoe, decide to camp on a desolate island.

As night falls, an uncanny feeling permeates the air—something is watching. The wind picks up, howling through the leaves of the willows, and strange shapes dance in the shadows. They discover their canoe has been tampered with, and eerie marks appear in the soil. One of them, gripped by terror, insists they leave at first light. In the dead of night, an otherworldly humming emerges, and the willows seem to close in, as if alive. Dawn breaks, revealing their campsite untouched, yet the sense of dread lingers.

6

Which choice best states the main purpose of the text?

A) To depict the contrast between dreams and reality in a supernatural setting.

B) To illustrate the friends' growing fear as they experience strange occurrences.

C) To depict the unsettling atmosphere of the remote island.

D) To highlight the tension between the friends as their relationship begins to deteriorate.

CONTINUE

Text 1:

Many historians argue that the primary cause of the American Civil War was the economic disparity between the industrialized North and the agrarian South. The North's economy was based on manufacturing and industry, while the South relied heavily on agriculture, particularly cotton production, which depended on slave labor. This economic difference created significant tension, leading to conflicts over tariffs, trade policies, and ultimately, the issue of slavery, which became the central point of contention and drove the nation to war.

Text 2:

Contrarily, historian James M. McPherson contends that the American Civil War was fundamentally a moral and political struggle over the institution of slavery. While economic factors played a role, McPherson argues that the war was primarily driven by the South's desire to maintain and expand slavery, which the North increasingly opposed on moral grounds. According to McPherson, the election of Abraham Lincoln, who was against the spread of slavery, was the tipping point that led Southern states to secede, triggering the war.

7

Based on the texts, how would James M. McPherson (Text 2) most likely respond to the view on the causes of the American Civil War presented in Text 1?

A) By arguing that the tension over tariffs and trade policies were as crucial as the moral issues surrounding slavery.

B) By calling into question the significance of economic disparities, asserting that the war was solely driven by moral and political issues surrounding slavery.

C) By acknowledging the economic differences but underscoring the election and the morality of slavery as more decisive factors.

D) By suggesting that the war could have been avoided entirely if both sides had compromised on the issue of slavery.

CONTINUE

Bees are known for their remarkable ability to communicate through dance. Researcher Karl von Frisch discovered that bees perform a "waggle dance" to convey the location of food sources to their hive mates. This dance includes specific movements and vibrations that indicate the direction and distance of the food. A bee, for instance, can waggle its abdomen while moving in a figure-eight pattern. The angle of the dance relative to the sun indicates the direction the other bees should travel, while the duration of the waggle phase, including specific buzzing sounds, indicates the approximate distance of the food source.

8

According to the text, what specific aspect of the waggle dance indicates the direction of the food source?

A) The vibrations made by the bee during the dance, such as a buzzing sound

B) The movement of the bee's abdomen during a figure-eight pattern of the dance

C) The angle of the bee's dance in relation to the position of the sun

D) The length of time it takes a bee to complete the waggle phase

CONTINUE

Dr. Lucy King's 2017 research concluded that the presence of bees significantly affects elephant behavior. Her study suggested that elephants avoid areas with bees, proposing bee fences as a solution to human-elephant conflicts. Despite these findings, the study was based on observations from only two herds in Kenya. In 2021, Dr. Richard Byrne and his team reviewed various studies on bees' impact on elephants and called into question the limited number of herds in King's research, suggesting the possibility of a flaw in research design and overstated results.

9

What does the text most directly suggest about Dr. Lucy King's conclusion?

A) It was influenced by earlier studies on animal behavior that also used a small sample size.

B) It has most likely been invalidated by findings gathered from later studies.

C) It emphasizes the importance of using a larger sample size in future studies on elephant behavior.

D) It may exaggerate the impact of the presence of bees on the behavior of elephants.

CONTINUE

Shaunae Miller-Uibo, a sprinter from the Bahamas, has faced numerous challenges throughout her life and athletic career, including injuries and fierce competition. Born and raised in Nassau, she showed early promise in track and field, quickly rising through the ranks despite limited resources. In an article for a sports column, a critic claims that Miller-Uibo's career is a testament to the power of resilience in overcoming obstacles to achieve remarkable feats. Her relentless training and mental fortitude have propelled her to the top of the track and field world, making her an inspiration to athletes everywhere and showcasing the true spirit of competition.

10

Which finding, if true, would most directly support the critic's claim?

A) Despite suffering several severe injuries, Miller-Uibo relentlessly returned to competition, culminating in gold at the 2016 Olympics.

B) On the world's biggest stages, Miller-Uibo set numerous national and world records, highlighting her exceptional talent and dedication to the sport.

C) Miller-Uibo often trained in challenging conditions, including intense heat and limited access to professional facilities.

D) Miller-Uibo often competed against some of the world's best sprinters, including Allyson Felix and Christine Ohuruogu, pushing her to improve continuously.

CONTINUE

Famous Bridges by Length and Year Built

Bridge	Country	Length (meters)	Year Built
Golden Gate Bridge	USA	2,737	1937
Tower Bridge	UK	244	1894
Akashi Kaikyō Bridge	Japan	3,911	1998
Brooklyn Bridge	USA	486	1883

A student is writing an essay about famous bridges for a history class and is interested in noting any observable patterns in bridge construction. As part of the research, the student examines how the materials and techniques used in building bridges have evolved over time. Early bridges, like the Tower Bridge in the UK, were often constructed using materials like stone and iron, which were durable but limited the bridge's length. With advances in physics and the introduction of steel and reinforced concrete, longer bridges became possible. For instance, the Golden Gate Bridge (USA, 1937) utilized steel to achieve a much greater span. Based on his findings, the student argues that _____

11

Which choice most effectively uses data from the table to complete the student's claim?

A) future bridges built in the 21st century will be longer than any built in the 20th century.

B) the use of stone and iron in bridge construction has led to the longest bridge spans in history.

C) the Akashi Kaikyō Bridge is shorter than both the Brooklyn Bridge and the Golden Gate Bridge.

D) bridges constructed in the 20th century tend to be longer than those built in the 19th century.

CONTINUE ➡

Monthly Rainfall and Average Rice Yield

Month	Average Rainfall (mm)	Average Rice Yield (kg/hectare)
June	110	3,300
July	250	4,150
August	390	2,600
September	80	3,000

Rice crops are highly dependent on rainfall for optimal growth and yield. A study conducted over three years in a Southeast Asian region analyzed the relationship between monthly rainfall and rice yield. The results indicate that rice yield increases with higher rainfall, peaking during months with moderate rainfall. However, excessive rainfall—defined as over 350 mm in a month—can reduce yield due to waterlogging. This excess can be seen most clearly _____.

12

Which choice most effectively uses data from the table to complete the statement?

A) in September, when rainfall was the lowest and the yield was only 3,000 kg/hectare of rice.

B) in August, when excessive rainfall led to a significant drop in rice yield.

C) in July, when the rainfall was 250 mm and the rice yield reached 4,150 kg/hectare.

D) in June, when rainfall and rice yield were greater than those in September.

CONTINUE

The Dumbo octopus, a rare and intriguing species of deep-sea octopus, is known for its ear-like fins that resemble the ears of Disney's Dumbo. Some researchers, fascinated by its unique appearance, have proposed that the evolution of the Dumbo octopus's unique fins is an adaptation for more efficient swimming in the high-pressure, low-light environments of the deep ocean. However, there is no consistent evidence showing a direct correlation between fin shape and swimming efficiency in various species of deep-sea octopus. For instance, Dumbo octopuses are found in regions with differing water currents and pressure levels: areas with strong currents and high pressure as well as those with relatively calm and low-pressure conditions, suggesting that _____

13

Which choice most logically completes the text?

A) fluctuations in water currents do not impact the distribution of Dumbo octopuses.

B) the evolution of the Dumbo octopus's fins is likely influenced by factors other than swimming efficiency.

C) water pressure in the deep ocean is too variable to influence the evolution of any deep-sea species.

D) Dumbo octopuses can only thrive in regions with stable environmental conditions.

CONTINUE

CRISPR technology, a powerful tool for editing genomes, allows scientists to alter DNA sequences and modify gene function. In the realm of medical ethics, the use of CRISPR for gene editing has sparked intense debate. Many bioethicists argue that while proponents emphasize the potential for CRISPR to eradicate genetic diseases, the most comprehensive ethical analyses also consider potential risks and societal implications. A societal consequence, for example, may include the possibility of exacerbating social inequalities, as access to gene-editing technologies might be limited to those who can afford them, creating a genetic divide between the wealthy and the less privileged. Approaching this technology with more holistic consideration could therefore _____

14

Which choice most logically completes the text?

A) promote wider acceptance and fairer distribution of CRISPR advancements across different socioeconomic groups.

B) help prevent the misuse of gene-editing technologies by establishing stricter regulatory frameworks.

C) ensure that gene-editing practices are only performed by highly qualified geneticists.

D) lead to the development of economic policies that limit access to gene-editing technologies.

CONTINUE

The caribou, a large herbivore found in the Arctic and Subarctic regions, embarks on one of the longest terrestrial migrations, traveling up to 3,000 miles annually. This journey is essential for their survival, as it allows them to access areas with abundant vegetation during the summer months and avoid unsuitable calving grounds during harsh winters. The humpback whale, likewise, undertakes an equally impressive migration—but in the ocean. These marine giants travel up to 16,000 miles each year, which ensures that they can feed on krill and small fish in nutrient-rich waters during the summer and reproduce in warmer, safer waters during the winter.

What is the main idea of the text?

A) The caribou travels a shorter distance than the humpback whale during their migrations.

B) The caribou and the humpback whale migrate in search of safety from predators and harsh environments.

C) The caribou and the humpback whale undertake long migrations to access food and suitable breeding grounds.

D) Although the caribou and the humpback whale embark on long migrations, the reasons for their journeys couldn't be more different.

CONTINUE

Dr. Jacob Lindell's study on the effects of urban green spaces on mental health, which was conducted over five years and across several continents, _____ that individuals who live near parks and gardens experience lower levels of stress and anxiety compared to those who live in urban areas with fewer natural spaces. The results have significant implications for urban planning and public health policies.

16

Which choice completes the text so that it conforms to the conventions of Standard English?

A) have revealed

B) reveal

C) revealed

D) was revealing

In his analysis of the protagonist in *The Shadow of Destiny*, literary critic Jonathan Smith argues that the character, while initially depicted as a tragic hero ensnared by fate, undergoes a transformation that challenges conventional narrative _____ argues, is further complicated by the author's intentional ambiguity in key scenes, which leaves readers grappling with the protagonist's true motivations.

17

Which choice completes the text so that it conforms to the conventions of Standard English?

A) structures, this, Smith

B) structures; this Smith

C) structures this, Smith,

D) structures; this, Smith

CONTINUE

Pigeons, often regarded as mere city dwellers, possess remarkable navigational abilities that have long intrigued scientists; _____ allow them to return to their nests over vast distances, with studies suggesting that they utilize the Earth's magnetic fields, the sun's position, and even the landscape's features as guides.

18

Which choice completes the text so that it conforms to the conventions of Standard English?

A) the birds homing instincts

B) the birds' homing instincts'

C) the bird's homing instincts

D) the birds' homing instincts

Despite their small size, ants have developed an extraordinarily complex system of communication that relies heavily on pheromones; these chemical _____ allow them to coordinate activities such as foraging, defense, and nest building with remarkable precision. Interestingly, different species of ants have evolved distinct pheromone languages—some even possess the ability to mimic the pheromones of other species—raising intriguing questions about the evolution of deception and cooperation in these social insects.

19

Which choice completes the text so that it conforms to the conventions of Standard English?

A) signals, which are produced by the ants, and released into the environment

B) signals, which are produced by the ants and released into the environment,

C) signals, which are produced, by the ants, and released into the environment,

D) signals, which are produced by the ants and released, into the environment,

CONTINUE

Living in cities at high altitudes, such as La Paz in Bolivia or Lhasa in Tibet, _____ some effect on residents' physical and mental health; while the body adapts to the lower oxygen levels by producing more red blood cells, some studies suggest that the constant challenge of living in such environments may also influence cognitive function and emotional well-being.

Which choice completes the text so that it conforms to the conventions of Standard English?

A) has

B) have

C) having

D) had

CONTINUE

Originally invented in ancient Greece to dispense holy water in temples, _____. This evolution reflects society's changing consumer habits, as well as advancements in technology that have allowed for increased customization and convenience.

Which choice completes the text so that it conforms to the conventions of Standard English?

A) the evolution of vending machines is such that they are now sophisticated devices that offer everything from gourmet meals to high-end electronics

B) offerings such as gourmet meals and high-end electronics demonstrate the evolution of vending machines into sophisticated devices

C) vending machines have evolved into sophisticated devices that now offer everything from gourmet meals to high-end electronics

D) the vending machines' sophisticated evolution is apparent with the gourmet meals and high-end electronics they now offer

CONTINUE ➡

In Einstein's theory of relativity, time is not an absolute, unchanging entity; rather, it is relative and can vary depending on the observer's speed and gravitational field. This revolutionary idea led to a profound realization in _____ time and space are intertwined, forming a four-dimensional continuum known as spacetime. The implications of this are vast: clocks moving at different speeds or in different gravitational fields will tick at different rates.

22

Which choice completes the text so that it conforms to the conventions of Standard English?

A) physics

B) physics,

C) physics, and

D) physics:

Traditional crafts, such as weaving, pottery, and metalwork, are more than just forms of artistic expression; they are also deeply intertwined with cultural identity and heritage. In many cultures, these crafts carry symbolic meanings and are used in rituals and ceremonies that mark important life events, from birth to marriage to death. _____ in an increasingly globalized world, these crafts are under threat from mass production and changing consumer preferences, leading to a loss of cultural diversity.

23

Which choice completes the text with the most logical transition?

A) For example,

B) Yet,

C) Furthermore,

D) In fact,

CONTINUE

In *The Melancholy of Fate*, the protagonist is initially portrayed as a brooding anti-hero trapped by circumstances beyond his control, yet as the narrative unfolds, it becomes clear that his actions are not merely the result of external forces; _____ they stem from deep-seated personal insecurities and a profound fear of failure, which he masks with a facade of stoicism.

Which choice completes the text with the most logical transition?

A) therefore,

B) for instance,

C) in other words,

D) rather,

Ancient grains such as quinoa, farro, and spelt have seen a resurgence in popularity in recent years. Unlike modern wheat, which has been heavily refined and processed, ancient grains retain more of their natural nutrients and fiber. They, _____ are often marketed as healthier alternatives to conventional grains. Additionally, these grains are more resilient to harsh growing conditions, making them an attractive option for sustainable agriculture.

Which choice completes the text with the most logical transition?

A) as a result,

B) nevertheless,

C) however,

D) for example,

CONTINUE

While researching a topic, a student has taken the following notes:

- *I Know Why the Caged Bird Sings* (1969) is Maya Angelou's autobiography focusing on her experiences of racism and identity in the segregated South.
- The autobiography brought widespread attention to the struggles of African American women.
- *Down in the Delta* (1998) is a film written and directed by Angelou, her first and only directorial project.
- The film follows a woman named Loretta as she returns to her ancestral home, seeking to reconnect with her heritage and discover who she truly is.
- *I Know Why the Caged Bird Sings* was recognized for its literary and cultural significance.
- *Down in the Delta* received praise for its powerful portrayal of African American family dynamics and the importance of heritage.

26

The student wants to highlight a similarity between the two works. Which choice most effectively uses relevant information from the notes to accomplish this goal?

A) Angelou's autobiography brought widespread attention to the struggles of African American women, whereas her film powerfully portrayed family dynamics.

B) *I Know Why the Caged Bird Sings* and *Down in the Delta* both explores themes of identity and heritage.

C) Angelou's film *Down in the Delta* follows a woman's return to her ancestral home, while her autobiography focuses on her experiences in the segregated South.

D) Angelou completed *I Know Why the Caged Bird Sings* in 1969 and *Down in the Delta* in 1998.

CONTINUE

While researching a topic, a student has taken the following notes:

- Used in healthcare, AI assists in diagnosing diseases and develops personalized treatment plans.
- AI optimizes trading strategies and detects fraudulent activities in the financial sector.
- AI-powered automation is expected to displace jobs in various sectors, particularly those involving routine tasks.
- Ethical concerns have been raised about AI, particularly regarding bias in algorithms and the potential for misuse in surveillance.
- AI-driven technologies have improved everyday life through smart home devices, virtual assistants, and personalized recommendations in e-commerce.

27

The student wants to make a generalization about the benefits and potential risks associated with the widespread adoption of AI. Which choice most effectively uses relevant information from the notes to accomplish this goal?

A) AI is increasingly used in healthcare, finance, and everyday life, improving efficiency and convenience across various sectors.

B) Technologies using AI include smart home devices and virtual assistants, but there might be biases in its algorithms and misuse in surveillance.

C) AI has optimized trading strategies in the finance industry, but jobs involving routine tasks likely will be displaced by AI.

D) The integration of AI in multiple industries offers significant benefits, but it also raises concerns about job displacement, privacy, and ethical implications.

If you finish before the time is called, you may check your work on this module only.
On Test Day, you will only be able to move to the next module when time expires.

🔑 Answer Key

Question Number	Correct Answer	Level of Difficulty	Question Type
1	A	Hard	**Craft and Structure:** *Words in Context*
2	C	Easy	**Craft and Structure:** *Words in Context*
3	D	Medium	**Craft and Structure:** *Words in Context*
4	B	Medium	**Craft and Structure:** *Interpreting Words in Context*
5	D	Hard	**Craft and Structure:** *Overall Structure*
6	B	Medium	**Craft and Structure:** *Main Purpose*
7	C	Hard	**Craft and Structure:** *Cross-Text Connections*
8	C	Easy	**Information and Ideas:** *Detail*
9	D	Medium	**Information and Ideas:** *Inference*
10	A	Hard	**Information and Ideas:** *Supporting a Claim*
11	D	Medium	**Information and Ideas:** *Cite Text as Evidence (Infographic)*
12	B	Medium	**Information and Ideas:** *Cite Text as Evidence (Infographic)*
13	B	Medium	**Information and Ideas:** *Inference (complete the text)*

Question Number	Correct Answer	Level of Difficulty	Question Type
14	A	Hard	**Information and Ideas:** *Inference (complete the text)*
15	C	Easy	**Information and Ideas:** *Main Idea*
16	C	Medium	**Standard English Conventions:** *Verbs*
17	D	Hard	**Standard English Conventions:** *Punctuation and Sentence Structure*
18	D	Easy	**Standard English Conventions:** *Punctuation (Apostrophes)*
19	B	Hard	**Standard English Conventions:** *Commas*
20	A	Hard	**Standard English Conventions:** *Verbs*
21	C	Medium	**Standard English Conventions:** *Modifiers*
22	D	Medium	**Standard English Conventions:** *Punctuation and Sentence Structure*
23	B	Medium	**Expression of Ideas:** *Transitions*
24	D	Hard	**Expression of Ideas:** *Transitions*
25	A	Medium	**Expression of Ideas:** *Transitions*
26	B	Medium	**Expression of Ideas:** *Rhetorical Synthesis*
27	D	Hard	**Expression of Ideas:** *Rhetorical Synthesis*

Raw Score Conversion Table

Raw Score (# of Correct Answers)	Reading and Writing Section Score	Raw Score (# of Correct Answers)	Reading and Writing Section Score
54	800	30	510
53	780	29	500
52	760	28	490
51	730	27	480
50	720	26	470
49	710	25	470
48	700	24	450
47	680	23	440
46	670	22	430
45	660	21	430
44	650	20	410
43	640	19	400
42	630	18	390
41	620		
40	610		
39	600		
38	590		
37	580		
36	570		
35	560		
34	550		
33	540		
32	530		
31	520		

 # Explanations

1. Words in Context: Hard

Answer: A) irrelevant

Step-by-Step Explanation:

1. Let's deconstruct the passage together. It discusses the scrutiny of historical accounts, emphasizing the importance of evaluating the credibility of sources, particularly when biases are apparent.

2. Notice the phrase "from a strictly logical perspective"—this indicates that the discussion is focusing on logic and reasoning rather than other considerations such as emotional appeal or subjective interpretation.

3. The information after the colon is key to understanding the correct answer because it serves to clarify or explain the point made earlier. It states that "it does not inherently determine the validity of the information presented," which suggests that the identity of the source doesn't logically affect the truthfulness of the claim. The SAT often includes important context clues after colons to provide critical explanations or clarifications that help in determining the correct answer.

4. Ask yourself, what word best describes something that doesn't affect or isn't relevant to the truth of a statement? "Irrelevant" fits perfectly because it means that the source is not directly connected to the logical validity of the information, aligning with the passage's logical approach.

Explanation of Incorrect Options:

B) pivotal: This is incorrect because it suggests that the source is of crucial importance, which contradicts the passage's assertion that the source does not inherently determine the information's validity.

C) detrimental: This is incorrect because it implies that the source negatively affects the validity of the information, which is not supported by what the passage is conveying.

D) factual: This is incorrect because it implies that the source itself is a fact, which doesn't fit with the idea that the source's identity doesn't inherently impact the validity of the information presented.

2. Words in Context: Easy

Answer: C) uneasy

Step-by-Step Explanation:

1. The narrator, Lockwood, describes his interactions with Mr. Heathcliff, noting that Heathcliff is a man of few words with intense expressions and that he remains aloof and cold despite Lockwood's attempts at conversation.

2. Notice the description of Mr. Heathcliff's "intense expressions" and his "aloof and cold" demeanor. These descriptions suggest that Mr. Heathcliff is not a welcoming or comforting presence, which would likely affect the narrator's feelings.

3. The word we need should capture the unsettling effect that Heathcliff's demeanor has on the narrator. The description of Heathcliff's intense and aloof nature is crucial because it helps clarify why the narrator might feel a certain way.

4. Ask yourself, what word best describes a feeling of discomfort when faced with someone who is intense, aloof, and cold? "Uneasy" fits perfectly because it means feeling nervous, anxious, or uncomfortable, which aligns with the atmosphere created by Heathcliff's demeanor.

Explanation of Incorrect Options:

A) exhausted: This is incorrect because it implies physical or mental fatigue, which doesn't directly relate to the emotional discomfort suggested by Heathcliff's intense and aloof behavior.

B) comforted: This is incorrect because it suggests a feeling of reassurance or relief, which contradicts the unsettling effect described in the passage.

D) enraged: This is incorrect because it implies intense anger, which is too extreme and doesn't align with the narrator's subtle sense of discomfort and unease in response to Heathcliff's demeanor.

3. Words in Context: Medium

Answer: D) inconsequential

Step-by-Step Explanation:

1. Let's take a moment to understand the passage. It contrasts two possible views of the scientific contributions made by Nikola Tesla and Marie Curie: that they were either revolutionary or something else. Regardless of how their contributions are viewed, the passage asserts that their impact on modern technology and medicine is undeniable.

2. Notice the contrast set up by the phrase "revolutionary or, conversely." This indicates that the word we need should be the opposite of "revolutionary." The key word "revolutionary" means something that brings about a major or fundamental change. This suggests that their contributions could be seen as impactful and transformative.

3. Therefore, the word we need should provide a direct contrast to "revolutionary," implying that their contributions could be viewed as minor or insignificant by some.

4. Ask yourself, what word best contrasts with "revolutionary" and suggests something that might be viewed as unimportant? "Inconsequential" fits perfectly because it means insignificant or not important, which aligns with the idea of downplaying the significance of their contributions, even though the passage ultimately refutes this view.

Explanation of Incorrect Options:

A) prolific: This is incorrect because it implies being highly productive or fruitful, which doesn't contrast with "revolutionary" in the way the passage requires.

B) stagnant: This is incorrect because it suggests a lack of movement or progress, which doesn't accurately convey the idea of something being viewed as unimportant or insignificant.

C) ingenious: This is incorrect because it means clever or inventive, which does not provide the necessary contrast to "revolutionary" that the passage sets up.

4. Interpreting Words in Context: Medium

Answer: B) clarified

Step-by-Step Explanation:

1. Let's understand the passage together. It describes how Elias Magnus Fries, a pioneering mycologist, published a seminal work that provided detailed descriptions and classifications of various fungal species.

2. The phrase in the second sentence "his detailed descriptions" serves as a crucial context clue, suggesting that Fries' careful and thorough work had some impact on the structures and reproductive mechanisms of fungi. The second sentence then states that Fries' work "illuminated the intricate structures and reproductive mechanisms" of fungi. The word "illuminated" in this context suggests that his work made these complex aspects of fungi more understandable and accessible. Thus, the word we need should convey the idea of making something clearer or easier to understand.

3. Ask yourself, what word best captures the idea of making complex information easier to understand? "Clarified" fits perfectly because it means to make something clear or easier to understand, which aligns with how Fries' descriptions helped to explain the intricate details of fungal structures and mechanisms.

Explanation of Incorrect Options:

A) simplified: This is incorrect because while Fries' work may have made the information clearer, the passage does not suggest that he made the complex structure and reproductive processes of fungi simpler.

C) disseminated: This is incorrect because it means to spread or distribute widely, which isn't supported by the context in the passage. What makes more logical sense is that his detailed descriptions made something clearer or easier to understand.

D) obscured: This is incorrect because it means to make something less clear or to hide it, which is the opposite of what Fries' work did according to the passage.

5. Overall Structure: Hard

Answer: D) It introduces a rare organism, proposes a hypothesis about its unique feature, and then presents findings that both support and challenge the hypothesis.

Logical Breakdown and Explanation:

This question asks you to identify the option that best describes the overall structure of the text. The correct choice should accurately reflect the way the passage is organized and the information is presented.

Option D is correct because it accurately describes the structure of the text. The passage begins by introducing a rare organism, the tripod fish. It then proposes a hypothesis about the fish's unique feature—its elongated fins—and how they might be used to detect prey. Finally, the passage presents findings from Dr. Anika Rao's research that both support the initial hypothesis (the fins are sensitive to vibrations) and challenge it (the fins are also used for navigation). This option correctly captures the progression from hypothesis to findings that both support and challenge the hypothesis.

Option A is incorrect because, while it mentions the introduction of the species and its environmental adaptations, it suggests that the passage explains how these adaptations contribute to its survival. The passage does not explicitly discuss how the adaptations contribute to survival; instead, it focuses on the hypothesis about the fins and the findings from the research, making this option only partially correct.

Option B is incorrect because it distorts the information in the passage. It suggests that the new data disproves the hypothesis, but the passage actually presents findings that both support and challenge the hypothesis rather than outright disproving it. This option inaccurately reflects the text's content.

Option C is incorrect because it inaccurately describes the hypothesis as "controversial." The passage does not suggest that the hypothesis about the tripod fish's fins is controversial; it is simply a hypothesis that the researchers aimed to test.

6. Main Purpose: Medium

Answer: B) To illustrate the friends' growing fear as they experience strange occurrences.

Logical Breakdown and Explanation:

This question asks you to identify the main purpose of the text. The correct choice should capture the central theme and focus of the passage, reflecting the progression of events and the mood established by the author.

Option B is correct because it best captures the main purpose of the text, which is to illustrate the friends' growing fear as they experience strange occurrences on the desolate island. The passage describes various unsettling events—such as the tampering with the canoe, eerie marks in the soil, and the otherworldly humming—that contribute to the friends' mounting terror, as evidenced by their insisting to "leave at first light." The focus is on their fear and how it intensifies throughout the night.

Option A is incorrect because it suggests that the text depicts a contrast between dreams and reality in a supernatural setting. However, the passage does not emphasize a distinction between dreams and reality; rather, it focuses on the real, tangible fear the characters feel in response to the strange events. This idea is unsupported by the passage.

Option C is incorrect because, while it mentions the unsettling atmosphere of the remote island, it is **incomplete** in capturing the main idea. The passage does more than just depict the atmosphere—it also focuses on the friends' growing fear as a result of the strange occurrences. Therefore, this option fails to fully encompass the main purpose of the text.

Option D is incorrect because it introduces the idea of tension between the friends and the deterioration of their relationship, which is **irrelevant** to the passage. The text does not mention any conflict or tension between the friends; instead, it focuses on their shared experience of fear. This option presents an idea that is not developed in the passage.

7. Cross-Text Connections: Hard

Answer: C) By acknowledging the economic differences but underscoring the election and the morality of slavery as more decisive factors.

Logical Breakdown and Explanation:

This question asks how James M. McPherson (Text 2) would likely respond to the view presented in Text 1 regarding the causes of the American Civil War. The correct answer should align with McPherson's emphasis on the moral and political issues surrounding slavery as the primary cause of the war.

Option C is correct because it aligns with McPherson's position in Text 2. McPherson acknowledges that economic differences between the North and South "played a role" in the lead-up to the Civil War, as discussed in Text 1. However, he emphasizes that the war was "fundamentally a moral and political struggle over the institution of slavery." He would likely argue that the "election of Abraham Lincoln, who was against the spread of slavery," and the moral opposition to slavery were more decisive factors in triggering the war.

Option A is incorrect because it suggests that McPherson would argue that tension over tariffs and trade policies was as crucial as the moral issues surrounding slavery. This contradicts McPherson's emphasis in Text 2, where he downplays economic factors in favor of moral and political issues, making this option unsupported by the passage.

Option B is incorrect because it suggests that McPherson would argue the war was solely driven by moral and political issues, completely dismissing economic disparities. While McPherson does emphasize the moral and political causes, Text 2 does acknowledge that economic factors played a role, making this option overly extreme and not fully supported by the passage.

Option D is incorrect because it introduces the idea that the war could have been avoided through compromise on slavery, which is **irrelevant** to McPherson's argument in Text 2. The passage does not suggest that McPherson believes the war could have been avoided, and this option does not accurately reflect his position.

8. Detail: Easy

Answer: C) The angle of the bee's dance in relation to the position of the sun

Logical Breakdown and Explanation:

This question asks you to identify which specific aspect of the waggle dance indicates the direction of the food source, based on the details provided in the passage. The correct answer should directly reflect the information in the text about how bees communicate direction through their dance.

Option C is correct because the passage clearly states that "the angle of the dance relative to the sun indicates the direction the other bees should travel." This information is explicitly provided in the text, making Option C the accurate choice that directly answers the question.

Option A is incorrect because, while the passage mentions "specific buzzing sounds," these sounds are associated with indicating the distance of the food source, not the direction. Choosing this option would contradict the passage's information about what the buzzing sounds represent.

Option B is incorrect because it misinterprets the passage's description of the bee's movements. The movement of the bee's abdomen during the figure-eight pattern is part of the dance but does not indicate the direction of the food source. This option distorts the information by attributing the directional aspect to the wrong part of the dance.

Option D is incorrect because the passage states that "the duration of the waggle phase" indicates the distance of the food source, not the direction. This option would be a misrepresentation of the passage, attributing the duration to the wrong aspect of the dance.

9. Inference: Medium

Answer: D) It may exaggerate the impact of the presence of bees on the behavior of elephants.

Logical Breakdown and Explanation:

This question asks you to determine what the text most directly suggests about Dr. Lucy King's conclusion regarding the impact of bees on elephant behavior. The correct answer should accurately reflect the concerns raised about her research based on the information provided.

Option D is correct because the text suggests that Dr. Lucy King's conclusion "may exaggerate the impact of the presence of bees on the behavior of elephants." This is supported by the information that Dr. Richard Byrne and his team questioned the limited number of herds in King's study and suggested that the results might be overstated. This option directly reflects the possibility that the conclusions drawn from a small sample size might not be as strong as initially presented.

Option A is incorrect because the text does not mention that Dr. King's conclusion was influenced by earlier studies on animal behavior with a small sample size. This idea is unsupported by the passage and introduces information that was never discussed.

Option B is incorrect because the text does not suggest that Dr. King's conclusion has been invalidated by later studies. Instead, it suggests there are concerns about the strength of her conclusion due to the small sample size, but it does not state that the conclusion has been entirely invalidated. This option distorts the text's meaning by overextending the criticism.

Option C is incorrect because, while the text indirectly touches on the importance of sample size by mentioning the small number of herds in King's study, it does not directly state that King's conclusion emphasizes the need for a larger sample size in future studies. This idea is not fully supported by the text.

10. Supporting a Claim: Hard

Answer: A) Despite suffering several severe injuries, Miller-Uibo relentlessly returned to competition, culminating in gold at the 2016 Olympics.

Logical Breakdown and Explanation:

This question asks you to determine which finding would most directly support the critic's claim that Shaunae Miller-Uibo's career is a testament to resilience in overcoming obstacles to achieve remarkable feats. The correct answer should provide evidence that validates the idea of resilience and overcoming challenges.

Option A is correct because it directly strengthens the critic's claim by illustrating Miller-Uibo's resilience. The finding that despite suffering several severe injuries, she relentlessly returned to competition and ultimately won gold at the 2016 Olympics clearly demonstrates her ability to overcome significant obstacles. This aligns perfectly with the critic's claim that her career showcases the power of resilience, resulting in a statement that makes the claim more likely to be true.

Option B is incorrect because, while it highlights Miller-Uibo's talent and dedication, it focuses on her achievements (setting national and world records) rather than on overcoming obstacles. This option does not directly relate to the theme of resilience in the face of challenges, making it less relevant to the critic's claim.

Option C is incorrect because, although it mentions that Miller-Uibo often trained in challenging conditions, it does not specifically relate to overcoming injuries or significant obstacles in the context of competition. This idea is somewhat related but does not directly address the critic's focus on resilience in overcoming major challenges, making it less supportive of the claim.

Option D is incorrect because it emphasizes the level of competition Miller-Uibo faced, but it does not directly support the idea of overcoming personal obstacles or resilience. Competing against top athletes is certainly challenging, but the option does not provide clear evidence of overcoming adversity or setbacks, which is central to the critic's claim.

11. Citing Text as Evidence (Infographic): Medium

Answer: D) bridges constructed in the 20th century tend to be longer than those built in the 19th century.

Logical Breakdown and Explanation:

This question asks you to choose the option that most effectively uses the data from the table to complete the student's claim about the evolution of bridge construction. The correct answer should reflect the trends in bridge length and construction techniques over time, as observed in the table.

Option D is correct because it accurately reflects the data in the table and the student's observations. The table shows that bridges constructed in the 20th century, such as the Golden Gate Bridge (2,737 meters) and the Akashi Kaikyō Bridge (3,911 meters), are significantly longer than those built in the 19th century, such as the Tower Bridge (244 meters) and the Brooklyn Bridge (486 meters). This trend aligns with the student's discussion of advances in materials and techniques allowing for longer bridge spans.

Option A is incorrect because it makes a prediction about future bridges that is unsupported by the data in the table. The table only provides information about bridges up to 1998, so there is no basis for claiming that future 21st-century bridges will be longer than those built in the 20th century.

Option B is incorrect because it contradicts the data in the table and the information in the passage. The table shows that the longest bridges, such as the Akashi Kaikyō Bridge and the Golden Gate Bridge, were built using modern materials like steel, not stone and iron. Stone and iron were used in earlier, shorter bridges like the Tower Bridge.

Option C is incorrect because it inaccurately describes the data. The Akashi Kaikyō Bridge is actually the longest bridge in the table (3,911 meters), so claiming it is shorter than the Brooklyn Bridge (486 meters) and the Golden Gate Bridge (2,737 meters) is incorrect and contradicts the data.

12. Citing Text as Evidence (Infographic): Medium

Answer: B) in August, when excessive rainfall led to a significant drop in rice yield.

Logical Breakdown and Explanation:

This question asks you to choose the option that most effectively uses the data from the table to complete the statement about how excessive rainfall can reduce rice yield. The correct answer should align with the observation that excessive rainfall (over 350 mm in a month) leads to a drop in rice yield due to waterlogging.

Option B is correct because it directly reflects the data from the table and supports the passage's point. In August, the rainfall was 390 mm, which is considered excessive, and this corresponds with a significant drop in rice yield to 2,600 kg/hectare. This choice clearly demonstrates the negative impact of excessive rainfall on rice yield, making it the most effective completion of the statement.

Option A is incorrect because it discusses September, when the rainfall was the lowest (80 mm) and the yield was 3,000 kg/hectare. This does not support the point being made about excessive rainfall leading to reduced yield, making it irrelevant to the passage's focus.

Option C is incorrect because, while it accurately states that the rice yield in July was 4,150 kg/hectare, it is irrelevant to the point being made in the passage. The passage focuses on the impact of excessive rainfall (over 350 mm) on reducing rice yield. July's rainfall of 250 mm is not considered excessive, so this data does not directly relate to the issue of waterlogging and its negative effect on rice yield, making it off-topic in the context of the passage's focus.

Option D is incorrect because it compares June and September, but neither month experienced excessive rainfall. June had 110 mm of rainfall and September had 80 mm, both of which are below the threshold for excessive rainfall (350 mm). This option does not support the passage's point about the impact of excessive rainfall, making it irrelevant.

13. Inference: Medium

Answer: B) the evolution of the Dumbo octopus's fins is likely influenced by factors other than swimming efficiency.

Logical Breakdown and Explanation:

This question asks you to choose the option that most logically completes the text, taking into account the information provided about the Dumbo octopus, its fins, and the varying environments it inhabits.

Option B is correct because it logically follows from the information provided in the passage. The text explains that Dumbo octopuses are found in regions with both strong currents and high pressure as well as calm and low-pressure conditions. This suggests that there isn't a direct correlation between fin shape and swimming efficiency. Therefore, it is logical to conclude that the evolution of the Dumbo octopus's fins is likely influenced by factors other than swimming efficiency. This option aligns with the passage's discussion of the lack of consistent evidence for a direct correlation.

Option A is incorrect because, while it mentions fluctuations in water currents, this idea is not the focus of the passage. The text is more concerned with the evolution of the Dumbo octopus's fins rather than their *distribution*. This makes the option **irrelevant** to the point being developed.

Option C is incorrect because it makes an **unsupported** generalization about water pressure being too variable to influence the evolution of *any deep-sea species*. The passage does not provide enough information to support such a broad statement, making this option illogical and unrelated in the context of the passage.

Option D is incorrect because it contradicts the information given in the passage. The text states that Dumbo octopuses are found in regions with varying environmental conditions, not just stable ones. Therefore, suggesting that they can only thrive in regions with stable conditions is **illogical** and unsupported by the passage.

14. Inference: Hard

Answer: A) promote wider acceptance and fairer distribution of CRISPR advancements across different socioeconomic groups.

Logical Breakdown and Explanation:

This question asks you to choose the option that most logically completes the text, focusing on the societal consequences and ethical considerations surrounding CRISPR technology.

Option A is correct because it logically follows from the discussion in the passage. The text highlights concerns about exacerbating social inequalities due to unequal access to CRISPR technology. Therefore, approaching the technology with more holistic consideration could logically "promote wider acceptance and fairer distribution of CRISPR advancements across different socioeconomic groups." This option aligns with the passage's focus on the potential societal implications of CRISPR and how broader ethical considerations could address these concerns.

Option B is incorrect because, while establishing stricter regulatory frameworks could help prevent misuse, this idea is not directly related to the passage's focus on social inequalities and access. The passage discusses societal consequences and ethical considerations rather than the need for stricter regulations, making this option **irrelevant** to the point being developed.

Option C is incorrect because ensuring that gene-editing practices are only performed by highly qualified geneticists is a narrower issue that doesn't directly address the broader societal concerns discussed in the passage. This option **introduces an idea that was never discussed** in the passage, making it irrelevant.

Option D is incorrect because it suggests the development of economic policies that limit access to gene-editing technologies, which contradicts the passage's concern about exacerbating social inequalities. Limiting access would likely worsen inequalities rather than address them, making this option **illogical** given the context.

15. Main Idea: Easy

Answer: C) The caribou and the humpback whale undertake long migrations to access food and suitable breeding grounds.

Logical Breakdown and Explanation:

This question asks you to identify the main idea of the text. The correct choice should capture the overall purpose and focus of the passage, reflecting the reasons behind the migrations of both the caribou and the humpback whale.

Option C is correct because it best captures the main idea of the passage. The text describes how both the caribou and the humpback whale undertake long migrations to access food and suitable breeding grounds. The caribou migrates to find abundant vegetation and avoid harsh calving grounds, while the humpback whale migrates to feed in nutrient-rich waters and reproduce in safer, warmer waters. This option encapsulates the overall purpose of their migrations, which is essential for their survival.

Option A is incorrect because it focuses on a minor detail—the difference in distance traveled by the caribou and the humpback whale—rather than the main purpose of their migrations. This option is **too minor** to capture the essence of the passage.

Option B is incorrect because it emphasizes the idea of migrating in search of safety from predators, which is **unsupported by the passage**. The passage focuses on the caribou and humpback whale migrating to access food and suitable breeding grounds, not on avoiding predators. While harsh environments are mentioned, the primary reasons for migration discussed in the passage are related to finding resources and favorable conditions for reproduction. Therefore, this option introduces an idea that is not supported by the text, making it inaccurate.

Option D is incorrect because it suggests that the reasons for the migrations of the caribou and the humpback whale are very different, which is **contradictory** to the passage. The passage actually highlights the similarities in their migration purposes—both species migrate to access food and suitable breeding grounds. This option introduces an idea that is not supported by the text.

16. Verbs: Medium

Answer: C) revealed

Logical Breakdown and Explanation:

This question asks you to choose the option that correctly completes the sentence, focusing on subject-verb agreement and proper verb tense.

Option C is correct because it uses the past tense verb "revealed," which correctly agrees with the singular subject "Dr. Jacob Lindell's study." The study has already been conducted, so the past tense is appropriate and conforms to the conventions of Standard English.

Option A is incorrect because it uses the plural verb "have revealed," which creates a **subject-verb disagreement**. The subject "study" is singular, so a plural verb is not appropriate.

Option B is incorrect because it uses the plural verb "reveal," which also creates a **subject-verb disagreement**. The singular subject "study" does not agree with the plural verb in this context, and the use of present tense is illogical since the study was conducted in the past.

Option D is incorrect because it uses "was revealing," which not only introduces a **tense issue** but also creates an awkward and incorrect construction. The phrase "was revealing" suggests a continuous action in the past, which doesn't fit the context where the study has already concluded and its results are now known.

17. Punctuation and Sentence Structure: Hard

Answer: D) structures; this, Smith

Logical Breakdown and Explanation:

This question asks you to choose the option that correctly completes the sentence, ensuring proper punctuation and avoiding run-on sentences.

Option D is correct because it uses a semicolon to correctly separate two independent clauses: "literary critic Jonathan Smith argues that the character undergoes a transformation that challenges conventional narrative structures" and "this is further complicated by the author's intentional ambiguity in key scenes." The semicolon appropriately separates the two independent clauses, and the commas correctly set off the nonessential phrase "Smith argues," making this option grammatically correct.

Option A is incorrect because it creates a run-on sentence by using a comma instead of a semicolon to separate the two independent clauses. The clauses "literary critic Jonathan Smith argues that the character... undergoes a transformation that challenges conventional narrative structures" and "this...is further complicated..." are both complete sentences and require a period, semicolon, or a comma and a FANBOYS word.

Option B is incorrect because, while it uses a semicolon to separate the two independent clauses, it fails to properly punctuate the nonessential phrase " Smith argues" (an intervening phrase) by omitting the necessary comma after "this." An intervening phrase is a type of nonessential information that introduces the 'source of the statement' (as in, "according to critics," "in my opinion," "my mom says," etc...) and is always surrounded off by commas when it appears inside an independent clause. In this case, the phrase "this, Smith argues," should be enclosed with commas to correctly indicate that it is nonessential. The lack of a comma after "this" violates this punctuation rule, making the sentence incorrect and the meaning awkward (*this Smith* argues, is...).

Option C is incorrect because it also creates a run-on sentence. There is no punctuation to separate the two independent clauses, and the extra comma after "Smith" creates an unnecessary pause that disrupts the flow of the sentence.

18. Punctuation: Easy

Answer: D) the birds' homing instincts

Logical Breakdown and Explanation:

This question asks you to choose the option that correctly completes the sentence, focusing on proper use of apostrophes to indicate possession.

Option D is correct because it uses the plural possessive form "birds'," which is appropriate given that the sentence refers to "Pigeons," a plural noun. The phrase "the birds' homing instincts" correctly indicates that the homing instincts belong to the pigeons.

Option A is incorrect because it uses "the birds" without an apostrophe, which is the plural noun form, not the possessive. Since the sentence needs to indicate that the homing instincts belong to the birds, the lack of an apostrophe makes this option incorrect.

Option B is incorrect because it places the apostrophe incorrectly in "instincts'." The phrase "the birds' homing instincts'" suggests that something belongs to the instincts, but no noun follows "instincts" to indicate what that might be. This creates a grammatical error.

Option C is incorrect because it uses the singular possessive form "bird's," which does not match the plural noun "Pigeons" referred to earlier in the sentence. The singular form is not supported by the context, making this option incorrect.

19. Commas: Hard

Answer: B) signals, which are produced by the ants and released into the environment,

Logical Breakdown and Explanation:

This question asks you to choose the option that correctly completes the sentence while following standard comma rules, particularly in the context of prepositional phrases and lists.

Option B is correct because it uses commas appropriately to set off the nonessential clause "which are produced by the ants and released into the environment." There are no unnecessary commas before prepositional phrases or between the two actions "produced by the ants" and "released into the environment," which are part of the same clause and should not be separated.

Option A is incorrect because it incorrectly adds a comma between "produced by the ants" and "released into the environment." This placement of a comma violates the rule that there should not be a comma between two parts of a list when only two items are present.

Option C is incorrect because it violates the comma rule by placing a comma between "produced" and "by the ants." The prepositional phrase "by the ants" belongs with the verb "produced" and specifies who is doing the producing. Since the phrase naturally blends with the previous words, no comma should be used to separate them. The unnecessary comma disrupts the flow of the sentence and creates an awkward pause.

Option D is incorrect because it incorrectly places a comma between "released" and "into the environment." The prepositional phrase "into the environment" specifies where the pheromones are released and should naturally blend with the verb "released." Since the prepositional phrase directly relates to the previous words, no comma should be used. The insertion of a comma here violates the rule and disrupts the sentence's clarity.

20. Verbs: Hard

Answer: A) has

Logical Breakdown and Explanation:

This question asks you to choose the option that correctly completes the sentence, focusing on subject-verb agreement and proper tense.

Option A is correct because it uses the singular verb "has," which agrees with the singular subject "Living" (-ing words are always singular when used as subjects). In this sentence, "Living in cities at high altitudes" is treated as a singular noun phrase, and therefore requires a singular verb. This choice also maintains the consistent present tense used in the passage.

Option B is incorrect because it uses the plural verb "have," which creates a **subject-verb disagreement**. The subject "Living" is singular, so it requires a singular verb, making this option incorrect.

Option C is incorrect because it uses "having," which creates a **sentence structure error**. "Having" is a participle and cannot function as the main verb in this sentence, resulting in a sentence fragment.

Option D is incorrect because it uses the past tense verb "had," which creates a **wrong tense** issue. The rest of the passage uses present tense, so "had" is inconsistent with the other verbs and disrupts the continuity of the text.

21. Modifiers: Medium

Answer: C) vending machines have evolved into sophisticated devices that now offer everything from gourmet meals to high-end electronics

Logical Breakdown and Explanation:

This question asks you to choose the option that correctly completes the sentence without creating a dangling modifier. The correct choice should ensure that the subject being modified by the phrase "Originally invented in ancient Greece to dispense holy water in temples" is logically placed at the beginning of the independent clause.

Option C is correct because it logically follows from the introductory phrase and places the appropriate subject, "vending machines," immediately after the modifying phrase. This ensures that the sentence clearly states that vending machines, originally invented in ancient Greece, have evolved into sophisticated devices. The sentence is grammatically correct and free of any dangling modifiers.

Option A is incorrect because it creates a dangling modifier. The phrase "Originally invented in ancient Greece to dispense holy water in temples" should logically modify "vending machines." However, in this option, the subject is "the *evolution* of vending machines," which is not something that could be "originally invented in ancient Greece." This makes the sentence illogical, as the noun "evolution" does not match the modifying phrase. What was originally invented in Ancient Greece? Vending machines, not their evolution.

Option B is incorrect because it also creates a dangling modifier. The phrase "Originally invented in ancient Greece to dispense holy water in temples" should modify "vending machines," but in this option, the subject is "*offerings* such as gourmet meals and high-end electronics." This does not make logical sense because these offerings were not "originally invented in ancient Greece."

Option D is incorrect because it creates a dangling modifier by starting the independent clause with "the vending machines' sophisticated *evolution*." The modifying phrase "Originally invented in ancient Greece to dispense holy water in temples" should describe "vending machines," not their "evolution."

22. Punctuation and Sentence Structure: Medium

Answer: D) physics:

Logical Breakdown and Explanation:

This question asks you to choose the option that correctly completes the sentence, focusing on avoiding sentence structure errors, using proper punctuation, and ensuring logical, clear meaning.

Option D is correct because it uses a colon to introduce the explanation that follows the statement. The colon appropriately separates the first independent clause "This revolutionary idea led to a profound realization in physics" from the elaboration "time and space are intertwined, forming a four-dimensional continuum known as spacetime." The colon indicates that the second part of the sentence is directly explaining or expanding upon the first part.

Option A is incorrect because it creates a run-on sentence. The sentence "This revolutionary idea led to a profound realization in physics" and the following explanation "time and space are intertwined" are both independent clauses. Without proper punctuation, this option results in a run-on sentence.

Option B is also incorrect because it creates a run-on sentence. Similar to Option A, it does not provide the necessary punctuation to separate the two independent clauses. The sentence structure is incorrect because a comma cannot be the only punctuation that separates the two ICs.

Option C is incorrect because it introduces "and" after "physics," which creates an awkward and illogical meaning. By adding "and," the sentence suggests that another independent clause or idea should follow, but instead, it continues with an explanation that directly relates to the realization in physics. This creates confusion, as the sentence structure implies a conjunction between two separate ideas rather than a clarification of the first idea. So, even though the sentence is grammatically correct, it creates an illogical meaning, something that is resolved in option D).

23. Transition: Medium

Answer: B) Yet,

Logical Breakdown and Explanation:

This question asks you to choose the transition that best connects the ideas in the passage logically. The correct transition should reflect the contrast between the importance of traditional crafts in cultural identity and the threat they face in a globalized world.

Option B is correct because "Yet" is a transitional word that introduces an idea that is unexpected or surprising given the preceding information. The passage first discusses the deep significance of traditional crafts in preserving cultural identity and heritage, which would lead one to assume that these practices are well-protected and enduring. However, "Yet" introduces the surprising and unexpected reality that, despite their importance, these crafts are under threat from mass production and changing consumer preferences. This shift from the anticipated preservation of cultural practices to their endangerment makes "Yet" the most precise and logical choice to connect these contrasting ideas.

Option A is incorrect because "For example" suggests that what follows will be an illustration or specific instance of the preceding statement. However, the sentence is not providing an example but rather presenting a contrasting idea, making this transition illogical.

Option C is incorrect because "Furthermore" is used to add additional information that supports the previous statement. However, the sentence is not adding information in support of the previous idea; instead, it introduces a contrasting situation, making this transition illogical.

Option D is incorrect because "In fact" is typically used to emphasize or reinforce the previous statement. The sentence following the blank does not reinforce the idea that traditional crafts are important; instead, it contrasts it by discussing the threat they face, making this transition illogical.

24. Transition: Hard

Answer: D) rather,

Logical Breakdown and Explanation:

This question asks you to choose the transition that best connects the ideas in the passage logically. The correct choice should emphasize the shift from the idea that the protagonist's actions are driven by external forces to the realization that they are actually rooted in his internal struggles.

Option D is correct because "rather" is a precise transitional word that provides an alternative to the idea presented in the previous statement. The text initially suggests that the protagonist's actions are driven by external circumstances beyond his control. However, "rather" introduces an alternative explanation, clarifying that his actions actually stem from deep-seated personal insecurities and a profound fear of failure.

Option A is incorrect because "therefore" implies a cause-and-effect relationship, which does not fit the context. The text is not explaining the result of the protagonist's circumstances but rather revising the understanding of his motivations, so this option produces an illogical meaning.

Option B is incorrect because "for instance" is used to introduce an example, which is not what the text is doing. The sentence is clarifying and correcting the earlier idea, not providing an example, making this transition illogical.

Option C is incorrect because "in other words" suggests a restatement or paraphrase of the previous idea. However, the text is not simply rephrasing the earlier statement; it is introducing a new and contrasting idea about the protagonist's motivations, so this option does not fit the context.

25. Transition: Medium

Answer: A) as a result,

Logical Breakdown and Explanation:

This question asks you to choose the transition that best connects the ideas in the passage logically. The correct choice should reflect the cause-and-effect relationship between the natural nutrients retained by ancient grains and their marketing as healthier alternatives.

Option A is correct because "as a result" effectively indicates a cause-and-effect relationship. The text explains that ancient grains retain more of their natural nutrients and fiber compared to modern wheat. The phrase "as a result" logically follows, suggesting that because of these retained nutrients, ancient grains are marketed as healthier alternatives to conventional grains.

Option B is incorrect because "nevertheless" introduces a contrast, which is illogical in this context. The sentence is not presenting an opposing idea but rather a consequence of the grains retaining their nutrients, so this option creates a contradictory meaning.

Option C is incorrect because "however" also introduces a contrast, which does not fit the context. The passage is explaining a direct relationship between the nutrient content of ancient grains and how they are marketed, not offering a counterpoint, making this option illogical.

Option D is incorrect because "for example" introduces a specific instance or illustration, which is not what the sentence is doing. The sentence is making a general statement about how ancient grains are marketed, not providing an example, so this option results in a nonsensical meaning.

26. Rhetorical Synthesis: Medium

Answer: B) *I Know Why the Caged Bird Sings* and *Down in the Delta* both explores themes of identity and heritage.

Logical Breakdown and Explanation:

This question asks you to identify the option that most effectively highlights a similarity between Maya Angelou's two works, using relevant information from the notes provided.

Option B is correct because it directly addresses the student's goal of highlighting a similarity between the two works. Both "I Know Why the Caged Bird Sings" and "Down in the Delta" explore themes of identity and heritage, as evidenced by the notes: the autobiography focuses on Angelou's experiences with "racism and identity," while the film follows a woman who seeks to "reconnect with her heritage and discover who she truly is." This option clearly and specifically identifies the shared themes between the two works.

Option A is incorrect because it contrasts the two works rather than highlighting a similarity. It focuses on the different impacts of the autobiography and the film, which does not accomplish the student's goal of finding a common theme.

Option C is incorrect because it is too vague and lacks specificity in achieving the goal of highlighting a similarity between the two works. While it mentions that the film follows a woman's return to her ancestral home and the autobiography focuses on experiences in the segregated South, it does not explicitly identify the common themes of identity and heritage that both works explore. This option fails to make a clear and direct connection between the two works, making it less effective in achieving the student's goal.

Option D is incorrect because it merely states the completion dates of the two works, which is irrelevant to the student's goal of highlighting a thematic similarity. This option does not use the relevant notes to draw a meaningful connection between the works and is therefore not as effective as the correct answer.

27. Rhetorical Synthesis: Hard

Answer: D) The integration of AI in multiple industries offers significant benefits, but it also raises concerns about job displacement, privacy, and ethical implications.

Logical Breakdown and Explanation:

This question asks you to choose the option that most effectively generalizes the benefits and potential risks associated with the widespread adoption of AI, using relevant information from the notes.

Option D is correct because it directly addresses both the benefits and potential risks of AI. The integration of AI in multiple industries offers significant benefits, such as improved efficiency and convenience, as noted in the healthcare, finance, and everyday life sectors. At the same time, it raises important concerns about job displacement, privacy, and ethical implications, which align with the notes on job displacement, bias in algorithms, and potential misuse in surveillance. This option effectively balances the discussion of AI's advantages with its potential downsides.

Option A is incorrect because it focuses solely on the benefits of AI, mentioning its use in healthcare, finance, and everyday life, and the improvements in efficiency and convenience. However, it fails to address the potential risks associated with AI, making it **incomplete** and less effective in achieving the student's goal of discussing both the benefits and risks.

Option B is incorrect because it introduces the potential risks associated with AI, such as bias in algorithms and misuse in surveillance, but it only mentions a few specific technologies like smart home devices and virtual assistants. This option is **too narrow** and does not effectively generalize the broader benefits and risks of AI across multiple industries, making it less effective than the correct answer.

Option C is incorrect because it narrowly focuses on AI's impact in the finance industry and job displacement, without adequately addressing the broader benefits and risks across multiple sectors. It also fails to discuss the ethical concerns and potential for misuse in other areas, making it **incomplete** and less effective in achieving the goal.

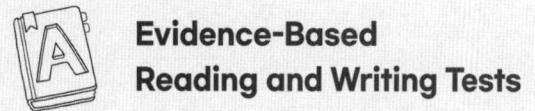

Practice Test

2

Reading and Writing

27 Questions, 32 Minutes

Inspired by the natural landscapes of his native Iceland, artist Olafur Eliasson creates installations that aim to _____ viewers' perceptions of their environment. His works often incorporate light, water, and air to create immersive experiences that redefine how art and nature interact and coexist for the viewer.

1

Which choice completes the text with the most logical and precise word or phrase?

A) distort

B) transform

C) degrade

D) narrow

CONTINUE

The Mimosa pudica, commonly known as the sensitive plant, responds to touch by rapidly folding its leaves. In 2021, researchers led by Dr. Anna Smirnova found that this plant's defensive reaction is triggered by a complex _____ mechanism that involves changes in turgor pressure within its cells. This rapid movement helps deter herbivores and protect the plant from damage.

Which choice completes the text with the most logical and precise word or phrase?

A) dehydration
B) respiration
C) manufactured
D) stimulation

Marie always found solace in the quiet library. The _____ environment allowed her to focus and escape the chaos of daily life. She cherished those peaceful moments, surrounded by books and the gentle rustling of pages, which provided a comforting backdrop to her thoughts.

Which choice completes the text with the most logical and precise word or phrase?

A) serene
B) frenetic
C) vibrant
D) raucous

CONTINUE

Dr. Aisha Khan's research at the University of Nairobi examines the impact of urbanization on local bird populations. She is investigating whether increasing levels of noise pollution in cities have _____ effect on the communication and mating behaviors of these birds—that is, to determine if heightened noise levels disrupt their ability to find mates and establish territories.

4

Which choice completes the text with the most logical and precise word or phrase?

A) a negligible

B) an invaluable

C) a detrimental

D) a transient

In her acclaimed novel *Half of a Yellow Sun*, Chimamanda Ngozi Adichie explores the complexities of the Nigerian Civil War through the intertwined lives of her characters. The book, which has received numerous awards, vividly portrays the era's turmoil and highlights the _____ experiences of the Igbo people, who faced profound struggles and demonstrated remarkable resilience throughout the conflict.

5

Which choice completes the text with the most logical and precise word or phrase?

A) superficial

B) harrowing

C) innocuous

D) whimsical

CONTINUE

The following text is from the 1912 poem "A Patch of Old Snow" by Robert Frost. Frost, a renowned American poet, is known for his use of natural imagery to explore themes of human experience.

> There's a patch of old snow in a corner,
> That I should have guessed
> Was a blow-away paper the rain
> Had brought to rest.
>
> It is speckled with grime as if
> Small print overspread it,
> The news of a day I've forgotten—
> If I ever read it.

6

Which choice best describes the overall structure of the text?

A) It begins by describing a scene, uses metaphors to reflect on its appearance, and ends with a contemplation on memory.

B) It introduces a natural scene, contrasts it with human activity, and concludes with a sense of nostalgia.

C) It depicts the changing seasons, relates them to human emotions, and ends with a reflection on impermanence.

D) It describes a landscape, explores the passage of time, and concludes with a hopeful message.

CONTINUE

The following text is adapted from *The Secret Garden*, a 1911 novel by Frances Hodgson Burnett. In the text, Mary Lennox discovers a hidden garden and begins to care for it.

Mary found herself at the threshold of a mysterious, overgrown garden. The walls were covered in ivy, and the once-beautiful flower beds were choked with weeds. Determined to bring it back to life, she began to pull out the weeds, uncovering delicate plants that had been suffocated. Each day, she returned to the garden, nurturing the plants with water and care. As the days passed, the garden slowly started to bloom, and Mary felt a deep sense of accomplishment.

7

Which choice best describes the function of the underlined sentence in the text as a whole?

A) To foreshadow the difficulties Mary will face in restoring the garden

B) To suggest that the garden is beyond repair due to its neglected condition

C) To highlight the contrast between the garden's past beauty and its current state

D) To emphasize the natural beauty of the garden despite its neglected condition

CONTINUE

The following text is adapted from anthropologist Dr. Jane Goodall's observations of the Hadza people, one of the last hunter-gatherer societies in Tanzania. Dr. Goodall notes that the Hadza's egalitarian social structure plays a crucial role in their survival. <u>Unlike in many modern societies, the Hadza do not accumulate personal wealth</u>. Resources are shared among all members of the group, ensuring that everyone has enough to eat. This practice of sharing is deeply embedded in their culture and is critical for their cohesion and resilience.

8

Which choice best describes the function of the underlined sentence in the text as a whole?

A) It elaborates on a claim about social structures in hunter-gatherer societies made earlier in the text.

B) It offers an example of a cultural practice among the Hadza discussed earlier in the text.

C) It notes a possible exception to the anthropologist's observations about egalitarianism.

D) It provides further details about the economic practices of the Hadza discussed earlier in the text.

CONTINUE

Text 1

In the past, neuroscientists believed that distinct regions of the human brain were responsible for specific functions, such as language, memory, and motor skills. This concept, known as localization of function, suggested a highly compartmentalized brain where different areas operated in isolation. These theories were primarily based on studies of brain injuries and lesions that caused deficits in particular abilities.

Text 2

Recent advances in neuroscience propose that humans possess not just one brain but multiple interconnected 'brains' that work together to process information and respond to the environment. This concept highlights the roles of the enteric nervous system (the 'second brain' in the gut) and the cardiac nervous system (the 'heart brain') in addition to the central nervous system in the skull. These systems communicate with the brain and each other, influencing emotions, decision-making, and overall health. The emerging view suggests a complex network of neural communication that extends beyond the skull.

9

Based on the texts, what would the author of Text 2 most likely say about Text 1's characterization of brain function theories?

A) It is outdated given the recent discoveries about the interconnectedness of various neural systems.

B) It is accurate given the established evidence supporting localization of function.

C) It is irrelevant given the new emphasis on the central nervous system.

D) It is groundbreaking considering the focus on brain injuries and lesions.

CONTINUE

In her 1989 novel, *The Joy Luck Club,* Amy Tan portrays the character Jing-mei (June) Woo as having a complex and evolving relationship with her mother, Suyuan Woo:

_____

10

Which quotation from *The Joy Luck Club* most effectively illustrates this claim?

A) "And then it occurs to me. They are frightened. In me, they see their own daughters, just as ignorant, just as unmindful of all the truths and hopes they have brought to America."

B) "I was six when my mother taught me the art of invisible strength. It was a strategy for winning arguments, respect from others, and eventually, though neither of us knew it at the time, chess games."

C) "My mother believed you could be anything you wanted to be in America. You could open a restaurant. You could work for the government and get good retirement. You could buy a house with almost no money down. You could become rich. You could become instantly famous."

D) "I had always assumed we had an unspoken understanding about these things; that she didn't have to ask me and I didn't have to answer. So maybe I never really knew what she had been feeling all those times. I know I was selfish, but I had no choice."

CONTINUE

Barcelona has emerged as a pioneer in smart city innovation, driven by the efforts of city planners-notably Antoni Vives and Pilar Conesa-spearheading initiatives to integrate advanced technologies like AI, IoT, and big data. Recognizing the complexities of urban management, they focused on creating an interconnected infrastructure. For example, they implemented smart lighting systems that adjust based on pedestrian activity. Their rationale was clear: to reduce energy consumption and enhance quality of life. Additionally, they introduced smart waste management, using sensors to optimize collection routes, thereby reducing operational costs and carbon emissions. These efforts exemplify a strategic, data-driven approach to urban planning.

11

According to the text, what were some benefits of the smart waste management system introduced in Barcelona?

A) The sensors increased the recycling rate among residents, leading to a more productive society.

B) The system automated waste sorting at disposal sites, which improved operations.

C) It reduced energy consumption, thereby improving the residents' quality of life.

D) The innovation increased efficiency of trash collection, resulting in lower operating costs.

CONTINUE

GDP Growth Rates of Selected Countries
(2019-2021)

Country	2019 GDP Growth (%)	2020 GDP Growth (%)	2021 GDP Growth (%)
United States	2.3	-3.4	5.7
China	6.1	2.3	8.1
Germany	0.6	-4.6	2.9
Brazil	1.1	-4.1	4.6

While researching the impact of the COVID-19 pandemic on global economies, a student noticed that most countries, including the United States, Germany, and Brazil, experienced negative GDP growth in 2020. The U.S. saw a contraction of -3.4%, Germany shrank by -4.6%, and Brazil's GDP declined by -4.1%. However, there was a surprising outlier: despite the widespread economic downturn, _____.

12

Which choice most effectively uses data from the table to complete the text?

A) China managed to minimize the impact of the pandemic and only saw a drop in GDP of -2.3% in 2020.

B) China not only avoided a GDP decline but actually experienced positive growth of 2.3% in 2020.

C) China's economy fell by 3.8% from 2019 to 2020.

D) China's GPD growth in 2020 was less than that in 2019.

CONTINUE

Number of Artifacts Discovered at Ancient Sites

Archaeological Site	Location	Number of Artifacts Found	Estimated Number of Undiscovered Artifacts
Machu Picchu	Peru	3,400	2,000+
Valley of the Kings	Egypt	5,800	1,000+
Terracotta Army	Xi'an, China	8,000+	Unknown
Pompeii	Italy	15,000	5,000+

Archaeologists frequently work with the understanding that the number of artifacts discovered at ancient sites represents only a small percentage of what remains buried. The numbers listed are often conservative estimates, as many areas of these sites remain unexplored. For example, _____

13

Which choice most effectively uses data from the table to complete the example?

A) the number of artifacts found at the Valley of the Kings (5,800) is likely an overestimate, as many sites have already been thoroughly explored.

B) the Terracotta Army's 8,000+ artifacts likely include all that remains, as the site has been fully excavated.

C) at Pompeii, the 15,000 artifacts found are likely just a fraction of what remains, as thousands more are believed to be buried.

D) the estimated 2000+ undiscovered artifacts at Machu Picchu is most likely an understatement, as the site has barely been explored.

CONTINUE ➡

The Pleistocene epoch, lasting from about 2.6 million years ago to approximately 11,700 years ago, saw significant changes in megafauna. Fossils of large animals from various periods of the Pleistocene have been discovered in different parts of the world. For instance, the Rancho La Brea Tar Pits in California, unearthed in the early 20th century, contain fossils dating back to approximately 40,000 years ago. Similarly, the Old Crow Basin in Canada, excavated in the 1960s, revealed animal fossils from around 20,000 years ago. Evidence, however, suggests that systematic hunting of smaller animals like squirrels by human tribes began around 25,000 years ago. This fact supports the conclusion that _____

14

Which choice most logically completes the text?

A) more recent archaeological sites than the Rancho La Brea Tar Pits are more likely to show evidence of smaller animals like squirrels.

B) neither the Rancho La Brea Tar Pits nor the Old Crow Basin contain evidence of systematic hunting of smaller animals.

C) the Old Crow Basin provides the earliest evidence of systematic hunting of smaller animals like squirrels by human tribes.

D) both the Rancho La Brea Tar Pits and the Old Crow Basin contain evidence of early human hunting practices involving megafauna.

CONTINUE ➡

In the early 20th century, the theory of spontaneous generation, which posited that living organisms could arise from non-living matter, was widely accepted by many scientists. According to this theory, maggots appeared in decaying meat through a process of spontaneous generation. However, Louis Pasteur claimed that this theory was flawed and that maggots actually came from eggs laid by flies. Pasteur's experiments demonstrated that when meat was protected from flies, no maggots would appear, providing strong evidence that living organisms arise from pre-existing life forms, not from non-living matter.

15

Which finding, if true, would most directly undermine Pasteur's claim about the theory of spontaneous generation?

A) Maggots develop into flies, which then lay eggs on decaying meat, leading to more maggots.

B) Maggots appear in decaying matter within a time frame too short for fly eggs to develop into maggots.

C) Maggots appear in other types of non-living matter, such as decaying vegetables and spoiled fruit.

D) Sealed containers of meat that have been sterilized and kept free from flies do not produce maggots, while open containers do.

CONTINUE

As one of the world's leading space exploration agencies, NASA has a long history of pushing the boundaries of what is known about our solar system. Its Mars missions, in particular, is part of a broader effort to uncover the mysteries of the Red Planet, and their aim is to answer a fundamental question: _____ Determining its answer could have profound implications for our understanding of life in the universe.

16

Which choice completes the text so that it conforms to the conventions of Standard English?

A) whether life ever existed on the Red Planet?

B) did life ever exist on the Red Planet.

C) whether life ever existed on the Red Planet.

D) did life ever exist on the Red Planet?

By studying the intricate beadwork and metalwork found in ancient African artifacts, historians can gain insights into the cultural exchanges of early African civilizations. When such artifacts aren't available, researchers turn to _____ practice of passing down cultural knowledge through spoken word from a tribe's storytellers (known as *Griots*), to piece together the historical narratives of African societies that left no written records.

17

Which choice completes the text so that it conforms to the conventions of Standard English?

A) oral tradition, the

B) oral tradition; the

C) oral tradition: the

D) oral tradition—the

CONTINUE

The elaborate footwork and passionate rhythms of Flamenco, a traditional Spanish dance form rooted in the Andalusian region, _____ beyond its cultural origins to inspire contemporary dance styles around the world, with choreographers incorporating Flamenco's intensity and expressive movements into modern performances.

Many of the ancient rock art sites in Australia's northern _____ depict various elements of Indigenous Australian culture, such as Dreamtime stories, ceremonial practices, and native wildlife. For example, the Gwion Gwion rock paintings in the Kimberley region are renowned for their detailed depictions of human figures adorned in ceremonial dress.

18

Which choice completes the text so that it conforms to the conventions of Standard English?

A) has spread
B) is spreading
C) have spread
D) was spread

19

Which choice completes the text so that it conforms to the conventions of Standard English?

A) regions that date back thousands of years,
B) regions, that date back thousands of years,
C) regions that date back thousands of years
D) regions, that date back thousands of years

CONTINUE

The orchid mantis, a remarkable insect native to Southeast Asia, mimics the appearance of a flower to lure unsuspecting _____ in South America, the leaf-tailed gecko, known for its remarkable camouflage abilities, employs a similar strategy, blending seamlessly into its environment by resembling dead leaves.

20

Which choice completes the text so that it conforms to the conventions of Standard English?

A) prey

B) prey,

C) prey and

D) prey;

As a behavioral economist, Dr. Dan Ariely studies consumer decision-making, a phenomenon that, _____ the often irrational ways people respond to pricing, marketing, and other economic factors, provides insights into how businesses can better understand their customers.

21

Which choice completes the text so that it conforms to the conventions of Standard English?

A) investigates

B) investigating

C) investigate

D) has investigated

CONTINUE ➡

The Arctic tern is known for its remarkable migration pattern, traveling from the Arctic to the Antarctic and back each year. This long journey covers approximately 44,000 miles annually. The Monarch butterfly, _____ undertakes a much shorter but still impressive migration from North America to central Mexico, where it hibernates for the winter.

22

Which choice completes the text with the most logical transition?

A) nonetheless,

B) for example,

C) though,

D) in addition,

A balanced diet includes the appropriate intake of macronutrients, which are essential for energy and bodily functions. _____ carbohydrates, proteins, and fats should be consumed in specific proportions to meet the body's daily energy needs and support overall health.

23

Which choice completes the text with the most logical transition?

A) That is,

B) Nevertheless,

C) Eventually,

D) Nowadays,

CONTINUE

Camels have evolved to survive in harsh desert environments by storing fat in their humps, which can be converted into water and energy when resources are scarce. _____, their thick coats protect them from the sun's heat during the day and keep them warm during the cold desert nights.

Which choice completes the text with the most logical transition?

A) However,

B) Nevertheless,

C) Thus,

D) In addition,

CONTINUE

While researching a topic, a student has taken the following notes:

- Sustainable architecture focuses on designing buildings that minimize environmental impact and maximize energy efficiency.
- The Bosco Verticale in Milan, Italy, is a prime example of sustainable architecture.
- The two residential towers are covered with over 900 trees and thousands of plants.
- The buildings were designed by Italian architect Stefano Boeri and completed in 2014.
- The vegetation helps to absorb CO_2, produce oxygen, and reduce energy consumption.

25

The student wants to provide a specific example of a sustainable architecture project. Which choice most effectively uses relevant information from the notes to accomplish this goal?

A) Minimizing environmental impact and maximizing energy efficiency are the goals of every sustainable architecture project.

B) Italian architect Stefano Boeri designed the Bosco Verticale in Milan, Italy, which was completed in 2014.

C) Designed by Stefano Boeri, the Bosco Verticale consists of over 900 trees and thousands of plants covering two residential towers.

D) Sustainable architecture includes features like vegetation that absorb CO_2, produce oxygen, and reduce energy consumption in buildings.

CONTINUE

While researching a topic, a student has taken the following notes:

- Cognitive-behavioral therapy (CBT) is a form of psychotherapy that helps individuals identify and change negative thought patterns.
- In a 2019 study, Dr. Michael Roberts conducted an experiment to assess the effectiveness of CBT in reducing anxiety levels in adolescents.
- Participants were randomly selected from a pool of high school students who had been identified as experiencing moderate to severe anxiety.
- Participants attended weekly CBT sessions for three months.
- Anxiety levels were measured before and after the treatment using standardized anxiety assessment tools.
- The study concluded that CBT significantly reduced anxiety levels in the majority of participants.

26

The student wants to present the study and its findings. Which choice most effectively uses relevant information from the notes to accomplish this goal?

A) In a 2019 study exploring CBT's effectiveness in reducing anxiety in teens, Dr. Roberts concluded that the therapy significantly alleviated anxiety symptoms in a majority of participants who attended weekly CBT sessions.

B) Participants were randomly selected high school students who identified with moderate to severe anxiety for Dr. Roberts' 2019 study on the effectiveness of CBT in treating anxiety.

C) To assess the efficacy of CBT in treating anxiety, Dr. Roberts instructed participants to attend weekly CBT sessions and measured their anxiety levels before and after treatment.

D) CBT helps individuals identify and change negative thought patterns, and findings from Dr. Roberts' 2019 study revealed that it also helps significantly reduce anxiety levels in those with moderate to severe forms of anxiety.

CONTINUE

While researching a topic, a student has taken the following notes:

- A 2021 study by Dr. Emily Stone examined the relationship between sleep duration and cognitive function in adults.
- She wanted to determine how different amounts of sleep affect memory, attention, and problem-solving abilities.
- Participants were divided into three groups: short sleepers (4-5 hours), moderate sleepers (6-7 hours), and long sleepers (8-9 hours).
- Cognitive performance tests were administered after one week of following the assigned sleep schedules.
- Results showed that moderate and long sleepers performed significantly better on cognitive tasks than short sleepers.
- The study suggests that adequate sleep is essential for maintaining optimal cognitive function.

27

The student wants to explain the purpose of Dr. Stone's study. Which choice most effectively uses relevant information from the notes to accomplish this goal?

A) The study by Dr. Stone found that those who slept between 6 and 9 hours performed significantly better on cognitive tasks than those who got 4 to 5 hours, highlighting the importance of adequate sleep.

B) Dr. Stone, in a 2021 study, examined the relationship between sleep duration and cognitive function in adults by having participants follow an assigned sleep schedule and administering cognitive tests thereafter.

C) In a 2021 study, Dr. Stone divided participants into three groups based on sleep duration to examine its effects on cognitive performance.

D) Dr. Stone's 2021 study aimed to determine how cognitive functions like memory, attention and problem-solving are impacted by varying amounts of sleep.

If you finish before the time is called, you may check your work on this module only.
On Test Day, you will only be able to move to the next module when time expires.

187

 **Answer Key**

Question Number	Correct Answer	Level of Difficulty	Question Type
1	B	Easy	**Craft and Structure:** *Words in Context*
2	D	Easy	**Craft and Structure:** *Words in Context*
3	A	Easy	**Craft and Structure:** *Words in Context*
4	C	Medium	**Craft and Structure:** *Words in Context*
5	B	Hard	**Craft and Structure:** *Words in Context*
6	A	Hard	**Craft and Structure:** *Overall Structure*
7	C	Medium	**Craft and Structure:** *Function of the Underlined Portion*
8	B	Medium	**Craft and Structure:** *Function of the Underlined Portion*
9	A	Medium	**Craft and Structure:** *Cross-Text Connections*
10	D	Hard	**Information and Ideas:** *Cite Text as Evidence*
11	D	Easy	**Information and Ideas:** *Detail*
12	B	Easy	**Information and Ideas:** *Cite Text as Evidence (Infographic)*
13	C	Medium	**Information and Ideas:** *Support a Claim (Infographic)*

Question Number	Correct Answer	Level of Difficulty	Question Type
14	A	Hard	**Information and Ideas:** *Inference (complete the text)*
15	B	Hard	**Information and Ideas:** *Weaken a Claim*
16	D	Medium	**Standard English Conventions:** *Punctuation (question mark)*
17	A	Hard	**Standard English Conventions:** *Punctuation and Sentence Structure*
18	C	Medium	**Standard English Conventions:** *Verbs*
19	C	Easy	**Standard English Conventions:** *Commas*
20	D	Medium	**Standard English Conventions:** *Punctuation and Sentence Structure*
21	B	Medium	**Standard English Conventions:** *Verbs*
22	C	Medium	**Expressions of Writing:** *Transitions*
23	A	Medium	**Expressions of Writing:** *Transitions*
24	D	Easy	**Expressions of Writing:** *Transitions*
25	C	Medium	**Expressions of Writing:** *Rhetorical Synthesis*
26	A	Hard	**Expressions of Writing:** *Rhetorical Synthesis*
27	D	Hard	**Expressions of Writing:** *Rhetorical Synthesis*

Instructions

Count the number of questions you got correct in Module 1.

Enter your score here: _____.

If your score is **18 or higher**, move on to the **HARD version** of Module 2.

If your score is **below 18**, proceed to the **EASY version** of Module 2.

 **Explanations**

1. Words in Context: Easy

Answer: B) transform

Step-by-Step Explanation:

1. Let's look at what the passage is saying. It describes how artist Olafur Eliasson is inspired by the natural landscapes of Iceland and how he creates installations that affect viewers' perceptions of their environment.

2. The passage mentions that Eliasson's works aim to "redefine how art and nature interact and coexist." The word "redefine" is a key context clue because if something is redefined, it implies that it is being given a new or different meaning or understanding, often in a profound way. This suggests that Eliasson's art doesn't just slightly alter perceptions; it fundamentally changes how viewers understand and experience the relationship between art and nature.

3. The word we need should convey the idea of changing or altering perceptions in a significant and positive way. "Transform" fits perfectly because it means to change something in a profound or fundamental way, which aligns with the idea of redefining perceptions as described in the passage.

4. Transform" is the most logical choice because it reflects the idea of a deep and impactful change in how viewers experience their environment.

Explanation of Incorrect Options:

A) distort: This is incorrect because it suggests altering something in a way that makes it less clear or accurate, which doesn't align with the positive and immersive effect described in the passage.

C) degrade: This is incorrect because it implies a reduction in quality or value, which contradicts the passage's description of the profound and immersive impact of Eliasson's art.

D) narrow: This is incorrect because it implies making something more limited or restricted, which does not logically fit the idea of profoundly changing perceptions as described in the passage.

2. Words in Context: Easy

Answer: D) stimulation

Step-by-Step Explanation:

1. Let's deconstruct the passage together. It describes how the Mimosa pudica, or sensitive plant, "responds to touch" by rapidly folding its leaves. The passage further explains that this reaction is triggered by a complex mechanism involving changes in turgor pressure within the plant's cells.
2. The key context clues are "responds to touch" and "this plant's defensive reaction is triggered." These phrases indicate that the plant's reaction is caused by an external stimulus, specifically touch.
3. The word "stimulation" is the most logical choice because it refers to the process of triggering a response, particularly in a biological context. The touch acts as a stimulus that initiates the plant's defensive mechanism, which aligns perfectly with the context provided.

Explanation of Incorrect Options:

A) dehydration: This is incorrect because it refers to the loss of water, which is unrelated to the context about the process of triggering a defensive reaction in response to touch.

B) respiration: This is incorrect because it refers to the process of breathing or energy production in cells, which is irrelevant to the passage whose context is about how the plant responds to an external stimulus like touch.

C) manufactured: This is incorrect because it suggests something is made or produced, which doesn't logically fit with the idea of triggering a reaction in response to an external stimulus.

3. Words in Context: Easy

Answer: A) serene

Step-by-Step Explanation:

1. Let's understand the passage. It describes how Marie finds solace in the quiet library. The library provides her with a space where she can focus and escape the chaos of daily life. The passage emphasizes the "peaceful moments" and the "gentle rustling of pages," which suggests a calm and tranquil environment.

2. Notice the phrases "quiet library" and "those peaceful moments." These phrases indicate that the environment is calm, soothing, and free from distractions. The setting is clearly one of tranquility, which allows Marie to relax and focus.

3. The word we need should reflect this calm and peaceful environment. The word should describe an atmosphere that is quiet and free from chaos, aligning with the overall tone of the passage.

4. Ask yourself, what word best describes a calm and peaceful environment? "Serene" fits perfectly because it means calm, peaceful, and untroubled, which aligns with the description of the library as a place where Marie finds solace.

Explanation of Incorrect Options:

B) frenetic: This is incorrect because it suggests frantic energy and activity, which contradicts the calm and peaceful environment described in the passage.

C) vibrant: This is incorrect because it implies liveliness and energy, which is inconsistent with the context of the tranquil setting of the library.

D) raucous: This is incorrect because it means loud and disorderly, which is the opposite of the quiet and peaceful environment described in the passage.

4. Words in Context: Medium

Answer: C) a detrimental

Step-by-Step Explanation:

1. Let's understand the passage. The passage describes Dr. Aisha Khan's research on the impact of urbanization, particularly noise pollution, on local bird populations. Specifically, she is investigating whether noise pollution affects the birds' communication and mating behaviors.
2. Notice the phrase "to determine if heightened noise levels disrupt their ability to find mates and establish territories." The word "disrupt" suggests that the noise pollution might have a negative impact on the birds' behaviors, possibly interfering with their ability to communicate and mate.
3. The word we need should reflect the potential negative impact of noise pollution on the birds' communication and mating behaviors.
4. Ask yourself, what word best describes a negative effect that disrupts or harms? "A detrimental" fits perfectly because it means causing harm or damage, which aligns with the passage's implication that noise pollution could be disrupting the birds' behaviors.

Explanation of Incorrect Options:

A) a negligible: This is incorrect because it implies that the effect is so small that it is insignificant, which doesn't logically fit the context regarding the concern about noise pollution disrupting bird behaviors.

B) an invaluable: This is incorrect because it means extremely valuable, which does not make sense in the context of discussing a potential negative effect.

D) a transient: This is incorrect because it means temporary or short-lived, which isn't supported by the context of determining if noise pollution is having a disruptive impact on the birds.

5. Words in Context: Hard

Answer: B) harrowing

Step-by-Step Explanation:

1. Let's look at what the passage is saying. The passage describes how Chimamanda Ngozi Adichie's novel *Half of a Yellow Sun* explores the Nigerian Civil War, focusing on the lives of her characters and the experiences of the Igbo people during this turbulent period. The passage mentions that the Igbo people "faced profound struggles and demonstrated remarkable resilience," indicating that their experiences were intense and challenging.
2. Notice the phrase "faced profound struggles and demonstrated remarkable resilience." This suggests that the experiences of the Igbo people during the conflict were deeply difficult and emotionally intense.
3. The word we need should capture the intense and challenging nature of the experiences described.
4. Ask yourself, what word best describes experiences that are extremely distressing and difficult? "Harrowing" fits perfectly because it means extremely distressing or terrifying, which aligns with the portrayal of the Igbo people's struggles during the Nigerian Civil War.

Explanation of Incorrect Options:

A) superficial: This is incorrect because it means shallow or lacking depth, which contradicts the intense and profound struggles described in the passage.

C) innocuous: This is incorrect because it means harmless or not likely to cause injury, which does not match the description of the difficult and challenging experiences faced by the Igbo people.

D) whimsical: This is incorrect because it suggests something light-hearted, playful, or fanciful, which is entirely inappropriate for the serious and intense context of the Nigerian Civil War.

6. Overall Structure: Hard

Answer: A) It begins by describing a scene, uses metaphors to reflect on its appearance, and ends with a contemplation on memory.

Logical Breakdown and Explanation:

This question asks you to identify the option that best describes the overall structure of the text, focusing on how the poem develops its ideas from beginning to end.

Option A is correct because it accurately captures the structure of the poem. The poem begins by describing a scene ("patch of old snow in a corner"), then uses a metaphor comparing the snow to a "blow-away paper" speckled with grime, suggesting that it resembles a forgotten newspaper. The poem ends with a contemplation on memory, as the speaker reflects on the "news of a day" they've forgotten—if they ever read it. This choice effectively describes the progression from observation to metaphor to reflection on memory.

Option B is incorrect because it suggests a contrast between the natural scene and human activity and concludes with a sense of nostalgia. While the poem does involve some reflection on memory, it doesn't specifically contrast nature with human activity or convey a strong sense of nostalgia. This option partially captures the reflection on memory but introduces ideas that aren't developed in the passage.

Option C is incorrect because it introduces the idea of the changing seasons, which is not present in the poem. The poem focuses on a single scene—a patch of old snow—and does not mention or depict the transition between seasons. By suggesting that the poem relates the changing seasons to human emotions, this option misinterprets the content of the poem. Since the mention of changing seasons is incorrect, the entire answer becomes invalid, as it introduces an off-topic idea. Isolating and challenging this incorrect detail effectively disqualifies the entire option.

Option D is incorrect because it introduces the idea of a hopeful message at the end of the poem, which is not present in the text. The poem concludes with a reflection on a forgotten or possibly unread piece of news, conveyed through the imagery of a speckled patch of old snow. This ending carries a sense of ambiguity or resignation rather than hope. By suggesting that the poem ends on a hopeful note, this option contradicts the actual tone and content of the poem's conclusion.

7. Function of the Underlined Portion: Medium

Answer: C) To highlight the contrast between the garden's past beauty and its current state

Logical Breakdown and Explanation:

This question asks you to identify the function of the underlined sentence within the text, focusing on how it contributes to the overall meaning and development of the passage.

Option C is correct because the phrase "once-beautiful" suggests that the garden used to be vibrant and well-maintained, while "choked with weeds" vividly describes its current state. The underlined sentence, "The walls were covered in ivy, and the once-beautiful flower beds were choked with weeds," highlights the contrast between the garden's past beauty and its current neglected state.

Option A is incorrect because the underlined sentence does not foreshadow the difficulties Mary will face. While the sentence does describe the garden's neglected condition, it does not suggest or predict specific challenges ahead. The verb "to foreshadow" implies a prediction or hint of future events, which is not the function of this sentence.

Option B is incorrect because it suggests that the garden is beyond repair, which is not supported by the passage. The text focuses on Mary's determination to bring the garden back to life, and the underlined sentence serves to describe its current state, not to imply that it cannot be restored.

Option D is incorrect because it suggests that the underlined sentence emphasizes the natural beauty of the garden despite its neglected condition. However, the sentence actually highlights the overgrown and neglected state of the garden, not its beauty. The verb "to emphasize" and the focus on "natural beauty" do not accurately describe what the underlined portion is doing in the text.

8. Function of the Underlined Portion: Medium

Answer: B) It offers an example of a cultural practice among the Hadza discussed earlier in the text.

Logical Breakdown and Explanation:

This question tests your ability to accurately interpret the role of specific sentences within a passage. The correct answer must reflect what the underlined sentence is "doing" in the context of the passage.

Option B is correct because the underlined sentence, "Unlike in many modern societies, the Hadza do not accumulate personal wealth," directly illustrates a key aspect of the Hadza's egalitarian social structure. By stating that the Hadza do not accumulate personal wealth, the sentence highlights how their social structure ensures that resources are shared equally among all members. This practice of avoiding personal wealth accumulation is a concrete example of the egalitarianism discussed earlier in the passage, showing how the Hadza's cultural values support the survival and cohesion of their community. The underlined sentence thus reinforces and exemplifies the broader theme of egalitarianism in Hadza society.

Option A is incorrect because it overgeneralizes the claim made about the Hadza to all hunter-gatherer societies. The passage specifically discusses the Hadza people, not all hunter-gatherer societies, so this option does not accurately reflect what the underlined sentence is doing.

Option C is incorrect because it suggests that the underlined sentence notes a possible exception to the anthropologist's observations about egalitarianism. However, the sentence reinforces the idea of egalitarianism by providing an example (how wealth is not a matter of personal accumulation), rather than introducing an exception. This option introduces an idea that is not supported by the passage.

Option D is incorrect because it suggests that economic practices were discussed *earlier in the text*. However, the earlier part of the passage does not specifically discuss "economic practices" but rather focuses on the social structure and resource-sharing practices of the Hadza. This option introduces a key idea that is not directly supported by the passage, making it incorrect.

9. Cross-Text Connections: Medium

Answer: A) It is outdated given the recent discoveries about the interconnectedness of various neural systems.

Logical Breakdown and Explanation:

This question asks you to determine how the author of Text 2 would likely respond to the characterization of brain function theories presented in Text 1.

Option A is correct because the author of Text 2 would likely consider Text 1's characterization of brain function theories as outdated. Text 2 presents a more recent and complex understanding of brain function, emphasizing the interconnectedness of various neural systems, including the enteric and cardiac nervous systems, which contrasts with the more compartmentalized view of brain function described in Text 1. This option correctly reflects the advancement in neuroscience that challenges the older theory of localization of function.

Option B is incorrect because it suggests that the author of Text 2 would find Text 1's characterization accurate. However, Text 2 emphasizes a more integrated and interconnected view of brain function, which disagrees with the compartmentalized approach described in Text 1. This option incorrectly presents the author's position by suggesting agreement instead of disagreement.

Option C is incorrect because it introduces the idea that the new emphasis is solely on the central nervous system, making the previous theories irrelevant. However, Text 2 discusses the interconnectedness of multiple neural systems, not just the central nervous system, and does not suggest that the older theories are irrelevant. This option introduces an idea not mentioned in the passage, making it incorrect.

Option D is incorrect because it suggests that Text 1's characterization is groundbreaking, which contradicts Text 2's position. The author of Text 2 presents a newer, more advanced theory that goes beyond the focus on brain injuries and lesions described in Text 1. This option incorrectly presents the author's position by suggesting that the older theory is innovative rather than outdated.

10. Citing Text as Evidence: Hard

Answer: D) "I had always assumed we had an unspoken understanding about these things; that she didn't have to ask me and I didn't have to answer. So maybe I never really knew what she had been feeling all those times. I know I was selfish, but I had no choice."

Logical Breakdown and Explanation:

This question asks you to identify the quotation from *The Joy Luck Club* that best illustrates the claim that Jing-mei (June) Woo has a complex and evolving relationship with her mother, Suyuan Woo.

Option D is correct because it most effectively illustrates the complex and evolving relationship between Jing-mei and her mother. The quote, "I had always assumed we had an unspoken understanding about these things; that she didn't have to ask me and I didn't have to answer," highlights Jing-mei's assumption that she and her mother shared a mutual understanding without the need for explicit communication. This reflects the complexity in their relationship, where unspoken expectations may have led to misunderstandings. The next part of the quote, "So maybe I never really knew what she had been feeling all those times," reveals Jing-mei's realization that she might not have truly understood her mother's emotions or intentions. This moment of self-awareness marks a shift in Jing-mei's perspective, showing the evolution of her relationship with her mother as she begins to recognize her own limitations in understanding Suyuan.

Option A is incorrect because it focuses on Jing-mei's realization about the fears of the older generation and how they see their daughters, but it does not directly address her relationship with her mother. The quote is more about generational concerns rather than the personal dynamic between Jing-mei and Suyuan, making it irrelevant to the specific claim.

Option B is incorrect because it describes a lesson Jing-mei learned from her mother about the "art of invisible strength," which is more about a specific skill rather than the complexity of their relationship. While it touches on an aspect of their interaction, it doesn't fully capture the evolving nature of their relationship as described in the claim.

Option C is incorrect because it describes Suyuan's beliefs about the opportunities available in America, which reflects her optimism and ambitions for Jing-mei but does not directly illustrate the complexity or evolution of their relationship. This quote is more about Suyuan's expectations than the dynamic between mother and daughter, making it irrelevant to the claim.

11. Detail: Easy

Answer: D) The innovation increased efficiency of trash collection, resulting in lower operating costs.

Logical Breakdown and Explanation:

This question asks you to identify the correct benefits of the smart waste management system introduced in Barcelona as described in the passage.

Option D is correct because it accurately reflects the benefits mentioned in the text. The passage states that the smart waste management system uses sensors to optimize collection routes, which results in "reducing operational costs and carbon emissions." This directly correlates to the increased efficiency of trash collection, leading to lower operating costs, making Option D the best choice.

Option A is incorrect because it introduces the idea that the sensors increased the recycling rate among residents, which was not mentioned in the passage. The passage discusses optimizing collection routes to reduce costs and emissions, but it does not mention any effect on recycling rates or societal productivity. This introduces information that was never discussed in the text.

Option B is incorrect because it suggests that the system automated waste sorting at disposal sites, which is not mentioned in the passage. The passage focuses on the use of sensors to optimize collection routes, not on the automation of waste sorting. This option attributes the wrong detail to the system's benefits.

Option C is incorrect because it confuses the relationship of ideas. The passage mentions that smart lighting systems were introduced to reduce energy consumption and enhance the quality of life, not the smart waste management system. This option incorrectly attributes the benefit of reduced energy consumption to the waste management system, which was never stated in the text.

12. Citing Text as Evidence (Inforgraphic): Easy

Answer: B) China not only avoided a GDP decline but actually experienced positive growth of 2.3% in 2020.

Logical Breakdown and Explanation:

This question asks you to choose the option that most effectively uses the data from the table to complete the text, focusing on how China's GDP growth in 2020 compares to that of other countries during the pandemic.

Option B is correct because it accurately reflects the data from the table and effectively contrasts China's economic performance with that of other countries. While most countries experienced negative GDP growth in 2020, China "not only avoided a GDP decline but actually experienced positive growth of 2.3%." This choice directly uses the data to highlight China as an outlier in the global economic downturn, making it the most effective completion of the text.

Option A is incorrect because it inaccurately states that China saw a drop in GDP of -2.3% in 2020. According to the table, China actually experienced positive growth of 2.3%, not a decline. This option is not true to the data provided, making it incorrect.

Option C is incorrect because, although it accurately calculates a 3.8% drop in China's GDP growth from 2019 to 2020, it misses the passage's focus on the year 2020. The passage emphasizes countries' economic performance during the pandemic in 2020, particularly noting how China was an outlier by experiencing positive growth while other countries faced declines. By focusing on the comparison between 2019 and 2020, this option introduces information that is not relevant to the passage's point about China's unique economic performance during the pandemic year.

Option D is incorrect because, while it is true that China's GDP growth in 2020 was less than in 2019, this detail is not directly related to the point the passage is making. The passage focuses on the surprising outlier of China's positive growth during a global downturn, so this option, which focuses only on the comparison between 2019 and 2020, provides an irrelevant detail that doesn't directly support the point being made.

13. Supporting a Claim (Infographic): Medium

Answer: C) at Pompeii, the 15,000 artifacts found are likely just a fraction of what remains, as thousands more are believed to be buried.

Logical Breakdown and Explanation:

This question asks you to choose the option that most effectively uses data from the table to complete the example, considering the passage's focus on the conservative nature of artifact counts and the likelihood that many more artifacts remain undiscovered.

Option C is correct because it accurately reflects the idea that the 15,000 artifacts found at Pompeii are likely just a fraction of what remains undiscovered. The table indicates that 5,000+ artifacts are still estimated to be buried, which supports the passage's point that many areas of these sites remain unexplored.

Option A is incorrect because it incorrectly suggests that the number of artifacts found at the Valley of the Kings (5,800) is likely an overestimate. The passage implies that the numbers are conservative and that more artifacts are likely undiscovered, so this option contradicts the passage's focus on the potential for more artifacts to be found.

Option B is incorrect because it falsely claims that the Terracotta Army's 8,000+ artifacts likely include all that remains, suggesting the site has been fully excavated. However, the table indicates the number of undiscovered artifacts is "Unknown," implying that the site is not fully excavated, and more artifacts could be discovered. This contradicts the point made in the passage about many areas remaining unexplored.

Option D is incorrect because it shifts the focus from the discovered artifacts, which the passage emphasizes, to the undiscovered ones. The passage is discussing the conservative nature of the numbers listed for artifacts that have already been found at ancient sites. By focusing on the estimated number of undiscovered artifacts at Machu Picchu, this option introduces information that is off-topic and not directly aligned with the passage's primary focus on the artifacts that have been discovered.

14. Inference (complete the text): Hard

Answer: A) more recent archaeological sites than the Rancho La Brea Tar Pits are more likely to show evidence of smaller animals like squirrels.

Logical Breakdown and Explanation:

This question asks you to choose the option that most logically completes the text, considering the information provided about the Pleistocene epoch, fossil discoveries, and the timing of systematic hunting of smaller animals.

Option A is correct because it logically suggests that more recent archaeological sites than the Rancho La Brea Tar Pits (which date back to 40,000 years ago) are more likely to show evidence of smaller animals like squirrels. Since systematic hunting of smaller animals began around 25,000 years ago, it makes sense that more recent sites, like the Old Crow Basin from 20,000 years ago, could contain such evidence.

Option B is incorrect because it illogically excludes the possibility that the Old Crow Basin could contain evidence of systematic hunting of smaller animals. The passage states that systematic hunting began around 25,000 years ago, and since the Old Crow Basin contains fossils from approximately 20,000 years ago, it is plausible that evidence of such hunting could exist there. Therefore, concluding that neither site contains evidence of hunting smaller animals contradicts the information provided.

Option C is incorrect because it incorrectly claims that the Old Crow Basin provides the *earliest* evidence of systematic hunting of smaller animals like squirrels. The passage does not specify that such evidence has been found at the Old Crow Basin and without more information from the text, this claim is unsupported and impossible to make.

Option D is incorrect because it does not logically follow from the information provided in the passage. The end of the passage shifts focus to the systematic hunting of smaller animals, such as squirrels, by human tribes around 25,000 years ago. Introducing the idea of megafauna (large animals) at this point is off-topic and does not align with the passage's development. Since the passage concludes by discussing small animals, presenting an idea about megafauna is not only irrelevant but also illogical in the context of the discussion.

15. Weaken a Claim: Hard

Answer: B) Maggots appear in decaying matter within a time frame too short for fly eggs to develop into maggots.

Logical Breakdown and Explanation:

This question asks you to identify which finding, if true, would most directly undermine Louis Pasteur's claim that maggots do not arise from non-living matter but instead come from eggs laid by flies.

Option B is correct because it presents a scenario where maggots appear in decaying matter within a time frame too short for fly eggs to develop into maggots. If this were true, it would directly challenge Pasteur's claim by suggesting that maggots could arise from non-living matter, as the short time frame would not allow for the typical life cycle from egg to maggot. This finding would provide evidence that spontaneous generation could still be possible, thereby undermining Pasteur's claim.

Option A is incorrect because it actually supports Pasteur's claim. It describes the process of maggots developing into flies, which then lay eggs on decaying meat, leading to more maggots. This reinforces the idea that maggots come from eggs laid by flies, not from non-living matter, and thus strengthens rather than weakens Pasteur's argument.

Option C is incorrect because it introduces the idea that maggots appear in other types of non-living matter, such as decaying vegetables and spoiled fruit. While this might expand the types of matter in which maggots appear, it does not directly challenge Pasteur's claim that maggots come from eggs laid by flies. The origin of the maggots in these other types of matter is still not addressed, making this option irrelevant to the claim.

Option D is incorrect because it supports Pasteur's claim. It suggests that maggots only appear in open containers where flies have access to lay eggs, while sealed containers do not produce maggots. This finding aligns with Pasteur's argument that maggots come from eggs laid by flies and not from spontaneous generation, generating an effect opposite to the purpose of the question.

16. Punctuation: Medium

Answer: D) did life ever exist on the Red Planet?

Logical Breakdown and Explanation:

This question focuses on whether the sentence should use a direct or indirect question. **Direct Questions** are used when the sentence itself is asking the question (e.g., "Did life ever exist on the Red Planet?"). They require subject-verb inversion (verb before subject) and end with a question mark. **Indirect Questions** are used when the sentence is reporting or discussing a question rather than asking it directly (e.g., "The aim is to determine whether life ever existed on the Red Planet."). They do not invert the subject and verb (subject before verb) and end with a period.

Option D is correct because it uses a direct question format, which is appropriate in the context of the sentence. The sentence in the passage ends with a colon, which introduces the fundamental question that NASA's Mars missions aim to answer: "Did life ever exist on the Red Planet?" This structure directly presents the question being considered, so a direct question format with subject-verb inversion and a question mark is required.

Option A is incorrect because it incorrectly uses an indirect question structure followed by a question mark. Since the sentence is presenting the question directly (we know this before the independent clause ends with a colon), a direct question format should be used instead of an indirect one.

Option B is incorrect because, although it correctly uses the direct question format, it ends the question with a period instead of the required question mark. Direct questions should always end with a question mark.

Option C is incorrect because it uses an indirect question format in a context where a direct question is needed. The sentence structure and the use of the colon indicate that the question is being asked directly, so the subject and verb should be inverted, and the sentence should end with a question mark.

17. Punctuation and Sentence Structure: Hard

Answer: A) oral tradition, the

Logical Breakdown and Explanation:

This question asks you to choose the option that correctly completes the sentence according to the conventions of Standard English, specifically focusing on punctuation and sentence structure.

Option A is correct because it uses commas to set off the nonessential information about Griots, creating a clear and logical sentence structure. The phrase "the practice of passing down cultural knowledge through spoken word from a tribe's storytellers (known as Griots)" provides additional information about "oral tradition" but is not essential to the main clause. The use of commas appropriately sets off this nonessential information, allowing the sentence to flow smoothly and logically.

Option B is incorrect because it uses a semicolon to separate the phrase "oral tradition" from the additional information. However, the information after the semicolon is not an independent clause (it does not stand alone as a complete sentence). A semicolon should only be used to separate two independent clauses, so this creates a sentence structure error.

Option C is incorrect because it uses a colon, which functions identically as a colon (on the SAT); a colon is used to provide a restatement or explanation of what was previously stated. However, in this context, the phrase following "oral tradition" is better treated as nonessential information that smoothly continues the main idea of the sentence ("researchers turn to oral tradition... to piece together the historical narratives of African societies that left no written records). Using a colon disrupts the sentence flow and creates an awkward structure, making it less effective than setting off the phrase with commas.

Option D is incorrect because it uses a dash, which can be used in the same way as a colon (on the SAT). However, in this context, the phrase following "oral tradition" is better treated as nonessential information that smoothly continues the main idea of the sentence ("researchers turn to oral tradition... to piece together the historical narratives of African societies that left no written records). Using a dash disrupts the sentence flow and creates an awkward structure, making it less effective than setting off the phrase with commas.

18. Verbs: Medium

Answer: C) have spread

Logical Breakdown and Explanation:

This question asks you to choose the option that correctly completes the sentence according to the conventions of Standard English, with a focus on subject-verb agreement.

Option C is correct because it uses the plural verb "have spread," which agrees with the compound subject "footwork and rhythms" (plural subject). The subject refers to two elements, "footwork" and "rhythms," which together require a plural verb. "Have spread" correctly matches the plural subject, making the sentence grammatically correct.

Option A is incorrect because it uses the singular verb "has spread," which does not agree with the plural subject "footwork and rhythms." The verb should be plural to match the compound subject, so "has" creates a subject-verb disagreement.

Option B is incorrect because it uses the singular verb "is spreading," which, like "has spread," does not agree with the plural subject "footwork and rhythms." The verb should be plural, making "is" incorrect.

Option D is incorrect because it uses the singular verb "was spread," which also does not agree with the plural subject "footwork and rhythms." Additionally, "was spread" implies a past action that was completed, which does not align with the context of the sentence describing the ongoing influence of Flamenco.

19. Commas: Easy

Answer: C) regions that date back thousands of years

Logical Breakdown and Explanation:

This question asks you to choose the option that correctly completes the sentence according to the conventions of Standard English, particularly focusing on the correct use of commas with essential and nonessential clauses.

Option C is correct because it treats the "that" clause as essential, which it is. The clause "that date back thousands of years" provides necessary information about the regions being discussed, specifically identifying them as ancient. Essential clauses should not be set off with commas, so no commas should appear before "that" or at the end of the clause. This makes Option C the grammatically correct choice.

Option A is incorrect because it incorrectly places a comma at the end of the clause ("years,"), which is unnecessary and incorrect. Essential clauses, like the "that" clause in this sentence, should not have commas separating them from the rest of the sentence.

Option B is incorrect because it incorrectly places a comma both before "that" and at the end of the clause ("years,"), treating the clause as nonessential. The "that" clause is essential to the meaning of the sentence, so no commas should be used.

Option D is incorrect because it incorrectly places a comma before "that," treating the clause as nonessential. Again, the "that" clause is essential to the sentence's meaning and should not be set off with commas.

20. Punctuation and Sentence Structure: Medium

Answer: D) prey;

Logical Breakdown and Explanation:

This question asks you to choose the option that correctly completes the sentence according to the conventions of Standard English, particularly focusing on sentence structure and avoiding run-on sentences.

Option D is correct because it uses a semicolon to separate two independent clauses (ICs). The first independent clause is "The orchid mantis mimics the appearance of a flower to lure unsuspecting prey," and the second independent clause is "the leaf-tailed gecko employs a similar strategy." A semicolon is the correct punctuation to separate these two ICs, preventing a run-on sentence.

Option A is incorrect because it creates a run-on sentence. It does not use any punctuation between the two independent clauses, which makes the sentence grammatically incorrect. The two ICs are "The orchid mantis...lure unsuspecting prey" and "the leaf-tailed gecko...employs a similar strategy."

Option B is incorrect because it only uses a comma to separate the two independent clauses. A comma alone is insufficient to separate two ICs, and this creates a comma splice, resulting in a run-on sentence.

Option C is incorrect because it uses "and" without a comma to separate the two independent clauses, which also results in a run-on sentence. When combining two ICs with "and," a comma is required before the conjunction, but even then, it would need to correctly address the full sentence structure.

21. Verbs: Medium

Answer: B) investigating

Logical Breakdown and Explanation:

This question asks you to choose the option that correctly completes the sentence according to the conventions of Standard English, particularly focusing on sentence structure and ensuring that the sentence is logical and grammatically correct.

Option B is correct because it uses "investigating" as a participial phrase, which correctly modifies "a phenomenon." The sentence structure becomes: "As a behavioral economist, Dr. Dan Ariely studies consumer decision-making, **a phenomenon that**, *investigating* the often irrational ways people respond to pricing, marketing, and other economic factors, **provides** insights into how businesses can better understand their customers." This structure is logical and grammatically correct, as "investigating" serves as nonessential information that elaborates on the "phenomenon" mentioned. A good tip to remember is that nonessential information can never begin with a verb that actually functions as a verb (not just a participle, a modifier).

Option A is incorrect because it creates a sentence with two main verbs ("investigates" and "provides"), which results in a nonsensical structure. The sentence would read: "Dr. Dan Ariely studies consumer decision-making, a phenomenon that investigates...provides..." This structure is illogical and ungrammatical and sounds ridiculous when read aloud.

Option C is incorrect because it also creates a sentence with two main verbs ("investigate" and "provides"), which similarly results in a nonsensical and ungrammatical structure. The sentence would read: "Dr. Dan Ariely studies consumer decision-making, a phenomenon that investigate...provides..." This structure is absurd and does not exist as a proper sentence structure.

Option D is incorrect because it uses "has investigated" as a second main verb in the sentence, creating the same issue of having two main verbs ("has investigated" and "provides"). The sentence would read: "Dr. Dan Ariely studies consumer decision-making, a phenomenon that has investigated...provides..." This structure is ungrammatical and illogical.

22. Transition: Medium

Answer: C) though,

Logical Breakdown and Explanation:

This question asks you to choose the option that most logically completes the text with an appropriate transition word or phrase, focusing on ensuring that the meaning remains clear and logical.

Option C is correct because "though" is used to introduce a contrast. The sentence contrasts the Arctic tern's long migration with the Monarch butterfly's shorter, yet still impressive, migration. The use of "though" signals that, despite the shorter distance, the Monarch butterfly's migration is noteworthy, which aligns with the intended comparison in the passage.

Option A is incorrect because "nonetheless" is used to introduce a statement that introduces something that unexpected or surprising based on what has just been said. However, in this context, the sentence is not setting up something surprising or unexpected but rather a comparison. Using "nonetheless" creates an illogical meaning.

Option B is incorrect because "for example" is used to introduce an example that supports or illustrates a point made in the previous sentence. Here, the passage is not giving an example of the Arctic tern's migration but is making a comparison between two different migrations. This makes "for example" an illogical choice.

Option D is incorrect because "in addition" is used to add another point or idea that supports what was previously mentioned (about the Arctic tern). However, the passage is contrasting the two migrations rather than simply adding information about the Monarch butterfly. Using "in addition" would create an illogical meaning and disrupt the intended contrast.

23. Transition: Medium

Answer: A) That is,

Logical Breakdown and Explanation:

This question asks you to choose the option that most logically completes the text with an appropriate transition word or phrase, ensuring that the sentence's meaning remains clear and logical.

Option A is correct because "That is," is used to restate or clarify a point just made. The sentence follows the mention of macronutrients by specifying which macronutrients—carbohydrates, proteins, and fats—are being referred to and how they should be consumed. This transition logically connects the general statement about macronutrients to the more specific details that follow.

Option B is incorrect because "Nevertheless" is used to introduce a contrasting idea or point. In this context, there is no contrast between the two statements; rather, the second statement clarifies the first. Using "Nevertheless" would create an illogical meaning.

Option C is incorrect because "Eventually" suggests a progression over time or something that will happen in the future. The sentence is not about a future event but is instead providing clarification on macronutrient consumption. This makes "Eventually" an illogical choice.

Option D is incorrect because "Nowadays" is used to refer to something happening in the present time, often in contrast to the past. The sentence is discussing general nutritional guidelines, not a change over time. Using "Nowadays" would create an illogical meaning and disrupt the flow of the text.

24. Transition: Easy

Answer: D) In addition,

Logical Breakdown and Explanation:

This question asks you to choose the option that most logically completes the text with an appropriate transition word or phrase, ensuring that the meaning is clear and logical.

Option D is correct because "In addition" is used to introduce information that continues the topic of the previous sentence in the same direction. The first sentence discusses one adaptation (fat storage in humps), and the second sentence adds another adaptation (thick coats), making "In addition" the most logical transition. These two sentences also discuss the adaptations in the same general direction (positive/valuable).

Option A is incorrect because "However" introduces a contrast or exception, which is not appropriate here since the two sentences are adding related information about the camel's adaptations.

Option B is incorrect because "Nevertheless" is also used to introduce something unexpected or surprising given the previous information, which is not the case in this passage. In the context of the passage, there is no contradiction between the two sentences. The first sentence talks about camels storing fat in their humps, while the second sentence discusses their thick coats. These are two different adaptations that complement each other, not opposing ideas.

Option C is incorrect because "Thus" is used to introduce a conclusion or result, but the second sentence is not a direct consequence of the first; instead, it provides additional information.The first sentence discusses how camels store fat in their humps, while the second sentence talks about their thick coats. These are separate adaptations, not a cause-and-effect relationship. Using "Thus" would incorrectly imply that the thick coat is a direct result of the fat storage, which is not the case, making this option illogical.

25. Rhetorical Synthesis: Medium

Answer: C) Designed by Stefano Boeri, the Bosco Verticale consists of over 900 trees and thousands of plants covering two residential towers.

Logical Breakdown and Explanation:

This question asks you to choose the option that most effectively uses relevant information from the notes to provide a specific example of a sustainable architecture project.

Option C is correct because it directly introduces the Bosco Verticale as a specific example of sustainable architecture. The choice provides relevant details about the project, including the name of the architect, the structure of the buildings, and the fact that they are covered with over 900 trees and thousands of plants. This information effectively illustrates a real-world application of sustainable architecture, which is the student's goal.

Option A is incorrect because it is too general and does not provide a specific example. While it mentions the goals of sustainable architecture, it does not reference the Bosco Verticale or any other project, making it irrelevant to the student's goal.

Option B is incorrect because, although it provides some details about the Bosco Verticale and its architect, it lacks specific information about the Bosco Verticale as an example of sustainable architecture. It mentions the architect and the completion date but fails to highlight the sustainability features that make the project relevant to the student's purpose. Tip: Compare the correct answer (C) to (B). Which choice is more *specific?* Definitely C). So, C) does a *more effective* job at achieving the goal in the question stem.

Option D is incorrect because, although it discusses the features of sustainable architecture, it does not mention the Bosco Verticale or any specific project. This makes the choice too vague and general when compared to the correct answer, which directly cites a specific example.

26. Rhetorical Synthesis: Hard

Answer: A) In a 2019 study exploring CBT's effectiveness in reducing anxiety in teens, Dr. Roberts concluded that the therapy significantly alleviated anxiety symptoms in a majority of participants who attended weekly CBT sessions.

Logical Breakdown and Explanation:

This question asks you to choose the option that most effectively presents the study and its findings using relevant information from the notes.

Option A s correct because it effectively presents both the study and its findings in a concise manner. The phrase "In a 2019 study exploring CBT's effectiveness in reducing anxiety in teens" provides an overview of the study, directly aligning with the note that Dr. Michael Roberts conducted this experiment to assess CBT's impact on adolescent anxiety. The phrase "*concluded that* the therapy significantly alleviated anxiety symptoms" signals the study's findings.

Option B is incorrect because it primarily focuses on the selection process of participants and does not fully present the study's findings. While it does mention the study, the specific detail about how the study was carried out is too narrow to be a general overview of the study. Moreover, it leaves out the crucial information about the study's conclusion that CBT significantly reduced anxiety levels, making it only partially correct.

Option C is incorrect because it primarily describes the methodology of the study (weekly CBT sessions and measuring anxiety levels before and after treatment) without clearly presenting the study's findings. This option is more focused on how the study was conducted rather than on the findings, making it less effective for the student's goal.

Option D is incorrect because it introduces information about how CBT helps individuals identify and change negative thought patterns, which is not directly relevant to the presentation of the study and its findings. While it does mention the study's conclusion, it does not adequately present the study itself, making this option less focused on the student's specific goal.

27. Rhetorical Synthesis: Hard

Answer: D) Dr. Stone's 2021 study aimed to determine how cognitive functions like memory, attention and problem-solving are impacted by varying amounts of sleep.

Logical Breakdown and Explanation:

This question asks you to choose the option that most effectively presents the study's purpose using relevant information from the notes.

Option D is correct because it directly addresses the purpose of Dr. Stone's study by stating the aim: "to determine how cognitive functions like memory, attention, and problem-solving are impacted by varying amounts of sleep." This choice effectively uses the relevant notes that describe Dr. Stone's goal of examining the relationship between sleep duration and cognitive function, specifically focusing on the aspects of memory, attention, and problem-solving.

Option A is incorrect because it focuses on the findings of the study rather than the purpose. It highlights the importance of adequate sleep based on the results, which is not the primary goal of explaining why the study was conducted.

Option B is incorrect because it emphasizes the methodology of the study—how participants were assigned to different sleep schedules and tested—rather than the purpose. While it mentions that Dr. Stone examined the relationship between sleep and cognitive function, it does not clearly articulate the study's aim.

Option C is incorrect because it describes how the participants were divided into groups based on sleep duration but does not clearly state the study's purpose. It focuses more on the procedure rather than explaining why the study was conducted.

Page Intentionally Left Blank

EASY: Reading and Writing

27 Questions, 32 Minutes

Marine biologists have long been fascinated by the communication patterns of dolphins, which employ a series of _____ clicks and whistles to convey messages. These sophisticated sounds are not merely for simple exchanges; they play a pivotal role in maintaining social bonds, coordinating hunting strategies, and navigating their aquatic environment. Researchers believe that the complexity of these vocalizations rivals that of human language.

1

Which choice completes the text with the most logical and precise word or phrase?

A) random
B) monotonous
C) elaborate
D) distinctive

CONTINUE

Polymath and astronomer Johannes Kepler, whose contributions to the scientific revolution were groundbreaking, believed that being _____ was essential to his discoveries. Because he meticulously observed planetary motions and rigorously tested his hypotheses, Kepler ensured that his laws of planetary motion were both comprehensive and accurate.

2

Which choice completes the text with the most logical and precise word or phrase?

A) imaginative

B) indifferent

C) honest

D) detail-oriented

One of the most intriguing cultural practices in Fiji is the traditional firewalking ceremony, which has been performed for centuries by the Sawau tribe on the island of Beqa. This ritual, deeply rooted in Fijian mythology to honor ancient gods and reinforce communal bonds, involves participants walking barefoot across hot embers. Such _____ displays, therefore, are not merely for spectacle: they represent a profound act of spiritual devotion that strengthens the community's cultural identity.

3

Which choice completes the text with the most logical and precise word or phrase?

A) reverent

B) mundane

C) ostentatious

D) ephemeral

CONTINUE

Historically, research on the Saami people, an indigenous group in northern Scandinavia, has _____ their reindeer herding practices. Recently, however, scholars have begun to explore other aspects of Saami culture, such as the intricate oral traditions and the unique yoik singing style of the Saami language. This shift aims to provide a more comprehensive understanding of the Saami's rich cultural heritage.

Which choice completes the text with the most logical and precise word or phrase?

A) primarily ignored

B) mainly criticized

C) predominantly emphasized

D) highly praised

In the bustling markets of Ho Chi Minh City, Vietnam, vendors and customers navigate through narrow alleys filled with vibrant goods. Each vendor strives to secure the best locations, their stalls laden with exotic fruits, fragrant spices, and intricate handicrafts. As vendors jostle for prime spots, the market comes alive with a palpable energy, and securing space becomes a daily challenge.

As used in the text, what does the phrase "jostle for" most nearly mean?

A) approve of

B) compete for

C) argue about

D) give up

Practice Test 2

CONTINUE

The following text is adapted from E. M. Forster's 1908 novel "A Room with a View." Lucy Honeychurch, a young woman on a trip to Italy, finds herself entranced by the beauty of Florence.

Lucy wandered through the narrow streets of Florence, soaking in the vibrant energy of the city. The cobblestone paths led her to hidden piazzas, where rows of artists displayed their works and street musicians played jaunty melodies. She marveled at the grandeur of the Duomo, its dome towering majestically over the city. Every corner seemed to offer a new delight, a fresh glimpse into the rich tapestry of Italian culture. For Lucy, this was more than just a vacation; it was an awakening.

6

Which choice best describes the function of the underlined sentence in the text as a whole?

A) It contrasts the busy streets of Florence with the quietness of Lucy's hometown.

B) It supports a description of Florence presented in the preceding sentence.

C) It introduces the historical significance of Florence.

D) It highlights Lucy's preference for quieter, hidden spots in the city.

CONTINUE →

Recent studies by Dr. Sarah Thompson have highlighted the crucial role of gut microbiota in overall health. The gut microbiota, comprising trillions of microorganisms, including bacteria, viruses, and fungi, is essential for digesting complex carbohydrates, synthesizing vitamins like B12 and K, and modulating the immune system. Disruptions to this ecosystem, due to poor diet, antibiotic use, or stress, can lead to inflammatory bowel disease (IBD), obesity, and neuropsychiatric disorders. Dr. Thompson emphasizes that a diet rich in fiber and fermented foods can foster a robust gut microbiota, enhancing overall health outcomes.

7

Which choice best states the main purpose of the text?

A) To discuss the negative effects of antibiotics on gut health

B) To propose dietary solutions for improving mental health through gut health

C) To analyze the role of gut microbiota in maintaining overall health

D) To highlight the importance of fiber and fermented foods in the diet

CONTINUE

The following text is from the poem "Flowers of a Moment" by Ko Un, a renowned Korean poet.

What is it you're searching for,
where the frost is falling?

Like me,
one day
you'll look back
and see the road you've taken
was always made of your own footprints.

Which choice best states the main purpose of the text?

A) To highlight the importance of self-reflection

B) To describe the beauty of frost-covered landscapes

C) To consider the significance of individual choices

D) To illustrate the inevitability of following a predetermined path

CONTINUE

The practice of haggling is a common behavior in the marketplaces of the Middle East; shoppers and vendors engage in animated negotiations, where the initial price is often inflated, and both parties exchange offers and counteroffers until a mutually agreeable price is reached. This ritual is characterized by lively verbal exchanges and strategic pauses. Researchers Dr. Yasmin Al-Rashid and Dr. Karim El-Sayed recorded interactions between buyers and sellers in various markets across the region, analyzing the frequency, duration, and tone of the negotiations. They also surveyed participants to gauge their emotional responses and perceived satisfaction with the outcomes. The researchers concluded that haggling is not merely a transactional activity but a social practice that reinforces relational bonds and community cohesion, as it establishes mutual respect and builds relationships between individuals.

9

Which finding, if true, would most directly weaken the researchers' conclusion?

A) Data showed that the frequency of haggling was significantly lower in urban areas with diverse populations.

B) Observational data revealed that a majority of haggling often included elements of storytelling, humor, and personal anecdotes.

C) Surveys revealed that a substantial number of buyers and sellers felt that haggling was an outdated practice.

D) Observational analysis indicated that haggling interactions were often brief and impersonal.

CONTINUE →

Text 1

Recent studies show that mindfulness meditation can significantly reduce stress levels in individuals. Participants who engaged in daily meditation reported lower levels of anxiety and improved overall well-being. These findings suggest that incorporating mindfulness practices into daily routines can have myriad benefits: reduced stress levels, better emotional regulation, improved sleep quality, and enhanced interpersonal relationships.

Text 2

Dr. Thomas Greene, a psychologist, argues that while mindfulness meditation can be helpful, it should not be seen as a cure-all for stress-related issues. He emphasizes that mindfulness meditation, although beneficial, is just one tool in a larger toolkit for mental health. Greene points out that stress often stems from complex and multifaceted sources, such as unresolved trauma, chronic illness, or ongoing interpersonal conflicts. By focusing solely on meditation, individuals might overlook these underlying problems that require more targeted interventions.

10

Based on the texts, what would Dr. Thomas Greene most likely say about the findings presented in Text 1?

A) They are overly optimistic and fail to consider the complexity of stress-related issues.

B) They are accurate but should be supplemented with additional mental health strategies.

C) They are misleading and ignore the potential risks of relying solely on meditation.

D) They are excessively exaggerated and provide an unrealistic view of mindfulness meditation's effectiveness.

CONTINUE ➡

In 1928, Alexander Fleming returned from vacation to his cluttered laboratory at St. Mary's Hospital and noticed something unusual: a petri dish containing Staphylococcus bacteria had been unintentionally contaminated by a blue-green mold, and the bacteria surrounding the mold had been destroyed. Intrigued, he isolated the mold and grew it in a pure culture to study its properties. Fleming carefully collected the mold's exudate, which he hypothesized contained the antibacterial substance, and conducted tests using this mold extract on various bacterial cultures, consistently observing its ability to kill a wide range of harmful bacteria. He named this moldy substance penicillin, marking the beginning of a revolutionary era in antibiotic treatment.

11

Which choice best states the main idea of the text?

A) Fleming conducted careful experiments and kept detailed notes of his observations in the hopes of making a breakthrough discovery.

B) Fleming's work demonstrated that the moldy substance, which would later be called penicillin, could destroy Staphylococcus bacteria.

C) The serendipitous finding of antibacterial properties in a mold by Alexander Fleming in 1928 eventually led to the discovery of penicillin.

D) Fleming's curious nature and relentless work ethic were the primary factors that led to the discovery of penicillin.

Practice Test 2

CONTINUE

Behavioral psychologists have theorized that the likelihood of individuals developing shopping addiction—defined as a compulsive need to shop and spend excessively—correlates with emotional gratification obtained from purchases. In a recent study of shopping behaviors, researchers found that, on average, individuals with shopping addiction experienced significant emotional highs from buying items, followed by guilt or regret. This pattern often leads to financial difficulties, strained relationships, and emotional distress, necessitating therapeutic interventions and support to manage impulses.

12

What do behavioral psychologists say about the correlation between shopping addiction and emotional gratification?

A) They think that shopping addiction is unrelated to emotional experiences and is purely a habit formed over time.

B) They believe that shopping addiction is related to the emotions shoppers experience after making purchases.

C) They are certain that emotional highs followed by emotional lows cause shopping addiction.

D) They conclude that shopping addiction is primarily due to financial instability and peer pressure rather than any emotional factors.

CONTINUE

The evolution of human language is a complex process that has fascinated linguists for centuries. It is believed that language began with simple sounds and gestures, gradually evolving into the diverse and sophisticated systems of communication we have today. Key milestones in this evolution include the development of syntax, which allowed for more complex sentence structures; the creation of a shared vocabulary, which enabled individuals within a community to convey specific ideas, emotions, and instructions more precisely; and the invention of writing, which enabled the preservation and dissemination of knowledge across generations.

13

It can most reasonably be inferred from the text that a shared vocabulary led to which outcome?

A) It allowed for the development of syntax, resulting in more complex sentence structures.

B) It facilitated cooperation clearer communication.

C) It led to the establishment of permanent settlements and agricultural practices.

D) It resulted in the publishing of books, which could preserve tradition and spread knowledge across generations.

CONTINUE

"Ain't I a Woman?" is a famous speech delivered by Sojourner Truth at the Woman's Rights Convention in Akron, Ohio, in 1851. In the speech, Truth speaks about the struggles and injustices women face: _____

Which quotation from Sojourner Truth's "Ain't I a Woman?" most effectively illustrates the claim?

A) "I have as much muscle as any man, and can do as much work as any man."

B) "If the first woman God ever made was strong enough to turn the world upside down all alone, these women together ought to be able to turn it back, and get it right side up again!"

C) "That man over there says that women need to be helped into carriages, and lifted over ditches, and to have the best place everywhere."

D) "If my cup won't hold but a pint, and yours holds a quart, wouldn't you be mean not to let me have my little half measure full?"

CONTINUE

_____ success often hinges on the sports agent's ability to navigate complex negotiations and secure lucrative opportunities. A skilled agent not only maximizes the athlete's earnings but also protects their interests during contract disputes. Furthermore, the agent's advice on personal branding can elevate the athlete's profile, enhancing their marketability and long-term prospects.

Capable of defying death itself, _____. By cycling between its adult and polyp stages, this tiny organism theoretically possesses the potential to live indefinitely, barring predation or disease.

15

Which choice completes the text so that it conforms to the conventions of Standard English?

A) Athletes

B) Athlete's

C) An athlete's

D) The athlete

16

Which choice completes the text so that it conforms to the conventions of Standard English?

A) the immortal jellyfish's ability enables it to revert its cells to a juvenile state after reaching maturity

B) the immortal jellyfish can revert its cells to a juvenile state after reaching maturity

C) it is the immortal jellyfish that can revert its cells to a juvenile state after reaching maturity

D) a juvenile state of its cells can be reverted to after reaching maturity by the immortal jellyfish

CONTINUE

In the early 20th century, physicists like Einstein and Bohr laid the groundwork for quantum mechanics, a field that puzzled and fascinated scientists for decades. Fast forward to the present, and quantum computing—a concept once considered purely theoretical—has become a burgeoning field with the potential to revolutionize technology. These computers, unlike classical ones, _____ qubits that exist in multiple states simultaneously, enabling them to solve complex problems at unprecedented speeds.

Which choice completes the text so that it conforms to the conventions of Standard English?

A) utilizing

B) utilized

C) utilize

D) had utilized

In the White Mountains of California, a grove of ancient bristlecone pines quietly endures the passage of millennia. Among them _____ Methuselah, the oldest known living tree, at approximately 4,800 years old. Methuselah trees have withstood countless storms, droughts, and even changes in climate.

Which choice completes the text so that it conforms to the conventions of Standard English?

A) stand

B) have stood

C) are standing

D) stands

CONTINUE

Antoni Gaudí, the renowned Catalan architect, is best known for his unique and whimsical designs that grace the city of Barcelona. His work is characterized by vibrant colors, organic shapes, and intricate details, often inspired by nature. One of his most famous creations, the Sagrada Família—which has been under construction since 1882—_____.

19

Which choice completes the text so that it conforms to the conventions of Standard English?

A) is a monumental basilica that combines Gothic and Art Nouveau styles

B) is a monumental basilica, that combines Gothic and Art Nouveau styles

C) is a monumental basilica; that combines Gothic, and Art Nouveau styles

D) is a monumental basilica that combines Gothic—and Art Nouveau styles

Scientists believe that dark matter makes up about 27% of the universe, yet _____ cannot be seen or directly detected with current technology. Despite their best efforts, astronomers have only been able to observe the effects of dark matter through its gravitational influence on visible matter. This enigma continues to puzzle the scientific community, driving them to explore new theories and experiments.

20

Which choice completes the text so that it conforms to the conventions of Standard English?

A) it's

B) one

C) they

D) it

CONTINUE

The walking culture in Japan is deeply ingrained in daily life, with many people choosing to walk as their primary mode of transportation. In 2010, a new trend emerged where urban walkers began exploring religious pilgrimage routes through modern _____ with community groups mapping out routes that blend cityscapes with nature, in 2018, a surge in interest led to the revival of forgotten pathways.

21

Which choice completes the text so that it conforms to the conventions of Standard English?

A) cities

B) cities;

C) cities:

D) cities—

Setting personal boundaries is crucial for maintaining healthy relationships and ensuring one's own well-being. When people respect each other's boundaries, they create a space where everyone feels safe and valued. However, if someone fails to respect _____, it can lead to feelings of discomfort or resentment, which can strain the relationship over time.

22

Which choice completes the text so that it conforms to the conventions of Standard English?

A) it

B) this

C) these boundaries

D) themselves

CONTINUE →

Sea turtles embark on long migrations across entire ocean basins, often traveling thousands of miles to return to the beaches where they were born to lay their eggs. _____ these migrations are perilous, with turtles facing threats from predators, fishing nets, and pollution along the way.

23

Which choice completes the text with the most logical transition?

A) In other words,

B) Consequently,

C) However,

D) In fact,

Keystone species, such as wolves in Yellowstone National Park, have a disproportionately large impact on their ecosystems. When wolves were reintroduced to Yellowstone, the populations of certain prey species, such as elk, were brought into balance. The presence of wolves, _____ led to the regeneration of vegetation, which in turn benefited other species in the ecosystem.

24

Which choice completes the text with the most logical transition?

A) moreover,

B) finally,

C) in contrast,

D) for example,

CONTINUE

The monarch butterfly undergoes a remarkable transformation during its lifecycle, starting as a tiny egg laid on a milkweed plant. The egg hatches into a caterpillar, which then feeds on the milkweed leaves, growing rapidly in size. After reaching its full size, the caterpillar forms a chrysalis, where it undergoes metamorphosis into a butterfly. _____ the adult monarch emerges from the chrysalis, ready to begin its migration to warmer climates.

Which choice completes the text with the most logical transition?

A) To illustrate,

B) Subsequently,

C) Indeed,

D) Still,

CONTINUE

While researching a topic, a student has taken the following notes:

- The growing popularity of plant-based diets has led to increased research on their health benefits.
- In 2020, Dr. James Nguyen conducted a study to explore whether a plant-based diet could positively impact mental health.
- Participants were randomly assigned to either a plant-based diet group or a control group following a standard diet.
- The study included 150 participants monitored over six months.
- Mental health was assessed before and after the study using standardized questionnaires.
- Results showed that those on the plant-based diet reported improved mood and reduced anxiety levels.

26

The student wants to explain how Dr. Nguyen's study was carried out. Which choice most effectively uses relevant information from the notes to accomplish this goal?

A) Participants in Dr. Nguyen's study were monitored over a period of six months to assess the impact of their diet on mental health.

B) Dr. Nguyen conducted the 2020 study to explore the potential mental health benefits of plant-based diets, reflecting their growing popularity.

C) The study, led by Dr. Nguyen, found that participants on a plant-based diet reported improved mood and reduced anxiety levels after six months.

D) In the 2020 study, 150 participants were randomly assigned to either a plant-based diet or a standard diet group and monitored for six months.

CONTINUE

While researching a topic, a student has taken the following notes:

- Rachel Carson's book *Silent Spring* is credited with highlighting the dangers of pesticides.
- Carson's work eventually resulted in policy changes, including the banning of DDT in the United States.
- John Muir was a passionate advocate for the preservation of wilderness in the United States and co-founded the Sierra Club in 1892.
- Muir's activism was instrumental in the establishment of Yosemite and Sequoia National Parks.
- Carson focused on chemical pollution and its impact on ecosystems.
- Muir emphasized the intrinsic value of nature and the need to protect it from commercial exploitation.

27

The student wants to emphasize the difference in the contributions of Rachel Carson and John Muir to environmental activism. Which choice most effectively uses relevant information from the notes to accomplish this goal?

A) Rachel Carson's *Silent Spring* raised awareness about pesticides, leading to policy changes, while John Muir co-founded the Sierra Club.

B) While Carson's work targeted chemical pollution, leading to the banning of DDT, Muir's efforts were centered on preserving wilderness and establishing national parks.

C) Rachel Carson and John Muir both made significant contributions to environmental activism, focusing on different aspects of environmental protection.

D) Rachel Carson and John Muir were both influential in the environmental movement, but Carson is more associated with pollution control, and Muir with national parks.

If you finish before the time is called, you may check your work on this module only.
On Test Day, you will only be able to move to the next module when time expires.

 **Answer Key**

Question Number	Correct Answer	Level of Difficulty	Question Type
1	C	Easy	**Craft and Structure:** *Words in Context*
2	D	Easy	**Craft and Structure:** *Words in Context*
3	A	Hard	**Craft and Structure:** *Words in Context*
4	C	Medium	**Craft and Structure:** *Words in Context*
5	B	Easy	**Craft and Structure:** *Interpreting Words in Context*
6	B	Medium	**Craft and Structure:** *Function of the Underlined Portion*
7	C	Medium	**Craft and Structure:** *Main Purpose*
8	A	Easy	**Craft and Structure:** *Main Purpose*
9	D	Hard	**Information and Ideas:** *Weaken a Claim*
10	A	Medium	**Craft and Structure:** *Cross-Text Connections*
11	C	Easy	**Information and Ideas:** *Main Idea*
12	B	Medium	**Information and Ideas:** *Detail*
13	B	Medium	**Information and Ideas:** *Detail*

Question Number	Correct Answer	Level of Difficulty	Question Type
14	D	Hard	**Information and Ideas:** *Cite Text as Evidence*
15	C	Medium	**Standard English Conventions:** *Punctuation (apostrophes)*
16	B	Easy	**Standard English Conventions:** *Modifiers*
17	C	Hard	**Standard English Conventions:** *Verbs*
18	D	Medium	**Standard English Conventions:** *Verbs*
19	A	Easy	**Standard English Conventions:** *Punctuation and Sentence Structure*
20	D	Easy	**Standard English Conventions:** *Pronouns*
21	B	Hard	**Standard English Conventions:** *Punctuation and Sentence Structure*
22	C	Medium	**Standard English Conventions:** *Pronouns*
23	C	Medium	**Expression of Ideas:** *Transitions*
24	A	Medium	**Expression of Ideas:** *Transitions*
25	B	Hard	**Expression of Ideas:** *Transitions*
26	D	Medium	**Expression of Ideas:** *Rhetorical Synthesis*
27	B	Hard	**Expression of Ideas:** *Rhetorical Synthesis*

Raw Score Conversion Table

Raw Score (# of Correct Answers)	Reading and Writing Section Score		Raw Score (# of Correct Answers)	Reading and Writing Section Score
54	N/A		30	470
53	N/A		29	470
52	N/A		28	450
51	N/A		27	450
50	N/A		26	440
49	N/A		25	430
48	N/A		24	430
47	N/A		23	410
46	N/A		22	410
45	N/A		21	400
44	600		20	390
43	590		19	390
42	580		18	380
41	570		17	360
40	560		16	350
39	550		15	330
38	540		14	300
37	530		13	300
36	530		12	270
35	520		11	260
34	510		10	250
33	500		9	240
32	490		8	220
31	480		7	210

Practice Test 2

 **Explanations**

1. Words in Context: Easy

Answer: C) elaborate

Step-by-Step Explanation:

1. Let's look at what the passage is saying. The passage discusses the communication patterns of dolphins, noting that they use "clicks and whistles" to convey messages. It emphasizes that these sounds are sophisticated and play a crucial role in various important activities, such as maintaining social bonds, coordinating hunting strategies, and navigating their environment.
2. Notice the phrases "these sophisticated sounds" and "complexity of these vocalizations rivals that of human language." These clues suggest that the communication patterns of dolphins are not simple or basic but rather intricate and detailed.
3. The word we need should reflect the complexity and sophistication of the dolphin communication described in the passage.
4. Ask yourself, what word best describes something that is complex, detailed, and sophisticated? "Elaborate" fits perfectly because it means intricate, detailed, and carefully arranged, which aligns with the description of the dolphin communication patterns in the passage.

Explanation of Incorrect Options:

A) random: This is incorrect because it implies a lack of pattern or purpose, which contradicts the idea of sophisticated and complex communication used by dolphins.

B) monotonous: This is incorrect because it means dull, repetitive, and lacking in variety, which does not match the intricate and sophisticated nature of dolphin communication described in the passage.

D) distinctive: While "distinctive" means unique or clearly different, there is nothing in the passage that supports the idea of standing out or being unique. On the other hand, the context, which mentions the complexity and sophistication of the dolphin's communication, makes "elaborate" a more precise fit.

2. Words in Context: Easy

Answer: D) detail-oriented

Step-by-Step Explanation:

1. Let's deconstruct the passage together. The passage discusses Johannes Kepler's contributions to the scientific revolution, emphasizing that his groundbreaking discoveries were a result of certain essential qualities. It highlights that Kepler "meticulously observed planetary motions" and "rigorously tested his hypotheses," which suggests that his approach to scientific work was thorough and precise.

2. Notice the phrases "meticulously observed" and "rigorously tested." These context clues indicate that Kepler paid close attention to detail and was careful in his scientific methods to ensure the accuracy of his discoveries.

3. The word we need should describe someone who is thorough, careful, and attentive to detail.

4. Ask yourself, what word best describes someone who is precise and careful in their work? "Detail-oriented" fits perfectly because it means being meticulous and focused on ensuring all aspects of a task are considered, which aligns with the description of how Kepler ensured his laws were comprehensive and accurate.

Explanation of Incorrect Options:

A) imaginative: This is incorrect because while imagination is important, the passage emphasizes meticulous observation and rigorous testing, which point more toward precision than creativity. In other words, the context in the passage does not support "imaginative" as the most precise word.

B) indifferent: This is incorrect because it implies a lack of interest or concern, which contradicts the careful and detailed approach Kepler took in his work.

C) honest: While honesty is a valuable trait, it does not specifically relate to the meticulous and rigorous approach described in the passage. "Detail-oriented" more precisely captures the quality that was essential to Kepler's discoveries.

3. Words in Context: Hard

Answer: A) reverent

Step-by-Step Explanation:

1. Let's look at what the passage is saying. The passage describes the traditional firewalking ceremony in Fiji, highlighting its deep roots in Fijian mythology and its significance in honoring ancient gods and reinforcing communal bonds. The passage emphasizes that this ritual is a "profound act of spiritual devotion" that strengthens the community's cultural identity.

2. Notice the phrases "profound act of spiritual devotion" and "not merely for spectacle." These clues indicate that the firewalking ceremony is not just a showy display but is instead a deeply meaningful and sacred practice.

3. The word we need should reflect the idea that the firewalking ceremony is a serious and respectful act of devotion, rather than something trivial or purely for show.

4. Ask yourself, what word best describes an act that is deeply respectful and devoted to spiritual beliefs? "Reverent" fits perfectly because it means showing deep respect and honor, especially in a religious or spiritual context, which aligns with the passage's description of the firewalking ceremony.

Explanation of Incorrect Options:

B) mundane: This is incorrect because it means ordinary or commonplace, which contradicts the description of the firewalking ceremony as a profound and spiritually significant ritual.

C) ostentatious: This is incorrect because it means showy or designed to attract attention, which conflicts with the passage's emphasis that the ceremony is "not merely for spectacle" but rather a serious act of devotion.

D) ephemeral: This is incorrect because it means short-lived or temporary, which is not supported by the passage. In other words, there is nothing in the context to suggest the short-lived nature of these fire walks.

4. Words in Context: Medium

Answer: C) predominantly emphasized

Step-by-Step Explanation:

1. Let's look at what the passage is saying. The passage describes how historical research on the Saami people has focused on a particular aspect of their culture—reindeer herding practices. It then mentions a recent shift in scholarly attention toward exploring other aspects of Saami culture, such as their oral traditions and unique singing style.
2. Notice the phrase "Recently, however, scholars have begun to explore other aspects of Saami culture." The word "however" indicates a contrast with what was done before, suggesting that previous research predominantly focused on one area.
3. The word we need should indicate that past research placed a strong emphasis on reindeer herding practices, in contrast to the more diverse cultural aspects being explored now.
4. Ask yourself, what word best describes something that was the main focus or heavily emphasized? "Predominantly emphasized" fits perfectly because it means that reindeer herding practices were the primary focus of earlier research, aligning with the passage's contrast between past and present scholarly interests.

Explanation of Incorrect Options:

A) primarily ignored: This is incorrect because it implies that reindeer herding practices were overlooked, which contradicts the idea that they were the main focus of previous research.

B) mainly criticized: This is incorrect because it suggests that reindeer herding practices were the subject of negative judgment, which doesn't align with the main idea of the passage, which is the aspects of the culture that are being studied.

D) highly praised: This is incorrect because it implies that reindeer herding practices were admired, which is not supported by the context provided in the passage. Instead, the context discusses the aspects of the Saami people that are being explored.

5. Interpreting Words in Context: Easy

Answer: B) compete for

Step-by-Step Explanation:

1. Let's look at what the passage is saying. The passage describes a busy market in Ho Chi Minh City where vendors strive to secure the best locations for their stalls. The phrase "jostle for prime spots" is used to convey the actions of these vendors as they navigate the competitive environment of the market.

2. Notice the context around the phrase "jostle for," which includes phrases like "securing space becomes a daily challenge" and "vendors jostle for prime spots." This context suggests that the vendors are actively competing with each other to get the best locations.

3. The phrase "jostle for" implies an active effort to secure something in a competitive situation. The word we need should reflect this idea of competition or striving for a desired outcome.

4. Ask yourself, what word best describes the act of competing to obtain something? "Compete for" fits perfectly because it captures the sense of vendors striving against each other to secure the best spots in the market.

Explanation of Incorrect Options:

A) approve of: This is incorrect because it means to agree with or accept something, which does not logically fit the competitive context described in the passage.

C) argue about: This is incorrect because while arguing could occur, the focus of the phrase "jostle for" is on the competition to secure a spot, not on verbal disagreements. In other words, because the context of the passage does not discuss the idea of arguing in any fashion, this answer is considered irrelevant, or unsupported by the passage.

D) give up: This is incorrect because it implies surrendering or quitting, which is the opposite of the active competition described by "jostle for."

6. Function of the Underlined Portion: Medium

Answer: B) It supports a description of Florence presented in the preceding sentence.

Logical Breakdown and Explanation:

This question asks you to choose the option that best describes the function of the underlined portion in the text as a whole by connecting key ideas from the answer choice to the passage.

Option B is correct because it supports the description of Florence presented in the preceding sentence. The underlined portion, "The cobblestone paths led her to hidden piazzas, where *rows of artists displayed their works* and street musicians *played jaunty melodies*," provides a vivid depiction of Florence's charm and liveliness, enhancing the description of the city as vibrant and culturally rich. This directly supports the earlier sentence that introduces Florence's vibrant energy and beauty.

Option A is incorrect because it mentions a contrast with Lucy's hometown, which is never discussed or implied in the passage. The underlined portion does not introduce or explore any comparison between Florence and another location.

Option C is incorrect because it refers to the historical significance of Florence, which is not the focus of the underlined portion. The passage is centered on Lucy's personal experience and the sensory details of the city, not on its historical context.

Option D is incorrect because it suggests that the underlined portion highlights Lucy's preference for quieter, hidden spots in the city. While the passage does mention hidden piazzas, it does not emphasize Lucy's *preference* for these spots over others. Instead, it showcases the lively and artistic atmosphere of Florence.

7. Main Purpose: Medium

Answer: C) To analyze the role of gut microbiota in maintaining overall health

Logical Breakdown and Explanation:

This question asks you to identify the main purpose of the text by determining which option best captures the overall focus of the passage.

Option C is correct because it captures the overall essence and big ideas of the passage, which is to analyze the role of gut microbiota in maintaining overall health. Key ideas such as "crucial role of gut microbiota," "digesting complex carbohydrates," and "modulating the immune system" all emphasize the central importance of gut microbiota in various aspects of health.

Option A is incorrect because it focuses narrowly on the negative effects of antibiotics, which are mentioned but not the main focus of the passage. This is a minor detail rather than the main purpose.

Option B is incorrect because it suggests that the passage proposes dietary solutions specifically for improving mental health through gut health. However, the passage does not focus solely on mental health or propose specific solutions for it, making this option too narrow and not supported by the text.

Option D is incorrect because it emphasizes the importance of fiber and fermented foods, which are discussed, but this is a small part of the passage and not the main purpose. The passage primarily analyzes the overall role of gut microbiota in health, making this option too narrow in scope.

8. Main Purpose: Easy

Answer: A) To highlight the importance of self-reflection

Logical Breakdown and Explanation:

This question asks you to identify the main purpose of the text by determining which option best captures the overall focus of the poem.

Option A is correct because it highlights the importance of self-reflection, which is central to the poem. The phrase "you'll look back" suggests a moment of introspection, while "the road you've taken was always made of your own footprints" emphasizes that the journey and choices one makes are personal and self-determined.

Option B is incorrect because it focuses on the frost-covered landscapes, which is only a minor detail in the poem. The poem's main purpose is not to describe the beauty of the landscape but to reflect on the journey of life.

Option C is incorrect because, while it touches on the significance of individual choices, it leaves out the crucial theme of self-reflection, which is a major element of the poem. The poem not only considers the importance of choices but also emphasizes looking back and reflecting on those choices, as seen in the line "you'll look back and see the road you've taken." Without incorporating the idea of self-reflection, **Option C** misses a key aspect of the poem's overall message.

Option D is incorrect because it suggests the inevitability of following a predetermined path, which is not supported by the text. The poem emphasizes the individual's role in shaping their own journey, rather than suggesting that the path is predetermined.

9. Weaken a Claim: Hard

Answer: D) Observational analysis indicated that haggling interactions were often brief and impersonal.

Logical Breakdown and Explanation:

This question asks you to identify which finding, if true, would most directly weaken the researchers' conclusion by determining which option most effectively challenges the idea that haggling is a social practice that reinforces relational bonds and community cohesion.

Option D is correct because it directly challenges the researchers' conclusion by indicating that haggling interactions were often brief and impersonal. The conclusion emphasizes that haggling builds relationships and mutual respect, but if the interactions are brief and lack personal connection, this would weaken the idea that haggling reinforces relational bonds and community cohesion. In other words, if D) is true, it makes the conclusion seem less likely to be valid (true).

Option A is incorrect because it focuses on the frequency of haggling in urban areas with diverse populations, which doesn't directly challenge the conclusion about the social aspects of haggling. While it introduces a different context, it doesn't undermine the conclusion that haggling builds relationships.

Option B is incorrect because it actually strengthens the conclusion. If haggling often includes storytelling, humor, and personal anecdotes, it would support the idea that haggling is a social practice that reinforces bonds.

Option C is incorrect because while it suggests that some participants view haggling as outdated, it does not directly weaken the conclusion about the social and relational aspects of haggling. The perception of haggling as outdated doesn't necessarily mean it doesn't build relationships.

10. Cross-Text Connections: Medium

Answer: A) They are overly optimistic and fail to consider the complexity of stress-related issues.

Logical Breakdown and Explanation:

This question asks you to determine how Dr. Thomas Greene would most likely respond to the findings presented in Text 1 by considering his perspective on mindfulness meditation and stress.

Option A is correct because it aligns with Dr. Greene's perspective that the findings in Text 1 are overly optimistic and fail to consider the complexity of stress-related issues. Key ideas from Text 2 include Greene's emphasis on the *multifaceted nature* of stress and his concern that focusing *solely on meditation might overlook underlying problems.* This suggests that Greene would likely view the findings in Text 1 as too simplistic.

Option B is incorrect because while it acknowledges that the findings are accurate, it suggests that additional mental health strategies should supplement them. This option doesn't capture Greene's critique, which focuses on the oversimplification of stress-related issues in Text 1, rather than just needing additional strategies. The idea of additonal. mental health strategies is never discussed in Text 2, so it's off topic and unsupported by the information in the passage.

Option C is incorrect because it introduces the idea that the findings are misleading and ignores potential risks, which is not the focus of Greene's argument. Greene's concern is more about the oversimplification of stress and not necessarily about the risks of meditation itself.

Option D is incorrect because it suggests that the findings are "excessively exaggerated" and provide an "unrealistic view" of mindfulness meditation's effectiveness, which goes beyond Greene's argument. Greene's critique is more about the narrow focus of the findings rather than an exaggeration of their effectiveness. This answer is too extreme based on the information presented to explain Dr. Greene's position.

11. Main Idea: Easy

Answer: C) The serendipitous finding of antibacterial properties in a mold by Alexander Fleming in 1928 eventually led to the discovery of penicillin.

Logical Breakdown and Explanation:

This question asks you to identify the main idea of the text by determining which option best captures the overall focus of the passage.

Option C is correct because it captures the overall essence of the text, which is that Alexander Fleming's serendipitous finding of antibacterial properties in mold led to the discovery of penicillin. The text emphasizes how this accidental discovery marked the beginning of a revolutionary era in antibiotic treatment.

Option A is incorrect because it focuses on Fleming's careful experiments and note-taking, which are only minor details in the passage. The passage centers more on the serendipitous discovery rather than the process of conducting experiments.

Option B is incorrect because it narrows the focus to Fleming's demonstration that the mold could destroy Staphylococcus bacteria. While this is part of the passage, it doesn't capture the broader significance of the discovery of penicillin, which is the main idea.

Option D is incorrect because it suggests that Fleming's curious nature and work ethic were the primary factors leading to the discovery of penicillin. However, the passage highlights the role of serendipity and the unexpected nature of the discovery rather than attributing it solely to Fleming's personal qualities.

12. Detail: Medium

Answer: B) They believe that shopping addiction is related to the emotions shoppers experience after making purchases.

Logical Breakdown and Explanation:

This question asks you to identify the correct interpretation of what behavioral psychologists say about the correlation between shopping addiction and emotional gratification based on the passage.

Option B is correct because it accurately reflects the passage's explanation that behavioral psychologists believe there is a correlation between shopping addiction and the emotional experiences associated with making purchases. The passage discusses how individuals with shopping addiction experience significant emotional highs from buying items, followed by guilt or regret, which relates directly to the emotional gratification that can lead to compulsive shopping behaviors.

Option A is incorrect because it suggests that shopping addiction is unrelated to emotional experiences, which contradicts the passage. The passage clearly states that there is a correlation between shopping addiction and emotional gratification.

Option C is incorrect because it reverses the relationship described in the passage. The passage states that emotional highs and lows are experienced as a result of making purchases, not that these emotions cause shopping addiction. The passage suggests that the emotional gratification obtained from purchases is what correlates with the development of shopping addiction, not the other way around. Therefore, **Option C** misinterprets the cause-and-effect relationship presented in the text.

Option D is incorrect because it introduces the idea that shopping addiction is primarily due to financial instability and peer pressure, which is not mentioned in the passage. The passage focuses on the emotional aspects related to shopping addiction.

13. Detail: Medium

Answer: B) It facilitated cooperation clearer communication.

Logical Breakdown and Explanation:

This question asks you to infer the outcome of a shared vocabulary based on the information provided in the passage.

Option B is correct because it directly aligns with the passage's explanation that a shared vocabulary "enabled individuals within a community to convey specific ideas, emotions, and instructions more precisely." This precise communication would naturally facilitate cooperation and clearer communication within the community.

Option A is incorrect because the passage does not suggest that a shared vocabulary led to the development of syntax. Instead, syntax is presented as a separate milestone in the evolution of language.

Option C is incorrect because the passage does not discuss the establishment of permanent settlements or agricultural practices as outcomes of a shared vocabulary. This option introduces ideas not mentioned in the passage.

Option D is incorrect because the passage attributes the preservation and dissemination of knowledge to the invention of writing, not to the development of a shared vocabulary. The shared vocabulary alone did not lead to the publishing of books or the preservation of tradition.

14. Cite Text as Evidence: Hard

Answer: D) "If my cup won't hold but a pint, and yours holds a quart, wouldn't you be mean not to let me have my little half measure full?"

Logical Breakdown and Explanation:

This question asks you to choose the quotation from Sojourner Truth's "Ain't I a Woman?" that most effectively illustrates her discussion about the struggles and injustices women face.

Option D is correct because it effectively illustrates the struggles and injustices women face, as described by Sojourner Truth in her speech. The quote, "If my cup won't hold but a pint, and yours holds a quart, wouldn't you be mean not to let me have my little half measure full?" metaphorically addresses the inequity women experience. It highlights the unfairness in how women are given fewer opportunities or resources (the "pint" versus the "quart") and the injustice of not allowing them even the small amount they deserve. This quote captures the essence of the struggles Truth discusses in her speech, making it the best illustration of the claim.

Option A is incorrect because, while it discusses women's strength and capabilities, it does not focus on the broader theme of systemic injustice and inequality that is central to the struggles described in the speech.

Option B is incorrect because it emphasizes women's collective strength and potential rather than directly addressing the specific struggles and injustices they face.

Option C is incorrect because it describes societal expectations rather than the direct struggles and injustices women face.

15. Punctuation: Medium

Answer: C) An athete's

Logical Breakdown and Explanation:

This question asks you to choose the option that completes the sentence in a way that conforms to the conventions of Standard English.

Option C is correct because it uses the singular possessive form "an athlete's," which is appropriate for describing the success that belongs to an individual athlete. The article "an" is necessary before the singular possessive "athlete's," making the sentence grammatically correct and logically clear.

Option A is incorrect because "Athletes" is a plural noun and does not have a possessive form, which is necessary to show that success belongs to the athletes.

Option B is incorrect because it uses the possessive "Athlete's," but it lacks an article (such as "an" or "the") before the singular possessive noun, which is required for grammatical correctness.

Option D is incorrect because "The athlete" creates an awkward and unclear sentence ("The athlete success"), which does not make logical sense in this context.

16. Modifiers: Easy

Answer: B) the immortal jellyfish can revert its cells to a juvenile state after reaching maturity

Logical Breakdown and Explanation:

This question asks you to choose the option that correctly completes the sentence, focusing on the proper use of modifiers. The goal is to ensure that the introductory modifier ("Capable of defying death itself") logically and grammatically connects to the subject of the sentence.

Option B is correct because it correctly places "the immortal jellyfish" as the subject of the sentence, which logically follows the opening phrase "Capable of defying death itself." The sentence is clear and makes logical sense: it is the immortal jellyfish that is capable of defying death.

Option A is incorrect because it creates a dangling modifier. The phrase "Capable of defying death itself" should logically modify the subject that follows, but "the immortal jellyfish's *ability*" does not make sense as the subject of the sentence. This results in an illogical meaning. The ability of the jellyfish is not what is capable of defying death; it is the jellyfish itself.

Option C is incorrect because it unnecessarily complicates the sentence structure with the phrase "it is the," making the sentence more awkward and less direct. Impersonal pronouns (pronouns that don't refer to a specific noun but are used as impersonal subjects, as in "*it* is a nice day") create a grammatical error. The jellyfish should be the subject and should appear at the start of the IC.

Option D is incorrect because it creates a dangling modifier. The phrase "Capable of defying death itself" should logically modify the subject that immediately follows, but in this option, "a state" becomes the subject. This creates an illogical meaning because "a state" cannot be capable of defying death. The sentence structure is awkward, and the meaning is unclear due to this misplaced subject.

17. Verbs: Hard

Answer: C) utilize

Logical Breakdown and Explanation:

This question asks you to choose the option that best completes the sentence according to the rules of Standard English, ensuring proper verb tense and sentence structure.

Option C is correct because it uses the present tense "utilize," which is consistent with the time reference "the present" given in the text. The sentence now reads logically: "These computers, unlike classical ones, utilize qubits that exist in multiple states simultaneously, enabling them to solve complex problems at unprecedented speeds."

Option A is incorrect because "utilizing" is not a complete verb form and creates a sentence fragment. The sentence would be missing a main verb, making it incomplete.

Option B is incorrect because "utilized" is in the past tense, which does not align with the time reference "the present" given in the text. The sentence requires a present tense verb to match the context.

Option D is incorrect because "had utilized" is in the past perfect tense, which is also inconsistent with the present time frame provided in the passage.

18. Verbs: Medium

Answer: D) stands

Logical Breakdown and Explanation:

This question asks you to choose the option that completes the sentence in a way that conforms to the conventions of Standard English. The focus here is on subject-verb agreement in an inverted sentence structure.

Option D is correct because the singular verb "stands" agrees with the singular subject "Methuselah." The sentence is inverted, meaning the subject ("Methuselah") follows the verb ("stands"). The prepositional phrase "Among them" does not affect the subject-verb agreement.

Option A is incorrect because "stand" is a plural verb, which does not agree with the singular subject "Methuselah."

Option B is incorrect because "have stood" is a plural verb phrase, which also does not agree with the singular subject "Methuselah."

Option C is incorrect because "are standing" is a plural verb phrase, which does not match the singular subject "Methuselah."

19. Punctuation and Sentence Structure: Easy

Answer: A) is a monumental basilica that combines Gothic and Art Nouveau styles

Logical Breakdown and Explanation:

This question asks you to choose the option that completes the sentence in a way that conforms to the conventions of Standard English. The focus here is on the correct use of punctuation and sentence structure.

Option A is correct because it properly introduces the essential "that" clause without unnecessary punctuation. The "that" clause ("that combines Gothic and Art Nouveau styles") is essential to the meaning of the sentence, so no comma is needed before "that."

Option B is incorrect because it incorrectly inserts a comma before "that." Since "that" introduces an essential clause, no comma should be used.

Option C is incorrect because it uses a semicolon before "that," which is inappropriate. A semicolon should separate two independent clauses, but the clause following the semicolon ("that combines Gothic, and Art Nouveau styles") is not independent; rather, it is a relative clause that blends with the previous information (modifying a monumental basilica).

Option D is incorrect because it uses a dash before "and Art Nouveau styles," which is unnecessary and creates a confusing structure: there are three dashes, in total, in the sentence. The sentence should flow naturally without additional punctuation that disrupts clarity.

20. Pronouns: Easy

Answer: D) it

Logical Breakdown and Explanation:

This question asks you to choose the option that completes the sentence in a way that conforms to the conventions of Standard English. The focus here is on correct pronoun usage to ensure clarity and proper agreement with the antecedent.

Option D is correct because the pronoun "it" appropriately refers back to "dark matter," which is a singular noun. The sentence maintains clarity and logical coherence with this choice.

Option A is incorrect because "it's" is a contraction of "it is" or "it has," which does not fit the context of the sentence. Tip: plug it's in the sentence and read it with the verb: "it is cannot be seen" doesn't make any sense.

Option B is incorrect because "one" is typically used to refer to an unspecified individual or object in a general sense, often when contrasting with another or when the specific identity is not important. In this context, however, "one" would create confusion because the sentence is specifically discussing "dark matter," a known entity. Thus, the meaning of the sentence would become illogical and unclear, especially when compared to the correct answer "it."

Option C is incorrect because "they" is a plural pronoun, which would not correctly refer to the singular noun "dark matter."

21. Punctuation and Sentence Structure: Hard

Answer: B) cities;

Logical Breakdown and Explanation:

This question asks you to choose the option that completes the sentence in a way that conforms to the conventions of Standard English, with a particular focus on punctuation and ensuring proper sentence structure. The key is to select the punctuation that accurately connects the ideas in the sentence while maintaining clarity and grammatical correctness.

Option B is correct because it uses a semicolon to correctly separate two independent clauses. The first clause is "a new trend emerged," and the second clause is "a surge in interest led to the revival of forgotten pathways." Both clauses are independent, making the semicolon the appropriate punctuation.

Option A is incorrect because it doesn't properly separate the two independent clauses, leading to a run-on sentence.

Options C and D are both incorrect for the same reason. If the only difference between two answers is a colon and a dash, and the passage doesn't have any dashes in it, you can safely eliminate both because colons and single dashes are considered functionally identical on the SAT. Since both can't be correct, they both must be wrong.

22. Pronouns: Medium

Answer: C) these boundaries

Logical Breakdown and Explanation:

The focus here is on ensuring that the pronoun used correctly refers to its antecedent, maintaining clarity and grammatical agreement.

Option C is correct because "these boundaries" clearly refers back to "each other's boundaries" mentioned earlier in the text. This choice ensures that the sentence remains clear and logical by correctly matching the plural noun "boundaries" with a plural pronoun.

Option A is incorrect because "it" is a singular pronoun, which does not agree with the plural noun "boundaries." Using "it" would create an unclear and grammatically incorrect sentence.

Option B is incorrect because "this" is a singular pronoun, and like "it," it does not correctly refer back to the plural noun "boundaries." This results in an illogical meaning.

Option D is incorrect because "themselves" does not clearly or logically connect to the noun "boundaries." This pronoun typically refers to people, not abstract concepts like boundaries, making it an ungrammatical choice in this context.

23. Transitions: Medium

Answer: C) However,

Logical Breakdown and Explanation:

This question asks you to choose the option that completes the sentence with the most logical transition, ensuring coherence and clarity in the passage.

Option C is correct because "However" is used to introduce a contrast or an exception to what was previously mentioned. The sentence discusses the long migrations of sea turtles, which is generally a remarkable feat, and then contrasts this with the dangers they face during these migrations.

Option A is incorrect because "In other words" is typically used to restate or clarify a point, not to introduce new or contrasting information. The sentence following the blank does not simply rephrase the previous sentence but instead introduces a new idea.

Option B is incorrect because "Consequently" suggests a cause-and-effect relationship. The text doesn't imply that the turtles' long migrations cause the threats; instead, it contrasts the migrations with the dangers. It's not logical to assume that traveling long distances is the reason threats exist. Threats could exist during short distances or in specific regions.

Option D is incorrect because "In fact" is used to emphasize or add evidence to a previous statement. It doesn't fit here because the sentence isn't adding evidence but rather introducing a contrasting idea.

24. Transitions: Medium

Answer: A) moreover,

Logical Breakdown and Explanation:

This question asks you to choose the option that completes the sentence with the most logical transition, ensuring coherence and clarity in the passage.

Option A is correct because "moreover" is used to add information that supports or expands on the previous statement. The sentence adds another result of the wolf reintroduction, explaining how it led to the regeneration of vegetation, which benefits the ecosystem further.

Option B is incorrect because "finally" suggests a conclusion or the last in a series of points, which doesn't align with the continuation of the explanation in the passage.

Option C is incorrect because "in contrast" is used to introduce information that opposes or contrasts with the previous statement. Here, the information provided supports and continues the explanation rather than contrasting it.

Option D is incorrect because "for example" is used to introduce an illustration of the previous statement. The sentence is not introducing an example but rather explaining the result of the presence of wolves, making this choice illogical.

25. Transitions: Hard

Answer: B) Subsequently,

Logical Breakdown and Explanation:

This question asks you to choose the option that completes the sentence with the most logical transition, ensuring the passage flows naturally from one idea to the next.

Option B is correct because "Subsequently" indicates that the next event in the sequence is the emergence of the adult monarch from the chrysalis, which follows the described stages of metamorphosis.

Option A is incorrect because "To illustrate" is typically used to introduce an example or further explanation of a previously mentioned idea. The passage is describing a sequence of events, not providing an example.

Option C is incorrect because "Indeed" is used to emphasize a point, but in this context, the sentence is moving on to the next stage in the lifecycle rather than emphasizing or reinforcing an earlier point.

Option D is incorrect because "Still" introduces something that is unexpected or surprising given the previous statement. In this context, there is no surprise or contrast being introduced; rather, the passage is simply describing the next step in the monarch butterfly's lifecycle. Therefore, "Still" does not fit logically in this sentence.

26. Rhetorical Synthesis: Medium

Answer: D) In the 2020 study, 150 participants were randomly assigned to either a plant-based diet or a standard diet group and monitored for six months.

Logical Breakdown and Explanation:

This question asks you to choose the option that most effectively explains how Dr. Nguyen's study was carried out, using relevant information from the notes provided.

Option D is correct because it clearly and effectively explains the methodology of Dr. Nguyen's study by stating that 150 participants were randomly assigned to either a plant-based diet group or a standard diet group and were monitored for six months. This choice directly aligns with the notes, focusing on how the study was conducted rather than its results or broader context.

Option A is incorrect because it only mentions that participants were monitored for six months but does not include details about the random assignment to different diet groups or the specific diets involved, which are crucial to understanding how the study was carried out. Additionally, it introduces irrelevant information by focusing on the purpose of the study ("to assess the impact of their diet on mental health"), which is not directly related to the question's goal of explaining how the study was conducted.

Option B is incorrect because it focuses more on the growing popularity of plant-based diets and the study's purpose rather than the actual methodology of the study. While this provides context, it does not clearly explain how the study was conducted.

Option C is incorrect because it primarily discusses the results of the study, stating that participants reported improved mood and reduced anxiety levels after six months. However, it does not detail the process or methodology of the study, which is the focus of the question.

27. Rhetorical Synthesis: Hard

Answer: B) While Carson's work targeted chemical pollution, leading to the banning of DDT, Muir's efforts were centered on preserving wilderness and establishing national parks.

Logical Breakdown and Explanation:

This question asks you to choose the option that most effectively emphasizes the difference in the contributions of Rachel Carson and John Muir to environmental activism by using relevant information from the notes.

Option B is correct because it clearly distinguishes the focus of Rachel Carson's and John Muir's contributions. Carson's work targeted chemical pollution, specifically leading to the banning of DDT, while Muir's efforts were centered on preserving wilderness and establishing national parks. This choice effectively uses the notes to highlight the different aspects of environmental protection that each individual focused on and the contributions each made.

Option A is incorrect because, while it mentions Carson's role in raising awareness about pesticides and Muir's co-founding of the Sierra Club, it does not clearly emphasize the distinct contributions of each figure to environmental activism, specifically the areas they each focused on. Tip: compare this answer to B) and ask yourself, which option is more effective at achieving the goal? You'll clearly see that B) is because "preserving wilderness and establishing national parks" is a clear contribution, whereas co-creating the Sierra Club isn't. We don't know whether the Sierra Club was contributive; we only know it was formed.

Option C is incorrect because it is too general, stating that both Carson and Muir made significant contributions to environmental activism without clearly emphasizing the difference in their contributions.

Option D is incorrect because, although it mentions the areas associated with each figure (pollution control for Carson and national parks for Muir), it does not provide the level of detail or specificity seen in Option B, making it less effective in highlighting the differences in their contributions.

Page Intentionally Left Blank

HARD: Reading and Writing

27 Questions, 32 Minutes

DIRECTIONS

The questions in this section address a number of important reading and writing skills. Each question includes one or more passages, which may include a table or graph. Read each passage and question carefully, and then choose the best answer to the question based on the passage(s).

All questions in this section are multiple-choice with four answer choices. Each question has a single best answer.

The following text is adapted from Amitav Ghosh's 2004 novel *The Hungry Tide*. The narrator describes a scene in the Sundarbans, a mangrove region in India and Bangladesh.

The fishermen of Lusibari, clad in their traditional lungis, were navigating the labyrinthine waterways of the Sundarbans. As they maneuvered their dinghies through the dense foliage, they were constantly _____ by the low-hanging branches and the swift currents of the tide, which made their journey longer than anticipated.

1

Which choice completes the text with the most logical and precise word or phrase?

A) guided

B) unaffected

C) rerouted

D) threatened

CONTINUE

The Yanomami tribe of the Amazon rainforest in Brazil and Venezuela and the Sami people of Northern Europe have developed some remarkable practices in response to their harsh environments. The Yanomami engage in shifting agriculture and sustainable hunting to thrive in the dense tropical forests, while the Sami practice reindeer herding and fishing to survive in the Arctic regions. These _____ allow them to navigate and endure the challenges of their distinct habitats.

2

Which choice completes the text with the most logical and precise word or phrase?

A) traditions

B) adaptations

C) dispositions

D) rituals

In her introduction to the anthology *Green Speculations: Science Fiction and Transformative Environmentalism*, which was written in the 1990s, editor Gerry Canavan highlights a shift toward more _____ addressed environmental themes, differing from science fiction stories of the 1960s to 1980s whose exploration of ecological issues were more subtle.

3

Which choice completes the text with the most logical and precise word or phrase?

A) assertively

B) passively

C) ambivalently

D) ambiguously

CONTINUE

While recent studies have challenged the notion that the diet of medieval European peasants was _____ that of the nobility, it is clear that their meals were largely composed of locally sourced grains and vegetables, contrasting with the more diverse and exotic foods available to the upper class.

4

Which choice completes the text with the most logical and precise word or phrase?

A) different from

B) dependent on

C) influenced by

D) comparable to

CONTINUE

The following text is from the 1923 poem "The Love Song of J. Alfred Prufrock" by T.S. Eliot.

> Let us go then, you and I,
> When the evening is spread out against the sky
> Like a patient etherized upon a table;
>
> Let us go, through certain half-deserted streets,
> The muttering retreats
> Of restless nights in one-night cheap hotels
> And sawdust restaurants with oyster-shells:
> Streets that follow like a tedious argument
> Of insidious intent
>
> To lead you to an overwhelming question…
> Oh, do not ask, "What is it?"
> Let us go and make our visit.

Which choice best describes the overall structure of the text?

A) The speaker describes a journey he has taken, then ends with a sense of achievement.

B) The speaker reflects on the desolation of the streets, then anticipates a significant revelation.

C) The speaker observes the evening setting, then resolves to confront an internal conflict.

D) The speaker details a hypothetical journey, then hints at an unresolved question.

CONTINUE

In the animal kingdom, different species exhibit a wide range of foraging behaviors. Some animals, like ants, are known for their cooperative efforts in gathering food. Ants work together in colonies, creating complex networks of trails to efficiently collect and transport food back to their nest. The solitary hunting habits of the tiger, however, demonstrate a very different approach: <u>tigers rely on stealth and strength to hunt alone, stalking their prey quietly before launching a powerful attack.</u> This behavior ensures that tigers secure their meals without competition from other predators or members of their species.

6

Which choice best describes the function of the underlined portion in the text as a whole?

A) It elaborates on the benefits of tigers hunting alone.

B) It connects a similarity between the animals discussed in the text.

C) It clarifies a point made earlier in the sentence.

D) It illustrates the tigers' inability to cooperate in groups to gather food.

CONTINUE

In the early 20th century, the prevailing theory of heredity was "blending inheritance," which suggested offspring were a mix of parental traits. However, this theory couldn't explain the reappearance of traits in later generations or the variation observed in populations. Through meticulous experiments with pea plants, Gregor Mendel demonstrated that traits are inherited as discrete units, known as genes, which do not blend. Although initially ignored, Mendel's work was rediscovered in the early 20th century. This led to the decline of blending inheritance and the acceptance of Mendelian inheritance.

7

Which choice best states the main purpose of the text?

A) To highlight the historical significance of blending inheritance and its lasting impact on genetics

B) To describe the limitations of a long-standing theory and present a more accurate alternative

C) To explain the reasons behind the initial acceptance and eventual decline of blending inheritance in scientific thought

D) To compare and contrast the methodologies used by early geneticists in their research

CONTINUE

Text 1

Cognitive psychologists have long studied how memory works, focusing on how information is encoded, stored, and retrieved. According to the multi-store model, memory consists of three distinct stores: sensory memory, short-term memory, and long-term memory. This model suggests that information passes through these stores sequentially, with rehearsal playing a crucial role in transferring data from short-term to long-term memory. Despite its widespread acceptance, this model has been criticized for its simplicity and lack of consideration for the complexities of memory processes.

Text 2

Dr. Elizabeth Loftus, a prominent cognitive psychologist known for her work on the malleability of human memory, has raised significant questions about the multi-store model. Loftus argues that memory is not a linear process but is instead highly reconstructive and susceptible to distortion. Her research

8

Based on the texts, how would Dr. Elizabeth Loftus (Text 2) most likely respond to the multi-store model discussed in Text 1?

A) By calling out the model's comprehensive explanation of the sequential nature of memory processes

B) By championing its linear and sequential processes and lauding its simplified approach to a complex topic

C) By recommending that additional research be done to explore how memory is influenced by social and environmental factors

D) By criticizing its sequential and simplistic approach to a dynamic and complex process

CONTINUE

"Ode to a Nightingale" is an 1819 poem by John Keats. The poem contrasts the immortality of the nightingale with the speaker's own fleeting experience, writing

_____

Which quotation from "Ode to a Nightingale" most effectively illustrates the claim?

A) "Away! away! for I will fly to thee, / Not charioted by Bacchus and his pards, / But on the viewless wings of Poesy,"

B) "Thou wast not born for death, immortal Bird! / No hungry generations tread thee down; / The voice I hear this passing night was heard"

C) "Darkling I listen; and, for many a time / I have been half in love with easeful Death, / Call'd him soft names in many a mused rhyme,"

D) "Fade far away, dissolve, and quite forget / What thou among the leaves hast never known, / The weariness, the fever, and the fret"

CONTINUE ➡

In the mountainous regions of northern Italy, a significant portion of the population has striking blue eyes. This physical trait is prominently observed in villages nestled within the Alps, where blue eyes are a common feature among the residents. Similarly, in the remote highlands of Scotland, blue eyes are also a prevalent trait, particularly among communities with deep historical roots in the area. Historical records indicate that both regions were once home to Celtic tribes who shared common ancestry and cultural practices. Geneticists, therefore, have concluded that _____

10

Which choice most logically completes the text?

A) the blue eye trait in northern Italy and the Scottish Highlands can be traced back to their shared Celtic ancestry.

B) people in northern Italy adopted the blue eye trait from their Scottish neighbors.

C) blue eyes will eventually become the dominant eye color in both Italy and Scotland.

D) the blue eye trait is a result of recent migration patterns between Italy and Scotland.

CONTINUE

In literary theory, the denouement is the final resolution of a narrative, while the obligatory scene is the pivotal moment that fulfills audience expectations. In Shakespeare's "Macbeth," the denouement occurs when Macbeth is slain by Macduff, restoring order with Malcolm's rise. The obligatory scene is Macbeth's encounter with the witches, igniting his ambition and setting the tragedy in motion. Literary theorist Northrop Frye argued that the interplay between denouement and obligatory scene can enhance the dramatic impact of a narrative. By carefully structuring these elements, Frye contends that writers can _____

11

Which choice most logically completes the text?

A)   create more intricate and confusing storylines that challenge the audience's understanding.

B)   ensure that every character has a significant backstory, regardless of their role in the plot.

C)   generate more powerful and emotionally resonant stories, heightening the audience's engagement and satisfaction.

D)   focus on a storyline that the audience will resonate with most but leave the story unresolved.

CONTINUE

Trends in Traditional Media Consumption
(2015-2023)

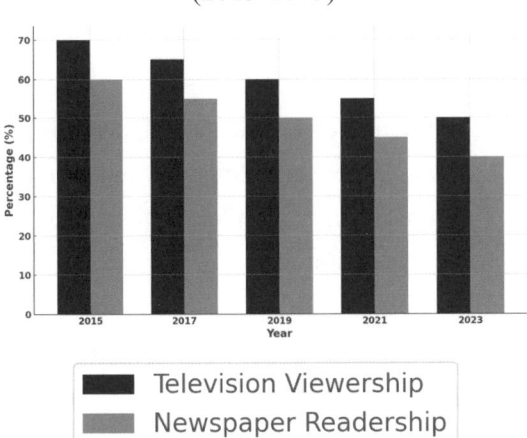

Recent research highlights a sharp increase in social media and digital platform consumption, especially among younger audiences. This rising trend comes at a cost: traditional media consumption. Researchers Maria Johnson and David Lee assessed the viewing habits of various age groups over the past decade. Their findings suggest a significant decline in television viewership and print newspaper readership, correlating with the growing preference for digital and social media platforms, which offer more convenience and personalized content.

12

Which choice best describes data from the graph that support the researchers' conclusion?

A) Television viewership was at its highest point in 2015 with about 70% of people claiming they watched tv, while newspaper readership's peak was at 60% in 2015.

B) Newspaper readership in 2017 was similar to television viewership in 2021.

C) Television viewership was consistently higher than newspaper readership throughout the five periods studied.

D) The percentage of newspaper readership shows a consistent decline in each of the five periods studied.

CONTINUE

Inflation Rate vs. Consumer Spending
(Dual-Axis Analysis)

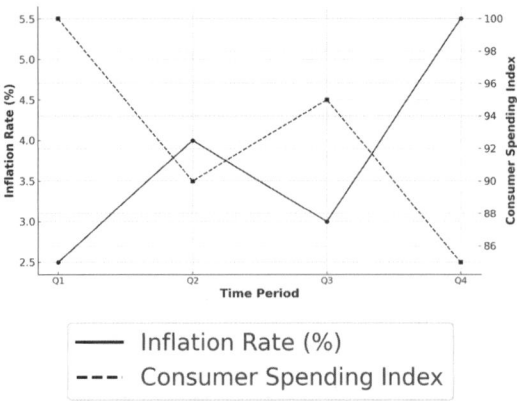

Inflation, characterized by the general increase in prices, can significantly influence consumer spending habits. An economics student analyzed the relationship between inflation rates and consumer spending over four quarters. In Q1, the inflation rate was 2.5%, with consumer spending at an index of 100. By Q2, inflation rose to 4.0%, leading to a drop in spending to an index of 90. Q3 saw a slight decrease in inflation to 3.0%, with spending recovering slightly to 95. However, by Q4, inflation spiked to 5.5%, causing consumer spending to drop further to an index of 85. The study concluded that _____

13

Which choice most effectively uses data from the graph to complete the student's conclusion?

A) fluctuations in consumer spending are largely unpredictable and do not consistently correlate with changes in inflation rates.

B) moderate inflation, such as the 3.0% in Q3, has little to no impact on consumer spending, which remained stable during this period.

C) inflation and consumer spending reflect an inverse correlation: that is, when inflation increases, consumer spending tends to decrease.

D) inflation and consumer spending reflect a direct correlation: that is, when inflation increases, consumer spending also tends to increase.

CONTINUE

Gastronomy encompasses the study of food and culture—including the preparation, presentation, and enjoyment of meals—and plays a crucial role in shaping and reflecting cultural identities. Traditional cuisines are often passed down through generations, preserving historical and cultural narratives within each recipe. In many cultures, food is central to community gatherings, rituals, and celebrations, reinforcing social bonds and cultural continuity. Additionally, the fusion of different culinary traditions can lead to the creation of new, hybrid cuisines that reflect the blending of cultures. This dynamic aspect of gastronomy not only honors the past; <u>it also allows for the amalgamation and evolution of cultural identities.</u>

14

Which statement about gastronomy, if true, would most directly support the underlined claim?

A) Chef Gordon Ramsay's television show focuses on improving struggling restaurants by refining their existing menus.

B) Chef Massimo Bottura's restaurant Osteria Francescana offers a dish called "Oops! I Dropped the Lemon Tart," which reinterprets a classic Italian dessert.

C) Chef Alice Waters emphasizes the importance of organic and locally sourced ingredients in her dishes at Chez Panisse.

D) Chef David Chang's restaurant Momofuku serves a dish called kimchi ramen, which fuses Korean and Japanese culinary traditions.

CONTINUE

15

To understand the role of microplastics in marine food webs, scientists have conducted extensive research on how these tiny plastic particles, less than 5 millimeters in diameter, are introduced into marine environments. Microplastics come from a variety of sources: cosmetic products, synthetic clothing fibers, and the breakdown of larger plastic debris. Once in the ocean, these particles are ingested by marine organisms at all levels of the food web, from plankton to large fish. The ingestion of microplastics can cause physical harm, such as blockages in digestive systems, and expose marine life to toxic chemicals. Additionally, microplastics can transfer up the food chain, potentially affecting human health.

Which choice best states the main idea of the text?

A) Microplastics originate from various sources and pose significant risks to marine organisms and possibly human health.

B) Plankton and large fish are equally affected by the ingestion of microplastics in marine environments.

C) The ingestion of microplastics by marine organisms is primarily caused by synthetic clothing fibers.

D) Scientists are primarily focused on finding ways to reduce the presence of microplastics in the ocean.

CONTINUE

The integration of artificial intelligence (AI) into medical diagnostics promises to revolutionize healthcare by improving accuracy and efficiency; however, it also raises significant ethical questions. For instance, when AI algorithms make decisions about patient care, who is ultimately responsible for those _____ Furthermore, the potential for AI to perpetuate existing biases in healthcare outcomes must be carefully considered.

16

Which choice completes the text so that it conforms to the conventions of Standard English?

A) decisions, the developers, the healthcare providers or the machines themselves.

B) decisions; the developers, the healthcare providers, or the machines themselves?

C) decisions—the developers, the healthcare providers, or the machines themselves.

D) decisions: the developers, the healthcare providers, or the machines themselves?

CONTINUE

The aye-aye—a nocturnal lemur native to Madagascar—is one of the most unusual creatures on the planet, with its elongated middle finger and large, radar-like ears designed for echolocation. Despite its bizarre appearance, the aye-aye plays a crucial role in its _____ its unique finger to extract insects from tree bark, which helps maintain the health of the forest. However, due to its odd features and nocturnal habits, local superstitions have led to the belief that the aye-aye is an omen of bad luck.

Which choice completes the text so that it conforms to the conventions of Standard English?

A) ecosystem using

B) ecosystem and using

C) ecosystem, using

D) ecosystem, uses

Competitive dog grooming showcases the artistry and precision involved in transforming dogs into living works of art. Competitions are held across the globe, with events like the Groom Expo in Hershey, Pennsylvania, in 2019; the Master Groom in Manchester, _____ the International Grooming Championship in Tokyo, Japan, in 2023, drawing participants from diverse backgrounds.

Which choice completes the text so that it conforms to the conventions of Standard English?

A) England, in 2021, and

B) England, in 2021; and

C) England, in 2021 and;

D) England, in, 2021; and

CONTINUE

In the culinary world, how food looks on the plate can be as important as how it tastes. This wasn't always the case; decades ago, flavor was king, and presentation was secondary. Today, however, chefs are expected to create visually stunning dishes that _____ the eye before they tantalize the taste buds. The rise of platforms like Instagram has only amplified this trend, turning chefs into visual artists who use ingredients as their medium.

Which choice completes the text so that it conforms to the conventions of Standard English?

A) has delighted

B) delighted

C) delighting

D) delight

Ever had a song stuck in your head that you just couldn't shake? This phenomenon, known as an earworm, is as annoying as it is common. Cognitive scientists have found that repetitive songs, especially _____ are the usual culprits. Decades from now, perhaps we'll have a clearer understanding of why some tunes cling to our minds so tenaciously while others slip away unnoticed.

Which choice completes the text so that it conforms to the conventions of Standard English?

A) those with simple, catchy melodies,

B) those with simple catchy melodies

C) those, with simple catchy melodies,

D) those with simple, catchy melodies

CONTINUE

Once confined to niche communities, _____. Over the past two decades, these online groups have evolved into powerful cultural entities, influencing everything from entertainment to politics. Whether it's creating fan art, debating plot theories, or organizing large-scale social campaigns, fans have shown that their passion can drive real-world change. The internet has transformed what it means to be a fan, making it a global phenomenon.

Which choice completes the text so that it conforms to the conventions of Standard English?

A) fandoms have exploded in the digital age

B) the explosion of fandoms in the digital age is apparent

C) the digital age has created an explosion of fandoms

D) fandoms' explosion is apparent in the digital age

Feared and misunderstood for centuries, sleep paralysis—a phenomenon where one wakes up unable to move—remains deeply unsettling even today. The brain wakes, but the body lags behind, leaving the sleeper trapped in a twilight state where reality and dreams blur. For ____ who've experienced it, the sensation of an unseen presence pressing down on their chest is something they're unlikely to forget.

Which choice completes the text so that it conforms to the conventions of Standard English?

A) them

B) those

C) one

D) they

CONTINUE

In today's digital age, the handwritten letter is nearly extinct. Once a primary means of communication, letters carried not only messages but also the writer's personality in the form of unique handwriting. Now, emails and text messages dominate, stripping away the tactile experience that once made written correspondence so intimate. _____ a small but dedicated group of enthusiasts continues to champion the art of letter writing, hoping to preserve it for future generations.

23

Which choice completes the text with the most logical transition?

A) To this end,

B) Despite this shift,

C) Instead,

D) Likewise,

Beloved for its tangy flavor and chewy texture, sourdough bread owes its unique characteristics to the wild yeast and bacteria found in sourdough starters. These living cultures are as individual as fingerprints; no two starters are exactly alike. Interestingly, the microorganisms in a starter can even change based on the environment in which they're kept: _____ what thrives in a San Francisco kitchen might struggle in a Parisian bakery.

24

Which choice completes the text with the most logical transition?

A) that is,

B) however,

C) alternatively,

D) rather,

CONTINUE

Have you ever felt your phone vibrate in your pocket, only to check and find no notifications? This experience, known as phantom phone vibration, is surprisingly common; it's a testament to how deeply our devices have integrated into our daily lives. Psychologists suggest that this phenomenon occurs because our brains become conditioned to expect constant communication; _____ we might perceive a vibration when none actually exists. It's a curious quirk of modern life, reflecting the way technology shapes our perceptions.

Which choice completes the text with the most logical transition?

A) still,

B) as a result,

C) moreover,

D) furthermore,

CONTINUE

While researching a topic, a student has taken the following notes:

- Uncontacted tribes are indigenous groups with little or no contact with the outside world.
- There are an estimated 100 uncontacted tribes in the Amazon rainforest and about 40 in Papua New Guinea.
- Isolated tribes are sometimes used interchangeably with uncontacted tribes, though isolated tribes may have had some contact.
- The Amazon rainforest is also home to approximately 400 contacted tribes.
- Papua New Guinea has about 300 contacted tribes.
- Many uncontacted tribes are at risk due to external threats like deforestation, illegal mining, and disease.

26

The student wants to contrast the number of uncontacted tribes in the Amazon rainforest with those in Papua New Guinea. Which choice most effectively uses relevant information from the notes to accomplish this goal?

A) Isolated tribes may have had some contact with the outside world, unlike the 100 uncontacted tribes in the Amazon rainforest.

B) Although about 400 contacted tribes exist in the Amazon rainforest, Papua New Guinea is home to approximately 300.

C) While Papa New Guinea has about 300 contacted and 40 uncontacted tribes, the Amazon rainforest is home to about 400 contacted and 100 uncontacted ones.

D) The Amazon rainforest contains approximately 100 uncontacted tribes, whereas Papua New Guinea is home to around 40.

CONTINUE

While researching a topic, a student has taken the following notes:

- Erwin Panofsky was an influential art historian focused on Renaissance art.
- Between 1930 and 1960, he conducted in-depth studies of several key artworks.
- In 1939, he analyzed "The Birth of Venus" by Sandro Botticelli, focusing on its symbolic use of mythological elements.
- In 1955, he studied "The School of Athens" by Raphael, examining the depiction of classical philosophers.
- Both "The Birth of Venus" and "The School of Athens" are iconic works of the Italian Renaissance.

27

The student wants to introduce Erwin Panofsky to an audience unfamiliar with him and emphasize his analysis of "The Birth of Venus." Which choice most effectively uses relevant information from the notes to accomplish this goal?

A) Erwin Panofsky, a prominent art historian known for his expertise in Renaissance art, conducted in-depth studies between 1930 and 1960, including an analysis of "The Birth of Venus."

B) An influential art historian who conducted in-depth studies of Renaissance art, Erwin Panofsky analyzed "The Birth of Venus" by Botticelli by focusing on its symbolic use of mythological elements.

C) Panofsky's analysis of "The Birth of Venus" in 1939 explored the symbolic use of mythological elements, one of many Renaissance works he studied.

D) Panofsky's analysis of "The Birth of Venus" focused on its symbolic use of mythological elements, while his study of "The School of Athens" examined the depiction of classical philosophers.

If you finish before the time is called, you may check your work on this module only.

On Test Day, you will only be able to move to the next module when time expires.

 **Answer Key**

Question Number	Correct Answer	Level of Difficulty	Question Type
1	C	Easy	**Craft and Structure:** *Words in Context*
2	B	Medium	**Craft and Structure:** *Words in Context*
3	A	Hard	**Craft and Structure:** *Words in Context*
4	D	Medium	**Craft and Structure:** *Words in Context*
5	D	Hard	**Craft and Structure:** *Overall Structure*
6	C	Medium	**Craft and Structure:** *Function of the Underlined Portion*
7	B	Medium	**Craft and Structure:** *Main Purpose*
8	D	Hard	**Craft and Structure:** *Cross-Text Connection*
9	B	Hard	**Information and Ideas:** *Cite Text as Evidence*
10	A	Medium	**Information and Ideas:** *Inference*
11	C	Medium	**Information and Ideas:** *Inference*
12	D	Easy	**Information and Ideas:** *Support a Claim (Infographic)*
13	C	Hard	**Information and Ideas:** *Complete the Text (Infographic)*

Question Number	Correct Answer	Level of Difficulty	Question Type
14	D	Medium	**Information and Ideas:** *Support a Claim*
15	A	Easy	**Information and Ideas:** *Main Idea*
16	D	Medium	**Standard English Conventions:** *Punctuation*
17	C	Hard	**Standard English Conventions:** *Sentence Structure*
18	B	Hard	**Standard English Conventions:** *Punctuation*
19	D	Medium	**Standard English Conventions:** *Verbs*
20	A	Hard	**Standard English Conventions:** *Commas*
21	A	Easy	**Standard English Conventions:** *Modifiers*
22	B	Medium	**Standard English Conventions:** *Pronouns*
23	B	Hard	**Expression of Ideas:** *Transitions*
24	A	Hard	**Expression of Ideas:** *Transitions*
25	B	Medium	**Expression of Ideas:** *Transitions*
26	D	Medium	**Expression of Ideas:** *Rhetorical Synthesis*
27	B	Hard	**Expression of Ideas:** *Rhetorical Synthesis*

Raw Score Conversion Table

Raw Score (# of Correct Answers)	Reading and Writing Section Score	Raw Score (# of Correct Answers)	Reading and Writing Section Score
54	800	30	510
53	780	29	500
52	760	28	490
51	730	27	480
50	720	26	470
49	710	25	470
48	700	24	450
47	680	23	440
46	670	22	430
45	660	21	430
44	650	20	410
43	640	19	400
42	630	18	390
41	620		
40	610		
39	600		
38	590		
37	580		
36	570		
35	560		
34	550		
33	540		
32	530		
31	520		

 **Explanations**

1. Words in Context: Easy

Answer: C) rerouted

Step-by-Step Explanation:

1. Let's look at what the passage is saying. The passage describes fishermen navigating through the challenging waterways of the Sundarbans, dealing with obstacles like low-hanging branches and swift currents. These conditions made their journey longer than expected, implying that the environment presented difficulties.

2. Notice the phrases "maneuvered their dinghies" and "made their journey longer than anticipated." These suggest that the obstacles, such as the low-hanging branches and swift currents, were regularly interfering with the fishermen's progress. These obstacles were not just occasional but persistent, causing delays and potentially forcing the fishermen to alter their course.

3. The word we need should describe or imply how the fishermen's journey took longer because of these obstacles.

4. Ask yourself, what word best describes the impact of the obstacles on the fishermen's journey? "Rerouted" is the most logical choice because it means having to change one's path or direction, which aligns with the idea that the fishermen's journey was made longer by the obstacles they encountered.

Explanation of Incorrect Options:

A) guided: This is incorrect because it implies that the obstacles helped direct the fishermen, which doesn't make logical sense and isn't consistent with the idea of their journey being more difficult and prolonged.

B) unaffected: This is incorrect because it suggests that the fishermen were not influenced by the obstacles, which contradicts the passage's description of their journey being extended.

D) threatened: This is incorrect because while the obstacles could pose a danger, the passage focuses on the practical challenges of navigation rather than on a sense of danger. Thus, "threatened" isn't supported by the context and isn't the most precise word.

2. Words in Context: Medium

Answer: B) adaptations

Step-by-Step Explanation:

1. Let's deconstruct the passage together. The passage describes how the Yanomami tribe and the Sami people have developed practices that help them survive and thrive in their respective environments. The Yanomami use shifting agriculture and sustainable hunting in the tropical rainforest, while the Sami practice reindeer herding and fishing in the Arctic regions.
2. Notice the phrase "developed some remarkable practices in response to their harsh environments." This suggests that these practices are not just cultural or traditional but are specifically tailored to help these groups survive in their challenging environments. The passage is focusing on how these practices help the tribes adapt to their surroundings.
3. The word we need should describe practices that are developed specifically to help these groups survive and navigate their difficult habitats.
4. Ask yourself, what word best describes practices that are developed in response to environmental challenges? "Adaptations" is the most logical choice because it refers to changes or strategies that allow organisms, or in this case, people, to survive and thrive in specific environments.

Explanation of Incorrect Options:

A) traditions: This is incorrect because traditions refer to cultural practices passed down through generations, but the passage is emphasizing practical strategies developed specifically in response to environmental challenges.

C) dispositions: This is incorrect because dispositions refer to a person's inherent qualities of mind and character, which does not fit the context of the passage discussing survival strategies.

D) rituals: This is incorrect because rituals refer to ceremonial practices, which are not related to the survival strategies being discussed in the passage.

3. Words in Context: Hard

Answer: A) assertively

Step-by-Step Explanation:

1. Let's look at what the passage is saying. The passage describes a shift in the way environmental themes are addressed in science fiction, specifically noting a change from the more subtle exploration of ecological issues in the 1960s to 1980s to a different approach in the 1990s.
2. Notice the contrast between "more subtle" and the phrase we need to complete the sentence. The passage is suggesting that in the 1990s, the approach to environmental themes became more direct and pronounced, contrasting with the earlier subtlety.
3. The word we need should describe how environmental themes are addressed in a more direct, stronger, or clearer manner, in contrast to the earlier subtle approach.
4. Ask yourself, what word best describes addressing something in a direct and strong way? "Assertively" is the most logical choice because it means addressing something in a confident and strong way, which aligns with the idea of a shift toward more direct environmental themes in the 1990s.

Explanation of Incorrect Options:

B) passively: This is incorrect because it implies a lack of active involvement or assertiveness, which contradicts the idea of a more direct and pronounced approach to environmental themes.

C) ambivalently: This is incorrect because it means having mixed or contradictory feelings, which does not fit the context of the passage describing a more direct approach to environmental themes. Thus, this option is irrelevant given what the passage talks about.

D) ambiguously: This is incorrect because it means unclear or open to interpretation, which is the opposite of the direct and clear approach suggested by the passage.

4. Words in Context: Medium

Answer: D) comparable to

Step-by-Step Explanation:

1. Let's look at what the passage is saying. The passage mentions that recent studies have challenged a certain belief about the diet of medieval European peasants compared to that of the nobility. It then contrasts the peasants' diet, mainly consisting of locally sourced grains and vegetables, with the more diverse and exotic foods available to the upper class.

2. Notice the contrast between the simple, locally sourced diet of the peasants and the diverse, exotic diet of the nobility. The passage implies that, despite these differences, there was a belief that the diets shared some level of similarity, which recent studies are now questioning.

3. Thus, the word we need should reflect the idea that the diets of peasants and nobility were once thought to be somewhat similar in nature, though the passage suggests this idea is being reconsidered.

4. Ask yourself, what word best captures the idea of comparing two things with some degree of similarity? "Comparable to" is the most logical choice because it suggests that the diets of peasants and nobility were considered similar enough to be compared, which aligns with the studies mentioned in the passage that challenge the notion of a clear difference.

Explanation of Incorrect Options:

A) different from: This is incorrect because it contradicts the passage's suggestion that the diets were once believed to have some similarities, not stark differences.

B) dependent on: This is incorrect because it suggests that the peasants' diet relied on the nobility's diet, which is not supported by the passage's discussion of the peasants' use of local grains and vegetables.

C) influenced by: This is incorrect because it implies that the peasants' diet was shaped by the nobility's diet, which is not what the passage is conveying. The passage instead highlights the contrast between the simplicity of the peasants' diet and the variety available to the nobility.

5. Overall Structure: Hard

Answer: D) The speaker details a hypothetical journey, then hints at an unresolved question.

Logical Breakdown and Explanation:

This question requires identifying the option that best describes the overall structure of the text, focusing on how the passage builds and develops its ideas from beginning to end.

Option D is correct because the speaker invites the reader on a hypothetical journey through the streets, as evidenced by the phrase "Let us go then, you and I." The journey is filled with imagery of desolate and unsettling streets, such as "half-deserted streets" and "one-night cheap hotels." "The passage ends with the mention of 'an overwhelming question.' Instead of revealing the question, the speaker responds by saying, 'Oh, do not ask, "What is it?"'" This indicates that the question remains unresolved." This choice accurately describes the progression from hypothetical journey to unanswered question, which leaves the poem open-ended.

Option A is incorrect because it introduces the idea that the speaker ends with a sense of achievement, which is not reflected in the passage. The passage does not describe a completed journey or resolution but instead hints at an unresolved question. This makes the option a **distortion** of the actual events in the passage, as it takes attractive words like "journey" but alters the meaning to suggest an outcome that isn't present.

Option B is incorrect because although it correctly identifies the speaker's reflection on the desolate streets, it suggests the anticipation of a significant revelation. The passage ends with the speaker telling the reader not to ask what the overwhelming question is, which implies no revelation is made. This answer is **partially correct** in capturing the desolate streets but introduces an off-topic idea about revelation that contradicts the actual conclusion of the passage.

Option C is incorrect because, while the speaker does observe the evening setting, the passage does not mention the speaker resolving to confront an internal conflict. Instead, it focuses on the hypothetical journey and an unresolved question. This makes the option **irrelevant**, as it introduces ideas about internal conflict that are unsupported by the passage.

6. Function of the Underlined Portion: Medium

Answer: C) It clarifies a point made earlier in the sentence.

Logical Breakdown and Explanation:

This question asks you to determine the function of the underlined portion within the overall passage, focusing on how it contributes to the main point of the sentence.

Option C is correct because the underlined portion—"tigers rely on stealth and strength to hunt alone, stalking their prey quietly before launching a powerful attack"—clarifies *how tigers hunt alone*, a point made earlier in the sentence. The use of the colon is important to note here because the information after the colon is meant to explain or clarify the independent clause that comes before it. In this case, the earlier part of the sentence introduces the idea of solitary hunting, and the underlined portion provides the specific methods tigers use, such as relying on stealth and strength.

Option A is incorrect because while the underlined portion does explain how tigers hunt, it does not focus specifically on the *benefits* of hunting alone. The text does not explicitly discuss the advantages of solitary hunting beyond mentioning the avoidance of competition—the following sentence talks about such benefits. Remember that this question asks what the *underlined portion* is "doing."

Option B is incorrect because the underlined portion does not connect a similarity between the animals discussed in the text. Instead, the passage contrasts the cooperative foraging of ants with the solitary hunting of tigers. This option **contradicts** information provided int he passage.

Option D is incorrect because it suggests that the underlined portion illustrates the tigers' inability to cooperate in groups. However, the text doesn't suggest that tigers are incapable of cooperating; it simply describes their solitary hunting habits. This makes **Option D unsupported by the passage** because it introduces an assumption that is not based on the content.

7. Main Purpose: Medium

Answer: B) To describe the limitations of a long-standing theory and present a more accurate
alternative

Logical Breakdown and Explanation:

This question asks you to identify the main purpose of the text by focusing on how it explains
the transition from one scientific theory to another.

Option B is correct because the passage explains the limitations of the blending inheritance
theory, such as its failure to account for the reappearance of traits and variation, and then
introduces Mendel's theory of inheritance as a more accurate alternative. The text centers on
describing why blending inheritance was insufficient and how Mendelian inheritance replaced
it, making this option the best reflection of the passage's purpose.

Option A is incorrect because it suggests that blending inheritance had a lasting impact on
genetics, which contradicts the information in the passage. The text explains that blending
inheritance was replaced by Mendelian inheritance and emphasizes its decline, not its enduring
influence. By claiming a lasting impact, this option directly **contradicts the ideas discussed
in the passage**.

Option C is incorrect because, while the passage mentions the decline of blending inheritance,
it does not explore the reasons behind its initial acceptance in detail. The passage focuses more
on the limitations of the theory and the rise of Mendelian inheritance, rather than a deep
exploration of blending inheritance's trajectory. This makes the option **partially correct but
ultimately off-topic**, as it emphasizes the wrong aspect of the passage.

Option D is incorrect because the passage does not compare or contrast different
methodologies used by geneticists. The focus is on explaining the shift from blending
inheritance to Mendelian inheritance, not on comparing research methods. This answer **uses
the wrong verb**, focusing on "contrast" where no such comparison exists in the passage.

8. Cross-Text Connections: Hard

Answer: D) By criticizing its sequential and simplistic approach to a dynamic and complex process

Logical Breakdown and Explanation:

This question asks how Dr. Elizabeth Loftus, based on her views in Text 2, would likely respond to the multi-store model described in Text 1.

Option D is correct because Dr. Loftus, in Text 2, critiques the multi-store model for presenting memory as a "linear process." She specifically argues that memory is instead "highly reconstructive and susceptible to distortion," emphasizing that the model's portrayal oversimplifies memory's complexity. By demonstrating that memories can be influenced by various factors, Loftus highlights how the multi-store model fails to account for these dynamic factors. Thus, she would most likely criticize the model for its overly "sequential and simplistic approach" to a more intricate and flexible process.

Option A is incorrect because it distorts the passage by suggesting that Dr. Loftus would "call out the model's comprehensive explanation." In fact, Text 1 describes the multi-store model as being criticized for its "simplicity" rather than being comprehensive. The argument made by Dr. Loftus is that memory is a "complex process" that the model fails to capture, not that it provides a thorough or complete view. This makes the option a **distortion** of the text's meaning, as it misrepresents both the model's limitations and Loftus's perspective.

Option B is incorrect because it implies that Loftus would support (champion) the model's sequential processes and its simplified approach. In reality, Text 2 clearly shows that Loftus criticizes this oversimplified view of memory. This option is a **contradiction** of her views, as it misinterprets her stance by suggesting she would advocate for the approach she actively challenges.

Option C is incorrect because it suggests that Loftus would recommend further research to explore how memory is influenced by social and environmental factors. While Loftus's research does indicate that memory is affected by these factors, the text does not imply that she would recommend more research. This makes the option **irrelevant**, as it introduces ideas not supported by the text.

9. Cite Text as Evidence: Hard

Answer: B) "Thou wast not born for death, immortal Bird! / No hungry generations tread thee down; / The voice I hear this passing night was heard"

Logical Breakdown and Explanation:

This question asks you to select the quotation that most effectively illustrates the contrast between the nightingale's immortality and the speaker's fleeting experience, as mentioned in the claim.

Option B is correct because it not only highlights the nightingale's immortality with the line "Thou wast not born for death, immortal Bird!" but also contrasts this with the speaker's own fleeting experience. The phrase "The voice I hear this passing night" emphasizes the speaker's temporary existence, as the nightingale's song endures across generations, while the speaker experiences it only briefly. This combination of the bird's eternal presence and the speaker's transient experience effectively illustrates the central contrast between immortality and mortality in the poem.

Option A is incorrect because it focuses on the speaker's desire to escape through poetry ("the viewless wings of Poesy") rather than contrasting the nightingale's immortality with the speaker's mortality. This option is **off-topic** to the claim, as it deals more with poetic imagination than with life and death.

Option C is incorrect because it focuses on the speaker's relationship with death, describing how the speaker has "been half in love with easeful Death," but it makes no mention of the nightingale or its immortality. The passage reflects the speaker's internal thoughts about death, not the contrast between the speaker's mortality and the bird's immortality, making it **irrelevant** to the claim.

Option D is incorrect because it distorts the intended contrast between the nightingale's immortality and the speaker's mortality. The lines focus on the speaker's desire to "fade far away" and escape the hardships of life, such as "the weariness, the fever, and the fret." While these lines express the speaker's yearning to forget life's struggles, they do not directly address the nightingale's immortality or compare it to the speaker's fleeting experience.

10. Inference: Medium

Answer: A) the blue eye trait in northern Italy and the Scottish Highlands can be traced back to their shared Celtic ancestry.

Logical Breakdown and Explanation:

This question asks for the most logical conclusion based on the information provided about the prevalence of blue eyes in both northern Italy and the Scottish Highlands, as well as the mention of shared Celtic ancestry.

Option A is correct because the passage notes that both regions were historically home to Celtic tribes who shared "common ancestry and cultural practices." Given this information, it is logical to conclude that the blue eye trait in both regions is likely inherited from this shared Celtic ancestry. The option directly connects the historical and genetic information provided in the passage.

Option B is incorrect because it suggests that people in northern Italy "adopted" the blue eye trait from their Scottish neighbors. There is no evidence in the passage to suggest that the trait was acquired through such a direct interaction or migration between the two regions. This makes the option **unsupported by the passage**.

Option C is incorrect because it introduces irrelevant information by predicting that blue eyes will "eventually become the dominant eye color" in both regions. The passage focuses on the historical and genetic origins of the blue eye trait, specifically related to shared Celtic ancestry, rather than speculating about future trends. This makes the option **irrelevant**, as it shifts the discussion from origins to a prediction not supported by the text.

Option D is incorrect because it introduces irrelevant information by suggesting that the blue eye trait is a result of "recent migration patterns" between Italy and Scotland. The passage makes no mention of any recent migrations, focusing instead on the historical presence of Celtic tribes as the likely source of the shared blue eye trait. This makes the option **irrelevant**, as it introduces a concept not discussed or supported by the text.

11. Inference: Medium

Answer: C) generate more powerful and emotionally resonant stories, heightening the audience's engagement and satisfaction.

Logical Breakdown and Explanation:

This question asks for the choice that logically completes the idea based on Northrop Frye's theory about the interplay between denouement and obligatory scenes enhancing the dramatic impact of a narrative.

Option C is correct because the passage describes how Northrop Frye argues that the careful structuring of the **denouement** (the final resolution) and the **obligatory scene** (the pivotal moment) enhances the narrative's dramatic impact. These elements work together to generate "more powerful and emotionally resonant stories," fulfilling audience expectations and leading to greater engagement and satisfaction. The denouement provides resolution, while the obligatory scene ignites the action, making the overall narrative more compelling. Thus, Frye's theory logically supports the idea of heightened emotional resonance and audience satisfaction as the purpose of this narrative structure.

Option A is incorrect because it introduces the idea of creating "intricate and confusing storylines." The passage does not suggest that the interplay of denouement and obligatory scenes is meant to confuse the audience, but rather to enhance the dramatic impact. This makes the option **illogical** based on the context.

Option B is incorrect because it suggests ensuring that "every character has a significant backstory." The passage discusses narrative structure, particularly the role of key scenes in driving the plot and engaging the audience, not character backstories. This option introduces **irrelevant** information.

Option D is incorrect because it suggests leaving the story unresolved, which contradicts the function of a denouement, which resolves the narrative. The passage emphasizes creating structure and satisfaction through resolution, making this option a **contradiction** of Frye's theory.

12. Support a Claim (Infographic): Easy

Answer: D) The percentage of newspaper readership shows a consistent decline in each of the five periods studied.

Logical Breakdown and Explanation:

This question asks for the choice that best supports the researchers' conclusion about the significant decline in traditional media consumption, including television viewership and newspaper readership, as audiences shift towards digital and social media platforms.

Option D is correct because it directly highlights the consistent decline in newspaper readership, which aligns with the researchers' conclusion about the reduction in traditional media consumption. This steady drop supports the overall trend of audiences moving away from traditional platforms like newspapers in favor of more convenient digital options. The consistent decline reflects the impact of the rise in social media and digital consumption, reinforcing the researchers' findings.

Option A is incorrect because it focuses on peak levels of viewership and readership in 2015, which do not illustrate the trend of **declining** media consumption over time. This makes the option **irrelevant** to the researchers' conclusion.

Option B is incorrect because the comparison between newspaper readership in 2017 and television viewership in 2021 does not provide meaningful insight into the overall trend of decline in both forms of traditional media. This makes it **irrelevant** to the conclusion as well.

Option C is incorrect because, while it points out that television viewership was higher than newspaper readership throughout the periods studied, it does not directly relate to the conclusion about the **decline** in traditional media consumption. The fact that one form of traditional media was consistently more popular than another does not support the idea of an overall decrease in traditional media use, making this option **irrelevant** to the conclusion.

13. Complete the Text (Infographic): Hard

Answer: C) inflation and consumer spending reflect an inverse correlation: that is, when inflation increases, consumer spending tends to decrease.

Logical Breakdown and Explanation:

This question asks you to select the conclusion that best reflects the relationship between inflation and consumer spending, as demonstrated by the data provided.

Option C is correct because the data shows an **inverse correlation** between inflation and consumer spending. As inflation increases (from 2.5% in Q1 to 5.5% in Q4), consumer spending consistently decreases (from an index of 100 to 85). This relationship is clearly reflected in the study's findings, making this the most effective conclusion.

Option A is incorrect because it suggests that fluctuations in consumer spending are "unpredictable" and do not correlate with inflation rates. However, the data shows a clear and predictable inverse relationship between inflation and spending, making this option **factually inaccurate**.

Option B is incorrect because it claims that moderate inflation has "little to no impact" on consumer spending. Although inflation decreased slightly in Q3 (to 3.0%), consumer spending did not remain stable; it recovered slightly, which suggests that spending is still impacted by inflation. This option is **unsupported by the data**.

Option D is incorrect because it suggests a **direct correlation**, claiming that when inflation increases, consumer spending also increases. The data shows the opposite—consumer spending decreases as inflation rises—making this option a **contradiction** of the relationship.

14. Support a Claim: Medium

Answer: D) Chef David Chang's restaurant Momofuku serves a dish called kimchi ramen, which fuses Korean and Japanese culinary traditions.

Logical Breakdown and Explanation:

This question asks for a statement that would most directly support the underlined claim that gastronomy allows for the "amalgamation and evolution of cultural identities" through the fusion of culinary traditions.

Option D is correct because it describes a dish, kimchi ramen, that merges elements of Korean (kimchi) and Japanese (ramen) culinary traditions. This fusion reflects the blending of cultures, which directly supports the idea of gastronomy as a dynamic force that evolves and combines different cultural identities, as mentioned in the underlined claim.

Option A is incorrect because Chef Gordon Ramsay's show focuses on refining existing menus, which doesn't emphasize the fusion of different culinary traditions. This option does not support the idea of cultural amalgamation and evolution, making it **irrelevant** to the claim.

Option B is incorrect because Chef Massimo Bottura's reinterpretation of a classic Italian dessert shows innovation within a single culinary tradition rather than the blending of different ones. While creative, it doesn't illustrate the fusion of multiple cultural identities, so it is **only partially relevant** to the claim.

Option C is incorrect because Chef Alice Waters emphasizes organic and locally sourced ingredients, which speaks to sustainability but not the blending or fusion of different culinary traditions. This option is **off-topic** for supporting the underlined claim about cultural amalgamation.

15. Main Idea: Easy

Answer: A) Microplastics originate from various sources and pose significant risks to marine organisms and possibly human health.

Logical Breakdown and Explanation:

This question asks for the choice that best captures the main idea of the text, which discusses how microplastics enter marine environments, their sources, and the harmful effects they have on marine life and potentially human health.

Option A is correct because it summarizes the key points of the text: microplastics come from "various sources" (cosmetic products, synthetic clothing fibers, and larger plastic debris), pose "significant risks" to marine organisms by causing physical harm, and can potentially transfer up the food chain to affect human health. This option effectively captures the main ideas presented in the text.

Option B is incorrect because it introduces **off-topic information** that is never discussed in the text. The passage does not focus on whether plankton and large fish are "equally affected" by microplastics, nor does it make this comparison. This option also focuses on **minor details** that do not capture the broader idea of microplastics' sources and harmful effects.

Option C is incorrect because, while it mentions that synthetic clothing fibers are one source of microplastic ingestion, this is **only partially correct**. The passage clearly lists other sources, such as cosmetic products and larger plastic debris, which are important to understanding the full picture. By focusing solely on one source, this option is **incomplete** and misses the broader discussion about the various sources and the overall impact of microplastics. Additionally, the passage never mentions that synthetic clothing fibers is the *primary cause* of microplastic ingestion, making this answer unsupported by information int he passage.

Option D is incorrect because the text does not mention that scientists are "primarily focused" on reducing microplastics in the ocean. Instead, the text explains the sources, effects, and risks of microplastics. This makes the option **irrelevant** to the main idea.

16. Punctuation: Medium

Answer: D) decisions: the developers, the healthcare providers, or the machines themselves?

Logical Breakdown and Explanation:

This question asks for the choice that best conforms to the conventions of Standard English, particularly in the context of punctuation and sentence structure.

Option D is correct because it uses a **colon** appropriately to introduce a list that elaborates on "who is ultimately responsible." The colon signals that the following list of options—developers, healthcare providers, or machines—explains the previous statement. Additionally, the sentence ends with a question mark, indicating that this is a direct question. This punctuation choice follows Standard English conventions for presenting a list within a question.

Option A is incorrect because the **comma** creates confusion by failing to clearly indicate the relationship between the initial statement and the list that follows. A comma makes it seem like "those decisions" is part of the list of options of people who may be responsible (developers, healthcare providers, or machines). Additionally, the sentence ends without a **question mark**, despite the fact that it is clearly asking a direct question—"Who is ultimately responsible?" This lack of a question mark further disrupts the clarity and completeness of the sentence.

Option B is incorrect because a **semicolon** is used incorrectly here. Semicolons are used to separate independent clauses or items in complex lists, but they are not used to introduce a list following a statement. This makes the punctuation inappropriate.

Option C is incorrect because, while the **dash** is acceptable to introduce a list, it omits the question mark needed at the end of the sentence. Since this is a direct question, the lack of a question mark means the sentence is incomplete and violates punctuation rules.

17. Sentence Structure: Hard

Answer: C) ecosystem, using

Logical Breakdown and Explanation:

This question asks for the choice that best completes the sentence in a way that conforms to Standard English conventions, focusing on proper sentence structure and clarity.

Option C is correct because the **comma** before "using" creates a logical modifier. The aye-aye "plays a crucial role in its ecosystem," and the phrase "using its unique finger to extract insects from tree bark" explains how it does so. The comma ensures that the reader understands that it's the aye-aye, not the ecosystem, that is using its finger. This structure is both clear and grammatically correct.

Option A is incorrect because without a comma, it suggests that the "ecosystem" is the subject "using" the aye-aye's unique finger. This **illogical modifier** makes the sentence confusing and implies a meaning that doesn't make sense.

Option B is incorrect because the addition of "and" creates a **nonsensical structure**. It suggests two separate actions ("plays a crucial role and using"), which breaks the parallel structure in the sentence, thus creating the wrong compound (*"and using"* must have another -ing word to create a proper compound).

Option D is incorrect because it introduces two main verbs ("plays" and "uses") without proper conjunction or structure to link them correctly. This results in a **nonsensical structure** ("the aye-aye *plays* a crucial role in its ecosystem, *uses* its unique finger...").

18. Punctuation: Hard

Answer: B) England, in 2021; and

Logical Breakdown and Explanation:

This question asks for the choice that correctly completes the sentence according to Standard English punctuation rules, particularly when dealing with complex lists.

Option B is correct because it uses a **semicolon** to separate the first item ("the Master Groom in Manchester, England, in 2021") from the second item in the list ("the International Grooming Championship in Tokyo, Japan, in 2023"). Semicolons are often used in complex lists where items themselves contain commas, ensuring clarity by preventing confusion between the internal commas and the commas separating the items. Additionally, the semicolon is placed before "and," which properly introduces the final item in the list, making this option conform to Standard English rules for punctuation in complex lists.

Option A is incorrect because it uses a **comma** instead of a semicolon to separate the second item from the third. In a complex list like this, where each item contains its own commas, a semicolon is necessary to avoid confusion and ensure clarity.

Option C is incorrect because it places "and;" at the end, which is a **grammatical error**. The semicolon should come before "and," not after it.

Option D is incorrect because it introduces a **comma** between "in" and "2021," which disrupts the natural flow of the phrase "in 2021." This phrase should be read smoothly as one thought, so adding a comma here is unnecessary and violates comma rules.

19. Verbs: Medium

Answer: D) delight

Logical Breakdown and Explanation:

This question asks for the choice that correctly completes the sentence while conforming to the conventions of Standard English, particularly subject-verb agreement, sentence structure, and verb tense.

Option D is correct because "delight" is a plural verb that agrees with the subject "stunning dishes." The sentence structure requires a verb in the present tense to indicate what these dishes do "today": they "delight the eye before they tantalize the taste buds." This choice ensures proper subject-verb agreement and tense.

Option A is incorrect because "has delighted" is a singular verb form, which does not agree with the plural subject "stunning dishes." This creates a **subject-verb agreement error**.

Option B is incorrect because "delighted" is in the **past tense**, while the sentence requires a present tense verb. The time reference "today" indicates that the action is ongoing in the present, so the verb should reflect this by being in the present tense ("delight"). Using the past tense misaligns with the sentence's intended meaning, making the verb tense incorrect.

Option C is incorrect because "delighting" is a **participle** and does not function as a complete verb in this context. The "that" clause is a dependent clause, which must always contain a verb, and "delighting" alone does not fulfill this requirement, leading to an **improperly structured dependent clause**.

20. Commas: Hard

Answer: A) those with simple, catchy melodies,

Logical Breakdown and Explanation:

This question asks for the choice that correctly completes the sentence while following Standard English punctuation rules, particularly when dealing with nonessential information and prepositional phrases.

Option A is correct because it properly uses commas to set off the nonessential phrase "especially those with simple, catchy melodies." This nonessential phrase provides additional information about the "usual culprits" of earworms, and the final comma correctly closes off the phrase. The use of the comma after the two adjectives "simple" and "catchy" is grammatical: according to the "and" test, if you can insert "and" between two adjectives and the phrase still makes sense, then a comma should be placed between them. In this case, "simple and catchy melodies" works, so a comma is needed between the adjectives.

Option B is incorrect because it violates the **comma rule** regarding nonessential information. When nonessential information appears inside a sentence, it must be enclosed by commas. In this case, "especially those with simple catchy melodies" is nonessential, so a comma is needed at the end to close the phrase. Without this final comma, the sentence is incomplete and grammatically incorrect.

Option C is incorrect because it places a **comma before "with"**, which introduces a prepositional phrase ("with simple, catchy melodies"). A comma is unnecessary before a prepositional phrase that blends with the previous information ("those with simple, catchy melodies"), making this a **violation of comma rules**.

Option D is incorrect because it does not include the necessary comma to close the nonessential phrase at the end of the sentence. Nonessential phrases should be separated by commas, so the omission of the final comma **violates a comma rule.**

21. Modifiers: Easy

Answer: A) fandoms have exploded in the digital age

Logical Breakdown and Explanation:

This question asks for the choice that best completes the sentence without creating any grammatical errors, particularly avoiding dangling modifiers.

Option A is correct because the noun "fandoms" logically modifies the phrase "Once confined to niche communities." The modifying phrase refers to something that was once limited, and "fandoms" fits as the subject that was confined to niche communities before expanding in the digital age. The sentence reads smoothly and makes logical sense.

Option B is incorrect because it creates a **dangling modifier**. The phrase "Once confined to niche communities" suggests that a noun should immediately follow to complete the thought. However, "the explosion of fandoms" does not logically match the initial phrase, making it grammatically incorrect.

Option C is incorrect because it also introduces a **dangling modifier**. The phrase "Once confined to niche communities" should be followed by the noun that was confined. "The digital age" is illogical in this context, as it suggests that the digital age was confined, which doesn't make sense.

Option D is incorrect because "fandoms' explosion" is awkward and creates a **dangling modifier** as well. The structure implies that "fandoms' *explosion*" was once confined, which is not a logical match for the opening phrase.

22. Pronouns: Medium

Answer: B) those

Logical Breakdown and Explanation:

This question asks for the choice that correctly completes the sentence according to Standard English, particularly in terms of pronoun agreement and clarity.

Option B is correct because the structure "those + modifiers" is grammatically acceptable. "Those" functions as a demonstrative pronoun that can be modified by the clause "who've experienced it," making it the correct choice in this sentence. This structure clearly refers to people who have experienced sleep paralysis and maintains grammatical consistency with the rest of the sentence.

Option A is incorrect because "them" is an **object pronoun**, and it is ungrammatical to use an object pronoun with a modifier. You cannot say "*them* who've experienced it" because object pronouns cannot be modified in this way. Instead, a **demonstrative pronoun** like "those" is required when using modifiers to modify the pronoun, making "*those* who've experienced it" the grammatically correct structure.

Option C is incorrect because "one" refers to a singular person, but the sentence later uses the plural pronoun "they're," creating a mismatch in number. This makes **one** grammatically inconsistent with the rest of the sentence.

Option D is incorrect because "they" is a **subject pronoun**, and it cannot be used after a preposition like "for." In this case, the sentence needs a demonstrative pronoun like "those" to follow the preposition and be modified by the clause "who've experienced it."

23. Transitions: Hard

Answer: B) Despite this shift,

Logical Breakdown and Explanation:

This question asks for the most logical transition to complete the sentence and connect the ideas in the paragraph.

Option B is correct because the transition "despite" introduces an unexpected or surprising idea. The passage explains how digital communication has largely replaced handwritten letters, so it's surprising that a small group of enthusiasts still champions letter writing. "Despite" doesn't just show contrast—it highlights the unexpected persistence of this group in the face of a shift toward digital communication. This transition effectively sets up the contrast and surprise that follows.

Option A is incorrect because "To this end" implies that the next sentence will elaborate on a solution or goal related to the previous idea. However, the sentence focuses on a contrasting group of people preserving letter writing, not continuing the trend of digital communication. This makes the transition illogical.

Option C is incorrect because "Instead" implies that the next idea should be a direct alternative to the one mentioned before. However, the small group of enthusiasts isn't an alternative to digital communication; they are a minority keeping a traditional practice alive despite the shift. This makes "Instead" illogical in this context.

Option D is incorrect because "Likewise" suggests similarity between the two ideas. However, the sentence presents a contrast between the dominance of digital communication and the small group dedicated to handwritten letters. Using "Likewise" creates an unclear and nonsensical connection.

24. Transitions: Hard

Answer: A) that is,

Logical Breakdown and Explanation:

This question asks for the most logical transition to complete the sentence and connect the ideas in the paragraph.

Option A is correct because "that is" introduces a clarification or elaboration on the previous statement. The sentence explains that the microorganisms in a starter can change based on the environment, and "that is" signals that what follows is a clarifying example of this concept: a starter thriving in a San Francisco kitchen might struggle in a Parisian bakery. This provides a specific illustration of how environmental factors can affect sourdough starters, making "that is" the most logical transition.

Option B is incorrect because "however" introduces a contrast, which isn't appropriate here. The second sentence isn't contrasting the idea that microorganisms change with the environment; it's clarifying it by offering an example. This makes "however" illogical in this context.

Option C is incorrect because "alternatively" suggests a choice between two possibilities, which doesn't fit the explanation being provided. The sentence is restating the original idea, not presenting an alternative option, making this transition inappropriate.

Option D is incorrect because "rather" is typically used to present an alternative to the topic of the previous statement. In this context, the second sentence is not providing an alternative to the first statement. Instead, it is elaborating on the idea that microorganisms in a sourdough starter change depending on the environment. Since "rather" implies a shift from one idea to another, its use here doesn't logically fit the flow of the passage.

25. Transitions: Medium

Answer: B) as a result,

Logical Breakdown and Explanation:

This question asks for the most logical transition to complete the sentence and connect the ideas in the paragraph.

Option B is correct because "as a result" is used to indicate a **consequence** of the previous statement. The passage explains that our brains become conditioned to expect constant communication, and the natural result of this conditioning is that we might perceive a vibration when none actually exists. This transition logically connects the cause (brain conditioning) to the effect (phantom phone vibrations), making it the most appropriate choice.

Option A is incorrect because "still" is similar to "nevertheless" and is typically used to introduce something unexpected or surprising given the previous statement. However, in this context, the second sentence is not introducing an unexpected idea but rather explaining the logical result of brain conditioning. Since the sentence is not surprising but a natural outcome, using "still" here wouldn't fit.

Option C is incorrect because "moreover" is used to add additional information that reinforces or expands on a point. However, the second sentence is not adding extra information but is explaining the result of the first statement, so "moreover" is inappropriate here.

Option D is incorrect because "furthermore" also adds additional information rather than showing a cause-and-effect relationship. The passage is not expanding on the previous point but explaining a consequence, so "furthermore" is misleading.

26. Rhetorical Synthesis: Medium

Answer: D) The Amazon rainforest contains approximately 100 uncontacted tribes, whereas Papua New Guinea is home to around 40.

Logical Breakdown and Explanation:

This question asks for the choice that most effectively contrasts the number of **uncontacted tribes** in the Amazon rainforest with those in Papua New Guinea, using relevant information from the student's notes.

Option D is correct because it directly contrasts the number of uncontacted tribes in both regions, stating that the Amazon rainforest has approximately 100 uncontacted tribes, while Papua New Guinea is home to around 40. This choice achieves the student's goal of providing a clear comparison based on the relevant notes.

Option A is incorrect because it focuses on the difference between isolated and uncontacted tribes rather than contrasting the number of uncontacted tribes in the two regions. This option does not achieve the goal and provides **irrelevant information**.

Option B is incorrect because it compares the number of **contacted tribes** in both regions, not uncontacted tribes, which is the focus of the student's goal. This makes the information **irrelevant** to the task.

Option C is incorrect because it provides **too much information**, including both contacted and uncontacted tribes. While it mentions the number of uncontacted tribes, it adds unnecessary details about contacted tribes, making it less effective for the specific goal of contrasting uncontacted tribes.

27. Rhetorical Synthesis: Hard

Answer: B) An influential art historian who conducted in-depth studies of Renaissance art, Erwin Panofsky analyzed "The Birth of Venus" by Botticelli by focusing on its symbolic use of mythological elements.

Logical Breakdown and Explanation:

This question asks for the choice that effectively introduces Erwin Panofsky to an audience unfamiliar with him while also emphasizing his analysis of "The Birth of Venus."

Option B is correct because it introduces Panofsky as an **influential art historian** known for his work on Renaissance art, providing context for the audience unfamiliar with him. It then directly emphasizes his analysis of "The Birth of Venus," specifically mentioning that he focused on the painting's symbolic use of mythological elements, which is the key point about his analysis from the notes.

Option A is incorrect because, while it introduces Panofsky and mentions his analysis of "The Birth of Venus," it provides less detail about the analysis itself. It does not emphasize the specific focus on the symbolic use of mythological elements, which is important to highlight according to the notes. This makes it **incomplete** in terms of the focus required and not as effective when compared to option B.

Option C is incorrect because it begins with Panofsky's analysis of "The Birth of Venus" but does not effectively introduce him to an unfamiliar audience. It assumes the audience already knows who he is, making the introduction **insufficient** for someone unfamiliar with his work and only achieving one of the two goals in the question stem.

Option D is incorrect because it not only introduces **irrelevant information** by discussing Panofsky's analysis of "The School of Athens," but it also fails to properly introduce Panofsky to an audience unfamiliar with him. There is no context provided about who Panofsky is, leaving the audience without a clear understanding of his background as an art historian. The lack of introduction and the addition of unnecessary information make this option ineffective for the intended purpose.

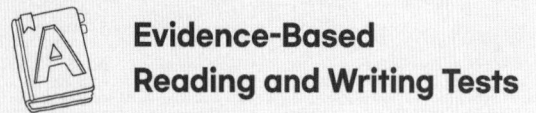

Practice Test

3

Reading and Writing

27 Questions, 32 Minutes

In many rural areas of Timor-Leste, traditional customs dictate various aspects of daily life. The practice of Tara Bandu, for instance, enforces community rules and environmental preservation through symbolic ceremonies. While Tara Bandu can help to _____ a sense of communal responsibility and environmental stewardship, rapid modernization and global cultural influences sometimes clash with these traditions, creating a complex social landscape.

1

Which choice completes the text with the most logical and precise word or phrase?

A) engender

B) mitigate

C) undermine

D) repudiate

CONTINUE

Educational research has shown that traditional methods of classroom instruction often have minimal impact on improving students' critical thinking skills, but these methods are not as _____ as this finding seems to suggest. Studies indicate that traditional instruction can provide a solid foundation of knowledge upon which more advanced skills can be built.

Which choice completes the text with the most logical and precise word or phrase?

A) outdated

B) biased

C) ineffectual

D) indisputable

In the realm of contemporary literature, many authors draw upon mythological themes to enrich their narratives. Norwegian writer Sigrid Undset, for instance, skillfully wove Norse mythology into her historical novels, thereby creating a vivid cultural tapestry. Similarly, Nigerian author Chimamanda Ngozi Adichie, known for her powerful storytelling, _____ Igbo folklore with contemporary issues, which resulted in critically acclaimed works.

Which choice completes the text with the most logical and precise word or phrase?

A) disregarded

B) integrated

C) compared

D) obfuscated

CONTINUE

Without significant economic reforms, we are unlikely to ever have _____ resolution to the ongoing unemployment crisis in many Middle Eastern countries. Issues such as persistent corruption, inadequate infrastructure investment, and political instability continue to impede progress, leaving the problem complex and unresolved.

Which choice completes the text with the most logical and precise word or phrase?

- A) a temporary
- B) a definitive
- C) a superficial
- D) a grandiose

In Marrakech, a city known for its busy marketplaces, the vivid tapestries and intricate pottery attract many tourists, admired for their craftsmanship and vibrant colors. However, the market experience is particularly _____ because of the lively interactions between vendors and customers, the aromatic scents of spices, and the melodic calls to prayer echoing through the air. These sensory elements combine to create a deeply immersive and emotionally rich atmosphere.

Which choice completes the text with the most logical and precise word or phrase?

- A) perplexing
- B) mundane
- C) prestigious
- D) affecting

CONTINUE

In 1840, the Treaty of Waitangi was signed between representatives of the British Crown, led by Captain William Hobson, and various Māori chiefs, including Hone Heke and Tamati Waka Nene. The treaty aimed to establish a legal framework for British settlement while recognizing Māori land ownership and granting them the rights of British subjects. However, the interpretation and implementation of the treaty have been contentious, leading to numerous land disputes and conflicts, such as the New Zealand Wars. Over the years, the Waitangi Tribunal was established to address grievances and ensure the treaty's promises were honored.

6

Which choice best states the main purpose of the text?

A) To evaluate the Treaty of Waitangi by considering its intentions and subsequent challenges

B) To detail the ongoing disputes and conflicts resulting from the Treaty of Waitangi

C) To question the validity of the Treaty of Waitangi and its historical significance

D) To catalogue the events leading up to the signing of the Treaty of Waitangi

CONTINUE

The following text is from the poem "The Sad Mother" by Gabriela Mistral, a Chilean poet.

> Sleep, sleep, my beloved,
> without worry, without fear,
> although my soul does not sleep,
> although I do not rest.
>
> Sleep, sleep, and in the night
> may your whispers be softer
> than a leaf of grass,
> or the sounds you make when you sigh.
>
> Now fly, gentle breath,
> rest in the river's silver,
> and in my arms, sleep deep,
> as the silent river passes by.

7

Which choice best describes the overall structure of the text?

A) It presents a series of commands, followed by expressions of longing

B) It gives assurances of safety and comfort, then describes a peaceful scene

C) It describes the natural environment, then explains its impact on the speaker's emotions

D) It introduces a moment of separation, then reflects on the pain it causes

CONTINUE

The phenomenon of Venice's sinking is often attributed to the city's unique construction on wooden pilings submerged in water. However, simply attributing the sinking to this feature is overly simplistic. The sinking of Venice involves a complex interplay of factors: as geologist Dr. Maria Rossi explains, these include the extraction of groundwater, the natural settling of sediments, and the rising sea levels due to climate change. While efforts have been made to address one or more of these issues, such as halting groundwater extraction, the multifaceted nature of the problem makes it challenging to find a comprehensive solution.

8

Which choice best describes the function of the underlined portion in the text as a whole?

A) It introduces a new hypothesis about the causes of Venice's sinking.

B) It contradicts a statement made previously in the sentence.

C) It offers a more comprehensive perspective on an issue mentioned earlier in the text.

D) It provides evidence that is later refuted in the text.

CONTINUE

The Rongorongo script of Easter Island remains one of the world's most mysterious writing systems. Discovered in the 19th century, Rongorongo consists of glyphs that were carved on wooden tablets. One notable glyph depicts a bird with a human head, believed by some scholars to represent a deity or important figure in Rapa Nui culture. Despite numerous attempts by linguists and historians, the script remains undeciphered, and its purpose and meaning are still unknown: some scholars believe it was used for religious or ceremonial purposes; others suggest it could have been a form of record-keeping; still others surmise that the script may have been used as a mnemonic device for teaching or oral storytelling. The tablets were found in various locations on the island, suggesting they had significant cultural importance to the Rapa Nui people.

9

According to the text, what is true about the Rongorongo script?

A) The Rongorongo script was deciphered in the 19th century when it was first discovered.

B) Some scholars believe that the Rongorongo script was primarily used for trade and commerce.

C) It has not been successfully interpreted, with scholars proposing various theories about its use.

D) The script was written on stone tablets and was used by other civilizations outside Easter Island.

Practice Test 3

CONTINUE

333

Text 1

Psychologists have long been intrigued by how different personality traits can coexist and thrive within a social environment. According to popular convention, certain dominant personality traits should emerge as more successful, outcompeting and overshadowing others. So why do a variety of personality traits continue to coexist within communities? Psychologists' numerous studies to explain this phenomenon still haven't uncovered a satisfactory explanation.

Text 2

Psychologist Dr. Carol Dweck and her colleagues have linked the diversity of personality traits to the concept of mindset. Dweck's research distinguishes between fixed and growth mindsets—beliefs about the malleability of personal attributes. People with a growth mindset view traits and abilities as improvable through effort and experience, while those with a fixed mindset see them as static. This distinction, says Dweck's team, creates a diverse range of behaviors and interactions that reduce direct competition among different personality types, as individuals focus more on personal growth rather than dominance.

10

Based on the texts, how would Dr. Carol Dweck and colleagues (Text 2) most likely respond to the "popular convention" discussed in Text 1?

A) By pointing out that it misunderstands how personality traits coexist and interact within social environments

B) By criticizing its limitations and ignoring the impact of social environments on the development of dominant personality traits

C) By asserting that it is accurate and correctly identifies how dominant personality traits become more successful than others

D) By demanding that it acknowledges the superiority of fixed mindsets in fostering dominant personality traits

CONTINUE

Creating antimatter begins by using a particle accelerator like the Large Hadron Collider (LHC) to collide protons at high speeds, producing antiprotons. These antiprotons are captured in Penning traps using electric and magnetic fields to prevent annihilation. They are then cooled to extremely low temperatures and combined with positrons to form antihydrogen. This requires incredibly precise instrumentation and control, as even the slightest contamination with matter could destroy the precious antimatter, making the process both a scientific and engineering marvel.

11

Which choice best states the main idea of the text?

A) The Large Hadron Collider (LHC) is used to collide protons at high speeds to produce antiprotons.

B) The process of creating antimatter involves capturing antiprotons in Penning traps and cooling them to form antihydrogen.

C) Creating antimatter requires expensive instrumentation, making it a costly scientific marvel

D) Creating antimatter through the process of producing and managing antiprotons involves extreme precision and control.

Practice Test 3

CONTINUE

335

"Cool Runnings" is a 1993 sports comedy film directed by Jon Turteltaub. The movie tells the uplifting true story of the first Jamaican bobsled team and their journey to compete in the 1988 Winter Olympics. Critics have praised the film for its heartwarming narrative and the compelling performances of its cast: _____

12

Which quote from a movie review most effectively illustrates the claim?

A) "The cinematography beautifully captures the snowy landscapes of Calgary, highlighting the contrast with the Jamaican team's tropical origins."

B) "The scene where the team members rally together after a devastating crash, lifting their sled and walking to the finish line, showcases the film's emotional core."

C) "John Candy's portrayal of the disgraced coach turned unlikely mentor provides depth to the story, but some of the supporting characters lacked development."

D) "While some of the jokes fell flat, the film's musical score did an excellent job of setting the tone for both comedic and serious moments."

CONTINUE

Health Markers after 6 Months
on Different Diets

Health Marker	Mean rating for participants on a plant-based diet	Mean rating for participants on a keto diet	Mean rating for participants on a paleo diet
Cholesterol level reduction	20%	15%	18%
Weight loss	12 pounds	15 pounds	14 pounds
Blood pressure improvement	10%	8%	12%

To evaluate the effectiveness of different diets on health markers, a research team conducted a study comparing the outcomes of participants following a plant-based diet, a keto diet, and a paleo diet. The study measured several health markers after six months. Higher percentages and greater weight loss indicate better outcomes in each measure. Compared to the mean ratings after 6 months for participants on a keto diet, the mean ratings for participants _____

Which choice most effectively uses data from the table to complete the statement?

A) on a plant-based diet were higher for cholesterol reduction but lower for weight loss.

B) on a paleo diet were lower across all three health markers.

C) on a plant-based diet were higher across all health markers.

D) on both the plant-based and paleo diets were higher in terms of weight loss.

CONTINUE ➡

Renewable Energy Projects and
Their Characteristics

Project Name	Energy Output (MW)	Type of Renewable Energy
Three Gorges Dam	22,500 MW	Hydroelectric
Alta Wind Energy Center	1,550 MW	Wind
London Array	630 MW	Offshore Wind
Ivanpah Solar Facility	392 MW	Solar Thermal

Renewable energy projects play a critical role in transitioning away from fossil fuels and mitigating climate change. These projects vary significantly in scale and type, ranging from massive hydroelectric dams to cutting-edge solar and wind installations. When evaluating these projects, researchers often emphasize the importance of energy output and the type of renewable energy used. Among the projects listed, the one with the highest energy output is the _____.

14

Which choice most effectively uses data from the table to complete the statement?

A) Alta Wind Energy Center, which is a wind energy project with an energy output of 1,550 MW

B) Three Gorges Dam, with an energy output of 22,500 MW, which is an offshore wind project

C) Three Gorges Dam, which is a hydroelectric project with an energy output of 22,500 MW

D) Ivanpah Solar Facility, with an energy output of 392 MW, which is a solar thermal project

CONTINUE

Hypothesizing that humans could possess the unique ability of echolocation—the ability to navigate and identify objects by producing sounds and listening to the echoes that bounce back—Dr. Lore Thaler carefully trained a group of twenty participants in echolocation techniques. Another group of twenty participants, who did not receive any echolocation training, served as the control group. Both groups were then tested in a dark maze, designed to assess their ability to navigate and identify objects without any visual cues. Dr. Thaler found that the echolocation-trained participants and the control group had similar success rates, concluding that humans are unable to develop the ability of echolocation.

15

Which finding, if true, would most directly weaken the researcher's conclusion?

A) Participants who received echolocation training were, on average, 15 years younger than those in the control group.

B) It was later revealed that a vast majority of participants in the control group received echolocation training prior to the experiment.

C) Statistical analysis revealed that the maze completion times for both groups had a standard deviation of 2.5 minutes.

D) The participants who received training from Dr. Thaler in echolocation techniques were trained for two weeks.

CONTINUE

Each year, sandhill cranes embark on a breathtaking migration, traveling from their breeding grounds in the northern U.S. and Canada to their wintering habitats in the southern United States and Mexico. What's truly captivating about _____ is not just the distance they cover, but the elaborate courtship dances they perform upon arrival—cranes bow, leap into the air, and flap their wings, a ritual that strengthens pair bonds and has been observed by ornithologists for decades.

Although it may seem like a simple yearning, nostalgia serves a complex psychological function: it helps individuals connect their past with their present. Studies have shown that when people feel nostalgic, they tend to view their lives with greater _____ their self-esteem and reduce feelings of loneliness. However, it's important not to dwell too much on what has been lost; while nostalgia can be comforting, living too much in the past can hinder one's ability to move forward.

16

Which choice completes the text so that it conforms to the conventions of Standard English?

A) these

B) them

C) it

D) these birds

17

Which choice completes the text so that it conforms to the conventions of Standard English?

A) positivity, which boosting

B) positivity, boosting

C) positivity, which can boost

D) positivity and boost

CONTINUE ➡

Black Friday, which occurs the day after Thanksgiving in the United States, has transformed from a simple shopping day into a cultural phenomenon that reflects consumer behavior and economic trends. Retailers offer steep _____ eager to take advantage of the deals, flood stores and websites in search of the best bargains.

18

Which choice completes the text so that it conforms to the conventions of Standard English?

A) discounts, and shoppers,

B) discounts, and shoppers

C) discounts and shoppers,

D) discounts and, shoppers

Daydreaming, often dismissed as a distraction, has been shown to have surprising cognitive benefits. When a person's mind wanders, they're not merely wasting _____ they're engaging in mental processes that can enhance creativity, problem-solving, and even empathy. Research suggests that the brain remains highly active during daydreaming, processing unresolved thoughts and emotions in the background.

19

Which choice completes the text so that it conforms to the conventions of Standard English?

A) time, instead,

B) time, instead;

C) time instead,

D) time; instead,

CONTINUE

Named after the American _____ Rube Goldberg machines are elaborate contraptions designed to perform a simple task in an overly complicated way. These machines often involve a series of chain reactions—each triggering the next in a whimsical, often unpredictable sequence. Despite their complexity, or perhaps because of it, Rube Goldberg machines have captivated the public's imagination for decades. Engineers, artists, and tinkerers alike enjoy the challenge of creating these intricate devices, which require both precision and creativity.

Which choice completes the text so that it conforms to the conventions of Standard English?

A) cartoonist, who popularized them,

B) cartoonist who popularized them—

C) cartoonist, who popularized them

D) cartoonist who popularized them,

Escape rooms, immersive experiences where participants solve puzzles to "escape" within a set time limit, _____ a global phenomenon in recent years. These rooms, often themed around mysteries or adventures, challenge participants to work together, think critically, and use their problem-solving skills under pressure.

Which choice completes the text so that it conforms to the conventions of Standard English?

A) have become

B) has become

C) and are becoming

D) becoming

CONTINUE

Color has a profound effect on human mood and behavior. Warm colors like red and yellow, _____ can evoke feelings of warmth and comfort, while cooler hues like blue and green often induce a sense of calm. This connection between color and emotion is why interior designers and marketers carefully consider color choices in their work; they know that the right palette can significantly influence how a space or product is perceived.

22

Which choice completes the text with the most logical transition?

A) though,

B) for instance,

C) moreover,

D) therefore,

Synchronized fireflies (found in certain regions of Southeast Asia) create one of nature's most mesmerizing displays by flashing their lights in unison. These fireflies, _____ are not just performing a random light show: their synchronization is a form of communication, primarily used to attract mates. While scientists have studied this phenomenon for years, the exact mechanisms that allow thousands of fireflies to synchronize so perfectly remain partially understood.

23

Which choice completes the text with the most logical transition?

A) however,

B) instead,

C) consequently,

D) similarly,

Practice Test 3

CONTINUE

343

Deep-sea gigantism, a phenomenon where marine animals grow to unusually large sizes, has puzzled scientists for decades. Because of the extreme pressures, frigid temperatures, and scarcity of food at these depths, one might expect smaller creatures to dominate the deep ocean. _____ giant squids, colossal crabs, and enormous isopods thrive in these harsh environments;

24

Which choice completes the text with the most logical transition?

A) Yet,

B) Additionally,

C) Hence,

D) Eventually,

The "runner's high" is a well-known phenomenon where long-distance runners experience a euphoric state, typically after intense physical exertion. This sensation, however, is not just a psychological effect. _____ it's caused by the release of endorphins and other neurotransmitters in the brain that reduce pain and promote a feeling of well-being.

25

Which choice completes the text with the most logical transition?

A) In other words,

B) Accordingly,

C) Rather,

D) Thus,

CONTINUE

While researching a topic, a student has taken the following notes:

- George Washington served as the first President of the United States from 1789 to 1797.
- Washington is known for his leadership during the American Revolutionary War.
- Abraham Lincoln served as the 16th President of the United States from 1861 to 1865.
- Lincoln is famous for leading the country during the Civil War and issuing the Emancipation Proclamation.
- Washington was a key figure in the drafting of the U.S. Constitution.
- Lincoln delivered the Gettysburg Address in 1863.

26

The student wants to provide specific details that compare the presidential achievements of George Washington and Abraham Lincoln. Which choice most effectively uses relevant information from the notes to accomplish this goal?

A) George Washington served as the first President of the United States during the 18th century, while Abraham Lincoln served as the 16th President during the 19th century.

B) Both George Washington and Abraham Lincoln played crucial roles during times of war.

C) George Washington played a prominent role in drafting the U.S. Constitution; likewise, Abraham Lincoln is known for issuing the Emancipation Proclamation.

D) As the 16th President of the United States, Abraham Lincoln led the country during the Civil War, issued the Emancipation Proclamation, and delivered the Gettysburg Address.

CONTINUE

While researching a topic, a student has taken the following notes:

- British archaeologist Howard Carter led the excavation of King Tutankhamun's tomb in the Valley of the Kings in 1922.
- King Tutankhamun, often referred to as "King Tut," ruled Egypt during the 18th dynasty, around 1332-1323 BC.
- The tomb was found largely intact, filled with treasures and over 5,000 artifacts, including the famous gold funerary mask.
- The discovery provided unprecedented insight into Ancient Egyptian burial practices and the wealth of the Pharaohs.
- The tomb's discovery sparked worldwide interest in Egyptology, with thousands of scholars engaging in further study.

27

Which choice most effectively uses information from the given sentences to emphasize the knowledge that was gained from the discovery of King Tutankhamun's tomb?

A)   The largely intact tomb provided an unprecedented look into the burial practices and material wealth of Ancient Egypt's Pharaohs.

B)   The tomb, excavated by British archaeologist Howard Carter in 1922, was found largely intact and contained the famous gold funerary mask of King Tutankhamun.

C)   King Tut was buried with over 5,000 artifacts and countless treasures, showcasing the wealth of the Pharaohs and offering new insights into Ancient Egyptian burial practices.

D)   The discovery of the tomb not only contained over 5,000 artifacts but also sparked a worldwide fascination with Egyptology, leading thousands of scholars to further study Ancient Egyptian history.

If you finish before the time is called, you may check your work on this module only.
On Test Day, you will only be able to move to the next module when time expires.

Answer Key

Question Number	Correct Answer	Level of Difficulty	Question Type
1	A	Medium	**Craft and Structure:** *Words in Context*
2	C	Easy	**Craft and Structure:** *Words in Context*
3	B	Medium	**Craft and Structure:** *Words in Context*
4	B	Easy	**Craft and Structure:** *Words in Context*
5	D	Hard	**Craft and Structure:** *Words in Context*
6	A	Medium	**Craft and Structure:** *Main Purpose*
7	B	Medium	**Craft and Structure:** *Overall Structure*
8	C	Hard	**Craft and Structure:** *Function of the Underlined Portion*
9	C	Medium	**Information and Ideas:** *Detail*
10	A	Hard	**Craft and Structure:** *Cross-Text Connections*
11	D	Medium	**Information and Ideas:** *Main Idea*
12	B	Easy	**Information and Ideas:** *Cite Text as Evidence*
13	A	Medium	**Information and Ideas:** *Cite Text as Evidence (Infographics)*

Question Number	Correct Answer	Level of Difficulty	Question Type
14	C	Easy	**Information and Ideas:** *Support a Claim (Infographics)*
15	B	Hard	**Information and Ideas:** *Weaken a Claim*
16	D	Easy	**Standard English Conventions:** *Pronouns*
17	C	Medium	**Standard English Conventions:** *Sentence Structure*
18	A	Hard	**Standard English Conventions:** *Commas*
19	D	Medium	**Standard English Conventions:** *Punctuation and Sentence Structure*
20	D	Easy	**Standard English Conventions:** *Punctuation*
21	A	Medium	**Standard English Conventions:** *Verbs*
22	B	Easy	**Expression of Ideas:** *Transitions*
23	A	Medium	**Expression of Ideas:** *Transitions*
24	A	Medium	**Expression of Ideas:** *Transitions*
25	C	Medium	**Expression of Ideas:** *Transitions*
26	C	Medium	**Expression of Ideas:** *Rhetorical Synthesis*
27	A	Hard	**Expression of Ideas:** *Rhetorical Synthesis*

Instructions

Count the number of questions you got correct in Module 1.

Enter your score here: _____.

If your score is **18 or higher**, move on to the **HARD version** of Module 2.

If your score is **below 18**, proceed to the **EASY version** of Module 2.

Explanations

1. Words in Context: Medium

Answer: A) engender

Step-by-Step Explanation:

1. Let's look at what the passage is saying. The passage describes how traditional customs, such as the practice of Tara Bandu in Timor-Leste, play an important role in enforcing community rules and environmental preservation. The passage also mentions that Tara Bandu can help foster certain positive outcomes, even though modernization and global cultural influences sometimes clash with these traditions.

2. Notice the phrases "dictate" and "enforces," which show that Tara Bandu actively promotes values like communal responsibility and environmental stewardship. The passage also mentions that Tara Bandu "can help to" foster these outcomes, suggesting it's a positive force in the community.

3. Thus, the word we need should reflect the idea of helping to create a sense of responsibility and stewardship in the community.

4. Ask yourself, what word best describes the act of creating or fostering something? "Engender" is the most logical choice because it means to cause or give rise to something, which fits the context of Tara Bandu helping to develop a sense of communal responsibility and environmental stewardship.

Explanation of Incorrect Options:

B) **mitigate:** This is incorrect because it means to make something less severe, which doesn't fit the context of creating or fostering a sense of responsibility and stewardship.

C) **undermine:** This is incorrect because it means to weaken or damage something, which is the opposite of what the passage suggests Tara Bandu is doing.

D) repudiate: This is incorrect because it means to reject or disown something, which does not make logical sense given the context in the passage about Tara Bandu fostering positive communal values.

2. Words in Context: Easy

Answer: C) ineffectual

Step-by-Step Explanation:

1. Let's deconstruct the passage together. The passage discusses how traditional classroom instruction methods are often found to have minimal impact on improving critical thinking skills. However, it also suggests that these methods are not completely ineffective because they provide a solid foundation for more advanced skills.
2. Notice the contrast in the passage: it starts by acknowledging the minimal impact of traditional methods on critical thinking but then argues that these methods still have value in building foundational knowledge. This implies that while traditional methods might not be the best for developing critical thinking, they are not entirely without merit.
3. The word we need should reflect the idea that traditional methods are not completely ineffective or useless, even if they aren't the most effective for critical thinking.
4. "Ineffectual" is the most logical choice because it means not producing the desired effect, which aligns with the passage's point that traditional methods may not be ideal for critical thinking but still have some value.

Explanation of Incorrect Options:

A) outdated: This is incorrect because it suggests that traditional methods are obsolete or old-fashioned, but the passage is discussing their effectiveness, not their relevance over time. So, this option is irrelevant given the information in the passage.

B) biased: This is incorrect because it refers to an unfair preference or prejudice, which does not fit the context of discussing the effectiveness of teaching methods.

D) indisputable: This is incorrect because it means something that cannot be argued or questioned, which contradicts the passage's discussion of the debated impact of traditional methods.

3. Words in Context: Medium

Answer: B) integrated

Step-by-Step Explanation:

1. Let's understand the passage together. The passage discusses how authors often use mythological themes to enhance their stories. It mentions Sigrid Undset, who incorporated Norse mythology into her novels, and then shifts to Nigerian author Chimamanda Ngozi Adichie, noting how she uses Igbo folklore alongside contemporary issues in her works.
2. Notice the transition "Similarly" at the beginning of the sentence discussing Adichie. This transition suggests that, like Undset, Adichie also blends cultural elements into her writing. The passage implies that Adichie skillfully combines Igbo folklore with modern themes, just as Undset wove Norse mythology into her historical novels.
3. Therefore, the word we need should describe how Adichie incorporates or combines Igbo folklore with contemporary issues in a way that contributes to her critically acclaimed works.
4. "Integrated" is the most logical choice because it means to combine or incorporate different elements into a whole, which fits perfectly with the idea of Adichie blending traditional folklore with modern themes in her writing.

Explanation of Incorrect Options:

A) disregarded: This is incorrect because it means to ignore or pay no attention to, which contradicts the passage's emphasis on how Adichie uses Igbo folklore in her works.

C) compared: This is incorrect because it suggests analyzing the similarities or differences between two things, which does not fit the context of blending folklore with contemporary issues.

D) obfuscated: This is incorrect because it means to make something unclear or obscure, which does not make logical sense given the passage's idea of effectively incorporating folklore into her narratives.

4. Words in Context: Easy

Answer: B) a definitive

Step-by-Step Explanation:

1. The passage discusses the ongoing unemployment crisis in many Middle Eastern countries and emphasizes that, without significant economic reforms, resolving this crisis will be difficult. It mentions persistent issues like corruption, inadequate infrastructure investment, and political instability that complicate the situation and prevent a straightforward solution.

2. Notice the focus on the complexity and unresolved nature of the problem, which suggests that the passage is discussing the need for a thorough and lasting solution, rather than a quick or partial fix.

3. Hence, the word we need should describe a resolution that is complete and conclusive, as the passage implies that only significant reforms can lead to a real solution to the crisis.

4. "A definitive" is the most logical choice because it means a final, complete, and conclusive solution, which aligns with the passage's emphasis on the need for significant reforms to fully resolve the crisis.

Explanation of Incorrect Options:

A) a temporary: This is incorrect because it implies a short-term solution, which contradicts the passage's emphasis on the need for a lasting resolution.

C) a superficial: This is incorrect because it suggests a solution that is only on the surface and not thorough, which does not fit the context of seeking a comprehensive solution to the crisis.

D) a grandiose: This is incorrect because it means overly elaborate or ambitious, which does not align with the passage's focus on finding an effective and conclusive resolution.

5. Interpreting Words in Context: Hard

Answer: D) affecting

Step-by-Step Explanation:

1. The passage describes the bustling and sensory-rich experience of the marketplaces in Marrakech. It highlights the vivid tapestries, intricate pottery, lively interactions between vendors and customers, aromatic scents of spices, and the melodic calls to prayer—all contributing to an immersive and emotionally rich atmosphere.

2. Notice the emphasis on how the marketplace experience is "particularly" something, due to these sensory and emotionally engaging elements. The passage suggests that the experience is not just visually stimulating but also deeply impactful on an emotional level.

3. Thus, the word we need should describe an experience that has a strong emotional impact on a person, aligning with the immersive and rich atmosphere described.

4. "Affecting" is the most logical choice because it means having a strong emotional impact, which fits perfectly with the description of the marketplace as a deeply immersive and emotionally rich environment.

Explanation of Incorrect Options:

A) perplexing: This is incorrect because it means confusing or puzzling, which does not match the context of the marketplace being emotionally rich and immersive.

B) mundane: This is incorrect because it means ordinary or dull, which is the opposite of the vibrant and emotionally engaging experience described in the passage.

C) prestigious: This is incorrect because it means having high status or respect, which doesn't align with the context of the marketplace experience being emotionally impactful.

6. Main Purpose: Medium

Answer: A) To evaluate the Treaty of Waitangi by considering its intentions and subsequent challenges

Logical Breakdown and Explanation:

This question requires identifying the primary purpose of the text, which discusses the Treaty of Waitangi, its initial intentions, and the challenges that arose from it.

Option A is correct because the text evaluates the Treaty of Waitangi by explaining both its intentions (establishing a legal framework for British settlement and recognizing Māori land rights) and the subsequent challenges (land disputes and conflicts such as the New Zealand Wars). The mention of the Waitangi Tribunal emphasizes the ongoing efforts to address these challenges, making this option the most comprehensive reflection of the text's purpose.

Option B is incorrect because it focuses exclusively on disputes and conflicts resulting from the treaty, which are only a part of the text's overall discussion. The text does not solely detail disputes but also addresses the treaty's initial goals and the attempts to resolve issues through the Waitangi Tribunal. This makes the option too narrow in scope.

Option C is incorrect because the text does not question the treaty's validity or its historical significance. Instead, it presents an evaluation of the treaty's challenges and the steps taken to address them, which is different from undermining its importance.

Option D is incorrect because the text does not focus on cataloging the events leading up to the signing of the treaty. Instead, it discusses the treaty's implications, its contested interpretation, and the actions taken to resolve its challenges, making this option irrelevant to the main purpose.

7. Overall Structure: Medium

Answer: B) It gives assurances of safety and comfort, then describes a peaceful scene

Logical Breakdown and Explanation:

This question requires identifying the structure of the poem by focusing on how its ideas develop and how the tone shifts from one part to another.

Option B is correct because the poem begins by providing assurances of safety and comfort, with the speaker telling the beloved to "sleep, sleep, my beloved, without worry, without fear." The second part of the poem transitions into describing a peaceful and gentle scene, with imagery like "whispers softer than a leaf of grass" and "rest in the river's silver." This progression from comforting the beloved to describing a peaceful atmosphere reflects the poem's overall structure.

Option A is incorrect because the poem does not consist of commands followed by expressions of longing. Instead, the speaker offers soothing assurances and describes a calm, peaceful scene. This makes Option A an **inaccurate** representation of the poem's structure.

Option C is incorrect because, while the poem uses some natural imagery, it does not describe how the environment impacts the speaker's emotions. The focus is more on providing comfort and describing peace, making this option **irrelevant** to the poem's actual structure.

Option D is incorrect because the poem does not introduce a moment of separation or reflect on the pain caused by it. Instead, it centers on providing reassurance and describing a peaceful setting. This option introduces **off-topic** ideas that are not present in the poem.

8. Function of the Underlined Portion: Hard

Answer: C) It offers a more comprehensive perspective on an issue mentioned earlier in the text.

Logical Breakdown and Explanation:

This question requires identifying the function of the underlined portion in relation to the larger text.

Option C is correct because the underlined portion offers a more complete explanation of Venice's sinking, expanding on the oversimplified idea that Venice's construction on wooden pilings is the sole cause. It introduces other contributing factors, such as groundwater extraction, sediment settling, and rising sea levels. This provides a more nuanced and detailed understanding of the issue.

Option A is incorrect because the underlined portion does not introduce a new hypothesis; instead, it builds on and expands the initial statement by adding more factors that contribute to the sinking of Venice. This makes **Option A** a misinterpretation of the text's function.

Option B is incorrect because the underlined portion does not contradict the previous statement. It elaborates on the initial idea rather than presenting an opposing argument, making this option **illogical**.

Option D is incorrect because the underlined portion is not later refuted. The text continues to support the more comprehensive explanation provided by the underlined section, so this option introduces an **irrelevant** idea.

9. Detail: Medium

Answer: C) It has not been successfully interpreted, with scholars proposing various theories about its use.

Logical Breakdown and Explanation:

This question requires identifying a fact about the Rongorongo script based on the text, focusing on its current undeciphered status and the various theories regarding its use.

Option C is correct because the text explicitly states that the Rongorongo script has not been deciphered and that scholars have proposed different theories about its use, including religious purposes, record-keeping, and as a mnemonic device. This matches the key points provided in the passage.

Option A is incorrect because the text clearly states that the script remains undeciphered, contradicting the idea that it was deciphered in the 19th century. This makes **Option A factually inaccurate**.

Option B is incorrect because there is no mention of trade or commerce in the text. The suggested uses of the script focus on cultural, religious, or educational purposes, making this option **irrelevant** to the text.

Option D is incorrect because nowhere in the text does it indicate that the script was used by other civilizations. Although the tablets were found in various locations, it doesn't mean other civilizations used them. This makes **Option D unsupported** by the information provided.

10. Cross-Text Connections: Hard

Answer: A) By pointing out that it misunderstands how personality traits coexist and interact within social environments

Logical Breakdown and Explanation:

This question requires identifying how Dr. Dweck and her colleagues would respond to the idea that dominant personality traits should outcompete and overshadow others, as mentioned in Text 1.

Option A is correct because Dr. Dweck's research challenges the notion that dominant traits should emerge as more successful. Instead, she argues that a diversity of personality traits is maintained because people with a growth mindset focus on personal growth rather than direct competition. This directly opposes the popular convention presented in Text 1.

Option B is incorrect because, while Dweck's research emphasizes the importance of mindset in personality development, there is no direct criticism of how social environments impact dominant traits. This makes **Option B partially correct** but ultimately off-topic.

Option C is incorrect because Dweck would not support the popular convention that dominant traits should overshadow others. Her research promotes diversity in personality traits and behaviors, making **Option C a contradiction** of her findings.

Option D is incorrect because Dweck's research does not promote fixed mindsets as superior. Instead, it highlights the benefits of a growth mindset in maintaining a variety of personality traits. This makes **Option D factually inaccurate**.

11. Main Idea: Medium

Answer: D) Creating antimatter through the process of producing and managing antiprotons involves extreme precision and control.

Logical Breakdown and Explanation:

This question asks for the option that best summarizes the main idea of the text, which describes the process of creating antimatter.

Option D is correct because it captures **the major ideas** of the text: creating antimatter involves producing antiprotons, capturing them in Penning traps, and cooling them to form antihydrogen. The text emphasizes the extreme precision and control required to manage the process, as contamination with matter could destroy the antimatter. This choice effectively encapsulates the process mentioned in the text.

Option A is incorrect because it focuses only on the first step of the process (colliding protons at high speeds) without mentioning the more critical details about capturing and cooling antiprotons, which are essential to creating antimatter. This option does not fully represent the complexity of the process, making it **incomplete** and focused too much on **minor details.**

Option B is incorrect because it describes part of the process—capturing antiprotons and cooling them—but it does not emphasize the extreme precision and control needed, which is a significant aspect of the text. This makes **Option B partially correct** but lacking the full picture.

Option C is incorrect because, while it mentions expensive instrumentation, the text focuses more on the precision and control required in the process rather than the cost of equipment. This makes **Option C off-topic** in relation to the text's main point.

12. Cite Text as Evidence: Easy

Answer: B) "The scene where the team members rally together after a devastating crash, lifting their sled and walking to the finish line, showcases the film's emotional core."

Logical Breakdown and Explanation:

This question requires selecting the quote that best reflects the claim that critics have praised *Cool Runnings* for its **heartwarming narrative** and **compelling performances**.

Option B is correct because it highlights a pivotal moment in the film—"the team members rally together after a devastating crash"—which showcases the emotional core of the story. The scene emphasizes the team's perseverance and unity, which contributes to the heartwarming narrative praised by critics.

Option A is incorrect because it focuses on the **cinematography** of the film, specifically the contrast between the snowy landscapes of Calgary and the team's tropical origins. While visually striking, this does not address the emotional or narrative aspects that critics highlighted, making this option **irrelevant** to the claim.

Option C is incorrect because it discusses John Candy's performance as the coach but introduces a critique about the development of the supporting characters. While John Candy's portrayal may be compelling, the negative comment about the supporting cast detracts from the overall praise. This makes the option **off-topic**.

Option D is incorrect because it focuses on the **musical score** rather than the heartwarming narrative or the performances of the cast. This option is **irrelevant** to the main point of the claim.

13. Cite Text as Evidence (Infographics): Medium

Answer: A) on a plant-based diet were higher for cholesterol reduction but lower for weight loss.

Logical Breakdown and Explanation:

This question requires selecting the option that accurately reflects the data from the table, comparing participants on a plant-based diet with those on a keto diet.

Option A is correct because the data shows that participants on a plant-based diet had a **higher cholesterol reduction** (20% vs. 15% for keto) but **lower weight loss** (12 pounds vs. 15 pounds for keto). This accurately matches the data presented in the table, making it the most effective completion of the statement.

Option B is incorrect because the data does not show that the paleo diet was lower across all three health markers. In fact, the paleo diet had **higher weight loss** than the plant-based diet (14 pounds vs. 12 pounds) and higher blood pressure improvement (12% vs. 10%). This makes **Option B factually incorrect**.

Option C is incorrect because participants on a plant-based diet did not have higher ratings across all health markers. They had higher cholesterol reduction but **lower weight loss** than the keto diet, making **Option C inaccurate**.

Option D is incorrect because participants on the plant-based diet did not have higher weight loss than those on the keto diet (12 pounds vs. 15 pounds). This makes **Option D incorrect based on the data**.

14. Support a Claim (Infographics): Easy

Answer: C) Three Gorges Dam, which is a hydroelectric project with an energy output of 22,500 MW.

Logical Breakdown and Explanation:

This question requires identifying which renewable energy project has the highest energy output based on the data in the table.

Option C is correct because the **Three Gorges Dam** is a **hydroelectric project** with an energy output of **22,500 MW**, making it the project with the highest energy output among those listed in the table. This option correctly reflects both the type of energy and the output.

Option A is incorrect because, while the Alta Wind Energy Center has a significant output (1,550 MW), it is not the highest on the list. The Three Gorges Dam has a much larger output of 22,500 MW, making **Option A factually incorrect**.

Option B is incorrect because it inaccurately states that the Three Gorges Dam is an **offshore wind project**, when it is actually a **hydroelectric project**. This makes **Option B factually inaccurate**.

Option D is incorrect because the **Ivanpah Solar Facility** has an energy output of **392 MW**, which is much lower than the Three Gorges Dam's 22,500 MW. This makes **Option D incorrect** in terms of output.

15. Weaken a Claim: Hard

Answer: B) It was later revealed that a vast majority of participants in the control group received echolocation training prior to the experiment.

Logical Breakdown and Explanation:

This question asks for the finding that would most directly weaken Dr. Thaler's conclusion that humans are unable to develop echolocation, based on the study.

Option B is correct because if the vast majority of the control group participants had received echolocation training prior to the experiment, then the comparison between the two groups would be flawed. The similar success rates between the echolocation-trained group and the control group would not accurately reflect the effects of the training, significantly weakening the researcher's conclusion and making the conclusion less likely to be true.

Option A is incorrect because the age difference between participants would not directly affect the validity of the conclusion about echolocation. The study is focused on training, and while age might play a role, it does not directly undermine the main finding. This makes **Option A less relevant**.

Option C is incorrect because the **standard deviation** in maze completion times does not provide direct evidence against the conclusion. It merely describes the variability in the results but does not explain why the control and trained groups had similar success rates. This makes **Option C less impactful**.

Option D is incorrect because the duration of the training (two weeks) is not enough to directly weaken the conclusion. The question focuses on comparing the two groups, and the duration of the training does not challenge the validity of the results. This makes **Option D irrelevant** to the conclusion.

16. Pronouns: Easy

Answer: D) these birds

Logical Breakdown and Explanation:

This question requires selecting the appropriate pronoun to complete the sentence, ensuring it agrees with the noun it refers to and fits grammatically.

Option D is correct because "these birds" logically refers back to "sandhill cranes," a plural noun. The sentence highlights what's captivating about the cranes, and using "these birds" keeps the reference clear, ensuring that the subject is understood.

Option A is incorrect because "these" is vague when used alone and does not clearly refer back to "sandhill cranes." This makes the pronoun unclear, violating **clarity**.

Option B is incorrect because "them" is a **vague pronoun** that lacks clarity. While "them" could refer to "sandhill cranes," there are multiple plural nouns in the previous sentence ("breeding grounds" and "winter habitats"), leaving the pronoun "them" ambiguous. Also, it does not explicitly provide the same level of specificity as "these birds," making the reference unclear to the reader. Using "them" without explicitly connecting it to "sandhill cranes" forces the reader to infer the subject, which can disrupt the flow and clarity of the sentence.

Option C is incorrect because "it" is a singular pronoun, but "sandhill cranes" is plural. This creates a **pronoun-antecedent disagreement**.

17. Sentence Structure: Medium

Answer: C) positivity, which can boost

Logical Breakdown and Explanation:

This question requires selecting the correct phrase that logically and grammatically connects the two ideas without creating a run-on sentence.

Option C is correct because "positivity, which can boost" uses a **relative clause** introduced by "which" to explain that positivity has the effect of boosting self-esteem and reducing loneliness. The relative clause adds **clarity** without creating a comma splice.

Option A is incorrect because "which boosting" is not a grammatically valid construction. It leaves the sentence without a proper verb form, creating an **improperly formed dependent clause,** a sentence structure error.

Option B is incorrect because it creates a **lack of parallel structure** with the phrases that follow. That portion reads, "boosting their self-esteem and reduce feelings of loneliness." The actions "boosting" and "reduce" are not parallel in form, as one is a gerund and the other is a verb. This disrupts the flow and consistency of the sentence, making it grammatically incorrect.

Option D is incorrect because it also breaks the **parallel structure**. The sentence would read, "tend to view their lives with greater positivity **and** boost their self-esteem **and** reduce feelings of loneliness." The "and" should only separate the second item ("boost their self-esteem") from the third item ("reduce feelings of loneliness"). Including an "and" between the first item ("view their lives") and the second item disrupts the parallel construction and creates an awkward sentence structure.

18. Commas: Hard

Answer: A) discounts, and shoppers,

Logical Breakdown and Explanation:

This question requires choosing the option that correctly punctuates a sentence with a compound subject, avoiding unnecessary commas that break the sentence flow.

Option A is correct because it properly uses the commas to separate the **compound sentence**: "Retailers offer steep discounts," followed by "and shoppers flood stores." The comma after "shoppers" introduces the nonessential phrase "eager to take advantage of the deals," and the second comma closes it, maintaining proper comma rules.

Option B is incorrect because it omits the necessary comma after "shoppers," leaving the nonessential clause unclosed. This creates a **punctuation error**.

Option C is incorrect because it places the comma before "shoppers" but doesn't close the nonessential clause properly. This results in a **comma splice (a run-on sentence)**.

Option D is incorrect because the comma after "discounts and" is unnecessary and breaks the flow of the sentence, treating "shoppers eager to take advantage of the deals" as nonessential information since the remaining sentence now becomes "retailers offer steep discounts and flood stores and websites in search of the best bargains," which doesn't make any sense. Retailers don't flood stores and websites to search for deals; shoppers do.

19. Punctuation and Sentence Structure: Medium

Answer: D) time; instead,

Logical Breakdown and Explanation:

This question focuses on the correct use of punctuation to introduce a contrasting clause while maintaining sentence flow.

Option D is correct because it uses a **semicolon** to separate two independent clauses: "they're not merely wasting time;" and "they're engaging in mental processes that can enhance creativity." The semicolon is appropriate here because it signals a close connection between the clauses without creating a run-on sentence.

Option A is incorrect because the phrase "time, instead," creates a **comma splice (a run-on sentence)** by linking two independent clauses with just a comma.

Option B is incorrect because placing the **semicolon after "instead"** creates an **illogical contrast** between the clauses. This structure suggests that "they're not merely wasting time" contrasts with the previous sentence, "daydreaming has been shown to have surprising cognitive benefits," which disrupts the logical flow. Rather, "instead" should introduce a relationship between "they're not merely wasting time" and the following independent clause, "they're engaging in mental processes that can enhance creativity." This would maintain a more logical and cohesive meaning, showing that the second clause supports the first rather than creating an unnecessary contrast.

Option C is incorrect because "time instead," does not provide the necessary punctuation to separate the two independent clauses. This creates a **run-on sentence**.

20. Punctuation: Easy

Answer: D) cartoonist who popularized them,

Logical Breakdown and Explanation:

This question requires proper punctuation to introduce a nonessential clause that provides additional information about the cartoonist without breaking sentence flow.

Option D is correct because the **"who" clause** is **essential** to the sentence. It specifies which cartoonist is being discussed by providing crucial information about him ("who popularized them"). Since the clause directly identifies the cartoonist, it should not be set off by commas. The absence of commas here is correct because the information is integral to the meaning of the sentence, not additional or nonessential.

Option A is incorrect because it places commas around the "who" clause, treating it as nonessential information. However, this clause is essential in identifying the cartoonist, so it should not be set off by commas. Using commas implies that the clause can be removed without altering the core meaning, which is not the case here.

Option B is incorrect because it uses a **dash** to set off the "who" clause, but the rule for using a single dash is that the information before the dash must be an **independent clause**. In this case, "Named after the American cartoonist who popularized them" is not an independent clause, violating this grammatical rule.

Option C is incorrect because it omits the necessary comma at the end of the "who" clause. The clause is treated as nonessential by the comma before "who," but since the clause is essential, there should be no commas at all. This results in inconsistent punctuation that misidentifies the role of the clause.

21. Verbs: Medium

Answer: A) have become

Logical Breakdown and Explanation:

This question requires selecting the correct verb form to agree with the subject "escape rooms," a plural noun.

Option A is correct because "have become" is the correct plural verb form to match the plural subject "escape rooms." The sentence reads: "Escape rooms... have become a global phenomenon." This ensures proper **subject-verb agreement**, as "have" matches the plural subject.

Option B is incorrect because "has become" is a singular verb, which does not agree with the plural subject "escape rooms." This creates a **subject-verb agreement error**.

Option C is incorrect because "and are becoming" creates an **incorrect compound** and results in an ungrammatical sentence. When "and" is used here, it suggests that "escape rooms" and "are becoming" are both parts of a compound subject, which doesn't make sense ("Escape rooms...and are becoming").

Option D is incorrect because "becoming" lacks the necessary auxiliary verb "are" or "have," making the sentence grammatically incomplete **(a fragment)**. The sentence would read, "Escape rooms...becoming a global phenomenon in recent years," which lacks a main verb and creates an incomplete sentence.

22. Transitions: Easy

Answer: B) for instance,

Logical Breakdown and Explanation:

This question requires selecting a transition that appropriately links the two ideas: the effect of warm colors and how cooler colors induce a different emotional response.

Option B is correct because "for instance" introduces an example of two types of color (warm and cool) and their effects on emotions ("warmth and comfort" and "a sense of calm").

Option A is incorrect because "though" is used to introduce a contrast, but in this case, the sentence is presenting examples, not contrasting ideas. This makes the transition **illogical**.

Option C is incorrect because "moreover" is used to add additional information rather than provide an example or illustration. The sentence is not adding more information but rather offering a specific example, making this transition **misleading**. In order for "moreover" to be used accurately, the sentence would have to provide another detail about colors in general, rather than diving into examples of specific colors.

Option D is incorrect because "therefore" is a cause-and-effect transition, which does not logically fit. The sentence is giving an example of how different colors affect emotions, not explaining a cause-and-effect relationship.

23. Transitions: Medium

Answer: A) however,

Logical Breakdown and Explanation:

The sentence begins by discussing the fireflies' synchronized light display, which could be seen as random, but the sentence aims to clarify that it has a purpose: communication.

Option A is correct because "however" introduces a **contrast** not only within the sentence but also with the **previous sentence**, which states that "synchronized fireflies create one of nature's most mesmerizing displays." The use of "however" contrasts this idea of mesmerizing synchronization with the clarification that their behavior is not a random light show. The sentence explains that despite the mesmerizing appearance, the synchronization serves a purpose, making "however" the most logical transition.

Option B is incorrect because "instead" suggests an alternative action, which is not the point of the sentence. The text isn't providing an alternative to random flashing but rather explaining the true purpose behind the flashing, making **"instead" illogical**.

Option C is incorrect because "consequently" implies a cause-and-effect relationship, which doesn't apply here. The sentence is not describing the result of something but correcting an incorrect assumption about the fireflies' behavior.

Option D is incorrect because "similarly" introduces a comparison between two related ideas, which is not relevant here. The sentence is not comparing two behaviors; it's providing a contrast between what seems random and what is actually a form of communication.

24. Transitions: Medium

Answer: A) Yet,

Logical Breakdown and Explanation:

The sentence discusses how one might expect smaller creatures to dominate the deep ocean because of the extreme environment, but instead, larger creatures thrive in those conditions.

Option A is correct because "Yet" introduces a **contrast** between what one might expect (smaller creatures in extreme conditions) and what actually occurs (giant squids, colossal crabs, and enormous isopods thrive). The transition signals the unexpected nature of the phenomenon, as the reader is led to believe that smaller creatures would survive better in such harsh conditions, but the reality is the opposite.

Option B is incorrect because "Additionally" suggests adding similar information. The sentence is not adding to the expectation of smaller creatures dominating but rather refuting it by showing that larger creatures thrive, so **"Additionally" is misleading**.

Option C is incorrect because "Hence" suggests a result, and the sentence is not presenting a cause-and-effect relationship. It's offering a contrast between expectation and reality, so **"Hence" doesn't fit**.

Option D is incorrect because "Eventually" refers to something that happens over time, which is not relevant here. The sentence is contrasting immediate expectations with an unexpected reality, not discussing a gradual development.

25. Transitions: Medium

Answer: C) Rather,

Logical Breakdown and Explanation:

This question requires selecting the transition that most logically connects the two ideas: the fact that the runner's high is not just psychological, and that it is caused by the release of endorphins and neurotransmitters.

Option C is correct because "Rather" introduces an **alternative explanation**, contrasting the previous assumption that the runner's high is purely psychological. The sentence explains that the sensation is **not psychological**, but instead caused by the release of endorphins and neurotransmitters, which offers a **biological** explanation. Using "Rather" highlights the shift from a psychological interpretation to a biological one, making it the most appropriate transition in this context.

Option A is incorrect because "In other words" suggests a rephrasing of the previous idea rather than introducing a new or alternative explanation. The second sentence is not merely restating the first; it's providing new information about the biological cause of the runner's high, making "In other words" inappropriate.

Option B is incorrect because "Accordingly" is used to introduce a result or consequence. However, the second sentence is explaining a biological cause, not discussing an outcome of the psychological explanation, so this transition doesn't logically fit.

Option D is incorrect because "Thus" indicates a conclusion or result, but the second sentence is providing a new explanation, not a direct consequence. "Thus" would imply that the biological explanation follows from the first statement, but instead, the second sentence offers a distinct alternative.

26. Rhetorical Synthesis: Medium

Answer: C) George Washington played a prominent role in drafting the U.S. Constitution; likewise, Abraham Lincoln is known for issuing the Emancipation Proclamation.

Logical Breakdown and Explanation:

This question requires comparing the **presidential achievements** of George Washington and Abraham Lincoln using the information provided in the student's notes.

Option C is correct because it directly compares the **specific achievements** of both presidents. It states that George Washington played a key role in drafting the U.S. Constitution, which is drawn directly from the notes, and compares it to Abraham Lincoln issuing the Emancipation Proclamation, another specific achievement from the notes. This comparison highlights their significant feats to American history, fulfilling the student's goal of comparing achievements.

Option A is incorrect because it focuses on the **time periods** during which each president served, not their specific achievements. While this information is factual, it doesn't provide a meaningful comparison of their presidential accomplishments. All we know is when they served as president.

Option B is incorrect because, although it mentions that both played roles during times of war, it is **too vague**. The notes provide more specific details about each president's actions, and this option misses the opportunity to highlight their concrete achievements. When compared to the correct answer, option C does a much more effective job in specifying the accomplishments.

Option D is incorrect because it only lists Lincoln's achievements without providing any information about Washington's. This option does not fulfill the task of comparing the presidential achievements of both individuals, leaving the answer **incomplete**.

27. Rhetorical Synthesis: Hard

Answer: A) The largely intact tomb provided an unprecedented look into the burial practices and material wealth of Ancient Egypt's Pharaohs.

Logical Breakdown and Explanation:

This question requires selecting the option that emphasizes what scholars learned from the discovery of King Tutankhamun's tomb, focusing on the knowledge it provided.

Option A is correct because it emphasizes the **unprecedented insight** into Ancient Egyptian burial practices and the material wealth of the Pharaohs, directly referencing the **knowledge gained** from the tomb's discovery. The notes specifically mention that the tomb provided valuable information about Egyptian burial practices and wealth, making this option the most relevant.

Option B is incorrect because it focuses on the **discovery of the tomb** and the famous gold funerary mask, but it does not emphasize what was learned from the tomb, which is the focus of the question. It presents factual information but doesn't address the **insights** gained.

Option C is incorrect because it introduces **unnecessary information** by emphasizing the 5,000 artifacts found in the tomb. While the number of artifacts is factual, the question focuses on the **knowledge gained** from the discovery. Additionally, the insight into Ancient Egyptian burial practices is placed in a **subordinate clause**, making it seem less important than the material wealth, which is contrary to the main point of the question. The insights should be the primary focus, not secondary to the number of artifacts.

Option D is incorrect because it focuses more on the **worldwide fascination** and the increase in Egyptology studies rather than the specific knowledge gained from the tomb's contents. While the note about sparking worldwide interest is relevant, it doesn't address the **core focus** on the knowledge gained from the discovery.

EASY: Reading and Writing

27 Questions, 32 Minutes

DIRECTIONS

The questions in this section address a number of important reading and writing skills. Each question includes one or more passages, which may include a table or graph. Read each passage and question carefully, and then choose the best answer to the question based on the passage(s).

All questions in this section are multiple-choice with four answer choices. Each question has a single best answer.

The following text is adapted from Mary Shelley's 1818 novel *Frankenstein*. Victor Frankenstein reflects on the aftermath of his creation's first moments of life.

Victor trembled as he gazed upon the lifeless form that now stirred with motion. The horror of his actions struck him deeply, and a realization dawned upon him like a shadow swiftly cast over the sun. The emotion was intense and clear, something he had never experienced so vividly before.

1

As used in the text, what does the word "vividly" most nearly mean?

A) faintly

B) distinctly

C) repeatedly

D) unwillingly

CONTINUE

From historic landmarks like the Lincoln Memorial, which honors one of America's greatest presidents, to modern installations like the National Gallery of Art, which celebrates artistic achievements, Washington, D.C., offers numerous sites to _____ the nation's rich cultural heritage and history.

2

Which choice completes the text with the most logical and precise word or phrase?

A) renovate

B) supplant

C) venerate

D) critique

Philosopher Martha Nussbaum argues that emotions are not just raw feelings but are deeply intertwined with our beliefs about the world. She posits that emotions like anger or grief are complex responses to our perceptions of events, often influenced by cultural narratives and personal values. This view challenges the more _____ understanding of emotions as purely physiological reactions.

3

Which choice completes the text with the most logical and precise word or phrase?

A) reductive

B) esoteric

C) sympathetic

D) constructive

CONTINUE

Frank Lloyd Wright, the visionary architect, championed a concept he called "organic architecture," emphasizing that buildings should harmonize with their environment. By integrating natural materials and following the land's natural contours, his designs achieved a seamless connection between the built and natural worlds. This innovative approach stood in stark contrast to the prevailing architectural trends of the time, which were largely _____, prioritizing form over environmental context.

4

Which choice completes the text with the most logical and precise word or phrase?

A) permanent

B) humdrum

C) holistic

D) conventional

The axolotl, an aquatic salamander native to Mexico, faces significant threats due to habitat loss and pollution. This unique creature, known for its ability to regenerate lost limbs and its perpetual juvenile appearance, has seen its population dwindle in recent years. Efforts to protect the axolotl have been challenging, given the urbanization of its natural habitat, Lake Xochimilco. However, conservationists have developed innovative solutions: floating gardens, known as chinampas, have been introduced to the lake to provide a cleaner and more stable environment. These gardens filter pollutants and create habitats that support both axolotls and local plant life.

5

Which choice best states the main purpose of the text?

A) To highlight the unique regenerative abilities of the axolotl

B) To discuss the challenges facing an aquatic animal and the efforts to mitigate them

C) To explain the role of the axolotl in the its natural habitat, Lake Xochimilco

D) To elaborate on the benefits of chinampas for both axolotls and native plant life in Lake Xochimilco

CONTINUE

The following text is from Jane Austen's 1815 novel Emma. Emma Woodhouse is reflecting on her recent conversation with Mr. Knightley.

Emma had always been confident in her social acumen, believing herself adept at reading people and orchestrating their lives. Her interaction with Mr. Knightley, however, had left her unsettled. <u>His straightforwardness and candor had pierced through her usual defenses, revealing to her flaws she had never acknowledged.</u> She felt a new sense of vulnerability, one that was both disconcerting and strangely invigorating. The assurance she once wore like a mantle now felt like a fragile veneer, easily shattered by a sincere word.

6

Which choice best describes the function of the underlined portion in the text as a whole?

A) It provides a glimpse into Emma's long-standing self-perception.

B) It contrasts Emma's interaction with Mr. Knightley to her other social encounters.

C) It highlights the impact a character's honesty has on another.

D) It explains why Emma values her social acumen.

CONTINUE

Dr. David Ludwig and several other nutritionists conducted a study aiming to understand the long-term health impacts of consuming processed foods. To achieve this, researchers divided lab rats into two groups: <u>one group was fed a diet high in processed foods, while the other group was given a diet of natural, whole foods.</u> After several months, the rats on the processed food diet showed significant weight gain, elevated blood sugar levels, and signs of metabolic syndrome, while the rats on the whole food diet maintained stable health markers.

7

Which choice best describes the function of the underlined portion in the text as a whole?

A) To introduce a challenge the team faced in conducting its study.

B) To summarize the findings of the research experiment.

C) To provide evidence of the results of the team's experiment.

D) To explain part of the methodology used in the study.

CONTINUE

The following text is from the poem "L'Hiver" by French poet Théodore de Banville, written in the 19th century.

In the heart of winter, I once lamented the cold and lifeless season, mourning the absence of spring's vibrant colors and summer's warmth. But as the days grew shorter and the snow blanketed the earth, a quiet revelation emerged: winter held its own austere beauty, a time for reflection and inner peace. The stark, silent landscape became a canvas for contemplation, and I found solace in the simplicity and stillness that winter brought.

8

Which choice best describes the overall structure of the passage?

A) It opens with a physical description of the narrator's current surroundings, then transitions to personal reflections.

B) It presents a current state of contentment, then recalls past difficulties.

C) It introduces a general question, then offers a specific answer.

D) It starts with a negative perspective, then shifts to a positive realization.

CONTINUE

"The Lottery" is a 1948 short story by Shirley Jackson. In the story, Jackson contrasts the town's idyllic setting with the brutal nature of the lottery, as evidenced by the following:

_____

Which quotation from "The Lottery" most effectively illustrates the claim?

A) "The morning of June 27th was clear and sunny, with the fresh warmth of a full-summer day; the flowers were blossoming profusely and the grass was richly green, as the villagers prepared for the lottery."

B) "Soon the men began to gather, surveying their own children, speaking of planting and rain, tractors and taxes."

C) "The sun shone brightly on the quaint village green, almost as if smiling upon the beauty it created, while little Dave Hutchinson waited to see if his fate would be determined by stoning."

D) "The children had stones, ready at hand. The villagers formed a circle and began to throw pebbles, the cloud's shadows masking the violence of the act."

CONTINUE

Text 1

Shipping food from distant locations has hidden costs that go beyond the price tag at the grocery store. These costs include environmental damage from the carbon emissions of transportation and the depletion of resources in exporting countries. Moreover, the reliance on imported goods can weaken local economies and reduce food security by making communities dependent on external sources for their food supply.

Text 2

Recent data from the International Food Logistics Association indicates that the environmental impact of shipping food is less severe than commonly believed. According to their 2023 report, advancements in shipping technology have reduced the carbon footprint of food transportation by 30% over the past decade. Additionally, statistical models show that food security in importing countries remains stable, with less than a 5% variance in local food production dependency.

10

Based on the texts, how would the author of Text 2 most likely respond to the concerns raised in Text 1 about the hidden costs of shipping food?

A) By agreeing with the notion that advancements in shipping technology have reduced the environmental impact of food transportation

B) By arguing that the concerns about food security in importing countries are overstated and not supported by recent data

C) By highlighting that the economic benefits of importing food outweigh the negative impacts on local economies

D) By acknowledging the idea that, although food security remains stable, there is still more research to be done before a definitive conclusion can be made

CONTINUE

Discoveries of Components of the
Antikythera Mechanism

Component	Function	Discovery Year
Main Gear Assembly	Calculates planetary positions	1902
Eclipse Prediction Dial	Predicts solar and lunar eclipses	1902
Date and Zodiac Scales	Tracks time and zodiac signs	1903
Front Plate	Displays the calendar and astronomical data	1903
Inscription Decoding	Revealed advanced understanding of astronomy	2006

The Antikythera Mechanism, discovered in a shipwreck off the coast of Greece in 1901, is an ancient Greek analog computer dating back to around 100 BC. This device was used to predict astronomical events and is considered one of the most advanced technological artifacts of antiquity. Its discovery has provided scholars with new insights into the technological capabilities of ancient Greek civilization. Over time, researchers have uncovered more details about its components, revealing the complexity and precision of its design. For example, in 1903, they discovered _____.

11

Which choice most effectively uses data from the table to complete the text?

A) the Eclipse Prediction Dial, which predicts solar and lunar eclipses

B) the Front Plate, which reveals an advanced understanding of astronomy

C) the Main Gear Assembly, which calculates planetary positions

D) the Date and Zodiac Scales, which track time and zodiac signs

CONTINUE

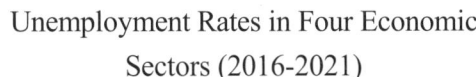

Unemployment Rates in Four Economic Sectors (2016-2021)

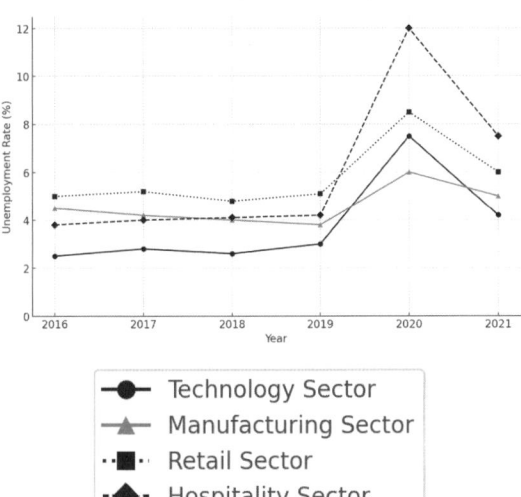

In recent years, layoffs across various economic sectors have fluctuated, reflecting broader economic conditions and industry-specific challenges. The technology sector, often seen as resilient, experienced relatively low layoff rates from 2016 to 2019, with a significant spike in 2020. This spike coincided with the global economic impact of the COVID-19 pandemic, which also led to an unprecedented surge in layoffs in the hospitality sector, as travel restrictions and lockdowns took a severe toll on the industry, as evidenced by _____

12

Which choice most effectively uses data from the table to complete the statement?

A) a double digit increase in unemployment rate in the hospitality sector from 2019 to 2020.

B) a declining trend in the unemployment rate across all four sectors from 2020 to 2021.

C) a nearly 8% increase in the hospitality sector's unemployment rate, rising from a little over 4% in 2019 to 12% in 2020.

D) a modest increase in the manufacturing sector's unemployment rate, which climbed from 3.8% in 2019 to 6% in 2020.

Practice Test 3

CONTINUE

Floating cities are emerging as a revolutionary solution to combat overpopulation and rising sea levels. Among the pioneers in this field, the city of Oceanus stands out for its full commitment to creating a self-sufficient floating metropolis. It plans to construct a network of interconnected platforms, each equipped with vertical gardens for sustainable agriculture, desalination plants to provide fresh water, and advanced waste recycling systems. The city will harness renewable energy sources, such as solar panels and wind turbines, to power its infrastructure.

13

According to the text, what is true about the city of Oceanus?

A) It intends to build systems for food, waste, and water within each interconnected platform.

B) The city will rely on imported fresh water for its residents.

C) Oceanus plans to use traditional farming techniques on its floating platforms.

D) By acknowledging the idea that, although food security remains stable, there is still more research to be done before a definitive conclusion can be made

CONTINUE

The rapid advancements in medical technology are transforming healthcare. One of the most significant developments is the use of artificial intelligence to diagnose diseases at earlier stages than traditional methods. AI algorithms can analyze vast amounts of data quickly and accurately, identifying patterns that might be missed by human doctors. To this end, _____

14

Which choice most logically completes the text?

A) many doctors are concerned that AI will completely replace human physicians.

B) the early diagnosis provided by AI can lead to more effective and timely treatments for patients.

C) traditional methods of diagnosis are becoming obsolete and are no longer taught in medical schools.

D) AI technology is primarily used for administrative tasks rather than diagnosing diseases.

CONTINUE

The rise of sustainable fashion is revolutionizing the clothing industry. Eco-friendly materials and circular fashion systems are at the forefront of this movement. Brands are increasingly adopting practices that minimize environmental impact, such as using organic fabrics, recycling old garments, and reducing water usage in production. However, the main challenge lies in scaling these sustainable practices to meet global demand while keeping costs affordable for consumers, making mainstream adoption difficult. Until costs are lowered, therefore, _____

Which choice most logically completes the text?

A) traditional fashion companies will likely increase their production of non-sustainable clothing.

B) designers will focus on incorporating more cultural heritage elements into their collections.

C) sustainable fashion will struggle to become a standard practice in the industry.

D) brands will stop creating sustainable fashion wear.

CONTINUE

Urban exploration, or "urbex," is the practice of exploring abandoned buildings and forgotten spaces within cities. Enthusiasts of this underground activity are drawn to the thrill of discovery and the opportunity to document decaying structures that were once full of life. Although the legality of urbex is often murky-since it usually involves _____ many explorers see themselves as preserving history by photographing these neglected sites before they disappear forever.

ASMR (Autonomous Sensory Meridian Response), a sensation triggered by specific sounds or visual stimuli, has become a cultural phenomenon on platforms like YouTube. Videos designed to induce ASMR _____ a variety of triggers-whispered voices, tapping, crinkling paper-that create a tingling sensation for some viewers. Interestingly, not everyone experiences ASMR; however, for those who do, it's a deeply relaxing experience that can help reduce stress and anxiety.

16

Which choice completes the text so that it conforms to the conventions of Standard English?

A) trespassing,

B) trespassing;

C) trespassing-

D) trespassing

17

Which choice completes the text so that it conforms to the conventions of Standard English?

A) feature

B) features

C) has featured

D) is featuring

CONTINUE

From their humble beginnings as collections of books in ancient civilizations, public libraries have evolved into community hubs that offer much more than just reading material. In the early 20th century, libraries _____ as quiet sanctuaries for study and research; however, today's libraries provide a range of services, from digital literacy programs to spaces for social gatherings.

18

Which choice completes the text so that it conforms to the conventions of Standard English?

A) serve

B) served

C) have served

D) will serve

Jazz music, which emerged in the early 20th century, is often celebrated for _____ improvisational style and ability to blend diverse musical traditions, including African rhythms, European harmonies, and American blues. As jazz evolved, it gave rise to various subgenres, each reflecting the cultural and social dynamics of its time—whether it be the swing era's exuberance, bebop's complexity, or the experimental nature of free jazz.

19

Which choice completes the text so that it conforms to the conventions of Standard English?

A) their

B) it's

C) its

D) one's

CONTINUE →

The ghost _____ is an eerie-looking plant that lacks chlorophyll, making it appear white and almost translucent. Unlike most plants that rely on photosynthesis, the ghost plant is a parasite, deriving its nutrients from mycorrhizal fungi that have a symbiotic relationship with nearby trees. This unique adaptation allows the ghost plant to thrive in dark, dense forests where sunlight is scarce.

_____, a mesmerizing display in summer, are a form of bioluminescence. This natural light production is not just for show—fireflies use it to attract mates. The enzyme luciferase, found in the insect's abdomen, interacts with oxygen to create the distinctive glow.

20

Which choice completes the text so that it conforms to the conventions of Standard English?

A) plant or "Indian pipe,"

B) plant, or "Indian pipe"

C) plant or "Indian pipe"

D) plant, or "Indian pipe,"

21

Which choice completes the text so that it conforms to the conventions of Standard English?

A) Fireflies glowing tails'

B) Fireflies' glowing tails

C) Firefly's glowing tails

D) Firefly glowing tails

CONTINUE

Synesthesia, a condition where one sensory experience triggers another, is both fascinating and perplexing. For some synesthetes, the letter "A" might evoke the color _____a piece of music could taste like chocolate. This neurological phenomenon challenges our conventional understanding of how the brain processes sensory information. The synesthete's world, filled with cross-wired perceptions, provides a unique perspective on the mind's complexity.

Which choice completes the text so that it conforms to the conventions of Standard English?

A) red,

B) red; or

C) red or

D) red, or

Quasicrystals are a rare form of matter that defies the traditional rules of crystallography. Unlike conventional crystals, which exhibit repeating patterns, quasicrystals possess a non-repeating, yet ordered, atomic structure. Discovered in the 1980s, _____.

Which choice completes the text so that it conforms to the conventions of Standard English?

A) these materials have challenged scientists' understanding of solid matter

B) scientists' understanding of solid matter have been challenged by these materials

C) it is these materials that have challenged scientists' understanding of solid matter

D) scientists have been challenged in terms of their understanding of solid matter because of Quasicrystals.

CONTINUE

Madagascar's biodiversity is astonishing, with over 90% of its wildlife found nowhere else on Earth. The island's lemurs, chameleons, and baobab trees are just a few examples of its unique fauna and flora. _____ Madagascar's ecosystems are under threat from deforestation, which is driven by the island's growing human population and agricultural expansion.

24

Which choice completes the text with the most logical transition?

A) Clearly,

B) Therefore,

C) Unfortunately,

D) Indeed,

The Great Pacific Garbage Patch is a massive accumulation of plastic waste in the Pacific Ocean. It spans an area twice the size of Texas and continues to grow. _____ this "island" of trash highlights the serious environmental impact of plastic pollution. Efforts to clean up the patch have intensified, but the challenge remains daunting due to its sheer size and location.

25

Which choice completes the text with the most logical transition?

A) In fact,

B) Still,

C) Previously,

D) However,

CONTINUE

The Bloop was an ultra-low frequency sound detected by underwater microphones in the South Pacific in 1997. _____ it was suspected to be of biological origin due to its resemblance to the sound of a living creature. However, later analysis suggested it was likely caused by the cracking of a large icequake in Antarctica.

Which choice completes the text with the most logical transition?

A) Eventually,

B) Initially,

C) On the other hand,

D) Consequently,

CONTINUE

While researching a topic, a student has taken the following notes:

- William Shakespeare is traditionally credited with writing iconic plays such as *Hamlet*, *Macbeth*, and *Romeo and Juliet*.
- Speculation exists that a contemporary of Shakespeare, Edward de Vere, the Earl of Oxford, may have been the true author of these works.
- Proponents of the Oxfordian theory argue that de Vere's education, literary background, and courtly experience better align with the themes and knowledge evident in the plays.
- Despite these claims, the majority of scholars support the view that Shakespeare of Stratford-upon-Avon was the genuine author.
- Proponents of the Shakespearean theory note that no conclusive evidence has been found to prove otherwise.

27

The student wants to specify the reasons some scholars believe Edward de Vere is the true author of the iconic plays Shakespeare is normally credited with. Which choice most effectively uses relevant information from the notes to accomplish this goal?

A) Edward de Vere, the Earl of Oxford, was a contemporary of William Shakespeare and is often speculated to be the true author of the plays.

B) The majority of scholars still support William Shakespeare as the genuine author of the iconic plays, despite alternative theories.

C) Some scholars believe Edward de Vere is the true author because his education, literary background, and courtly experience better align with the knowledge and themes present in the plays.

D) Supporters of the Shakespearean theory point to the fact that no conclusive evidence exists to disprove Shakespeare as the author of the plays.

STOP

If you finish before the time is called, you may check your work on this module only.
On Test Day, you will only be able to move to the next module when time expires.

🔑 Answer Key

Question Number	Correct Answer	Level of Difficulty	Question Type
1	B	Easy	**Craft and Structure:** *Interpreting Words and Phrases*
2	C	Medium	**Craft and Structure:** *Words in Context*
3	A	Hard	**Craft and Structure:** *Words in Context*
4	D	Medium	**Craft and Structure:** *Words in Context*
5	B	Easy	**Craft and Structure:** *Main Purpose*
6	C	Medium	**Craft and Structure:** *Function of the Underlined Portion*
7	D	Easy	**Craft and Structure:** *Function of the Underlined Portion*
8	D	Medium	**Craft and Structure:** *Overall Structure*
9	C	Hard	**Information and Ideas:** *Cite Text as Evidence*
10	B	Medium	**Craft and Structure:** *Cross-Text Connection*
11	D	Easy	**Information and Ideas:** *Cite Text as Evidence (Infographics)*
12	C	Medium	**Information and Ideas:** *Cite Text as Evidence (Infographics)*
13	A	Easy	**Information and Ideas:** *Detail*

Question Number	Correct Answer	Level of Difficulty	Question Type
14	B	Easy	**Information and Ideas:** *Inference*
15	C	Medium	**Information and Ideas:** *Inference*
16	C	Medium	**Standard English Conventions:** *Punctuation and Sentence Structure*
17	A	Easy	**Standard English Conventions:** *Verbs*
18	B	Easy	**Standard English Conventions:** *Verbs*
19	C	Easy	**Standard English Conventions:** *Pronouns*
20	D	Medium	**Standard English Conventions:** *Commas*
21	B	Easy	**Standard English Conventions:** *Punctuation*
22	D	Medium	**Standard English Conventions:** *Punctuation and Sentence Structure*
23	A	Easy	**Standard English Conventions:** *Modifiers*
24	C	Medium	**Expression of Ideas:** *Transitions*
25	A	Easy	**Expression of Ideas:** *Transitions*
26	B	Medium	**Expression of Ideas:** *Transitions*
27	C	Hard	**Expression of Ideas:** *Rhetorical Synthesis*

Raw Score Conversion Table

Raw Score (# of Correct Answers)	Reading and Writing Section Score	Raw Score (# of Correct Answers)	Reading and Writing Section Score
54	N/A	30	470
53	N/A	29	470
52	N/A	28	450
51	N/A	27	450
50	N/A	26	440
49	N/A	25	430
48	N/A	24	430
47	N/A	23	410
46	N/A	22	410
45	N/A	21	400
44	600	20	390
43	590	19	390
42	580	18	380
41	570	17	360
40	560	16	350
39	550	15	330
38	540	14	300
37	530	13	300
36	530	12	270
35	520	11	260
34	510	10	250
33	500	9	240
32	490	8	220
31	480	7	210

 # Explanations

1. Interpreting Words in Context: Easy

Answer: B) distinctly

Step-by-Step Explanation:

1. Let's look at what the passage is saying. The passage describes Victor Frankenstein's intense and clear realization as he witnesses his creation coming to life. The emotion he feels is described as something he had never experienced so "vividly" before, suggesting that this emotion is exceptionally strong and clear.

2. Notice the context surrounding the word "vividly." The passage describes Victor's emotional experience as intense and unprecedented, which suggests that "vividly" is meant to convey how sharply and powerfully these emotions are felt. The phrase "something he had never experienced so vividly before" emphasizes that this moment stands out in his memory with exceptional clarity and strength, indicating that the word should imply a strong, clear, and unforgettable experience.

3. The word we need should reflect the idea of experiencing something in a clear, powerful, or memorable way.

4. Ask yourself, what word best describes experiencing something in a clear, powerful, or memorable way? "Distinctly" is the most logical choice because it means clearly or in a way that stands out, which fits the context of Victor experiencing his emotions in a very clear and intense manner.

Explanation of Incorrect Options:

A) **faintly:** This is incorrect because it means weakly or with little intensity, which contradicts the strong and clear emotion described in the passage.

C) **repeatedly:** This is incorrect because it suggests something happening multiple times, which does not fit the context of the emotion being experienced in a clear and intense way.

D) unwillingly: This is incorrect because it means without wanting to, which does not align with the description of how clearly and powerfully Victor is experiencing his emotions. In other words, there is no information in the context to support this choice.

2. Words in Context: Medium

Answer: C) venerate

Step-by-Step Explanation:

1. Let's deconstruct the passage together. The passage highlights Washington, D.C., as a city rich with historic landmarks and modern installations that honor and celebrate America's cultural heritage and history. The examples given—the Lincoln Memorial and the National Gallery of Art—suggest a focus on respect, admiration, and celebration of the nation's past and artistic achievements.

2. Notice the context surrounding the sentence: The passage emphasizes the idea of honoring and celebrating important aspects of the nation's history and culture. This suggests that the word we need should reflect an act of showing deep respect or admiration for these significant sites.

3. Thus, the word we need should align with the idea of honoring or showing reverence for the nation's cultural heritage.

4. Ask yourself, what word best describes the act of honoring or deeply respecting something? "Venerate" is the most logical choice because it means to regard with great respect or reverence, which fits perfectly with the context of appreciating and honoring the nation's rich cultural heritage and history.

Explanation of Incorrect Options:

A) renovate: This is incorrect because it means to restore or update something, which doesn't fit the context of honoring or respecting historical and cultural sites. Therefore, this option should be considered irrelevant to the ideas talked about in the passage.

B) supplant: This is incorrect because it means to replace something, which is not relevant to the idea of celebrating or honoring the nation's history.

D) critique: This is incorrect because it means to evaluate or analyze something, often finding faults, which contradicts the passage's focus on admiration and respect for the nation's cultural heritage.

3. Words in Context: Hard

Answer: A) reductive

Step-by-Step Explanation:

1. Let's understand the passage together. The passage describes philosopher Martha Nussbaum's view that emotions are complex and deeply connected to our beliefs, cultural narratives, and personal values. This view contrasts with a different understanding of emotions that the passage suggests is more simplistic or limited.
2. Notice the phrase "This view challenges," which indicates that Nussbaum's perspective is different from a simpler or more basic understanding of emotions. The passage contrasts Nussbaum's complex view of emotions with another, less nuanced perspective.
3. Therefore, the word we need should describe the simpler, more basic understanding of emotions that Nussbaum's view challenges.
4. "Reductive" is the most logical choice because it means simplifying something complex to the point of minimizing its true nature to its most basic form, which fits the context of Nussbaum challenging a simplistic view of emotions as merely physiological reactions.

Explanation of Incorrect Options:

B) esoteric: This is incorrect because it means something that is understood by only a small, specialized group, which doesn't fit the context of a more simplistic understanding of emotions that is challenged by Nussbaum's complex view of emotions.

C) sympathetic: This is incorrect because it means feeling or showing compassion, which does not align with the idea of a simplistic or basic understanding of emotions.

D) constructive: This is incorrect because it means serving a useful purpose or helping to improve something, which does not fit the context of challenging a simplistic understanding of emotions.

4. Words in Context: Medium

Answer: D) conventional

Step-by-Step Explanation:

1. The passage describes Frank Lloyd Wright's innovative approach to architecture, which emphasized harmony between buildings and their natural environment. His designs integrated natural materials and followed the land's contours, contrasting with the architectural trends of his time.

2. Notice the phrase "stood in stark contrast" and how Wright's approach is described as innovative. This implies that the architectural trends of the time were the opposite of his, likely more traditional or ordinary in comparison to his groundbreaking methods.

3. The word we need should reflect the idea that the prevailing architectural trends were more traditional or standard, lacking the innovation and environmental sensitivity that Wright championed.

4. Ask yourself, what word best describes something that is ordinary or follows traditional norms? "Conventional" is the most logical choice because it means adhering to accepted standards or norms, which fits the context of contrasting Wright's innovative approach with the more traditional architectural trends of his time.

Explanation of Incorrect Options:

A) permanent: This is incorrect because it refers to something lasting or enduring, which doesn't fit the context of architectural trends being contrasted with Wright's innovative approach.

B) humdrum: While this means boring or monotonous, it doesn't precisely capture the idea of traditional or standard practices in architecture, making it less fitting than "conventional."

C) holistic: This is incorrect because it means considering something as a whole, especially in a way that is more integrated and comprehensive, which would be closer to Wright's approach rather than the traditional trends he contrasted with.

5. Interpreting Words in Context: Hard

Answer: D) affecting

Step-by-Step Explanation:

1. The passage describes the bustling and sensory-rich experience of the marketplaces in Marrakech. It highlights the vivid tapestries, intricate pottery, lively interactions between vendors and customers, aromatic scents of spices, and the melodic calls to prayer—all contributing to an immersive and emotionally rich atmosphere.
2. Notice the emphasis on how the marketplace experience is "particularly" something, due to these sensory and emotionally engaging elements. The passage suggests that the experience is not just visually stimulating but also deeply impactful on an emotional level.
3. Thus, the word we need should describe an experience that has a strong emotional impact on a person, aligning with the immersive and rich atmosphere described.
4. "Affecting" is the most logical choice because it means having a strong emotional impact, which fits perfectly with the description of the marketplace as a deeply immersive and emotionally rich environment.

Explanation of Incorrect Options:

A) perplexing: This is incorrect because it means confusing or puzzling, which does not match the context of the marketplace being emotionally rich and immersive.

B) mundane: This is incorrect because it means ordinary or dull, which is the opposite of the vibrant and emotionally engaging experience described in the passage.

C) prestigious: This is incorrect because it means having high status or respect, which doesn't align with the context of the marketplace experience being emotionally impactful.

6. Function of the Underlined Portion: Medium

Answer: C) It highlights the impact a character's honesty has on another.

Logical Breakdown and Explanation:

To determine the function of the underlined portion, we need to understand how it contributes to the overall passage. The passage focuses on Emma's reflection after a conversation with Mr. Knightley. The underlined portion—"His straightforwardness and candor had pierced through her usual defenses, revealing to her flaws she had never acknowledged"—shows how Mr. Knightley's honesty challenges Emma's self-perception, making her realize aspects of herself she had not confronted.

Option C is correct because the underlined portion directly describes the **impact of Mr. Knightley's honesty** (one character) on Emma (another character), showing how his words revealed her hidden flaws. This emphasizes the effect of one character's honesty on another, making it central to Emma's emotional shift.

Option A is incorrect because, although the passage touches on Emma's self-perception, the underlined portion is more focused on how Mr. Knightley's straightforwardness influences her. This option is **off-topic** as it misidentifies the focus of the underlined portion.

Option B is incorrect because there is no comparison between Mr. Knightley's interaction with Emma and her interactions with others. The passage is specific to *this* interaction. This answer is a **distortion** because it introduces a comparison that doesn't exist in the text.

Option D is incorrect because the underlined portion does not explain why Emma values her social acumen. Instead, it focuses on how Mr. Knightley's words challenge her usual confidence. This makes it **irrelevant** to the function of the underlined portion.

7. Function of the Underlined Portion: Easy

Answer: D) To explain part of the methodology used in the study.

Logical Breakdown and Explanation:

To determine the function of the underlined portion, we need to assess how it contributes to the overall structure of the passage. The underlined portion—"one group was fed a diet high in processed foods, while the other group was given a diet of natural, whole foods"—describes the **methodology** used in the experiment. It explains the key difference in the diets given to each group of rats, which is crucial for understanding how the experiment was structured.

Option D is correct because the underlined portion explains **part of the methodology** used in the study, specifically the division of the rats into two groups with different diets. This information sets up the experiment and allows readers to understand how the study was conducted.

Option A is incorrect because the underlined portion does not introduce a challenge faced by the research team. This answer is **off topic,** as it suggests an issue that isn't present in the passage.

Option B is incorrect because the underlined portion does not summarize the findings of the study. It focuses on the **process** rather than the results, making this option **inaccurate.**

Option C is incorrect because the underlined portion does not provide evidence of the experiment's results. It describes the experimental setup, not the outcomes, making it **irrelevant** to the function of the underlined portion.

8. Overall Structure: Medium

Answer: D) It starts with a negative perspective, then shifts to a positive realization.

Logical Breakdown and Explanation:

To determine the overall structure, we need to consider how the passage develops from beginning to end. The passage starts with the narrator expressing negative feelings about winter, lamenting the cold and lifeless season. As the passage progresses, the narrator experiences a shift in perspective, recognizing winter's unique beauty and finding peace in the simplicity it brings.

Option D is correct because the passage starts with a **negative perspective** on winter ("I once lamented the cold...") and then shifts to a **positive realization** about the season's beauty and peace. The passage is structured around this change in attitude, making it the most logical answer.

Option A is incorrect because the passage does not open with a physical description of the narrator's surroundings. Instead, it begins with an emotional reflection on winter. This makes it **off-topic** in terms of the passage's structure.

Option B is incorrect because the passage does not begin with contentment. The narrator's initial reaction to winter is negative, making this option a **contradiction** to the structure of the passage.

Option C is incorrect because there is no general question posed in the passage. The passage is about a change in perspective, not about answering a question. This answer is **irrelevant** to the structure of the passage.

9. Cite Text as Evidence: Hard

Answer: C) "The sun shone brightly on the quaint village green, almost as if smiling upon the beauty it created, while little Dave Hutchinson waited to see if his fate would be determined by stoning."

Logical Breakdown and Explanation:

To determine which quotation best illustrates the claim, we need to find a quote that shows the **contrast** between the idyllic setting of the town and the brutal nature of the lottery. The most effective quote should include both a description of the peaceful setting and a reference to the violence of the lottery.

Option C is correct because it effectively captures the **juxtaposition** between the beauty of the setting and the brutal nature of the lottery. The peaceful description of the "sun shone brightly" contrasts with the grim reality of Dave Hutchinson awaiting his fate, which is determined by stoning. This contrast is the core of the claim, making it the most fitting choice.

Option A is incorrect because it only describes the idyllic setting ("clear and sunny," "flowers were blossoming") without addressing the violent nature of the lottery. While it effectively sets the scene, it is **incomplete** as it fails to highlight the brutality that contrasts with the town's peaceful appearance.

Option B is incorrect because it focuses on mundane details ("surveying their own children, speaking of planting and rain") without capturing the brutality of the lottery. This makes it **off-topic** as it doesn't address the claim.

Option D is incorrect because it emphasizes the brutality of the act ("the villagers formed a circle and began to throw pebbles") but does not include a description of the peaceful setting. This makes it **incomplete** because it leaves out the contrast between the idyllic setting and the violence.

10. Cross-Text Connections: Medium

Answer: B) By arguing that the concerns about food security in importing countries are overstated and not supported by recent data

Logical Breakdown and Explanation:

To determine how the author of Text 2 would respond to Text 1, we need to examine the concerns raised in Text 1 and see how they are addressed in Text 2. Text 1 focuses on the hidden costs of shipping food, such as environmental damage and weakened food security. Text 2, however, presents data that downplays these concerns, showing that the environmental impact has been reduced and that food security remains stable.

Option B is correct because the author of Text 2 would likely argue that the **concerns about food security** raised in Text 1 are **overstated**. Text 2 provides data showing that food security remains stable, with less than a 5% variance, which directly contradicts Text 1's claim of reduced food security.

Option A is incorrect because it focuses only on the environmental aspect, whereas the more relevant point in Text 2 is about food security. This answer is **incomplete** as it does not fully address the concerns raised in Text 1.

Option C is incorrect because it introduces an **off-topic** focus on the economic benefits of importing food. Text 2 focuses on environmental and food security issues, not the economic benefits.

Option D is incorrect because Text 2 confidently presents data that disputes the concerns in Text 1. There is no mention of the need for further research, making this answer **irrelevant** and unsupported by the ideas presented in the text.

11. Cite Text as Evidence (Infographics): Easy

Answer: D) the Date and Zodiac Scales, which track time and zodiac signs

Logical Breakdown and Explanation:

To determine which choice completes the text most effectively, we need to match the **year**, **component**, and **function** mentioned in the text to the data provided in the table. The text mentions a discovery made in 1903, so we must select a component from the table that was discovered in that year.

Option D is correct because the **Date and Zodiac Scales**, which track time and zodiac signs, were discovered in 1903 according to the table. This fits the context of the passage and provides the most relevant information.

Option A is incorrect because the **Eclipse Prediction Dial** was discovered in 1902, not 1903. This makes it **factually inaccurate** based on the table data.

Option B is incorrect because the **Front Plate** was discovered in 1903, but the function described in this option ("reveals an advanced understanding of astronomy") is **inaccurate** based on the table, which attributes that function to Inscription Decoding discovered in 2006.

Option C is incorrect because the **Main Gear Assembly** was discovered in 1902. This makes it **factually incorrect** for the date given in the passage.

12. Cite Text as Evidence (Infographics): Medium

Answer: C) a nearly 8% increase in the hospitality sector's unemployment rate, rising from a little over 4% in 2019 to 12% in 2020.

Logical Breakdown and Explanation:

To complete the statement effectively, we need to find a **specific data point** from the table that shows a significant change in the **hospitality sector**'s unemployment rate during the impact of the COVID-19 pandemic, particularly from 2019 to 2020.

Option C is correct because it accurately describes the **8% increase** in the hospitality sector's unemployment rate, rising from just over 4% in 2019 to 12% in 2020. This data directly correlates with the impact of the pandemic on the hospitality industry, making it the most relevant choice.

Option A is incorrect because it inaccurately describes the increase as a **double-digit** rise. The actual increase in the hospitality sector's unemployment rate from 2019 to 2020 is **approximately 8%** (from just over 4% to 12%), which is not a double-digit increase. This makes the description **factually inaccurate** based on the data.

Option B is incorrect because it refers to a **declining trend** in 2020-2021 across all sectors, which is not the focus of the passage. This makes it **off-topic**.

Option D is incorrect because it discusses the **manufacturing sector**, not the hospitality sector. This choice is **irrelevant** to the specific topic of the sentence.

13. Detail: Easy

Answer: A) It intends to build systems for food, waste, and water within each interconnected platform.

Logical Breakdown and Explanation:

To determine which choice is correct, we need to focus on the details provided in the text about the city of Oceanus. The text states that the city will create interconnected platforms with systems for **sustainable agriculture, desalination plants for fresh water, and advanced waste recycling systems**.

Option A is correct because it accurately reflects the city's intention to build systems for food **(agriculture)**, waste **(advanced waste recycling system)**, and water **(desalination plants for fresh water)** within each interconnected platform, as described in the text.

Option B is incorrect because the city plans to have **desalination plants** to provide fresh water, meaning it will not rely on imported fresh water. This makes it **factually inaccurate**.

Option C is incorrect because there is no mention of **traditional farming techniques**. Instead, the text emphasizes **vertical gardens**, which are not traditional. This option is **unsupported** by the information provided.

Option D is incorrect because it introduces an unrelated claim about food security and additional research, which is not discussed in the text. This makes it **off-topic** and unsupported by the context.

14. Inference: Easy

Answer: B) the early diagnosis provided by AI can lead to more effective and timely treatments for patients.

Logical Breakdown and Explanation:

To complete the text logically, we need to find the option that aligns with the idea that artificial intelligence (AI) is transforming healthcare by diagnosing diseases at earlier stages than traditional methods. The final sentence should logically build on this concept.

Option B is correct because it explains the consequence of AI's ability to diagnose diseases early: leading to more effective and timely treatments. This logically follows from the claim that AI can analyze data faster and more accurately than human doctors.

Option A is incorrect because it introduces concerns about AI replacing doctors, which is not relevant to the passage's focus on early diagnosis. This makes it **off topic**.

Option C is incorrect because it claims that traditional methods of diagnosis are becoming obsolete and are no longer taught in medical schools, which is not mentioned or implied in the passage. The text focuses on how AI is enhancing early diagnosis, but it doesn't suggest that traditional methods are being replaced or discarded. This option is **irrelevant** because it introduces an idea that is not supported by the passage.

Option D is incorrect because the idea that AI is primarily used for administrative tasks does not logically follow from the information provided in the passage. The text focuses on how AI is being used to diagnose diseases and identify patterns that may be missed by human doctors. Introducing a claim that AI is used for administrative purposes is **irrelevant** and disrupts the logical flow of the passage. The topic of administrative tasks is not mentioned or supported by the preceding sentences, making this option an illogical completion of the text.

15. Inference: Medium

Answer: C) sustainable fashion will struggle to become a standard practice in the industry.

Logical Breakdown and Explanation:

To complete the text logically, we need to focus on the challenges that sustainable fashion faces in scaling up its practices while keeping costs affordable for consumers. The passage discusses how the high costs of sustainable fashion make mainstream adoption difficult, so the correct completion should reinforce this idea.

Option C is correct because it logically concludes that sustainable fashion will struggle to become a standard practice in the industry due to the high costs associated with scaling. This directly follows from the passage's focus on the difficulties of expanding sustainable practices while keeping them affordable for a wide range of consumers.

Option A is incorrect because it introduces an unrelated idea about traditional fashion companies increasing the production of non-sustainable clothing. The passage doesn't discuss what traditional fashion companies might do in response to sustainable fashion's challenges, making this option **off-topic** and irrelevant to the passage's main argument.

Option B is incorrect because it shifts the focus to designers incorporating more cultural heritage elements into their collections. This option is **irrelevant** of the passage because it introduces a concept (cultural heritage) that is not discussed in the text, and it doesn't logically connect to the problem of scaling sustainable practices.

Option D is incorrect because it goes too far beyond the scope of what the passage says. The passage discusses the challenges of scaling sustainable fashion due to high costs, but it doesn't suggest that brands will completely stop creating sustainable fashion. This option makes an extreme claim that is not supported by the passage, as correct answers should provide a **logical conclusion** based on the information given, rather than introducing a conclusion that extends beyond the passage's focus. Therefore, Option D is both **factually unsupported** and an overreach.

16. Punctuation and Sentence Structure: Medium

Answer: C) trespassing—

Logical Breakdown and Explanation:

To determine the correct choice, we need to focus on the punctuation rule for dashes. In the passage, there is already a dash before the underlined portion, which sets up a potential nonessential clause. The rule for a single dash is that an independent clause (IC) must appear before the dash. If the sentence does not have an independent clause, using only one dash is a punctuation error.

Option C is correct because it provides the second dash, turning the additional information ("since it usually involves trespassing") into a **nonessential clause**. The use of two dashes creates the proper sentence structure (a dependent clause + nonessential information + an independent clause).

Option A, **Option B**, and **Option D** are all incorrect because they leave the passage with only **one dash**. This creates a punctuation error, as the information before the dash is not an independent clause. A single dash should be preceded by an independent clause, and without it, these options break the rule, making them **grammatically flawed**.

17. Verbs: Easy

Answer: A) feature

Logical Breakdown and Explanation:

To determine the correct answer, we need to focus on **subject-verb agreement**. The subject of the sentence is "videos", which is plural. Therefore, the verb must also be plural to maintain correct agreement between the subject and the verb.

Option A is correct because "feature" is the plural form of the verb, which agrees with the plural subject "videos." This makes it the grammatically correct choice.

Option B is incorrect because "features" is a singular verb form, which does not agree with the plural subject "videos." This creates a subject-verb agreement error.

Option C is incorrect because "has featured" uses a singular subject (has), which creates a subject-verb disagreement with the plural subject "videos". The verb should match the plural subject "videos," so using the singular "has" results in an incorrect grammatical structure.

Option D is incorrect because "is featuring" is also a singular verb (is), which does not agree with the plural subject "videos." Like Option C, this creates a subject-verb disagreement, making it grammatically incorrect.

18. Verbs: Easy

Answer: B) served

Logical Breakdown and Explanation:

To determine the correct answer, we need to focus on verb tense and consider the time reference provided in the sentence, which is "in the early 20th century." This indicates that the action being described took place in the past, so the verb must match this time frame.

Option B is correct because "served" is in the past tense, which is appropriate for describing how libraries functioned in the early 20th century. The past tense fits the time reference and correctly contrasts with the present-day functions of libraries discussed in the next part of the sentence.

Option A is incorrect because "serve" is in the present tense, which does not fit with the time reference of the early 20th century. The sentence is describing something that happened in the past, so the present tense is grammatically incorrect.

Option C is incorrect because "have served" is in the present perfect tense, which implies that the action continues up to the present. However, the sentence contrasts the past function of libraries with their current roles, so the present perfect tense creates a tense mismatch.

Option D is incorrect because "will serve" is in the future tense, which is inconsistent with the time frame of the early 20th century. The sentence refers to a past action, not a future one, making this option illogical.

19. Pronouns: Easy

Answer: C) its

Logical Breakdown and Explanation:

To determine the correct answer, we need to focus on the possessive form of the subject. The subject of the sentence is "jazz music," which is singular. Therefore, we need to use the singular possessive pronoun that correctly refers to jazz music's improvisational style and its blending of musical traditions.

Option C is correct because "its" is the singular possessive pronoun that refers to jazz music. It correctly indicates that jazz is known for its improvisational style and its ability to blend musical traditions.

Option A is incorrect because "their" is a plural possessive pronoun. The subject, "jazz music," is singular, so using "their" creates a subject-pronoun disagreement.

Option B is incorrect because "it's" is a contraction for "it is" or "it has." The sentence requires the possessive form of "it" to show that the improvisational style belongs to jazz music. Using "it's" here creates a grammatical error and a nonsensical sentence.

Option D is incorrect because "one's" is unclear and illogical in this context. "One's" refers to a general or hypothetical person, which doesn't logically fit when discussing the specific qualities of jazz music. This makes the option inappropriate for the sentence.

20. Commas: Medium

Answer: D) plant, or "Indian pipe,"

Logical Breakdown and Explanation:

To determine the correct choice, we need to focus on the rules regarding nonessential information, specifically when a synonym is added after the noun to clarify or describe it further. Nonessential information should be set off by commas to indicate that it is additional but not necessary for the meaning of the sentence. The sentence discusses the ghost plant, also known as "Indian pipe", which is a synonym that needs to be marked as nonessential.

Option D is correct because it places commas around the synonym "Indian pipe," indicating that this phrase is nonessential information. It correctly follows the rule of surrounding nonessential synonyms with commas and avoids placing a comma between the subject ("plant") and the verb ("is"). This option properly signals that "Indian pipe" is an alternative name for the ghost plant.

Option A and **Option B** are incorrect because they each use only one comma, which results in placing a comma between the subject ("plant") and the verb ("is"). This violates the rule that **a single comma should never separate a subject and its verb**, making both options grammatically incorrect.

Option C is incorrect because it uses no commas around the phrase "Indian pipe," making it seem like "plant or Indian pipe" refers to two different plants rather than being two names for the same plant. This creates an **illogical meaning** in the context of the sentence.

21. Punctuation: Easy

Answer: B) Fireflies' glowing tails

Logical Breakdown and Explanation:

To determine the correct choice, we need to focus on the **correct use of apostrophes** to indicate possession. The phrase is describing the **glowing tails of fireflies**, so the correct possessive form should be used to show that the glowing tails belong to the fireflies.

Option B is correct because "Fireflies' glowing tails" uses the **plural possessive** form of "fireflies" (with the apostrophe after the "s") to show that the glowing tails belong to the fireflies. This option is grammatically correct and makes sense in context, as the sentence refers to multiple fireflies.

Option A is incorrect because "Fireflies glowing tails'" places the apostrophe after "tails," which indicates possession but lacks a noun to show what "tails" is possessing. This creates a grammatical error by leaving the **possessive form incomplete**.

Option C is incorrect because "Firefly's glowing tails" uses a **singular possessive** form ("firefly's"), but the sentence is referring to **multiple fireflies**. Additionally, the singular possessive form would typically require an article like **"the"** or **"a"** before it to make the sentence grammatically correct, which is missing here.

Option D is incorrect because "Firefly glowing tails" does not use any possessive form, which makes the meaning unclear and illogical. It reads as though "firefly" is being used as an adjective, which creates confusion and doesn't fit the context of the sentence.

22. Punctuation and Sentence Structure: Medium

Answer: D) red, or

Logical Breakdown and Explanation:

To determine the correct choice, we need to focus on how to properly connect two independent clauses (ICs). The first clause, "the letter 'A' might evoke the color red," is an IC, and the second clause, "a piece of music could taste like chocolate," is another IC. A **comma plus a FANBOYS word** (for, and, nor, but, or, yet, so) is required to connect these two ICs properly.

Option D is correct because it uses a **comma plus "or"** (a FANBOYS word) to connect the two independent clauses. This creates a grammatically correct sentence, properly linking the two related but separate ideas.

Option A is incorrect because it only uses a **comma** without a FANBOYS word, resulting in a **run-on sentence**. A comma by itself is not strong enough to join two independent clauses.

Option B is incorrect because it uses a **semicolon** followed by "or." A semicolon should not be used with a FANBOYS conjunction like "or." Instead, a semicolon is appropriate when used with **conjunctive adverbs** like "however" or "instead," making this option grammatically inappropriate.

Option C is incorrect because it only uses "or" without a comma. This also results in a **run-on sentence** since it doesn't properly link the two independent clauses.

23. Modifiers: Easy

Answer: A) these materials have challenged scientists' understanding of solid matter

Logical Breakdown and Explanation:

To determine the correct choice, we need to focus on avoiding a **dangling modifier**. The phrase **"discovered in the 1980s"** is a modifying phrase that must logically modify the **noun** that appears immediately after it. The subject of the independent clause should be the **quasicrystals**, which were discovered in the 1980s.

Option A is correct because it places **"these materials"** (referring to quasicrystals) immediately after the modifying phrase. This correctly matches the modifier to the subject, making the sentence logical and grammatically correct.

Option B is incorrect because it places **"scientists' understanding of solid matter"** after the modifier. The phrase **scientists'** is a possessive form and does not represent something that was discovered. This creates an illogical sentence, as understanding was not discovered in the 1980s.

Option C is incorrect because **"it is these materials"** starts with an impersonal subject (**"it"**), which creates a mismatch between the modifier and the subject of the sentence. The subject should be the quasicrystals, but this option makes the sentence unnecessarily indirect and confusing.

Option D is incorrect because it places **"scientists"** after the modifier, suggesting that scientists were discovered in the 1980s, which is obviously illogical. The modifier needs to refer to the quasicrystals, not the scientists.

24. Transitions: Medium

Answer: C) Unfortunately,

Logical Breakdown and Explanation:

To determine the correct transition, we need to focus on the **relationship between the two sentences**. The first sentence highlights Madagascar's incredible biodiversity, while the second sentence discusses a **negative consequence**—the threat to its ecosystems caused by deforestation. The transition should reflect this shift from a **positive** to a **negative** idea.

Option C is correct because **"Unfortunately"** introduces the unfavorable situation of deforestation threatening Madagascar's ecosystems. This transition reflects the **contrast** between the initial admiration of Madagascar's biodiversity and the negative impact of deforestation, making it the most logical choice.

Option A is incorrect because **"Clearly"** suggests a sense of **certainty or obviousness**, but it doesn't make sense to use this transition after a sentence that highlights the **positive** aspect of Madagascar's biodiversity. Following a positive statement with **certainty** about a **negative** situation (deforestation) creates an awkward and illogical flow.

Option B is incorrect because **"Therefore"** implies a **cause-and-effect relationship**, which doesn't fit here. The first sentence talks about biodiversity, and the second mentions deforestation, but there is no direct causal link between the two ideas.

Option D is incorrect because **"Indeed"** is used to reinforce or emphasize an earlier point. However, the second sentence is introducing new, contrasting information (the threat of deforestation), not reinforcing the idea of biodiversity.

25. Transitions: Easy

Answer: A) In fact,

Logical Breakdown and Explanation:

To determine the correct transition, we need to analyze the relationship between the sentences. The first two sentences describe the **massive size** and **growth** of the Great Pacific Garbage Patch, emphasizing the serious environmental impact of plastic pollution. The following sentence shifts to **reinforce** and **emphasize** this impact by discussing the ongoing efforts to clean up the patch, which have intensified due to the severity of the problem. Therefore, the appropriate transition should reinforce the seriousness of the issue.

Option A is correct because **"In fact"** provides additional **emphasis** on the environmental significance of the patch, reinforcing the idea that the garbage patch is an alarming issue. This transition works well in this context because it supports and **builds on** the previous sentence's description of the growing problem.

Option B is incorrect because **"Still"** typically conveys the idea of something **unexpected** happening despite prior statements. However, in this case, the sentence is emphasizing the seriousness of the problem with the growing garbage patch, not something surprising. There is no shift in expectation; rather, the sentence is reinforcing the environmental impact, so "Still" doesn't fit logically.

Option C is incorrect because **"Previously"** refers to something that **happened in the past**, but the passage is discussing an ongoing issue. Using "Previously" would disrupt the timeline and create confusion in the narrative.

Option D is incorrect because **"However"** suggests a **contrast**, but the sentence is not introducing a contrasting idea. The sentences flow logically from describing the **problem** to emphasizing the seriousness of the issue.

26. Transitions: Medium

Answer: B) Initially,

Logical Breakdown and Explanation:

To determine the correct transition, we need to focus on how the first sentence (about the Bloop being detected) connects to the second sentence, which describes the initial hypothesis that the sound was biological in origin. The appropriate transition should signal the **starting point** of the investigation, which is later revised by the analysis in the third sentence.

Option B is correct because **"Initially"** signals the **first assumption** or **early belief** about the origin of the Bloop. The sentence goes on to explain that scientists initially suspected the sound was biological, which sets up the contrast with the later analysis that attributed the sound to an icequake. This creates a logical and chronological flow, where the **initial assumption** is revised after further analysis.

Option A is incorrect because **"Eventually"** suggests a **final conclusion** or something happening later in time, but the sentence is describing the first assumption scientists made about the sound. It doesn't logically fit with the context, as the initial assumption must come before the later analysis.

Option C is incorrect because **"On the other hand"** indicates a **contrast** or a **different perspective**, but the sentence isn't introducing a contrasting idea. It's simply describing the first step in the analysis (suspecting a biological origin), not offering an opposing view.

Option D is incorrect because **"Consequently"** suggests a **cause-and-effect relationship**, which doesn't make sense here. The sentence is not describing the result of something; it's explaining the initial hypothesis that scientists formed when they first detected the Bloop.

27. Rhetorical Synthesis: Hard

Answer: C) Some scholars believe Edward de Vere is the true author because his education, literary background, and courtly experience better align with the knowledge and themes present in the plays.

Logical Breakdown and Explanation:

To determine the correct choice, we need to focus on the goal of the question: specifying the **reasons** why some scholars believe **Edward de Vere** may have authored the iconic plays attributed to William Shakespeare. The correct choice should draw on relevant details from the notes.

Option C is correct because it directly addresses the reasons some scholars support the idea that Edward de Vere is the true author. It clearly mentions his **education, literary background, and courtly experience**, aligning with the themes and knowledge present in the plays. This information comes straight from the notes, fulfilling the requirement to specify the reasons behind the belief in de Vere's authorship.

Option A is incorrect because it only **mentions the speculation** that de Vere may be the true author but does not **specify the reasons** why some scholars believe this. It lacks the detailed support (education, literary background, etc.) needed to explain why the Oxfordian theory exists.

Option B is incorrect because it focuses on the **majority opinion** supporting Shakespeare as the genuine author. This contradicts the goal of the question, which is to specify the **reasons for supporting de Vere**, not the reasons for rejecting alternative theories.

Option D is incorrect because it discusses the **Shakespearean theory** and the **lack of evidence against Shakespeare**, which is irrelevant to the question's goal of explaining the reasons **for supporting de Vere** as the true author. It focuses on defending Shakespeare rather than addressing the Oxfordian theory.

HARD: Reading and Writing

27 Questions, 32 Minutes

DIRECTIONS

The questions in this section address a number of important reading and writing skills. Each question includes one or more passages, which may include a table or graph. Read each passage and question carefully, and then choose the best answer to the question based on the passage(s).

All questions in this section are multiple-choice with four answer choices. Each question has a single best answer.

The intricate social structure of honeybee colonies has long fascinated scientists. Among the many complex behaviors exhibited by these insects, one of the most remarkable is their method of communication. The waggle dance performed by foraging bees is crucial to the survival of the hive. This behavior not only communicates the location of food sources but is also _____ ensuring the colony thrives even in challenging environments.

1

Which choice completes the text with the most logical and precise word or phrase?

A) integral to

B) reliant on

C) subjected to

D) inessential to

CONTINUE →

Shonda Rhimes' television series *Bridgerton* has captivated audiences worldwide with its opulent settings, intricate plotlines, and a meticulously crafted ensemble cast. The series, indeed, has become a cultural phenomenon, lauded for its innovative approach to period drama. In fact, *Bridgerton* _____ one of television's most prestigious accolades: the Primetime Emmy Award for Outstanding Drama Series.

2

Which choice completes the text with the most logical and precise word or phrase?

A) achieved

B) completed

C) received

D) renounced

One way to _____ the influence of a philosopher's theories is to examine the extent to which these theories are incorporated into contemporary academic discourse. For example, the works of Friedrich Nietzsche, known for his profound impact on existentialism and postmodernism, are frequently referenced and debated, highlighting their enduring relevance.

3

Which choice completes the text with the most logical and precise word or phrase?

A) promulgate

B) ascertain

C) trivialize

D) undermine

CONTINUE

The following text is adapted from *The Book of Chuang Tzu* (translated by Martin Palmer, 1996), an ancient Chinese text attributed to the philosopher Zhuangzi.

"I once dreamed I was a butterfly, fluttering happily among the flowers, carefree and unaware of my human life. When I awoke, I was astonished by the vividness of the dream and spent days reflecting on the nature of reality. After traveling inward into the <u>recesses</u> of my mind and soul, I was left with profound questions: was I Zhuangzi who had dreamed of being a butterfly or a butterfly dreaming I was Zhuangzi?"

The following text is from the poem "To a Poet" by Alice Meynell. In this poem, the speaker is addressing another poet.

Thou hast given thy thoughts to the
endless sea,
And the stars above in the sky,
With words that dance upon the page,
Revealing truths both far and nigh.
Thy verses speak of a world unseen,
Of beauty beyond compare,
And in thy lines, a gentle grace,
That few can ever share.

4

As used in the text, what does the word "recesses" most nearly mean?

A) luxuries

B) breaks

C) surfaces

D) depths

5

Which choice best states the main purpose of the text?

A) To reflect on the profound impact of a poet's words and conclude with admiration

B) To discuss the poet's influence on the natural world and celestial bodies

C) To describe the poet's meticulous approach to writing about nature

D) To narrate an encounter between the speaker and the poet

Practice Test 3

CONTINUE

Economists led by Dr. Rebecca Adams and Dr. Michael Chen, aiming to analyze the impact of remote work on productivity and employee satisfaction, conducted a two-year study, collecting data from 1,500 employees across 50 companies to test the previous assumptions that remote work would lead to decreased productivity and lower job satisfaction. The findings were revealing: productivity increased by an average of 15% among remote workers, with 85% reporting higher job satisfaction compared to their in-office counterparts, challenging the traditional belief that remote work is detrimental to both productivity and employee satisfaction.

6

Which choice best describes the function of the underlined portion in the text as a whole?

A) To provide details that reveal the purpose of the study

B) To summarize the findings of the study, emphasizing both their positive and negative implications

C) To present the relevant results of the study that contradict a previously held assumption

D) To introduce the hypothesis tested by the researchers

CONTINUE ➡

In a review of Charlotte Brontë's "Jane Eyre," literary critic Mary Thompson notes that Jane Eyre's moral integrity and independence profoundly shape her interactions with the enigmatic Mr. Rochester. Despite her growing feelings for him, Jane maintains a strong sense of self-worth and principles. This is evident in her declaration: _____

7

Which quote from Jane Eyre would most strongly support the critic's claim?

A) "I care for myself. The more solitary, the more friendless, the more unsustained I am, the more I will respect myself."

B) "My bride is here... because my equal is here, and my likeness."

C) "He made me love him without looking at me."

D) "I could not unlove him now, merely because I found that he had ceased to notice me."

CONTINUE

Universal Basic Income (UBI) is a policy proposal that suggests providing regular, unconditional payments to all citizens: perhaps to reduce poverty, or to address job displacement caused by automation, or to ensure a basic level of economic security for everyone. In a detailed report published in the Journal of Economic Perspectives, a prominent economist recently argued that while UBI could offer significant benefits, its implementation is riddled with formidable challenges, such as securing sustainable funding, navigating political resistance, and mitigating concerns about its effects on work incentives.

8

Which quotation from the report best illustrates the economist's argument?

A) "Preliminary experiments in several countries have indicated that UBI enhances financial stability for those involved."

B) "The idea of UBI has been the subject of much debate among policymakers, with varied opinions on its practicality."

C) "Implementing UBI would necessitate significant reforms to existing tax policies and social welfare programs, presenting substantial logistical and political obstacles."

D) "UBI is viewed by many as a promising approach to securing economic stability in an era of increasing automation."

CONTINUE

Text 1

Author Ayn Rand, in her book "The Fountainhead," emphasizes the importance of individualism and personal achievement. She argues that true success is measured by one's ability to pursue and achieve personal goals, regardless of societal expectations or norms. Rand's philosophy, known as Objectivism, posits that the highest moral purpose is the pursuit of one's own happiness and self-interest. According to Rand, focusing solely on individual achievements and personal pursuits defines the essence of a successful life.

Text 2

Philanthropist and business magnate Bill Gates advocates for a broader definition of success that includes both personal achievement and societal contribution. Gates, through his work with the Bill & Melinda Gates Foundation, emphasizes the importance of using personal success to benefit others. He argues that true success is not only about achieving personal goals but also about making a positive impact on society.

9

Based on the texts, how would Bill Gates (Text 2) most likely respond to Ayn Rand's (Text 1) perspective on the meaning of success?

A) As shortsighted, because it focuses on immediate personal goals rather than the longer timeframes needed for meaningful societal contributions

B) As insightful, because disregarding societal expectations to pursue one's goals is important

C) As flawed, because true success is primarily about making a positive impact on society and disregarding one's personal goals

D) As incomplete, because, although personal achievement is indeed a significant aspect of success, it neglects the importance of contributing to society

Practice Test 3

CONTINUE

The following text is from Aldous Huxley's 1932 novel "Brave New World.".

"Every one belongs to every one else," whispered the voice in the sleeping-tube. The students nodded, emphatically agreeing with a statement which upwards of sixty-two thousand repetitions in the dark had made them accept, not merely as true, but as axiomatic, self-evident, utterly indisputable. The Director smiled at them indulgently, ever so pleased with the effect of his words. "They'll grow up with what the psychologists used to call an instinctive hatred of books and flowers," he remarked.

10

According to the text, why does the Director smile at the students?

A) He is impressed by the students' critical thinking skills.

B) He is pleased with the students' acceptance of the conditioning.

C) He is happy that the students are excited about their future careers as psychologists.

D) He is amused by the students' rebellion against traditional education.

CONTINUE ➡

Key Performance Metrics Across Online Learning Platforms

Measure	Platform A	Platform B	Platform C
Average Improvement in Test Scores	12%	8%	15%
Student Satisfaction Rating	4.2/5	3.8/5	4.5/5
Retention Rate	85%	78%	90%

A research team conducted a study comparing three popular platforms to determine their effectiveness. Platform A is known for its rigorous test questions that challenge students to apply concepts in practical scenarios. Platform B emphasizes interactive learning models designed to engage students actively. Platform C offers a personalized learning experience, adapting the course material to each student's pace and comprehension level. The researchers gathered and recorded data on several key metrics, including average improvement in test scores, student satisfaction ratings, and retention rates after participants completed courses on each platform. After analyzing the results, the researchers concluded that the most effective platform was _____

11

Which choice most effectively uses data from the table to complete the researchers' conclusion?

A) Platform C, with its interactive learning models, achieving a 12% improvement in test scores and a retention rate at 85%.

B) Platform A, known for its rigorous test questions, achieving to a significant 12% improvement in test scores and a retention rate of 85%

C) Platform C, with its personalized learning experience, achieving a 15% improvement in test scores and a retention rate at 90%.

D) Platform B, with its interactive learning models, achieving an average of 8% improvement in test scores and a retention rate at 78%.

CONTINUE

Economic Impact of Tourism
in Different Regions

Region	Increase in Local GDP (%)	Job Creation (in thousands)	Infrastructure Development Rating (1-10)
Coastal Areas	15%	120	8.5
Urban Centers	20%	200	9.2
Rural Areas	8%	50	6.5

Over the past decade, different areas have experienced varying levels of economic benefits from tourism, influenced by their unique attractions and infrastructure. Coastal areas, known for their beaches and resorts, boast well-developed infrastructure that supports high visitor traffic. Urban centers, with their rich cultural and historical attractions, feature extensive infrastructure, including transportation networks and accommodations, which can support large numbers of tourists. In contrast, rural areas, despite their natural beauty and potential for eco-tourism, have relatively underdeveloped infrastructure. After collecting data, researchers concluded that the economic impact of tourism is closely related to the region's existing infrastructure and its capacity to attract and accommodate visitors effectively.

12

Which choice most effectively uses data from the table to support the researchers' conclusion?

A) Coastal areas, with their popular beaches and resorts, attract more tourists than rural areas, with 120,000 visitors compared to 50,000.

B) Rural areas, despite their low infrastructure development rating of 6.5, have begun investing heavily in infrastructure, so they'll see more economic growth.

C) Despite their natural attractions, rural areas, with an infrastructure development rating of 6.5, saw only an 8% increase in local GDP, whereas urban centers, with a higher infrastructure rating of 9.2, experienced a 20% increase in GDP.

D) Urban centers have seen the largest increase in infrastructure development rating, a score of 9.2, which has led to a 20% increase in GDP growth.

CONTINUE ⟶

In the mysterious depths of the ocean, certain species of octopuses, such as the mimic octopus, display extraordinary abilities; these clever creatures can transform their appearance to imitate a variety of marine animals they encounter, including lionfish, flatfish, and even venomous sea snakes. This mimicry serves dual purposes: protection from predators and an enhanced ability to hunt. However, a marine biologist warns that the loss of biodiversity in marine environments could severely undermine the mimic octopus's survival strategy, giving them fewer animals to transform into.

13

Which finding, if true, would most directly weaken the biologist's claim?

A) Studies have shown that mimic octopuses possess advanced memory capabilities, allowing them to remember and replicate mimicry patterns and predator responses from birth.

B) Mimic octopuses have been observed adapting their mimicry to entirely new species within a short period, demonstrating a remarkable ability to transform within seconds.

C) While mimic octopuses can imitate a variety of species, they primarily rely on the most common and abundant species in their habitat.

D) In ecosystems with high biodiversity, mimic octopuses thrive by mimicking a wide variety of species, thus reducing their risk of predation.

CONTINUE

Etched into the arid plains of southern Peru, the Nazca Lines are a series of ancient geoglyphs depicting various shapes and figures, some stretching over hundreds of meters. One specific aspect that has intrigued researchers is the depiction of animals. Some scholars have suggested that these animal figures were created for religious or ceremonial purposes, believing that they were offerings to the gods. However, archaeologist Maria Reiche, who spent decades studying the Nazca Lines, proposed that the geoglyphs might have been an astronomical calendar. Her theory, therefore, suggests that _____

14

Which choice most logically completes the text?

A) each animal figure may correspond to a different deity in Nazca mythology.

B) the depiction of animals is primarily a form of artistic expression without any deep religious significance.

C) each animal figure possibly aligns with specific celestial events that correspond to important seasonal activities like hunting and harvesting.

D) the geoglyphs were created to serve as a map for travelers, helping them navigate the jagged terrain of Peru.

CONTINUE

In a 2014 study published in the journal "Pain," researchers at Harvard Medical School aimed to investigate the power of the placebo effect-when patients experience real improvements in their condition after receiving a treatment that has no proven effect-on pain relief. They conducted an experiment involving 60 participants suffering from chronic lower back pain. The participants were randomly assigned to two groups: one group received a sugar pill they were told was a powerful painkiller, while the other group received no treatment. Remarkably, 59% of those who took the sugar pill reported a significant reduction in pain levels, while only 16% of the untreated group reported any improvement. Thus, researchers concluded that _____

15

Which choice most logically completes the text?

A) that sugar pills can be effective treatments for a variety of medical conditions.

B) the participants in the untreated group were more susceptible to chronic pain.

C) the placebo effect is a myth and has no real impact on pain relief.

D) the expectation of relief can lead to actual improvement in symptoms.

Practice Test 3

CONTINUE

The Voynich _____ most enigmatic books; discovered in the early 20th century, its pages are filled with strange illustrations and undeciphered text. Despite decades of study, no one has cracked the code. Therefore, the manuscript remains a puzzle, fascinating both cryptographers and historians.

Which choice completes the text so that it conforms to the conventions of Standard English?

A) Manuscript, one of the world's

B) Manuscript is the world's

C) Manuscript is one of the world's

D) Manuscript being one of the world's

The Moon, Earth's faithful satellite, has a hidden side that always faces away from us. This "far side" _____ a mystery until 1959 when the Soviet Luna 3 spacecraft captured the first images of it. Surprisingly, the far side is heavily cratered and lacks the large, smooth maria that are visible on the near side. This discovery, in fact, reshaped our understanding of the Moon's formation.

Which choice completes the text so that it conforms to the conventions of Standard English?

A) remains

B) would have remained

C) has remained

D) had remained

CONTINUE

Deep in the ocean, near Japan's Susami Bay, lies the world's deepest postbox-10 meters below the surface. Divers, seeking a novel experience, send waterproof postcards from this submerged mailbox. Indeed, it has become a popular attraction for _____ the postbox has received tens of thousands of letters-proof that even in the depths of the sea, communication thrives.

In Cameroon, there are two lakes-Lake Nyos and Lake _____ they can explode. These lakes, situated atop volcanic craters, trap vast amounts of carbon dioxide beneath their surfaces; when disturbed, this gas can be released in a catastrophic eruption-known as a limnic eruption. In 1986, Lake Nyos experienced such an event; a massive cloud of CO_2 erupted from the lake, suffocating over 1,700 people and thousands of livestock.

18

Which choice completes the text so that it conforms to the conventions of Standard English?

A) adventurers installed in 1999,

B) adventurers installed in 1999;

C) adventurers; installed in 1999,

D) adventurers, installed in 1999,

19

Which choice completes the text so that it conforms to the conventions of Standard English?

A) Monoun—that hold a deadly secret:

B) Monoun; that hold a deadly secret:

C) Monoun—that hold a deadly secret,

D) Monoun—that hold a deadly secret

Practice Test 3

CONTINUE

The catacombs-an underground ossuary containing the remains of over six million people-stretch for miles, hidden beneath the bustling streets of Paris. Originally created to address the city's overflowing cemeteries in the 18th century, _____.

20

Which choice completes the text so that it conforms to the conventions of Standard English?

A) tourists now flock to the catacombs, drawn by its macabre appeal.

B) the catacombs have since become a macabre tourist attraction

C) it is the catacombs that have since become a macabre tourist attraction

D) the catacombs' macabre appeal has made them a popular tourist destination.

There are several natural phenomena that baffle and amaze scientists: the Catatumbo Lightning in Venezuela, where lightning storms occur almost 300 nights a year; the Blood Falls in Antarctica, where iron-rich water seeps out of the ice, turning red when it hits the air; the Sailing Stones of Death Valley, which move across the desert floor on their own, leaving tracks behind _____ in Australia, a rare meteorological event where a massive, tubular cloud stretches across the sky.

21

Which choice completes the text so that it conforms to the conventions of Standard English?

A) them, and the Morning Glory Cloud

B) them; and the Morning Glory Cloud

C) them; and the Morning Glory Cloud,

D) them, and the Morning Glory Cloud;

CONTINUE

On the frozen surface of Lake Baikal-the world's deepest freshwater lake-_____ mysterious formations known as "Baikal Zen stones." These stones, balanced atop thin pillars of ice, appear as if placed by a careful hand; however, they are a natural phenomenon.

22

Which choice completes the text so that it conforms to the conventions of Standard English?

A) exist

B) exists

C) existing

D) has existed

The Voynich Manuscript, an illustrated codex written in an unknown script, has baffled cryptographers, linguists, and historians for centuries. Some believe it's a hoax, created to fool scholars; _____ others are convinced it holds the secrets of a lost language or contains alchemical knowledge.

23

Which choice completes the text with the most logical transition?

A) on the other hand,

B) similarly,

C) moreover,

D) thus,

CONTINUE

The theory of plate tectonics explains how continents drift, earthquakes occur, and mountains form and unifies many previously disconnected geological phenomena under a single, comprehensive framework. The theory was initially met with skepticism; scientists were reluctant to abandon earlier models that had dominated the field. _____, as evidence mounted, the scientific community embraced plate tectonics as a fundamental principle of geology.

24

Which choice completes the text with the most logical transition?

A) Consequently

B) Previously

C) Furthermore

D) Eventually

The invention of the printing press by Johannes Gutenberg in the mid-15th century revolutionized the way information was disseminated. _____ this invention, books were painstakingly copied by hand; thus, they were expensive and accessible only to the wealthy or the clergy. With the printing press, however, books could be produced quickly and in large quantities, leading to an unprecedented spread of knowledge.

25

Which choice completes the text with the most logical transition?

A) Despite

B) After

C) Prior to

D) Because of

CONTINUE

While researching a topic, a student has taken the following notes:

- Giant pandas are native to China and primarily eat bamboo, which constitutes over 99% of their diet.
- Habitat loss due to deforestation and agricultural expansion threatens the panda population.
- A bamboo die-off in the 1980s caused a significant decline in panda numbers.
- China established panda reserves in the 1990s to protect and increase the panda population.
- Zoos worldwide collaborate on breeding programs to support panda conservation.
- The giant panda was reclassified from "Endangered" to "Vulnerable" on the IUCN Red List in 2016.

26

The student wants to provide a specific example of an event after which the panda population drastically decreased. Which choice most effectively uses relevant information from the notes to accomplish this goal?

A) Deforestation and agricultural expansion have led to significant habitat loss, threatening the survival of the giant panda.

B) In 2016, the giant panda's status was changed from "Endangered" to "Vulnerable" on the IUCN Red List.

C) During the 1980s, a large-scale die-off of bamboo occurred, which caused a drastic decline in panda numbers.

D) Global breeding initiatives in zoos have played a key role in efforts to boost the panda population.

CONTINUE

While researching a topic, a student has taken the following notes:

- The Burj Khalifa is the tallest building in the world, standing at 828 meters, located in Dubai, UAE.
- The Great Wall of China stretches over 13,000 miles, originally built to protect Chinese states from invasions.
- The Sagrada Familia is an unfinished basilica in Barcelona, designed by architect Antoni Gaudí; construction began in 1882.
- The Sydney Opera House is a UNESCO World Heritage Site, known for its distinctive shell-like design, located in Sydney, Australia.
- The Panama Canal is an engineering marvel completed in 1914, connecting the Atlantic and Pacific Oceans, revolutionizing global maritime trade.
- The Colosseum is an ancient Roman amphitheater in Rome, Italy, famous for gladiatorial games, completed in AD 80.

27

The student wants to provide a specific example of an architectural project that has not been completed for over a century. Which choice most effectively uses relevant information from the notes to accomplish this goal?

A) The Sagrada Familia in Barcelona, designed by Antoni Gaudí, started construction in 1882.

B) Connecting the Atlantic and Pacific Oceans, the Panama Canal is an engineering marvel completed in 1914.

C) Designed by Antoni Gaudí, the Sagrada Familia is an unfinished basilica that began construction in 1882.

D) Stretching over 13,000 miles, the Great Wall of China was constructed to defend against invasions.

If you finish before the time is called, you may check your work on this module only.

On Test Day, you will only be able to move to the next module when time expires.

Answer Key

Question Number	Correct Answer	Level of Difficulty	Question Type
1	A	Medium	**Craft and Structure:** *Words in Context*
2	C	Medium	**Craft and Structure:** *Words in Context*
3	B	Hard	**Craft and Structure:** *Words in Context*
4	D	Easy	**Craft and Structure:** *Interpreting Words and Phrases*
5	A	Hard	**Craft and Structure:** *Main Purpose*
6	C	Hard	**Craft and Structure:** *Function of the Underlined Portion*
7	A	Easy	**Information and Ideas:** *Support a Claim*
8	C	Medium	**Information and Ideas:** *Cite Text as Evidence*
9	D	Hard	**Craft and Structure:** *Cross-Text Connection*
10	B	Easy	**Information and Ideas:** *Detail*
11	C	Medium	**Information and Ideas:** *Cite Text as Evidence (Infographics)*
12	C	Hard	**Information and Ideas:** *Support a claim (Infographics)*
13	A	Hard	**Information and Ideas:** *Weaken a Claim*

Question Number	Correct Answer	Level of Difficulty	Question Type
14	C	Medium	**Information and Ideas:** *Inference (Complete the Text)*
15	D	Medium	**Information and Ideas:** *Inference (Complete the Text)*
16	C	Medium	**Standard English Conventions:** *Sentence Structure*
17	D	Hard	**Standard English Conventions:** *Verbs*
18	C	Hard	**Standard English Conventions:** *Punctuation and Sentence Structure*
19	A	Medium	**Standard English Conventions:** *Punctuation and Sentence Structure*
20	B	Easy	**Standard English Conventions:** *Modifiers*
21	B	Hard	**Standard English Conventions:** *Punctuation*
22	A	Medium	**Standard English Conventions:** *Verbs*
23	A	Easy	**Expression of Ideas:** *Transitions*
24	D	Hard	**Expression of Ideas:** *Transitions*
25	C	Hard	**Expression of Ideas:** *Transitions*
26	C	Medium	**Expression of Ideas:** *Rhetorical Synthesis*
27	C	Easy	**Expression of Ideas:** *Rhetorical Synthesis*

Raw Score Conversion Table

Raw Score (# of Correct Answers)	Reading and Writing Section Score	Raw Score (# of Correct Answers)	Reading and Writing Section Score
54	800	30	510
53	780	29	500
52	760	28	490
51	730	27	480
50	720	26	470
49	710	25	470
48	700	24	450
47	680	23	440
46	670	22	430
45	660	21	430
44	650	20	410
43	640	19	400
42	630	18	390
41	620		
40	610		
39	600		
38	590		
37	580		
36	570		
35	560		
34	550		
33	540		
32	530		
31	520		

 Explanations

1. Words in Context: Medium

Answer: A) integral to

Step-by-Step Explanation:

1. The passage discusses the social structure and complex behaviors of honeybee colonies, with a particular focus on the waggle dance performed by foraging bees. This dance is described as crucial for the hive's survival because it communicates the location of food sources.
2. Notice the emphasis on the waggle dance being "crucial to the survival of the hive." This indicates that the dance is not just important but essential for the bees' ability to find food and, therefore, for the overall success and survival of the colony.
3. The word we need should reflect the idea that the waggle dance is a necessary and fundamental part of the colony's survival and ability to thrive in challenging environments.
4. Ask yourself, what word best describes something that is essential or absolutely necessary? "Integral to" is the most logical choice because it means being an essential part of something, which fits perfectly with the idea that the waggle dance is crucial for the survival of the honeybee colony.

Explanation of Incorrect Options:

B) reliant on: This is incorrect because, when plugged into the sentence, it suggests that the waggle dance depends on something else, which makes no sense given that the context of the passage is about the bees' reliance on the waggle dance.

C) subjected to: This is incorrect because it implies being under the control or influence of something, which doesn't fit the context of the waggle dance being essential for survival.

D) inessential to: This is incorrect because it means not necessary, which directly contradicts the passage's emphasis on the waggle dance being crucial to the colony's survival.

2. Words in Context: Medium

Answer: C) received

Step-by-Step Explanation:

1. Let's deconstruct the passage together. The passage describes how Shonda Rhimes' television series *Bridgerton* has gained widespread acclaim, becoming a cultural phenomenon and being praised for its innovative approach to period drama. The passage then mentions that the series has been recognized with one of television's most prestigious awards.

2. Notice the context around the award being described as "one of television's most prestigious accolades," which indicates that the series was honored with this recognition. The word we need should convey that *Bridgerton* was given or awarded the Primetime Emmy Award for Outstanding Drama Series.

3. As a result, the word we need should reflect the idea that the series was formally given or honored with the Emmy Award.

4. Ask yourself, what word best describes the act of being given or awarded something? "Received" is the most logical choice because it means being given something, especially as a form of recognition or honor, which fits perfectly with the context of *Bridgerton* being honored with the Primetime Emmy Award.

Explanation of Incorrect Options:

A) achieved: While *Bridgerton* indeed achieved great success, "achieved" implies accomplishment through effort. When plugged into the sentence, it doesn't fit the context of being awarded or given an accolade. The sentence is emphasizing the receipt of an honor, not the process of achieving it.

B) completed: This is incorrect because "completed" means finishing something, which doesn't fit the context of being awarded an honor. Inserting "completed" into the sentence would make the sentence illogical, as it suggests the series finished an award, which doesn't make sense.

D) renounced: This is incorrect because it means to formally give up or reject something, which is the opposite of receiving an award.

3. Words in Context: Hard

Answer: B) ascertain

Step-by-Step Explanation:

1. Let's understand the passage together. The passage discusses the idea of evaluating a philosopher's influence by examining how much their theories are incorporated into contemporary academic discourse. The example of Friedrich Nietzsche is given, showing that his works are frequently referenced and debated, which emphasizes their continued importance.

2. Notice the phrase "to examine the extent to which these theories are incorporated into contemporary academic discourse." This indicates that the passage is focused on determining how much impact a philosopher's theories have had over time. The example of Nietzsche, whose works have had a "profound impact" and are "frequently referenced and debated," underscores the importance of assessing how often and in what context these theories are discussed, as this reflects their influence.

3. Thus, the word we need should reflect the process of determining or measuring the influence of a philosopher's theories.

4. Ascertain" is the most logical choice because it means to find out or determine something with certainty, which fits perfectly with the context of examining how much a philosopher's theories are incorporated into academic discourse.

Explanation of Incorrect Options:

A) promulgate: This is incorrect because it means to promote or spread ideas, which isn't supported by the context of the passage. The passage focuses on evaluating the impact of a philosopher's work on academic discourse, not on the spread of ideas. For "promulgate" to be correct, the passage would need to discuss the dissemination of ideas rather than their influence on other works.

C) trivialize: This is incorrect because it means to make something seem less important, which contradicts the idea of evaluating the significant influence of a philosopher's theories.

D) undermine: This is incorrect because it means to weaken or damage something, which does not align with the context of determining the extent of influence.

4. Interpreting Words in Context: Easy

Answer: D) depths

Step-by-Step Explanation:

1. Let's look at what the passage is saying. The passage describes Zhuangzi reflecting on a vivid dream where he was a butterfly. After waking, he spends time contemplating the nature of reality and embarks on an introspective journey into the "recesses" of his mind and soul, which leaves him with profound existential questions.

2. Notice the phrase "traveling inward into the recesses of my mind and soul." The context indicates that Zhuangzi is engaging in deep, thoughtful introspection, as he tries to understand the profound questions about reality that the dream has stirred within him. The fact that he spends "days reflecting" implies that this exploration is not superficial or brief; instead, it suggests a journey into the deeper, more hidden parts of his mind and soul.

3. Therefore, the word we need should describe a part of the mind or soul that is deep, hidden, or internal.

4. "Depths" is the most logical choice because it refers to the deepest or most profound parts, which aligns with the context of Zhuangzi exploring the deeper aspects of his mind and soul.

Explanation of Incorrect Options:

A) luxuries: This is incorrect because it isn't supported by the passage. The passage does not mention or develop the idea of indulgence, which is what "luxuries" refers to.

B) breaks: This is incorrect because it implies interruptions or pauses, which the passage does not support. The context describes continuous, deep reflection rather than intermittent pauses. Hence, we would consider B) irrelevant and not directly related to the topic of the passage.

C) surfaces: This is incorrect because it refers to the outer or external parts of something, which the passage does not focus on. Instead, the passage is concerned with deep, internal exploration, the opposite of "surfaces."

5. Main Purpose: Hard

Answer: A) To narrate an encounter between the speaker and the poet

Logical Breakdown and Explanation:

To determine the main purpose of the text, we need to focus on the **big picture** of the poem, including the speaker's overall tone and the themes expressed. In the poem, the speaker reflects on the **poet's ability to convey deep, universal truths** through their words. The admiration for the poet's skill and the impact of their poetry is evident throughout the lines.

Option A is correct because the poem reflects on the **profound impact** of the poet's words, particularly in the lines like "Thy verses speak of a world unseen" and "Revealing truths both far and nigh." The poem concludes with a note of **admiration**, as shown by the phrase "And in thy lines, a gentle grace, / That few can ever share." This indicates the speaker's deep **respect and admiration** for the poet's unique ability to express beauty and truth.

Option B is incorrect because while the poem mentions celestial imagery such as the "stars above in the sky" and the "endless sea," it does not suggest that the poet **influences** these natural elements. Instead, the poet's words are inspired by these elements, making this option a **misinterpretation** of the relationship between the poet and the natural world.

Option C is incorrect because the poem does not focus on the poet's **meticulous approach** to writing about nature. While natural imagery is present, the poem centers more on the **impact of the poet's words** and the truths they reveal, rather than on the poet's specific **technique** or approach to writing.

Option D is incorrect because the poem is not **narrating an encounter** between the speaker and the poet. Instead, it is a reflection on the poet's work and the admiration the speaker has for the poet's ability to express beauty and truth. There is no mention of a personal meeting or interaction between the speaker and the poet.

6. Function of the Underlined Portion: Hard

Answer: C) To present the relevant results of the study that contradict a previously held assumption

Logical Breakdown and Explanation:

To determine the function of the underlined portion, we need to focus on **what the information accomplishes** within the context of the text. The passage is about a study conducted by economists to test the assumption that remote work leads to **decreased productivity** and **lower job satisfaction**. The underlined portion provides the **actual findings** of the study, which **contradict** this prior assumption by showing **increased productivity** and **higher job satisfaction** among remote workers.

Option C is correct because the underlined portion **presents the relevant results** of the study, specifically showing that productivity increased by **15%** and that **85%** of remote workers reported **higher job satisfaction**. These findings **challenge the traditional belief** that remote work harms productivity and satisfaction. The results directly contradict the **previous assumption**, making this option the most accurate description of the function.

Option A is incorrect because the underlined portion does not focus on **revealing the purpose of the study**. The purpose of the study—testing assumptions about remote work—was already introduced earlier in the text, so this is not the main function of the underlined portion.

Option B is incorrect because while the underlined portion emphasizes the **positive findings**, it does not discuss any **negative implications** of the study. The text highlights increased productivity and job satisfaction, with no mention of adverse results, making this option a **misinterpretation** of the text.

Option D is incorrect because the underlined portion does not introduce the **hypothesis**. The hypothesis—remote work might lead to decreased productivity and job satisfaction—is introduced in the earlier part of the passage. The underlined portion instead **presents the findings** that challenge this hypothesis.

7. Support a Claim: Easy

Answer: A) "I care for myself. The more solitary, the more friendless, the more unsustained I am, the more I will respect myself."

Logical Breakdown and Explanation:

To determine the best quote supporting the critic's claim, we need to analyze the critic's main argument: **Jane Eyre's moral integrity and independence shape her interactions with Mr. Rochester**, especially in maintaining her **sense of self-worth** despite her growing feelings for him.

Option A is correct because it directly reflects Jane's strong sense of self-worth and her determination to maintain her principles, even in challenging circumstances. In the quote, Jane declares, "I care for myself. This phrase directly highlights **Jane's independence** and **self-reliance**. Jane is affirming that, regardless of external circumstances, her primary concern is her **own self-respect**. This connects to the critic's point that Jane maintains her sense of self-worth, even when her feelings for Mr. Rochester grow stronger. The other part of the quote states "The more solitary, the more friendless, the more unsustained I am, the more I will respect myself." Here, Jane is declaring that even in the face of **isolation and hardship**, she will continue to respect herself. This reflects her **moral integrity**: Jane will not sacrifice her principles or sense of worth for the sake of her relationship with Mr. Rochester or anyone else.

Option B is incorrect because while it mentions **equality** between Jane and Mr. Rochester, it focuses more on **mutual respect** within their relationship, not on Jane's **independence** or her ability to **maintain her self-worth**. The critic's claim centers on Jane's **personal integrity**, so this quote doesn't fully capture the essence of that argument.

Option C is incorrect because it emphasizes Jane's **feelings of love** for Mr. Rochester without referencing her **moral integrity** or **independence**. The critic's claim highlights Jane's **strength of character**, and this quote is more about the **power of love** rather than her sense of **self-worth**.

Option D is incorrect because it portrays Jane's **enduring love** for Mr. Rochester, even when he ceases to notice her, but it does not reflect her **moral integrity** or **self-respect**. This quote focuses on her **emotional attachment** rather than her ability to **stand by her principles**, which is the central point of the critic's argument.

8. Cite Text as Evidence: Medium

Answer: C) "Implementing UBI would necessitate significant reforms to existing tax policies and social welfare programs, presenting substantial logistical and political obstacles."

Logical Breakdown and Explanation:

To determine which quotation best illustrates the economist's argument, we need to focus on the **argument** presented in the passage. The passage describes both the benefits and challenges of Universal Basic Income (UBI). While UBI could offer significant benefits, the economist argues that its **implementation faces formidable challenges**, including issues like **securing sustainable funding**, **political resistance**, and the **effects on work incentives**.

Option C is correct because it best illustrates the economist's argument by directly addressing the significant challenges of implementing UBI. The quotation highlights the need for "significant reforms to existing tax policies and social welfare programs," pointing to the complexity of adjusting current systems to accommodate UBI. It also references "substantial logistical and political obstacles," aligning with the economist's concern about navigating political resistance and structural changes. This makes it the most relevant quote, as it encapsulates the core argument that, despite UBI's potential benefits, its **practical implementation presents formidable difficulties**.

Option A is incorrect because while it discusses **financial stability** as a potential benefit of UBI, it does not address the implementation challenges or logistical obstacles. The economist's argument in the passage acknowledges UBI's benefits, but this quotation **leaves out** the formidable difficulties that the economist emphasizes.

Option B is incorrect because it is **too vague** and does not specifically address the economist's focus on **challenges** to UBI. Although it mentions the debate surrounding UBI, it doesn't illustrate the practical or logistical difficulties that are central to the economist's argument.

Option D is incorrect because, like Option A, it only discusses the **promising aspects** of UBI, such as its potential to secure **economic stability**. However, it leaves out the difficulties and political obstacles that are key to the economist's critique of UBI.

9. Cross-Text Connection: Hard

Answer: D) As incomplete, because, although personal achievement is indeed a significant aspect of success, it neglects the importance of contributing to society

Logical Breakdown and Explanation:

To determine how Bill Gates would most likely respond to Ayn Rand's perspective, we need to examine the key differences in their definitions of success. Rand focuses on **individual achievement** and **self-interest** as the essence of a successful life (Text 1), while Gates advocates for using personal success to **benefit society** (Text 2).

Option D is correct because Gates would likely argue that while personal achievement is important, success must also include societal contribution, which Rand's perspective neglects. This aligns with Gates' philosophy that success involves both personal and societal achievements.

Option A is incorrect because Gates does not criticize Rand's focus on immediate personal goals, but rather her exclusion of societal impact, making it **off-topic**.

Option B is incorrect because Gates would not support Rand's disregard for societal expectations. This response **contradicts** Gates' belief in societal contributions.

Option C is incorrect because Gates does not disregard personal goals; he believes success includes both personal achievements and societal impact, making this **distorted**.

10. Detail: Easy

Answer: B) He is pleased with the students' acceptance of the conditioning.

Logical Breakdown and Explanation:

To determine why the Director smiles at the students, we need to look at how the passage describes the students' reaction and the Director's response to their behavior.

Option B is correct because the text clearly indicates that the Director is pleased with the success of the conditioning. The phrase "the students nodded, emphatically agreeing with a statement which upwards of sixty-two thousand repetitions in the dark had made them accept" shows that the students have been conditioned to accept the statement as "axiomatic, self-evident, utterly indisputable." This suggests that the Director is pleased with how well the conditioning process has worked, which is why he smiles "indulgently" at them. His satisfaction is directly tied to their unquestioning acceptance of the idea, confirming that he is pleased with their conditioned response.

Option A is incorrect because the text does not mention anything about the students' critical thinking skills. In fact, the students' acceptance of the statement is a result of conditioning, not critical thinking.

Option C is incorrect because the passage does not mention anything about the students' future careers as psychologists, nor does it suggest that the Director's smile is related to their career aspirations.

Option D is incorrect because the students are not rebelling against traditional education. Instead, they are fully accepting the conditioning they have undergone, which is the opposite of rebellion.

11. Cite Text as Evidence (Infographic): Medium

Answer: C) Platform C, with its personalized learning experience, achieving a 15% improvement in test scores and a retention rate at 90%.

Logical Breakdown and Explanation:

To determine the most effective platform, we need to consider the key performance metrics provided in the table, including improvement in test scores, student satisfaction, and retention rates. The most effective platform would likely be the one with the highest overall performance in these areas.

Option C is correct because Platform C shows the highest average improvement in test scores at 15% and the highest retention rate at 90%. This makes Platform C the most effective based on the data provided, as it performs best across all the key metrics.

Option A is incorrect because it misrepresents the information. Platform C offers a 15% improvement in test scores, not 12%, and it is not focused on interactive learning models (that is Platform B).

Option B is incorrect because although Platform A has a 12% improvement in test scores and an 85% retention rate, it does not outperform Platform C, which has higher scores across the board.

Option D is incorrect because Platform B has the lowest improvement in test scores at 8% and the lowest retention rate at 78%, making it the least effective of the three platforms based on the data.

12. Support a Claim (Infographic): Hard

Answer: C) Despite their natural attractions, rural areas, with an infrastructure development rating of 6.5, saw only an 8% increase in local GDP, whereas urban centers, with a higher infrastructure rating of 9.2, experienced a 20% increase in GDP.

Logical Breakdown and Explanation:

To determine the best answer, we need to focus on how the data from the table supports the researchers' conclusion, which is that the economic impact of tourism is closely tied to the infrastructure of each region. The best answer should link the regions' infrastructure ratings with their economic growth.

Option C is correct because it directly reflects the information provided in both the table and the passage. The passage states that **urban centers** feature **"extensive infrastructure."** This matches the data in the table, where urban centers have a high infrastructure development rating of **9.2** and saw a **20%** increase in local GDP. On the other hand, the passage also highlights that **rural areas** have **"relatively underdeveloped infrastructure."** This aligns with the table's data showing that rural areas have a lower infrastructure rating of **6.5** and only experienced an **8%** increase in GDP. This comparison effectively supports the conclusion that economic growth from tourism is closely related to the level of infrastructure development, as indicated in the passage.

Option A is incorrect because it inaccurately compares visitors instead of focusing on infrastructure and GDP growth, which is not mentioned in the table. The 120,000 vs. 50,000 visitor figures are not provided in the table.

Option B is incorrect because it introduces information not mentioned in the table about rural areas investing in infrastructure, which goes beyond the data provided. The table does not suggest future predictions about growth.

Option D is incorrect because it goes beyond what the data provides. The statement that "urban centers have seen the largest increase in infrastructure development rating" is misleading since the table only provides the current infrastructure development rating (**9.2**) but does not show any previous ratings or data about an increase. Thus, this is unsupported by the data in the table and the informaiton in the passage.

13. Weaken a Claim: Hard

Answer: A) Studies have shown that mimic octopuses possess advanced memory capabilities, allowing them to remember and replicate mimicry patterns and predator responses from birth.

Logical Breakdown and Explanation:

To determine the correct answer, we need to examine the biologist's claim that the **loss of biodiversity** would **undermine the mimic octopus's survival strategy** by leaving fewer animals for the octopuses to mimic. The correct answer will directly challenge this claim by presenting evidence that makes it less likely to be true.

Option A is correct because it presents evidence that mimic octopuses have **advanced memory capabilities**, allowing them to **remember and replicate mimicry patterns and predator responses from birth**. This suggests that even if biodiversity decreases, mimic octopuses could still successfully imitate species they've already encountered or learned from, weakening the biologist's concern that a loss of biodiversity would severely affect their survival. This information challenges the idea that mimic octopuses need a wide variety of species to mimic, thereby reducing the impact of biodiversity loss on their survival strategy.

Option B is incorrect because, although it highlights the octopus's ability to **adapt its mimicry to new species**, it doesn't specifically weaken the claim that a reduction in available species would undermine their survival. Adapting to new species doesn't refute the biologist's concern about the overall reduction in species due to biodiversity loss.

Option C is incorrect because it actually **supports the biologist's claim**. If mimic octopuses **primarily rely on common and abundant species**, then a loss of biodiversity would likely reduce the number of species they can mimic, confirming the biologist's concern.

Option D is incorrect because it focuses on **ecosystems with high biodiversity**, which is consistent with the biologist's claim. It implies that in high-biodiversity environments, mimic octopuses thrive by mimicking many species, but it does not weaken the claim about what happens when biodiversity is lost.

14. Inference (Complete the Text): Medium

Answer: C) each animal figure possibly aligns with specific celestial events that correspond to important seasonal activities like hunting and harvesting.

Logical Breakdown and Explanation:

To determine the correct answer, we need to focus on Maria Reiche's theory that the Nazca Lines might have been an **astronomical calendar**. The correct answer will logically extend this idea by connecting the **animal figures** to **celestial events** or seasonal patterns.

Option C is correct because it directly supports Reiche's theory that the geoglyphs might have functioned as an **astronomical calendar**. It suggests that **each animal figure aligns with specific celestial events** that are connected to **important seasonal activities like hunting and harvesting**. This explanation fits with the idea that the geoglyphs were not just art or religious symbols but had a practical, astronomical purpose.

Option A is incorrect because it suggests that the animal figures represent **different deities** in Nazca mythology, which contradicts Reiche's theory of the astronomical calendar. This explanation aligns more with the religious interpretation, which is not supported by Reiche's findings.

Option B is incorrect because it claims that the animal depictions are **purely artistic**, without religious significance. This does not align with Reiche's theory, which implies that the figures had a practical purpose related to the movement of celestial bodies rather than just being art.

Option D is incorrect because it suggests the geoglyphs served as a **map for travelers**, which is unrelated to Reiche's theory of the geoglyphs being an astronomical calendar. There is no evidence in the passage to suggest that the Nazca Lines were designed for navigation, making this answer off topic and unsupported by the text.

15. Inference (Complete the Text): Medium

Answer: D) the expectation of relief can lead to actual improvement in symptoms.

Logical Breakdown and Explanation:

To determine the correct answer, we need to focus on how the **placebo effect** is described and what the researchers discovered in their experiment. The text highlights that **59% of participants** who took the sugar pill reported a **significant reduction in pain**, even though the sugar pill had no proven medical effect. This result suggests that the **expectation of relief** played a significant role in the participants' improvement.

Option D is correct because it directly ties the researchers' conclusion to the idea that the **expectation of relief** (from the sugar pill) can lead to **actual improvement in symptoms**, as shown by the high percentage of participants who reported less pain despite receiving no active treatment.

Option A is incorrect because the researchers are only focusing on the **specific experiment** described in the passage, which investigates the placebo effect on chronic lower back pain. Making a broader claim that sugar pills could be effective for a **variety of medical conditions** extends beyond the scope of the study, which is not supported by the details provided. This makes it **off-topic** and an overgeneralization based on the experiment.

Option B is incorrect because the focus of the study is not about the **susceptibility** of participants to chronic pain but about the difference between those who took a placebo and those who did not. This option is off topic and unsupported by the ideas developed in the passage.

Option C is incorrect because it contradicts the findings. The experiment shows that the placebo effect **does** have an impact on pain relief, as seen in the significant difference between the treated and untreated groups.

16. Sentence Structure: Medium

Answer: C) Manuscript is one of the world's

Logical Breakdown and Explanation:

To determine the correct choice, focus on sentence structure and ensure the sentence contains a main verb to make it complete and uses the proper phrasing.

Option C is correct because it provides a **complete sentence** with the main verb "is," making the structure "The Voynich Manuscript is one of the world's most enigmatic books." This properly connects the subject ("Voynich Manuscript") to the predicate, forming a grammatically sound sentence.

Option A is incorrect because it forms a **fragment**, lacking a main verb. The phrase "one of the world's most enigmatic books" is a descriptive phrase, but without a verb, the sentence remains incomplete. Remember that a semicolon connects two independent clauses. However, there is no IC before the semicolon.

Option B is incorrect because "is the world's most" requires a **singular noun** to follow it. The noun "books" is **plural**, creating a grammatical mismatch.

Option D is incorrect because it results in a **fragment**; "being one of the world's" lacks the necessary main verb to complete the sentence, making it incomplete. Remember that -ing words do not function as verbs.

17. Verbs: Hard

Answer: D) had remained

Logical Breakdown and Explanation:

To determine the correct answer, we must focus on the tense of the verb in relation to the context provided in the passage.

Option D is correct because the past perfect tense "had remained" is used to describe an action that occurred **before** a specific point in the past ("until 1959"), when the Soviet Luna 3 spacecraft captured the first images of the far side of the Moon. The use of "had remained" appropriately conveys that the far side was a mystery **up until** that moment in the past.

Option A ("remains") is incorrect because it uses the **present tense**, which suggests that the far side is **still** a mystery today, contradicting the fact that it was revealed in 1959.

Option B ("would have remained") is incorrect because it suggests a **hypothetical** situation, which is not appropriate since the far side **was** a mystery until it was revealed by the Soviet Luna 3 spacecraft.

Option C ("has remained") is incorrect because the **present perfect tense** ("has remained") implies that the far side of the Moon **continues to be** a mystery up to the present moment. However, the passage specifically refers to a **past event**—the discovery in 1959 by the Soviet Luna 3 spacecraft. Since the mystery was resolved in 1959, the present perfect tense would be inappropriate here, as it suggests that the mystery is still ongoing. The passage needs to emphasize that the mystery was resolved in the past, which is why the past perfect ("had remained") is the correct choice.

18. Punctuation and Sentence Structure: Hard

Answer: C) adventurers; installed in 1999,

Logical Breakdown and Explanation:

To determine which choice correctly completes the sentence, we need to focus on proper sentence structure and punctuation rules, especially how independent clauses (ICs) should be separated.

Option C is correct because it appropriately uses a semicolon to separate two independent clauses: "Indeed, it has become a popular attraction for adventurers" and "the postbox has received tens of thousands of letters." The semicolon creates a logical break between these complete ideas, making the sentence grammatically correct.

Option A is incorrect because it creates a run-on sentence by improperly connecting two independent clauses with just a comma. The clause after "adventurers" ("installed in 1999") does not have proper separation.

Option B is incorrect because the semicolon placement makes it sound as though the adventurers were installed in 1999, which is illogical ("it has become a popular attraction for adventurers installed in 1999").

Option D is also incorrect because it creates another run-on sentence. The comma after "adventurers" does not separate the two independent clauses, which leads to a sentence structure error.

19. Punctuation and Sentence Structure: Medium

Answer: A) Monoun—that hold a deadly secret:

Logical Breakdown and Explanation:

To determine which choice correctly completes the sentence, we need to focus on how the punctuation separates and connects clauses, ensuring that independent and dependent clauses are correctly joined.

Option A is correct because the dash is the second of two dashes that is used to close the nonessential information ("Lake Nyos and Lake Monoun"). The colon then properly introduces the explanation of the secret, which is the potential for an explosion. This structure avoids run-ons and provides clarity between the parts of the sentence.

Option B is incorrect because it uses a semicolon improperly. Semicolons should only be used between two independent clauses, and "that hold a deadly secret" is a dependent clause, so it cannot stand alone as a sentence.

Options C and **D** create run-on sentences because they fail to properly separate the two independent clauses: "there are two lakes that hold a deadly secret" and "they can explode." Both the comma and lack of punctuation lead to incorrect sentence structures.

20. Modifiers: Easy

Answer: B) the catacombs have since become a macabre tourist attraction

Logical Breakdown and Explanation:

To determine which choice correctly completes the sentence, we need to ensure that the modifying phrase "originally created to address the city's overflowing cemeteries in the 18th century" correctly describes the subject at the beginning of the independent clause. In this case, the catacombs are what were created, so they must be the subject of the independent clause.

Option B is correct because "**the catacombs**" are **placed at the beginning of the independent clause**, making it clear that they were created to address the city's cemeteries. The structure maintains grammatical clarity and avoids any confusion about the noun being modified.

Option A is incorrect because it begins with "**tourists**," which shifts the focus away from what the modifying phrase is referring to. This creates a disconnect between the modifier and the subject it is meant to describe, resulting in a dangling modifier (a grammatical error) and an illogical meaning (**tourists** weren't created to address the city's cemetery issue).

Option C is incorrect because it unnecessarily complicates the sentence with "**it** is the catacombs." This phrasing is less direct and adds confusion to the sentence structure.

Option D is incorrect because the possessive form "the catacombs' macabre **appeal**" does not count as the subject of the sentence. Instead, the subject becomes "appeal," which does not logically connect with the modifying phrase "originally created to address the city's overflowing cemeteries." The **appeal** was not created to address cemetery issues—the catacombs were—so this structure leads to confusion and a dangling modifier.

21. Punctuation: Hard

Answer: B) them; and the Morning Glory Cloud

Logical Breakdown and Explanation:

To determine the correct punctuation for this sentence, we need to focus on how to **separate complex items in a list**. **Semicolons** are used to separate items in a list when the **items themselves contain commas**.

Option B is correct because it uses a semicolon to separate the final item in the list, "the Morning Glory Cloud in Australia," from the previous items. This keeps the list of items consistent (a semicolon is used to separate each of the items in the list). Here's the breakdown of the list:

1. The Catatumbo Lightning in Venezuela, where lightning storms occur almost 300 nights a year;
2. The Blood Falls in Antarctica, where iron-rich water seeps out of the ice, turning red when it hits the air;
3. The Sailing Stones of Death Valley, which move across the desert floor on their own, leaving tracks behind them;
4. The Morning Glory Cloud in Australia, a rare meteorological event where a massive, tubular cloud stretches across the sky.

Option A is incorrect because it uses a comma, which doesn't provide sufficient separation between the complex items in the list. The use of a semicolon is needed here for consistency since semicolons are used to separate the items in the list.

Option C is incorrect because it adds an unnecessary comma after "the Morning Glory Cloud." Remember that commas should not be placed before prepositional phrases that blend naturally with the previous information. The prepositional phrase "in Australia" specifies the place where the Morning Glory Cloud occurs and creates one fluid idea. Note: the prepositional phrases in the other items in the list ("in Venezuela" and "in Antarctica") don't have commas before them.

Option D is incorrect because it adds a semicolon after "the Morning Glory Cloud," which is the wrong placement. The semicolon should appear before the name of the phenomenon, not after.

22. Verbs: Medium

Answer: A) exist

Logical Breakdown and Explanation:

To determine the correct verb, we need to focus on the **subject-verb agreement** and identify the subject of the sentence, which is "mysterious formations." Since the subject is plural, the verb must also be plural.

Option A is correct because "exist" is the **plural form of the verb** and agrees with the **plural subject** "mysterious formations." The sentence is also in an **inverted form**, where the verb appears before the subject ("On the frozen surface of Lake Baikal... exist mysterious formations..."). Remember that a prepositional phrase can't contain the subject of a sentence, and since "Lake Baikal" is part of the prepositional phrase "on the frozen surface of Lake Baikal," we know the subject must appear after the verb in this sentence.

Option B is incorrect because "exists" is a **singular verb**, which does not agree with the plural subject "mysterious formations."

Option C is incorrect because "existing" **does not function as a verb** (-ing words by themselves do not function as verbs). This leads to a **fragment** (an incomplete sentence).

Option D is incorrect because "has existed" is a **singular verb**, which does not agree with the plural subject "mysterious formations."

23. Transitions: Easy

Answer: A) on the other hand,

Logical Breakdown and Explanation:

To determine the most logical transition, we need to understand the relationship between the two independent clauses. The first clause discusses **one belief** about the Voynich Manuscript being a hoax, while the **second presents a differing view** that it may hold valuable knowledge.

Option A is correct because "**on the other hand**" introduces a **contrast between the two perspectives**—one group thinks the manuscript is a hoax, while the other believes it has significant knowledge. This transition clearly signals the opposing viewpoints.

Option B is incorrect because "**similarly**" indicates a **comparison** between two sentences along the same lines, which is not logical here since the second clause presents a contrasting idea.

Option C is incorrect because "**moreover**" is used **to add information that continues the discussion of the previous statement**, not to introduce a contrasting viewpoint.

Option D is incorrect because "**thus**" implies a **conclusion or result**, which doesn't fit the sentence structure or the relationship between the two ideas.

24. Transitions: Hard

Answer: D) Eventually

Logical Breakdown and Explanation:

To determine the most logical transition, we need to focus on how the passage describes the **shift from skepticism to acceptance over time**. The first sentence sets up the **initial skepticism** toward the theory, and the second sentence describes the growing acceptance as evidence mounted.

Option D is correct because **"eventually"** signals a **progression of time**, indicating that the scientific community gradually came to accept the theory as more evidence accumulated. This aligns perfectly with the passage's development.

Option A is incorrect because **"consequently"** suggests a **cause-and-effect relationship**, but the passage emphasizes a slow progression, not an immediate consequence.

Option B is incorrect because **"previously"** refers to an earlier time, which **doesn't logically fit here**, as the sentence is describing a change that occurred at a later point in time.

Option C is incorrect because **"furthermore" continues the discussion of the previous statement** rather than indicating a progression or change in views, which is the focus of the passage. In order for C) to be correct, the sentence started by "furthermore" would need to provide another detail about the *initial theory*, which is not the topic of the sentence.

25. Transitions: Hard

Answer: C) Prior to

Logical Breakdown and Explanation:

To determine the most logical transition, we need to examine how the **passage contrasts the time before and after** the invention of the printing press. The sentence following the blank describes the process of copying books by hand, which occurred before Gutenberg's invention.

Option C is correct because **"Prior to"** accurately sets up the contrast between the time before the printing press, when books were laboriously copied by hand, and the change brought about by the invention.

Option A is incorrect because **"Despite"** introduces a contradiction or something unexpected in relation to what comes before or after it. However, in this context, the passage is explaining the natural progression from the era when books were hand-copied to the transformative effects of the printing press. There is no contradiction or opposition between these two ideas; rather, they are logically sequential. "Despite" would suggest that even though the printing press existed, books were still copied by hand, which is the opposite of the passage's intent.

Option B is incorrect because **"After"** would imply the hand-copying of books happened after the invention of the printing press, which is **illogical** given the context. Why would books be copied by hand *after* the invention of the printing press? It doesn't make any sense when plugged in to the passage.

Option D is incorrect because "Because of" implies a causal relationship, suggesting that the hand-copying of books was caused by the invention of the printing press. This is illogical. The passage is explaining how, before the printing press, books were manually copied, and it was only after the press was invented that books could be mass-produced. "Because of" in this context would confuse the cause-and-effect relationship by implying that the printing press led to more hand-copying, which is not true.

26. Rhetorical Synthesis: Medium

Answer: C) During the 1980s, a large-scale die-off of bamboo occurred, which caused a drastic decline in panda numbers.

Logical Breakdown and Explanation:

To determine which option best provides **a specific example** of an event that led to a drastic decline in the panda population, we need to identify the option that references a clear, time-specific event connected to the population decrease.

Option C is correct because it directly mentions the **bamboo die-off in the 1980s**, which, according to the notes, **caused a significant decline** in panda numbers. This provides a specific, causal example that fits the criteria in the question stem.

Option A is incorrect because, although it mentions **threats to the panda population** (deforestation and agricultural expansion), it does not provide a specific example or event that led to a drastic decline in the population.

Option B is incorrect because it introduces **irrelevant** information about the panda's status change in 2016. This doesn't address the student's goal of providing a specific example of an event that caused a drastic decrease in the panda population.

Option D is incorrect because it discusses global breeding initiatives in zoos, which focus on increasing the panda population. This information is irrelevant to the student's goal of highlighting an event that caused a significant population decline.

27. Rhetorical Synthesis: Easy

Answer: C) Designed by Antoni Gaudí, the Sagrada Familia is an unfinished basilica that began construction in 1882.

Logical Breakdown and Explanation:

To determine which choice best provides an example of an architectural project that has remained unfinished for over a century, we need to focus on the specific details from the notes about ongoing or incomplete construction. The student's goal is to highlight a structure that fits this description, and only one of the notes clearly points to such a project.

Option C is correct because it directly states that the Sagrada Familia is an unfinished basilica that began construction in 1882, fulfilling the requirement of being a project that has not been completed for over a century.

Option A is incorrect because while it mentions the Sagrada Familia and the start of its construction in 1882, it does not emphasize that the project remains unfinished, **missing the crucial detail** needed to meet the student's goal.

Option B is incorrect because it focuses on the Panama Canal, which was completed in 1914, and **does not relate** to the concept of an ongoing or unfinished project.

Option D is incorrect because it describes the length of the Great Wall of China and why it was constructed. However, there is no mention of an uncompleted project and therefore does not meet the student's objective.

Practice Test

4

Reading and Writing

27 Questions, 32 Minutes

DIRECTIONS

The questions in this section address a number of important reading and writing skills. Each questions includes one or more passages, which may include a table or graph. Read each passage and question carefully, and then choose the best answer to the question based on the passage(s).

All questions in this section are multiple-choice with four answer choices. Each question has a single best answer.

Geologists often utilize remote sensing technology to identify and monitor geothermal activity. These techniques can detect subtle variations in temperature and surface composition. If a geologist has _____ that a new geothermal hotspot is developing in an unexplored area, remote sensing data can confirm this suspicion by revealing increased thermal emissions and alterations in surface minerals.

1

Which choice completes the text with the most logical and precise word or phrase?

A) proof

B) an assertion

C) an inkling

D) a synopsis

CONTINUE ➡

The price of rare heirloom tomatoes in the late 2000s surged dramatically. Paradoxically, this led to _____ demand: consumers who had never been interested in purchasing expensive tomatoes flocked to farmers' markets. They believed the higher prices indicated superior quality and anticipated that the tomatoes could become a lucrative investment.

2

Which choice completes the text with the most logical and precise word or phrase?

A) increased

B) decreased

C) affected

D) appraised

Collecting oral histories from marginalized communities, documenting the vernacular architecture of rural villages, and preserving folk music traditions might appear to be frivolous hobbies more than worthwhile activities. Yet, these endeavors are pivotal for understanding the breadth of human experience—they can _____ perspectives and experiences that are often overlooked by mainstream historical records.

3

Which choice completes the text with the most logical and precise word or phrase?

A) fabricate

B) elucidate

C) induce

D) conceal

CONTINUE

Coined as a task designed for only 'the bravest of people,' the mapping of the entire human genome seemed _____ to many scientists. They doubted it could be accomplished within their lifetimes. However, with the advent of new technologies and international collaboration, the Human Genome Project was successfully completed in 2003.

Which choice completes the text with the most logical and precise word or phrase?

A) inevitable

B) daunting

C) irreproachable

D) undervalued

Unlike most animals, the wood frog can enter a state of suspended animation, where up to 70% of its body water turns to ice. As temperatures drop, the frog's liver converts glycogen into glucose, which is then distributed throughout its body. This glucose acts as a natural antifreeze, <u>preventing ice crystals from forming inside cells and causing damage</u>. Instead, ice forms in the spaces outside cells, while the high concentration of glucose protects the cells themselves. When spring arrives and temperatures rise, the ice melts, and the frog's bodily functions gradually resume.

Which choice best describes the function of the underlined portion in the text as a whole?

A) To highlight the process by which the wood frog converts glycogen into glucose

B) To contrast the wood frog's adaptation with that of other animals

C) To explain a benefit of glucose distribution in the wood frog's body

D) To explain why ice forms outside the cells rather than inside them

The following text is adapted from "The Wretched and the Beautiful," a short story by E. Lily Yu. In the text, the arrival of mysterious celestial beings causes a stir in a small seaside town.

In the quiet town by the sea, the arrival of the strange, celestial beings caused quite a stir. These visitors, with their iridescent skin and otherworldly grace, were unlike anything the townsfolk had ever seen. Though they communicated through melodies and light, their intentions remained a mystery. Some residents, moved by curiosity and empathy, approached the beings with offerings of food and shelter. Others, however, were wary and kept their distance, whispering rumors of hidden dangers and potential threats.

6

Which choice best describes the function of the underlined portion in the text as a whole?

A) It depicts the response of a portion of the townsfolk.

B) It illustrates the overall mystery surrounding the beings' intentions.

C) It suggests that the celestial beings required sustenance and shelter.

D) It contrasts the benevolent actions of some residents with the malevolence of the beings.

CONTINUE

A cultural study compared work-life balance in Spain and Argentina by interviewing 500 participants from each country and analyzing labor statistics. In Spain, the siesta tradition allows for a mid-afternoon break-extending the workday into the evening-while Argentina follows a conventional work schedule with strong emphasis on family time. Spaniards reported higher satisfaction due to flexible schedules, whereas Argentinians, valuing the separation between work and family life, felt it enhanced their overall well-being. The study concluded that cultural norms significantly influence work-life balance perceptions.

7

Which choice best states the main purpose of the text?

A) To challenge conventional views on work-life balance by comparing two cultures

B) To explain the different work schedules in Spain and Argentina

C) To encourage other countries to adopt a work-life balance closer to that of Spain

D) To discuss the impact of cultural practices on two countries

The following text is adapted from Cho Nam-joo's 2016 novel *Kim Jiyoung, Born 1982*. Kim Jiyoung, a young woman in South Korea, navigates societal expectations and personal challenges.

Jiyoung often felt confined by the expectations placed upon her. From a young age, she observed the different ways her brother was treated compared to her. While he was encouraged to pursue his interests, she was expected to help with household chores and excel in her studies, but not too much as to overshadow her brother. Despite her achievements, she felt her life choices were limited by societal norms.

Which choice best states the main idea of the text?

A) Jiyoung feels satisfied with the opportunities she has.

B) Jiyoung observes how her brother is treated differently but feels grateful for her confined situation.

C) Jiyoung is aware of the gender-based disparities in expectations and feels limited by them.

D) Jiyoung believes that excelling in her studies will lead to more freedom and fewer responsibilities at home.

CONTINUE

Text 1

Sociologist Dr. Elizabeth Sweet argues that pop culture has the biggest influence on teens within a society. According to Dr. Sweet, the pervasive nature of media and entertainment shapes teenagers' values, behaviors, and aspirations. Dr. Sweet's research, which spans several decades, suggests that the messages conveyed through pop culture are internalized by teens: these messages play a significant role in their development and identity formation.

Text 2

Although he acknowledges that pop culture sets the stage for many aspects of teen behavior, psychologist Dr. Laurence Steinberg contends that teens are most influenced by their immediate environment, including their peer group and friends. Dr. Steinberg's studies reveal that the behaviors and attitudes of close friends have a more direct impact on teenagers' decision-making processes and self-esteem. He points to data showing that peer pressure and social interactions within a teen's immediate circle are critical in shaping their choices and actions.

9

Based on the texts, how would Dr. Steinberg (Text 2) most likely respond to the claim discussed in Text 1?

A) By asserting that Dr. Sweet overestimates the influence of pop culture and underestimates the role of peer groups and friends

B) By suggesting that pop culture and immediate environments equally influence teens' behaviors and decisions

C) By agreeing that pop culture is the primary influence on teens but adding that peer groups also play a significant role

D) By challenging the idea that pop culture has any impact on teens and instead focusing solely on the influence of their immediate surroundings

CONTINUE →

The following text is from Ama Ata Aidoo's 1965 play *The Dilemma of a Ghost*. The scene is a dialogue between Eulalie and her husband, Ato.

EULALIE: I wish I could understand why they are all so concerned about how many children I have and when. It's my life, isn't it? Back in the States, women can decide for themselves, but here, it seems everyone has an opinion about my womb. How am I supposed to deal with this constant pressure?

ATO: I know it's hard, Eulalie. But family is very important here, and having children is seen as a crucial part of our identity. They don't mean to pressure you; they just don't understand your perspective.

According to the text, what is "this constant pressure" in regard to?

A) The familial pressure that Eulalie should return to the States to broaden her perspective

B) The consistent need for Eulalie to get her family to understand her perspective

C) The societal expectation about Eulalie's reproductive choices

D) The cultural norms of getting married and having children

CONTINUE

In her extensive research on the human brain, neuroscientist Dr. Suzana Herculano-Houzel and her team investigated the function of gray matter, which consists mainly of neuronal cell bodies. Gray matter was once thought to primarily occupy space without significant function. However, studying brain scans and neuronal densities in various mammals, including humans, the team discovered that regions with higher concentrations of gray matter are critically involved in cognitive functions such as memory, attention, and decision-making. Furthermore, Dr. Herculano-Houzel's research revealed that individuals with denser gray matter in specific brain areas tend to perform better on cognitive tests. Based on these findings, Herculano-Houzel hypothesized that gray matter likely _____

11

Which choice most logically completes the text?

A) was once thought to be more abundant in ancient human species but has since diminished in modern humans.

B) plays a more important role than previously believed in facilitating higher-order mental processes.

C) will increase in volume as humans continue to evolve and develop higher cognitive abilities.

D) is more abundant in mammals with larger brains, suggesting it primarily supports basic motor functions.

CONTINUE

Social Media Usage and Reported Mental Health Effects by Age Group

Age Group	Average Daily Time Spent on Social Media (Hours)	Percentage Reporting Negative Mental Health Effects	Percentage Reporting Positive Social Connections
13-18 years	4.5	64%	22%
19-25 years	3.8	43%	31%
26-40 years	2.5	28%	52%
41-60 years	1.2	15%	65%

Studies have shown that while social media can foster positive social connections, it is also associated with negative mental health effects, particularly in younger users. Researchers have concluded that the amount of time spent on social media tends to correlate positively with the likelihood of experiencing these negative effects: that is, the two variables move in the same direction—either both increasing or both decreasing together.

12

Which choice best describes data from the table that support the researchers' conclusion?

A) The 41-60 years age group spends the least time on social media (1.2 hours daily) but reports the highest percentage of positive social connections at 65%.

B) As social media usage decreases from the 13-18 years age group (4.5 hours daily) to the 26-40 years age group (2.5 hours daily), the percentage of reported negative mental health effects also decreases significantly (from 64% to 28%).

C) The 41-60 years age group spends less time, on average, on social media than does the 13-18 years age group.

D) As social media usage increases from the 26-40 years age group (2.5 hours daily) to the 13-18 years age group (4.5 hours daily), the percentage of positive social connections drastically decreases (from 52% to 22%).

CONTINUE

Psychologist Daniel Goleman, renowned for his work on emotional intelligence (EI), posits that leaders with high EI can enhance organizational profitability by mitigating employee stress and burnout. His research highlights that emotionally intelligent leaders foster supportive work environments, which in turn lower stress levels, reduce sick days, cut healthcare costs, and boost overall productivity. To test Goleman's hypothesis, researchers conducted a comprehensive study involving several companies. They assessed the EI levels of company leaders and meticulously tracked indicators of employee well-being and organizational profitability, including the number of sick days taken, healthcare costs, and revenue growth over a year.

13

Which finding from the researchers' study, if true, would most strongly support Goleman's hypothesis?

A) On average, employees in companies with leaders who had high EI perceived their leaders as more empathetic compared to those with leaders who had moderate or low EI.

B) On average, companies with leaders who had high EI reported a 30% reduction in workplace conflicts and a saving of $75,000 in conflict resolution and legal costs annually compared to those with leaders who had moderate or low EI.

C) On average, companies with leaders who had high EI spent $50,000 more annually on employee wellness programs compared to those with leaders who had moderate or low EI.

D) On average, companies with leaders who had high EI showed no significant difference in employee turnover rates compared to those with leaders who had moderate or low EI.

Practice Test 4

CONTINUE →

493

"A Good Man is Hard to Find" is a 1953 short story by Flannery O'Connor. In the story, a grandmother tries to convince an escaped convict, known as The Misfit, that he is inherently good. The grandmother's moment of grace and realization about her own faults occurs just before her death, which becomes clear when she says, _____

14

Which choice most effectively uses a quotation from "A Good Man is Hard to Find" to illustrate the claim?

A) "You wouldn't shoot a lady, would you?"

B) "I know you're a good man. You don't look a bit like you have common blood."

C) "Forgive me...I've been wrong all my life."

D) "I've always tried to be good. I've always tried to do the right thing. Why is this happening to me?"

CONTINUE

Saturn's largest _____ is home to vast lakes-not of water, but of liquid methane and ethane. These alien lakes, which glisten under Titan's thick, hazy atmosphere, have intrigued scientists since their discovery by the Cassini spacecraft in 2004; in fact, they offer a rare glimpse into the chemistry of a world completely different from our own.

The ancient baobab trees of Madagascar-often called "the upside-down trees" due to their root-like branches-can live for over a thousand years. _____ massive trunks, which store water during the dry season, serve as a lifeline for local communities and wildlife.

15

Which choice completes the text so that it conforms to the conventions of Standard English?

A) moon, Titan,

B) moon Titan

C) moon Titan,

D) moon, Titan

16

Which choice completes the text so that it conforms to the conventions of Standard English?

A) There

B) It's

C) Their

D) Its

CONTINUE

In the grand temples of ancient Egypt, cats were revered as sacred beings, believed to possess divine qualities and to serve as the earthly companions of the goddess Bastet. These feline deities, adorned with gold jewelry and housed in elaborate tombs, were so cherished that harming them was punishable by death. In the _____ homes alike, cats roamed freely, their presence a constant reminder of the gods' favor.

17

Which choice completes the text so that it conforms to the conventions of Standard English?

- A) pharaohs courts' and the citizens'
- B) pharaohs' courts and the citizens
- C) pharaoh's courts and the citizen's
- D) pharaohs' courts and the citizens'

In the vast expanse of the universe beyond the reach of our telescopes and probes resides a structure known as the cosmic web—a vast network of galaxies, dark matter, and interstellar gas that _____ the backbone of the cosmos. The web's filaments, stretching across billions of light-years, are where galaxies are born and evolve.

18

Which choice completes the text so that it conforms to the conventions of Standard English?

- A) form
- B) have formed
- C) forms
- D) are forming

CONTINUE →

Nikola Tesla, the brilliant inventor who gave the world alternating current electricity (AC), was a man ahead of his time. His visionary _____ were never fully realized, included wireless energy transmission and a global communication network.

Which choice completes the text so that it conforms to the conventions of Standard English?

A) ideas, many of them

B) ideas; many of them

C) ideas many of which

D) ideas, many of which

In sports, the underdog is often overlooked, yet nothing captivates audiences more than when an unlikely team rises to victory. Whether it's a last-minute goal or a record-breaking run, these moments remind us that anything is possible. The thrill of the unexpected triumphs and the joy of seeing the improbable come to life _____ what make sports so compelling.

Which choice completes the text so that it conforms to the conventions of Standard English?

A) are

B) is

C) were

D) was

CONTINUE

Fans can turn a simple movie into a cultural phenomenon. Take *Star Wars*, for instance. What began as a space _____ became a global empire. Fans dress as characters, attend conventions, and create their own stories, keeping the saga alive. Fandom shows the enduring power of storytelling and its ability to connect people across generations.

21

Which choice completes the text so that it conforms to the conventions of Standard English?

A) opera in 1977,

B) opera in 1977;

C) opera, in 1977,

D) opera in 1977

Bees play an essential role in the pollination of crops, making them crucial to global food production. Without bees, many of the fruits, vegetables, and nuts we rely on would be _____ bee populations are declining due to pesticides, habitat loss, and disease.

22

Which choice completes the text so that it conforms to the conventions of Standard English?

A) scarce, however,

B) scarce however

C) scarce; however,

D) scarce, however;

CONTINUE →

Language, a living, dynamic entity, constantly evolves to reflect the changes in society. New words are coined, old ones fade into obscurity, and meanings shift over time. The word "cool," _____ has transitioned from describing temperature to expressing approval. Similarly, technological advancements have introduced terms like "selfie" and "hashtag" into our everyday vocabulary.

23

Which choice completes the text with the most logical transition?

A) however,

B) for instance,

C) nevertheless,

D) in addition,

Social media has drastically altered the way we communicate, connecting people across the globe in real-time. However, it has also introduced new challenges, such as the spread of misinformation and the erosion of privacy. _____, the constant exposure to curated, idealized versions of others' lives can lead to feelings of inadequacy and anxiety.

24

Which choice completes the text with the most logical transition?

A) Additionally

B) Still

C) Hence

D) In other words

Practice Test 4

CONTINUE

Quantum computing is poised to transform technology by offering solutions to problems that classical computers cannot efficiently tackle. _____ quantum computers leverage the principles of superposition and entanglement to perform complex calculations at unprecedented speeds.

CONTINUE ➡

25

Which choice completes the text with the most logical transition?

A) In contrast,

B) Regardless,

C) In comparison,

D) In fact,

While researching a topic, a student has taken the following notes:

- The Yuchi language, spoken by the Yuchi people of Oklahoma, is one of the most critically endangered languages in the world.
- Language revitalization efforts are taking place within the Yuchi community in Oklahoma, using immersion programs and digital tools.
- Reviving the Yuchi language is seen as crucial for preserving cultural identity and passing down traditional knowledge to future generations.
- These revitalization efforts began intensifying in the early 2000s after the number of fluent speakers dropped to fewer than 10.
- The Yuchi Language Project, a community-led initiative, plays a central role in teaching the language to younger generations.
- Despite the challenges, there has been a gradual increase in the number of Yuchi language learners, with new educational resources being developed regularly.

26

The student wants to explain the significance of the Yuchi language revitalization efforts. Which choice most effectively uses relevant information from the notes to accomplish this goal?

A) Revitalization efforts for the Yuchi language, which began intensifying in the early 2000s, are using immersion programs and digital tools within the Yuchi community in Oklahoma.

B) In response to the rapid decline in fluent speakers to fewer than 10, the Yuchi Language Project intensified its efforts in the early 2000s and has since seen a gradual increase in the number of Yuchi language learners.

C) The Yuchi Language Project plays a central role in teaching the language to younger generations so as to preserve cultural identity and pass down traditional knowledge to future generations.

D) Despite challenges, the Yuchi community is developing new educational resources to revive its language, which is one of the most critically endangered languages in the world.

While researching a topic, a student has taken the following notes:

- Fast fashion refers to the rapid production of inexpensive clothing, often inspired by the latest trends.
- The fashion industry is responsible for 10% of global carbon emissions, largely due to fast fashion practices.
- Approximately 85% of textiles produced annually end up in landfills or are incinerated.
- The use of synthetic fibers like polyester, which are derived from fossil fuels, contributes to microplastic pollution in oceans.
- Some fashion brands are adopting sustainable practices, such as using recycled materials and reducing water consumption in production.
- Consumer awareness and demand for sustainable fashion alternatives have been growing in recent years.

27

The student wants to emphasize the efforts being made to address the environmental problems caused by fast fashion. Which choice most effectively uses relevant information from the notes to accomplish this goal?

A) Fast fashion is known as the rapid production of inexpensive clothing, which often leads to textiles being incinerated or ending up in landfills.

B) The fashion industry, driven by fast fashion practices, is responsible for 10% of global carbon emissions, and the use of synthetic fibers like polyester contributes to microplastic pollution.

C) As consumer awareness of the environmental impact of fast fashion has grown, more fashion brands have responded by adopting sustainable practices such as using recycled materials and reducing water consumption in their production processes.

D) In response to the carbon emissions, textile waste and microplastic pollution created by fast fashion, some fashion brands have adopted sustainable practices like using recycled materials and reducing water consumption.

If you finish before the time is called, you may check your work on this module only.
On Test Day, you will only be able to move to the next module when time expires.

🔑 Answer Key

Question Number	Correct Answer	Level of Difficulty	Question Type
1	C	Medium	**Craft and Structure:** *Words in Context*
2	A	Hard	**Craft and Structure:** *Words in Context*
3	B	Medium	**Craft and Structure:** *Words in Context*
4	B	Easy	**Craft and Structure:** *Words in Context*
5	C	Hard	**Craft and Structure:** *Function of the Underlined Portion*
6	A	Easy	**Craft and Structure:** *Function of the Underlined Portion*
7	D	Medium	**Craft and Structure:** *Main Purpose*
8	C	Easy	**Information and Ideas:** *Main Idea*
9	A	Medium	**Craft and Structure:** *Cross-Text Connection*
10	C	Easy	**Information and Ideas:** *Detail*
11	B	Hard	**Information and Ideas:** *Inference*
12	B	Hard	**Information and Ideas:** *Support a Claim (Infographics)*
13	B	Medium	**Information and Ideas:** *Support a Claim*

Practice Test 4

Question Number	Correct Answer	Level of Difficulty	Question Type
14	C	Medium	**Information and Ideas:** *Cite Text as Evidence*
15	A	Medium	**Standard English Conventions:** *Commas*
16	C	Easy	**Standard English Conventions:** *Pronouns*
17	D	Medium	**Standard English Conventions:** *Punctuation*
18	C	Medium	**Standard English Conventions:** *Verbs*
19	D	Hard	**Standard English Conventions:** *Sentence Structure*
20	A	Medium	**Standard English Conventions:** *Verbs*
21	D	Easy	**Standard English Conventions:** *Punctuation and Sentence Structure*
22	C	Medium	**Standard English Conventions:** *Punctuation*
23	B	Easy	**Expression of Ideas:** *Transitions*
24	A	Hard	**Expression of Ideas:** *Transitions*
25	D	Hard	**Expression of Ideas:** *Transitions*
26	C	Medium	**Expression of Ideas:** *Rhetorical Synthesis*
27	D	Medium	**Expression of Ideas:** *Rhetorical Synthesis*

Instructions

Count the number of questions you got correct in Module 1.

Enter your score here: _____.

If your score is **18 or higher**, move on to the **HARD version** of Module 2.

If your score is **below 18**, proceed to the **EASY version** of Module 2.

📑 Explanations

1. Words in Context: Medium

Answer: C) an inkling

Step-by-Step Explanation:

1. The passage describes how geologists use remote sensing technology to detect and monitor geothermal activity by identifying subtle temperature changes and surface composition variations. It then discusses a scenario where a geologist suspects that a new geothermal hotspot is developing and suggests that remote sensing data can confirm this suspicion by revealing specific indicators like increased thermal emissions.

2. Notice the phrase "can confirm this suspicion" in the passage. This indicates that the geologist initially has a suspicion or a sense that something might be happening, which is not yet confirmed. The context suggests that the geologist has a preliminary or vague idea about the possible development of a geothermal hotspot, rather than definitive proof or a strong assertion.

3. The word we need should describe a preliminary, less certain feeling or suspicion that a geologist might have before confirmation through data.

4. "An inkling" is the most logical choice because it means a slight or vague idea, which fits perfectly with the context of a geologist having an initial, unconfirmed sense that a new geothermal hotspot might be developing.

Explanation of Incorrect Options:

A) proof: This is incorrect because it suggests definitive evidence, which the passage indicates comes later, after remote sensing data confirms the suspicion.

B) an assertion: This is incorrect because it implies a strong statement of fact or belief, which is not supported by the passage. The context implies that the geologist only has a vague suspicion, not a firm declaration.

D) a synopsis: This is incorrect because it refers to a summary, which doesn't make logical sense given the context of a geologist having an initial, unconfirmed suspicion about a geothermal hotspot.

2. Words in Context: Hard

Answer: A) increased

Step-by-Step Explanation:

1. Let's deconstruct the passage together. The passage describes a situation where the price of rare heirloom tomatoes surged dramatically in the late 2000s. Despite the higher prices, which might typically discourage buyers, the passage notes a paradoxical effect where more consumers became interested in purchasing these expensive tomatoes.

2. Notice the word "Paradoxically," which indicates that the result was unexpected or contrary to what one might assume. Normally, when prices increase, demand might decrease, but here the opposite happened. The passage explains that consumers flocked to farmers' markets, driven by the belief that the higher prices signified superior quality and that the tomatoes could be a good investment.

3. The word we need should reflect the idea that demand for the tomatoes actually went up, despite the price increase.

4. Ask yourself, what word best describes an increase in demand in this context? "Increased" is the most logical choice because it directly describes the rise in consumer interest and demand for the heirloom tomatoes, despite their higher prices.

Explanation of Incorrect Options:

B) decreased: This is incorrect because it contradicts the passage's description of more consumers becoming interested in buying the tomatoes, which indicates increased demand.

C) affected: This is incorrect because it is too vague and does not specifically describe the nature of the change in demand, which the passage clearly states was an increase. Plus, affected doesn't make logical sense because the paradox isn't that the demand was affected. The paradox is that demand went up.

D) appraised: This is incorrect because it refers to evaluating or assessing something, which is not directly related to the context of describing the change in consumer demand.

3. Words in Context: Medium

Answer: B) elucidate

Step-by-Step Explanation:

1. Let's understand the passage together. The passage discusses activities such as collecting oral histories, documenting vernacular architecture, and preserving folk music traditions, which might be dismissed as trivial. However, the passage emphasizes that these endeavors are crucial for gaining a comprehensive understanding of human experience, particularly by highlighting perspectives that are often ignored by mainstream historical records.

2. Notice the phrase "pivotal for understanding the breadth of human experience" and "perspectives and experiences that are often overlooked." The context suggests that these activities help to reveal or bring to light important aspects of history and culture that might otherwise remain hidden.

3. Thus, the word we need should describe the act of making something clearer or bringing it to light, in this case, perspectives and experiences that are usually ignored.

4. "Elucidate" is the most logical choice because it means to make something clear or to shed light on it, which fits perfectly with the context of these activities helping to reveal overlooked perspectives and experiences.

Explanation of Incorrect Options:

A) fabricate: This is incorrect because it is unsupported by the passage. The passage does not develop or discuss the idea of making something up, which is what "fabricate" implies.

C) induce: This is incorrect because it is irrelevant to the passage. The passage does not discuss bringing about an effect or causing something, which is the meaning of "induce."

D) conceal: This is incorrect because it means to hide or keep something secret, which is the opposite of what the passage suggests these activities do.

4. Interpreting Words in Context: Easy

Answer: B) daunting

Step-by-Step Explanation:

1. The passage describes the mapping of the entire human genome as a task initially perceived as requiring immense bravery. Many scientists doubted that this task could be completed within their lifetimes, suggesting that it was viewed as extremely difficult or challenging.
2. Notice the phrases "task designed for only 'the bravest of people'" and "doubted it could be accomplished within their lifetimes." These context clues indicate that the task was seen as highly challenging and intimidating to many scientists, which sets the stage for a word that conveys a sense of difficulty.
3. The word we need should describe a task that is seen as extremely challenging and intimidating.
4. "Daunting" is the most logical choice because it means something that seems difficult to deal with or intimidating, which fits perfectly with the context of the passage.

Explanation of Incorrect Options:

A) inevitable: This is incorrect because it means something that is certain to happen, which contradicts the passage's emphasis on the doubt and challenge surrounding the project.

C) irreproachable: This is incorrect because it means beyond criticism or faultless, which is irrelevant to the context of a task being perceived as difficult.

D) undervalued: This is incorrect because it means something that is not given enough recognition or worth, which is not discussed or supported by the passage.

5. Function of the Underlined Portion: Hard

Answer: C) To explain a benefit of glucose distribution in the wood frog's body

Logical Breakdown and Explanation:

This question asks you to determine the role the underlined portion, "preventing ice crystals from forming inside cells and causing damage," plays within the context of the passage, specifically focusing on how it fits into the description of the wood frog's adaptation to freezing conditions.

Option C is correct because the underlined sentence explains how the glucose distributed throughout the frog's body acts as antifreeze, which prevents damage by stopping ice crystals from forming inside cells. This is a direct benefit of glucose distribution, as it protects the frog's cells from the harmful effects of freezing, which is crucial to the frog's survival in cold temperatures.

Option A is incorrect because the underlined portion does not explain the conversion of glycogen into glucose. Instead, it explains the role of glucose once it has already been produced and distributed in the frog's body. The focus of the underlined portion is on preventing ice crystals, not the process of glycogen conversion.

Option B is incorrect because the passage does not compare the wood frog's adaptation to that of other animals. The focus is solely on the wood frog's unique ability to survive freezing temperatures, and the underlined portion is part of that description rather than a contrast with other animals.

Option D is incorrect because, although the underlined portion mentions ice crystals, it does not directly explain why ice forms outside the cells. The text addresses that ice forms outside the cells in a separate part, while the underlined sentence focuses specifically on how glucose prevents ice from forming inside the cells.

6. Function of the Underlined Portion: Easy

Answer: A) It depicts the response of a portion of the townsfolk.

Logical Breakdown and Explanation:

This question asks you to determine how the underlined portion, "Some residents, moved by curiosity and empathy, approached the beings with offerings of food and shelter," functions within the overall context of the passage. You should focus on the role this sentence plays in the description of the townsfolk's reaction to the arrival of the celestial beings.

Option A is correct because the underlined sentence describes how a specific group of the townsfolk responded to the beings. It highlights that some residents, driven by curiosity and empathy, offered food and shelter to the celestial beings, providing insight into a portion of the townsfolk's reaction: a positive response.

Option B is incorrect because the underlined portion does not directly focus on the overall mystery of the beings' intentions. Instead, it highlights a specific response by some residents, rather than delving into the mystery of why the beings arrived or what they want.

Option C is incorrect because the underlined portion does not suggest that the celestial beings actually required sustenance or shelter. It only describes the townsfolk's offer of food and shelter, which was motivated by curiosity and empathy, not by any indication that the beings needed these resources.

Option D is incorrect because the underlined sentence does not contrast benevolent actions with malevolence. The celestial beings' intentions remain a mystery throughout the passage, and there is no mention of malevolent actions by the beings. The sentence focuses solely on the residents' offerings, without suggesting any conflict or malevolence from the beings.

7. Main Purpose: Medium

Answer: D) To discuss the impact of cultural practices on two countries

Logical Breakdown and Explanation:

Main purpose questions require identifying the overarching idea or message conveyed by the entire passage. In this case, the passage discusses how cultural practices in Spain and Argentina affect perceptions of work-life balance.

Option D is correct because the passage discusses the impact of cultural practices on work-life balance in Spain and Argentina. The text focuses on how cultural norms, such as Spain's siesta tradition and Argentina's conventional schedule with an emphasis on family time, shape the perceptions of work-life balance in each country. People in Spain take a break in the middle of their day and work into the evening, which shows a work-life balance that blends tradition into their workday. In contrast, people in Argentina clearly separate work from life, as they value family. This highlights the role culture plays in influencing these perceptions.

Option A is incorrect because the passage does not challenge conventional views on work-life balance. Instead, it describes and compares how work-life balance is experienced in two specific cultures without attempting to challenge any traditional views.

Option B is incorrect because, while the text does explain the different work schedules in Spain and Argentina, this is not the main purpose. The primary focus is on how cultural practices influence work-life balance perceptions, not merely on describing work schedules. This is a minor detail that only captures part of the overall focus of the passage.

Option C is incorrect because the passage does not suggest that other countries should adopt a work-life balance similar to that of Spain. The passage is descriptive, explaining how cultural norms influence work-life balance, rather than advocating for one system over another.

8. Main Idea: Easy

Answer: C) Jiyoung is aware of the gender-based disparities in expectations and feels limited by them.

Logical Breakdown and Explanation:

Main idea questions ask you to identify the central focus or overall message of the passage. In this case, the text is about Jiyoung's experiences with societal expectations, especially gender-based disparities, and how these limitations make her feel.

Option C is correct because the passage describes how Jiyoung is aware of the gender-based differences in expectations, particularly when comparing herself to her brother. She feels confined and "limited by these societal norms," which shape her life choices (she was unable to pursue her interests). This captures the overall message that Jiyoung is conscious of the disparities and feels restricted by them.

Option A is incorrect because the passage does not suggest that Jiyoung feels satisfied with her situation. On the contrary, the text emphasizes her feelings of confinement and limitation due to societal expectations, particularly those based on gender.

Option B is incorrect because, while Jiyoung does observe the different treatment between her and her brother, the passage does not indicate that she feels grateful for her confined situation. Instead, she feels restricted by it.

Option D is incorrect because the text does not mention Jiyoung believing that excelling in her studies will lead to more freedom. In fact, the passage suggests that she is expected to excel, but not to the point of overshadowing her brother, which reinforces her feeling of limitation rather than offering a path to more freedom.

9. Cross-Text Connections: Medium

Answer: A) By agreeing that pop culture is the primary influence on teens but adding that peer groups also play a significant role

Logical Breakdown and Explanation:

This question asks you to determine how Dr. Steinberg from Text 2 would likely respond to Dr. Sweet's claim in Text 1. To answer correctly, you need to focus on Dr. Steinberg's position and the key ideas mentioned in both passages.

Option A is correct because Dr. Steinberg emphasizes the influence of a teen's immediate environment, particularly their peer group and friends, over pop culture. This suggests that Dr. Steinberg would likely argue that Dr. Sweet overestimates the influence of pop culture and underestimates the critical role peer groups play in shaping teens' behaviors and decision-making. Text 2 specifically points to peer pressure and social interactions as more direct influences on teenagers than pop culture.

Option B is incorrect because Dr. Steinberg does not suggest that pop culture and immediate environments equally influence teens. While he acknowledges pop culture's role, he clearly argues that peer groups have a more direct and stronger influence on teens.

Option C is incorrect because Dr. Steinberg does not agree that pop culture is the primary influence. Instead, he asserts that the immediate environment, particularly peer groups, has the most significant impact on teens, which contradicts Dr. Sweet's view.

Option D is incorrect because Dr. Steinberg does not claim that pop culture has no impact at all. He acknowledges its influence but believes that the immediate environment, especially peer groups, is more critical in shaping teens' behavior and decisions.

10. Detail: Easy

Answer: C) The societal expectation about Eulalie's reproductive choices

Logical Breakdown and Explanation:

This question asks you to interpret what "this constant pressure" refers to in the passage, based on the conversation between Eulalie and Ato. You need to focus on what Eulalie is describing and the specific issue she's addressing.

Option C is correct because the passage clearly shows that Eulalie is feeling societal pressure about her reproductive choices. She expresses frustration that people are concerned with how many children she has and when, which makes her feel pressured about her decisions regarding motherhood. The phrase "everyone has an opinion about my womb" reinforces that this pressure is focused on her reproductive choices.

Option A is incorrect because there is no mention of anyone pressuring Eulalie to return to the States. The passage is centered on the societal pressure regarding her having children, not about her location or need to broaden her perspective.

Option B is incorrect because, while Eulalie expresses frustration that her family doesn't understand her perspective, the "constant pressure" she refers to is specifically about her reproductive choices, not about getting her family to understand her.

Option D is incorrect because the pressure is not about cultural norms around getting married. Eulalie and Ato are already married, and the focus of the pressure is on having children, not on marriage itself.

11. Inference: Hard

Answer: B) plays a more important role than previously believed in facilitating higher-order mental processes.

Logical Breakdown and Explanation:

This question asks you to infer how to logically complete the passage based on Dr. Herculano-Houzel's research on gray matter and its role in cognitive functions. The correct answer should be consistent with the key ideas presented in the text, particularly the discovery that gray matter is critically involved in higher-order mental processes like memory, attention, and decision-making.

Option B is correct because the passage emphasizes that gray matter is "critically involved in cognitive functions" and that individuals with denser gray matter perform better on cognitive tests. This strongly suggests that gray matter plays a more important role than was previously believed, especially in higher-order mental processes. Therefore, this choice logically follows from the text's discussion of the function of gray matter.

Option A is incorrect because the passage does not discuss ancient human species or suggest that gray matter has diminished in modern humans. There is no information provided to support this conclusion.

Option C is incorrect because the passage does not mention gray matter increasing in volume as humans evolve. While the research suggests gray matter plays an important role, there is no mention of future changes in gray matter volume as part of human evolution.

Option D is incorrect because the passage specifically links gray matter to cognitive functions, not basic motor functions. Additionally, the passage does not suggest that mammals with larger brains have more gray matter primarily for motor functions. This contradicts the focus on cognitive abilities.

12. Support a Claim (Infographics): Hard

Answer: B) As social media usage decreases from the 13-18 years age group (4.5 hours daily) to the 26-40 years age group (2.5 hours daily), the percentage of reported negative mental health effects also decreases significantly (from 64% to 28%).

Logical Breakdown and Explanation:

This question asks you to identify which choice best supports the researchers' conclusion that time spent on social media correlates positively with the likelihood of experiencing negative mental health effects. The conclusion is that as social media usage increases, negative mental health effects tend to increase as well. You need to look for a pattern in the data where both social media usage and negative mental health effects either increase or decrease together.

Option B is correct because it directly supports the researchers' conclusion. The data show that as social media usage decreases (from 4.5 hours daily in the 13-18 years group to 2.5 hours daily in the 26-40 years group), the percentage of reported negative mental health effects also decreases significantly (from 64% to 28%). This clearly aligns with the researchers' conclusion that the two variables move in the same direction—both decreasing together.

Option A is incorrect because it highlights positive social connections rather than focusing on the relationship between social media usage and negative mental health effects, which is the focus of the researchers' conclusion.

Option C is incorrect because, while it mentions that the 41-60 years age group spends less time on social media than the 13-18 years age group, it does not connect this fact to the percentage of reported negative mental health effects, which is essential to supporting the researchers' conclusion.

Option D is incorrect because it focuses on the relationship between social media usage and positive social connections, not negative mental health effects. The researchers' conclusion is about the correlation between social media usage and negative effects, not positive connections.

13. Support a Claim: Medium

Answer: B) On average, companies with leaders who had high EI reported a 30% reduction in workplace conflicts and a saving of $75,000 in conflict resolution and legal costs annually compared to those with leaders who had moderate or low EI.

Logical Breakdown and Explanation:

The question asks you to identify which finding would most strongly support Daniel Goleman's hypothesis that leaders with high emotional intelligence (EI) enhance organizational profitability by reducing employee stress and burnout. The claim implies that high-EI leaders create supportive environments that lead to better employee well-being and financial benefits for the company, such as fewer sick days, lower healthcare costs, and increased productivity.

Option B is correct because it directly links high-EI leadership to tangible financial benefits for companies. The finding that companies with high-EI leaders experienced a 30% reduction in workplace conflicts and saved $75,000 annually in conflict resolution and legal costs strongly supports Goleman's hypothesis. It shows that emotionally intelligent leadership can reduce stressors such as workplace conflicts, which in turn improves overall organizational efficiency and profitability.

Option A is incorrect because, although it suggests that employees perceive high-EI leaders as more empathetic, it does not provide direct evidence of how this empathy leads to measurable financial outcomes like reduced healthcare costs or increased productivity. Empathy alone is not enough to support Goleman's hypothesis about profitability.

Option C is incorrect because, although it mentions that high-EI leaders spend more on employee wellness programs, it does not show how these programs contribute to reducing stress, sick days, or improving profitability. Spending more on wellness does not automatically lead to increased profits.

Option D is incorrect because it suggests no significant difference in employee turnover rates between companies with high-EI leaders and those with moderate or low-EI leaders. This finding does not support Goleman's hypothesis, as turnover rates are often linked to employee well-being, and a lack of difference weakens the idea that high EI leadership enhances profitability through improved employee well-being.

14. Cite Text as Evidence: Medium

Answer: C) "Forgive me...I've been wrong all my life."

Logical Breakdown and Explanation:

This question asks you to select the quotation that most effectively illustrates the grandmother's moment of grace and realization about her own faults just before her death in Flannery O'Connor's "A Good Man is Hard to Find." The correct answer will directly reflect her moment of self-awareness and repentance before she dies.

Option C is correct because the quote "Forgive me...I've been wrong all my life" directly shows the grandmother's moment of grace and realization. In this moment, she acknowledges her faults, signaling a significant change in her character. This admission of wrongdoing aligns with the claim that she experiences a moment of clarity about her own moral failings just before her death.

Option A is incorrect because the quote "You wouldn't shoot a lady, would you?" does not show any realization or admission of fault. Instead, it reflects the grandmother's earlier manipulative and superficial behavior, appealing to The Misfit's sense of decency to spare her life. This does not illustrate a moment of grace or self-awareness.

Option B is incorrect because the quote "I know you're a good man. You don't look a bit like you have common blood" reflects the grandmother's superficial judgments based on appearance and social class. This statement does not reflect any acknowledgment of her own faults or a moment of grace.

Option D is incorrect because the quote "I've always tried to be good. I've always tried to do the right thing. Why is this happening to me?" shows the grandmother questioning her circumstances rather than admitting any faults. It reflects confusion and self-righteousness, not the moment of grace or realization described in the passage.

15. Commas: Medium

Answer: A) moon, Titan,

Logical Breakdown and Explanation:

This question is testing your understanding of nonessential appositives. In this case, "Titan" is an appositive that renames "Saturn's largest moon." Since there is only **one** Saturn's largest moon, "Titan" is considered nonessential information. Nonessential appositives should be set off by commas.

Option A is correct because "Titan" is nonessential and should be surrounded by commas: **"Saturn's largest moon, Titan,** is home to vast lakes..." This correctly sets off the appositive according to the rules of Standard English.

Option B is incorrect because it does not place commas around "Titan," making the appositive essential when it is actually nonessential.

Option C is incorrect because the comma is misplaced. The comma should come before and after "Titan," not just after it.

Option D is incorrect because it does not include a comma after "Titan," which is required to close the nonessential appositive.

16. Pronouns: Easy

Answer: C) Their

Logical Breakdown and Explanation:

This question is testing your understanding of pronoun-noun agreement. The subject of the sentence is "The ancient baobab trees," which is plural, so the correct pronoun must also be plural to agree with the noun.

Option C is correct because "Their" is the correct plural possessive pronoun, referring to the "ancient baobab trees." It correctly indicates that the trunks belong to the trees: "**Their** massive trunks, which store water during the dry season, serve as a lifeline..."

Option A is incorrect because "There" refers to a place or existence and does not indicate possession.

Option B is incorrect because "It's" is the contraction for "it is" or "it has," which does not fit the sentence and is singular, while the subject is plural.

Option D is incorrect because "Its" is a singular possessive pronoun, but the subject "baobab trees" is plural.

17. Punctuation: Medium

Answer: D) pharaohs' courts and the citizens'

Logical Breakdown and Explanation:

This question is testing your understanding of plural and possessive forms, especially when referring to more than one individual or entity. The sentence discusses "pharaohs' courts" and "citizens' homes," so both "pharaohs" and "citizens" should be plural possessive because the courts belong to multiple pharaohs and the homes belong to multiple citizens.

Option D is correct because "pharaohs'" is the correct plural possessive form (referring to courts belonging to multiple pharaohs), and "citizens'" is the correct plural possessive form (referring to homes belonging to multiple citizens). Therefore, **"pharaohs' courts and the citizens' homes"** correctly conveys the idea of possession for both groups.

Option A is incorrect because "pharaohs courts' and the citizens'" misplaces the apostrophe in "courts'," which suggests the courts possess something, but the phrase should indicate the courts belong to the pharaohs.

Option B is incorrect because "citizens" is not possessive, while the sentence is referring to the homes belonging to the citizens. It should be "citizens'."

Option C is incorrect because both "pharaoh's" and "citizen's" use the singular possessive form, while the sentence refers to multiple pharaohs and citizens. It doesn't make logical for the passage to be referring to a singular citizen, so it needs to be plural possessive.

18. Verbs: Medium

Answer: C) forms

Logical Breakdown and Explanation:

This question is testing subject-verb agreement. The subject of the sentence is "a vast network," which is singular. Therefore, the verb must also be singular to agree with the subject.

Option C is correct because "forms" is the correct singular verb that agrees with the singular subject "a vast network": "a vast network...**forms** the backbone of the cosmos."

Option A is incorrect because "form" is a plural verb, but the subject "a vast network" is singular.

Option B is incorrect because "have formed" is a plural verb phrase and uses the past perfect tense, which does not fit the present description of the cosmic web.

Option D is incorrect because "are forming" is a plural verb phrase, and the subject is singular.

19. Sentence Structure: Hard

Answer: D) ideas, many of which

Logical Breakdown and Explanation:

This question is testing your understanding of punctuation rules, specifically the correct use of commas and clauses. The phrase that follows "ideas" is a nonessential clause starting with "which," so it must be set off by a comma.

Option D is correct because "ideas, many of which" correctly uses a comma to introduce the nonessential clause "many of which were never fully realized." The comma is necessary before "which" to conform to Standard English rules.

Option A is incorrect because it creates a run-on sentence without proper punctuation between the two clauses. Remember that the pronoun "them," as in "many of them" creates a complete sentence when paired with a verb. This is not the case when the relative pronoun "which" is used. In these cases, "many of which" creates a dependent clause, not an independent clause.

Option B is incorrect because the use of a semicolon is not appropriate here. A semicolon is used to separate two independent clauses, but there is no IC before the semicolon.

Option C is incorrect because it omits the necessary comma before "which." The "which" clause is nonessential and must be preceded by a comma.

20. Verbs: Medium

Answer: A) are

Logical Breakdown and Explanation:

This question is testing subject-verb agreement and verb tense. The subject of the sentence is "The thrill of the unexpected triumphs and the joy of seeing the improbable come to life," which refers to two ideas ("thrill" and "joy"). Since the subject is plural, the verb must also be plural.

Option A is correct because "are" is the correct plural verb that agrees with the compound subject "thrill" and "joy" (a plural subject). The sentence reads: "The thrill of the unexpected triumphs and the joy of seeing the improbable come to life **are** what make sports so compelling."

Option B is incorrect because "is" is a singular verb, but the subject is plural.

Option C is incorrect because "were" is in the past tense, while the sentence is in the present tense.

Option D is incorrect because "was" is singular and in the past tense, while the sentence needs a plural verb in the present tense since the passage provides general facts about the underdog and uses present tense verbs to discuss it.

21. Punctuation and Sentence Structure: Easy

Answer: D) opera in 1977

Logical Breakdown and Explanation:

This question tests your understanding of proper punctuation, specifically the use of commas and semicolons in sentences. The phrase "in 1977" is a prepositional phrase that specifies when the event occurred and should naturally blend into the sentence without additional commas unless needed for clarity.

Option D is correct because it correctly integrates the prepositional phrase "in 1977" without unnecessary punctuation. The sentence reads: "*What* began as a space opera in 1977 *became* a global empire." The phrase fits smoothly without breaking up the subject and verb.

Option A is incorrect because the comma after "1977" creates an unnecessary separation between the subject ("What began as a space opera") and the verb ("became"). A single comma should never separate the subject and its verb.

Option B is incorrect because semicolons should separate two independent clauses, and "What began as a space opera in 1977" is not an independent clause.

Option C is incorrect because the comma after "opera" and before "in 1977" is unnecessary, as no comma is needed before a prepositional phrase that specifies time in this context. "In 1977" specifies *when* this occurred and naturally blends with the previous information, so no comma is needed.

22. Punctuation: Medium

Answer: C) scarce; however,

Logical Breakdown and Explanation:

This question is testing your understanding of punctuation with conjunctive adverbs (like "however"). To determine whether to use a semicolon or commas, you need to check if the sentence contains one or two independent clauses (ICs). In this case, the second part of the sentence ("bee populations are declining due to pesticides, habitat loss, and disease") is an independent clause, while the first part ("Without bees, many of the fruits, vegetables, and nuts we rely on would be scarce") is also an independent clause.

Option C is correct because a semicolon is needed to separate two independent clauses, and a comma should follow "however." The sentence would read: "Without bees, many of the fruits, vegetables, and nuts we rely on would be scarce; however, bee populations are declining due to pesticides, habitat loss, and disease."

Option A is incorrect because the conjunction "however" separates two independent clauses, which requires a semicolon, not just commas. This creates a run-on sentence, a sentence structure error.

Option B is incorrect because it lacks the necessary comma after "however" and doesn't use a semicolon to separate the two independent clauses.

Option D is incorrect because there should not be a semicolon after "however" because it creates an illogical meaning. When a comma is placed after "however" it contrasts *that* IC with the one *before* it. However, the first IC, "Bees play an essential role in the pollination of crops," is not expressing a contrasting idea with the second IC, " many of the fruits, vegetables, and nuts we rely on would be scarce." Instead, they show a cause-and-effect relationship, making D) illogical.

23. Transitions: Easy

Answer: B) for instance,

Logical Breakdown and Explanation:

Transition questions test your ability to choose words or phrases that logically connect ideas within a passage, ensuring smooth flow and coherence between independent clauses (ICs). The second IC is explaining how the word "cool" has evolved in meaning, shifting from temperature to approval. It's providing an example of how language changes over time (the first IC).

Option B ("for instance") is correct because it introduces the word "cool" as an example of how language evolves, which aligns with the first independent clause's purpose of illustrating a change in word meaning.

Option A ("however") is incorrect because it suggests a contrast or contradiction, which does not fit the context of providing an example of linguistic evolution.

Option C ("nevertheless") is incorrect because it also signals contrast, which is not the intended relationship here.

Option D ("in addition") is incorrect because the sentence is not adding a new idea that continues the discussion of the previous topic along the same lines, but rather providing a specific example of the previous statement about evolving language. If D) were correct, the second IC would be providing a general detail about language, but instead, it gives a specific example of a type of language (the word "cool").

24. Transitions: Hard

Answer: A) Additionally

Logical Breakdown and Explanation:

Transition questions test your ability to choose words or phrases that logically connect ideas within a passage, ensuring smooth flow and coherence between independent clauses (ICs). The second IC explains that exposure to idealized lives on social media can lead to feelings of inadequacy and anxiety. The first IC mentions the challenges social media brings, such as the spread of misinformation and erosion of privacy.

Option A ("Additionally") is correct because it logically adds another negative effect of social media to the first IC's discussion of challenges. The second IC builds on the first by introducing an additional challenge that social media poses, aligning with the purpose of expanding the list of difficulties.

Option B ("Still") is incorrect because it suggests a contrast or pause between ideas, while both independent clauses discuss challenges. There is no contrast here.

Option C ("Hence") is incorrect because it signals a cause-and-effect relationship, which is not the case. The second IC introduces a separate challenge rather than explaining the result of the first.

Option D ("In other words") is incorrect because it suggests the second IC is a restatement or clarification of the first IC, but it is actually introducing a new and separate challenge.

25. Transitions: Hard

Answer: D) In fact,

Logical Breakdown and Explanation:

Transition questions test your ability to choose words or phrases that logically connect ideas within a passage, ensuring smooth flow and coherence between independent clauses (ICs). The second IC explains how quantum computers leverage superposition and entanglement to perform complex calculations at unprecedented speeds. The first IC discusses quantum computing's potential to transform technology by solving problems classical computers cannot.

Option D ("In fact") is correct because it reinforces the first IC's statement by providing specific details about how quantum computing achieves its transformative power. The second IC directly supports the claim made in the first IC, making "in fact" the logical transition to emphasize this point.

Option A ("In contrast") is incorrect because it introduces a comparison or contrast, but the second IC is not contrasting the first—it is expanding on it.

Option B ("Regardless") is incorrect because it suggests dismissal or a shift away from the first idea, which is not the case here.

Option C ("In comparison") is incorrect because there is no comparison being made between two ideas in this passage. The second IC provides additional explanation, not a comparison.

26. Rhetorical Synthesis: Medium

Answer: C) The Yuchi Language Project plays a central role in teaching the language to younger generations so as to preserve cultural identity and pass down traditional knowledge to future generations.

Logical Breakdown and Explanation:

Rhetorical synthesis questions ask you to identify the answer that best synthesizes information from multiple notes to achieve the intended purpose—in this case, explaining the significance of the Yuchi language revitalization efforts. The correct answer should highlight both the challenges and the importance of preserving the language for cultural identity and future generations.

Option C is correct because it effectively synthesizes the notes by explaining the importance of the Yuchi Language Project in preserving cultural identity and passing down traditional knowledge to future generations. This response captures both the significance of the revitalization efforts and their impact on preserving Yuchi culture, which is central to the purpose of the student's explanation.

Option A is incorrect because it focuses more on the methods of revitalization (immersion programs and digital tools) and the timeline rather than on the significance of the efforts.

Option B is incorrect because it focuses primarily on the increase in language learners and the timeline of the decline in fluent speakers, but it does not explain why these revitalization efforts are significant.

Option D is incorrect because, while it mentions challenges and efforts to revive the language, it does not emphasize the central idea of preserving cultural identity and traditional knowledge, which is a key part of the significance of the revitalization efforts.

27. Rhetorical Synthesis: Medium

Answer: D) In response to the carbon emissions, textile waste and microplastic pollution created by fast fashion, some fashion brands have adopted sustainable practices like using recycled materials and reducing water consumption.

Logical Breakdown and Explanation:

The question asks for the best choice that emphasizes the efforts being made to address the environmental problems caused by fast fashion. The correct answer should focus on the specific actions taken to mitigate the environmental damage caused by fast fashion practices.

Option D is correct because it directly addresses the environmental issues created by fast fashion—carbon emissions, textile waste, and microplastic pollution—and highlights how some fashion brands are responding to these specific challenges. The use of recycled materials and the reduction of water consumption are concrete examples of how brands are adopting sustainable practices to tackle these environmental problems. This option frames the response appropriately, focusing on efforts aimed at addressing environmental concerns.

Option A is incorrect because it only discusses fast fashion's negative consequences, such as textiles being incinerated or ending up in landfills, without mentioning any efforts to address these issues.

Option B is incorrect because it focuses solely on the environmental damage caused by fast fashion, such as carbon emissions and microplastic pollution, without highlighting any efforts to mitigate these problems.

Option C is incorrect because it frames the response by fashion brands as a reaction to **consumer awareness** rather than the actual **environmental issues**. While it mentions sustainable practices, it suggests that these efforts are primarily driven by consumer awareness, which doesn't align with the focus of the question—addressing the environmental problems directly.

EASY: Reading and Writing

27 Questions, 32 Minutes

The groundbreaking theories of physicist Niels Bohr are now _____ in academic textbooks and university lectures worldwide, underscoring their importance in modern physics. However, during his lifetime, Bohr often faced skepticism from the scientific community, and his ideas were initially met with resistance.

1

Which choice completes the text with the most logical and precise word or phrase?

A) rejected

B) replicated

C) adjusted

D) emphasized

CONTINUE

From vibrant trapunto paintings like *Filipina: A Racial Identity Crisis* to intricate textile works such as *Singapore Art Bridge*, Filipino artist Pacita Abad's pieces are celebrated for their bold use of color and texture. Her art, often inspired by her travels around the world and her deep connection to Filipino culture and history, showcases a unique blend of personal and cultural experiences. Thus, her creations are _____ direct experiences and cultural heritage.

2

Which choice completes the text with the most logical and precise word or phrase?

A) detached from

B) influenced by

C) revered for

D) limited to

In a landmark study on social conformity, conducted in the 1950s, psychologist Solomon Asch revealed that individuals often conform to group opinions—even when those opinions are clearly incorrect. Critics, at first, suggested that the participants' conformity might simply be _____; however, Asch's controlled experiments, which meticulously measured responses, demonstrated the opposite: social pressure had a significant influence on their judgments.

3

Which choice completes the text with the most logical and precise word or phrase?

A) fleeting

B) inconsequential

C) observable

D) deliberate

CONTINUE ➡

The following text is adapted from the 1914 story "The Lady or the Tiger?" by Frank R. Stockton, an American writer and humorist.

In a distant kingdom, the princess was torn by a dreadful choice. She knew the secret of the two doors in the arena: one held a lady, the other a tiger. The young man she loved stood before the doors, ready to choose. The princess gave a subtle nod. Trusting her, the young man advanced, unaware of what lay behind.

4

As used in the text, what does the word "advanced" most nearly mean?

A) Surpassed

B) Proceeded

C) Hesitated

D) Preceded

The following text is adapted from Bertrand Russell's 1932 essay *In Praise of Idleness*.

Modern methods of production have given us the possibility of ease and security for all; we have chosen, instead, to have overwork for some and starvation for others. Too much work is done in the world, immense harm is caused by the belief that work is virtuous. The road to happiness and prosperity lies in an organized diminution of work. Leisure is essential to civilization, and we should aspire to a society where leisure is valued.

5

Which choice best states the main purpose of the text?

A) To argue that hard work is essential for a life of leisure

B) To praise technological advancements that reduce work hours and increase leisure time

C) To call attention to reducing certain types of work and embracing leisurely pursuits

D) To recount the societal impacts of work and leisure

Practice Test 4

CONTINUE

535

The following text is from the 1922 poem "The Heart of a Woman" by Georgia Douglas Johnson.

> The heart of a woman goes forth with the dawn,
> As a lone bird, soft-winging, so restlessly on,
> Afar o'er life's turrets and vales does it roam
> In the wake of those echoes the heart calls home.
>
> The heart of a woman falls back with the night,
> And enters some alien cage in its plight,
> And tries to forget it has dreamed of the stars
> While it breaks, breaks, breaks on the sheltering bars.

Which choice best describes the overall structure of the text?

A) It contrasts the heart's freedom during the day with its confinement at night.

B) It summarizes a journey taken by a woman's heart through various landscapes.

C) It portrays the heart's dreams of freedom followed by its acceptance of reality.

D) It makes an extended comparison of the heart to a bird in flight.

CONTINUE

For centuries, it was believed by both doctors and patients alike that ulcers were primarily caused by stress and spicy foods. In the 1980s, however, Dr. Barry Marshall and Dr. Robin Warren discovered that a bacterium called Helicobacter pylori (H. pylori), which could easily be eradicated with antibiotics, was responsible for most peptic ulcers. Initially met with skepticism, their findings eventually revolutionized the understanding and treatment of ulcers: ulcers were not merely a symptom of lifestyle factors but a curable bacterial infection.

7

Which choice best describes the function of the underlined portion in the overall structure of the text?

A) It emphasizes the initial skepticism faced by Marshall and Warren's discovery.

B) It compares the old and new beliefs about ulcer treatment.

C) It underscores a significant shift in the understanding of ulcer causes.

D) It undermines the treatment methods used in curing bacterial infections with ulcers.

The following text is adapted from Kao Kalia Yang's memoir, *The Latehomecomer*.

In the quiet hours of the night, as the family gathered around the fire, Grandma told stories of the old country. Her voice, a gentle whisper, carried the weight of generations. The flickering flames cast shadows on the walls, dancing to the rhythm of her words. Through her tales, the children saw the lush green mountains and heard the rushing rivers of Laos, a homeland they had never seen but knew intimately through her vivid descriptions.

8

Which choice best states the main purpose of the text?

A) To question the historical accuracy of Grandma's stories

B) To demonstrate the impact of Grandma's storytelling on certain members of the family

C) To create a sense of nostalgia in the family as Grandma vividly describes stories of her homeland

D) To consider the importance of storytelling in maintaining traditions

CONTINUE ➡

Digital detox retreats, where participants disconnect from all electronic devices, have long been a common practice in some wellness-focused communities. In these retreats, participants often gather in serene natural settings such as secluded forests, tranquil beaches, or picturesque mountains. Activities typically include guided meditation sessions at dawn, yoga classes under the open sky, and group hikes through scenic trails. Meals are prepared using locally sourced organic ingredients, encouraging mindfulness and appreciation of nature's bounty. Evenings are spent around a campfire, where participants share stories, engage in reflective discussions, and enjoy the simplicity of life without digital distractions. Recently, these retreats have become increasingly popular in urban areas worldwide.

9

What question does the text most effectively attempt to answer?

A) What types of settings are used for digital detox retreats?

B) What makes digital detox retreats so unique compared to typical retreats?

C) Why have digital detox retreats become popular in cities around the world?

D) What activities and experiences are offered at digital detox retreats?

CONTINUE

The Singing Sand Dunes, located in various parts of the world including Qatar, Mongolia, and California, are a rare and fascinating natural phenomenon. These dunes produce a low-frequency hum or roar when the sand is disturbed, creating a sound that has captivated scientists and tourists alike. The sound is generated by the unique properties of the sand grains, including their size, shape, and the way they interact with each other. In recent years, these dunes have drawn increasing attention from researchers who are eager to understand the exact mechanisms behind the phenomenon. According to a study, the sound produced by the dunes can vary depending on factors such as humidity, temperature, and the speed at which the sand grains move.

10

Which finding, if true, would most directly support the underlined claim?

A) The dunes cause significant temperature changes in their immediate environment, leading to fluctuations in local weather patterns.

B) During periods of high humidity, the dunes produce a lower-pitched hum, while during dry conditions, they generate a higher-pitched roar.

C) The sand dunes move quickly (up to 80 mph) during dry, windy days, but when the temperature drops at night, the dunes are still.

D) Scientists discovered that the sand grains in the dunes are primarily composed of quartz, which can enhance the resonance and amplification of sound.

CONTINUE

Economic Impact of Cultural Events
on Local Economies

Event	Number of Visitors (in thousands)	Total Revenue Generated (in millions)	Change in Local Business Activity (%)
Annual Music Festival	150	$75	+28%
Local Food Fair	60	$5	+2%
City Marathon	50	$20	+13%
Historic Reenactment Fair	30	$10	+7%
International Film Festival	80	$50	+15%

Cultural events such as music festivals, film festivals, and marathons can significantly boost local economies by attracting visitors and increasing spending in local businesses. Generally, events that draw more visitors tend to generate higher revenue and lead to greater increases in local business activity. However, this pattern is not always consistent across all events. For instance, _____

Which choice most effectively uses data from the table to complete the example?

A) The Annual Music Festival attracted the most visitors and led to the greatest change in local business activity (+28%) and total revenue generated ($75 million).

B) The Local Food Fair attracted 60,000 visitors, which is twice as many as the Historic Reenactment Fair, but it generated only half the revenue.

C) The International Film Festival drew more visitors and generated $30 million more in revenue than did the City Marathon.

D) The Historic Reenactment Fair, despite attracting fewer visitors than the City Marathon, resulted in a higher percentage increase in local business activity.

Practice Test 4

CONTINUE

Text 1

A widely held belief about ancient Egyptian society posits a rigid social class structure that was almost impossible to transcend. This perspective suggests that ancient Egyptians were born into their social status—whether pharaohs, priests, scribes, artisans, or laborers—and remained in that class for life. According to this view, social mobility was extremely limited, and one's position in society was largely determined by birth.

Text 2

Historian Dr. Joyce Tyldesley, in her book "Hatchepsut: The Female Pharaoh," presents compelling evidence that ancient Egyptian society allowed for more social mobility than previously thought. Dr. Tyldesley's research, which includes analysis of burial sites and ancient records, reveals numerous instances of individuals who rose in rank through personal achievement and royal favor. She highlights examples of artisans becoming priests and commoners attaining administrative positions, indicating that merit and opportunity played a significant role in social advancement.

12

Based on the texts, what would Dr. Joyce Tyldesley (Text 2) most likely say about the widely held belief presented in Text 1?

A) It exaggerates the rigidity of Egyptian social class structure and overlooks evidence of social mobility.

B) It accurately depicts the limitations of social mobility in ancient Egyptian society.

C) It provides a comprehensive explanation of how social classes functioned in ancient Egypt.

D) It acknowledges some aspects of social mobility in Egyptian society but fails to consider the role of merit and opportunity.

CONTINUE

As the deer population in a given habitat increases, it provides more food for wolves, resulting in an increase in the wolf population. This direct relationship enhances the predatory pressure on the deer. Conversely, as the wolf population grows, predation intensifies, leading to a decrease in the deer population, exemplifying an inverse relationship. This reduction in deer numbers subsequently leads to _____

13

Which choice most logically completes the text?

A) wolves increasing their hunting territory to find more deer.

B) an increase in vegetation due to reduced grazing by deer.

C) a decrease in the wolf population due to a scarcity of food.

D) wolves seeking out smaller animals to prey on instead of deer.

Traditional crafts are a significant repository of cultural heritage. The intricate beadwork of the Maasai people in Kenya and Tanzania represents their social status and history, while the quilting traditions of the Amish communities in the United States convey stories and community values. Efforts to preserve cultural heritage have been made over the years—for example, the UNESCO Intangible Cultural Heritage Lists. Such attempts, however, have typically focused on preserving tangible artifacts even though some cultural expressions are best understood through their creation process. Therefore, if those involved in such efforts want to ensure that a comprehensive range of cultural heritage is secured, they must _____

14

Which choice most logically completes the text?

A) acknowledge that traditional crafts are largely influenced by contemporary artistic trends.

B) understand that preserving cultural heritage requires attention to both the finished crafts and the methods used to create them.

C) promote the commercial sale of traditional crafts to ensure their financial sustainability.

D) focus exclusively on documenting and preserving the physical artifacts of traditional crafts.

Practice Test 4

CONTINUE →

Elephants are often referred to as "ecosystem engineers" because of their significant impact on their environments. By uprooting trees and trampling vegetation, _____.
Furthermore, their dung disperses seeds and provides nutrients to the soil, fostering plant growth.

Which choice completes the text so that it conforms to the conventions of Standard English?

A) other species are able to thrive because elephants help maintain the savanna ecosystem

B) the savanna ecosystem is maintained by the elephants, which allow other species to thrive

C) the elephants' role in the savanna ecosystem is to maintain it, which allows other species to thrive

D) they help maintain the savanna ecosystem, allowing other species to thrive

Henna, a natural dye made from the Lawsonia inermis plant, has been used for centuries in cultural _____ the Middle East, South Asia, and North Africa. Traditionally, henna is applied in intricate patterns on the skin for weddings, religious festivals, and rites of passage.

Which choice completes the text so that it conforms to the conventions of Standard English?

A) ceremonies: across

B) ceremonies—across

C) ceremonies, across

D) ceremonies across

CONTINUE

K-Pop, or Korean pop music, has taken the world by storm over the past decade. Groups like BTS and BLACKPINK have amassed millions of fans _____ to their catchy music, intricate choreography, and highly polished music videos, they have become cultural icons, influencing not only the music industry but also fashion, beauty trends, and social media culture across the globe.

The mass adoption of autonomous vehicles raises important ethical questions. As these vehicles become more widespread, society must grapple with issues such as decision-making in life-and-death situations and the allocation of liability in accidents. For example, if an autonomous vehicle is faced with an unavoidable collision, _____

Which choice completes the text so that it conforms to the conventions of Standard English?

A) globally thanks

B) globally, thanks

C) globally; thanks

D) globally; thanks,

Which choice completes the text so that it conforms to the conventions of Standard English?

A) should it prioritize the safety of its passengers or pedestrians.

B) should it prioritize the safety of its passengers or pedestrians?

C) it should prioritize the safety of its passengers or pedestrians?

D) it should prioritize the safety of its passengers or pedestrians.

CONTINUE

Plant-based diets, which emphasize _____ have gained popularity in recent years. This shift is driven by growing concerns about health, animal welfare, and environmental sustainability.

19

Which choice completes the text so that it conforms to the conventions of Standard English?

A) vegetables: fruits, grains and legumes,

B) vegetables, fruits, grains, and legumes—

C) vegetables, fruits, grains, and legumes

D) vegetables, fruits, grains, and legumes,

In the quiet moments before bed, many people find solace in reading for pleasure. Among the many benefits of this habit, improved cognitive function and reduced stress are perhaps the most notable. Research has _____ engaging with a good book can increase empathy, expand vocabulary, and even improve sleep quality.

20

Which choice completes the text so that it conforms to the conventions of Standard English?

A) shown:

B) shown, that

C) shown

D) shown; that

CONTINUE ➡

At the core of Einstein's groundbreaking work, the theory of relativity challenges our perceptions of time and space. Within this framework, time is not a constant, but rather, it can slow down or speed up depending on the observer's velocity relative to the speed of light. Of great importance to physicists _____ the way this theory explains the behavior of objects in gravitational fields.

Which choice completes the text so that it conforms to the conventions of Standard English?

A) is

B) are

C) was

D) were

Since _____ invention in the early 19th century, photography has dramatically evolved. What began as a complex, time-consuming process has become accessible to everyone, thanks to digital technology. With the advent of smartphones, anyone can capture moments instantly.

Which choice completes the text so that it conforms to the conventions of Standard English?

A) it's

B) their

C) its

D) one

CONTINUE

Regular physical activity is essential for children's healthy development. Exercise not only strengthens their bodies but also improves their cognitive function and concentration. For instance, children who engage in regular physical activities tend to perform better academically. Exercise, _____ helps them develop social skills as they interact with peers in team sports.

Which choice completes the text with the most logical transition?

A) therefore,

B) nevertheless,

C) additionally,

D) as a result,

Cuttlefish are fascinating creatures known for their ability to change color and texture almost instantaneously. These adaptations help them evade predators and communicate with each other. Additionally, their intelligence rivals that of octopuses, allowing them to solve complex problems and demonstrate learning capabilities. _____ despite their cleverness and camouflage, cuttlefish have relatively short lifespans, typically living only one to two years in the wild.

Which choice completes the text with the most logical transition?

A) Finally,

B) Consequently,

C) For example,

D) Nevertheless,

CONTINUE

Bioluminescence is a natural phenomenon where organisms produce light through chemical reactions within their bodies. This ability is most commonly observed in deep-sea creatures, where light is scarce. Certain terrestrial species, such as fireflies, _____ also exhibit bioluminescence, using it for communication and mating purposes.

Which choice completes the text with the most logical transition?

A) for example,

B) in fact,

C) similarly,

D) thus,

CONTINUE

While researching a topic, a student has taken the following notes:

- Cymatics is the study of visible sound and vibration.
- It often involves using a medium like sand or water on a vibrating surface to visualize sound waves.
- Different sound frequencies produce different patterns, often geometric in shape.
- The artist David creates cymatic art by projecting these sound-induced patterns onto large canvases.
- His installation "Resonance" features patterns formed by varying frequencies of sound waves.

26

The student wants to provide a definition and example of "cymatics." Which choice most effectively uses relevant information from the notes to accomplish this goal?

A) The term "cymatics" refers to the study of visible sound and vibration and is often demonstrated using mediums like sand or water.

B) Cymatics, the study of visible sound and vibration, is used by the artist David in his installation "Resonance," where sound-induced geometric patterns are projected onto large canvases.

C) The artist David's installation "Resonance" features patterns formed by varying sound frequencies, which is an example of cymatics.

D) Cymatics involves using mediums like sand or water on vibrating surfaces to visualize sound waves and different sound frequencies to produce various patterns.

CONTINUE

While researching a topic, a student has taken the following notes:

- Maya Lin is a renowned architect and artist.
- She designed the Vietnam Veterans Memorial at the age of 21 while still a student at Yale University.
- The memorial is known for its V-shaped black granite walls inscribed with the names of over 58,000 fallen soldiers.
- Lin's design was initially met with controversy due to its stark, minimalist aesthetic.
- Over time, the memorial has been praised for its emotional impact and its innovative use of reflective surfaces to create a personal and contemplative experience.
- Lin has said that her goal was to create a space that acknowledged the pain of loss while allowing for reflection and healing.

27

The student wants to emphasize Maya Lin's unique approach to designing the Vietnam Veterans Memorial. Which choice most effectively uses relevant information from the notes to accomplish this goal?

A) Maya Lin's design for the Vietnam Veterans Memorial is praised for its innovative use of reflective surfaces, which creates a personal and contemplative experience.

B) The goal of Maya Lin's design for the Vietnam Veterans Memorial was to create a space for visitors that acknowledged the pain of loss while allowing for reflection and healing.

C) The Vietnam Veterans Memorial, designed by Maya Lin at the age of 21, is now a celebrated site in Washington, D.C., known for its minimalist design and the use of black granite walls.

D) Maya Lin, a Yale University student at the time, designed the Vietnam Veterans Memorial, which features over 58,000 names inscribed on black granite walls.

If you finish before the time is called, you may check your work on this module only.

On Test Day, you will only be able to move to the next module when time expires.

🔑 Answer Key

Question Number	Correct Answer	Level of Difficulty	Question Type
1	D	Medium	**Craft and Structure:** *Words in Context*
2	B	Easy	**Craft and Structure:** *Words in Context*
3	B	Medium	**Craft and Structure:** *Words in Context*
4	B	Easy	**Craft and Structure:** *Words in Context*
5	C	Easy	**Craft and Structure:** *Main Purpose*
6	A	Hard	**Craft and Structure:** *Overall Structure*
7	C	Hard	**Craft and Structure:** *Function of the Underlined Portion*
8	B	Medium	**Craft and Structure:** *Main Purpose*
9	D	Medium	**Information and Ideas:** *Main Idea*
10	B	Hard	**Information and Ideas:** *Support a Claim*
11	B	Medium	**Information and Ideas:** *Cite Text as Evidence (Infographics)*
12	A	Medium	**Craft and Structure:** *Cross-Text Connection*
13	C	Easy	**Information and Ideas:** *Inference*

Question Number	Correct Answer	Level of Difficulty	Question Type
14	B	Medium	**Information and Ideas:** *Inference*
15	D	Easy	**Standard English Conventions:** *Modifiers*
16	D	Easy	**Standard English Conventions:** *Punctuation*
17	C	Hard	**Standard English Conventions:** *Punctuation and Sentence Structure*
18	B	Medium	**Standard English Conventions:** *Punctuation*
19	D	Easy	**Standard English Conventions:** *Punctuation*
20	C	Medium	**Standard English Conventions:** *Punctuation and Sentence Structure*
21	A	Medium	**Standard English Conventions:** *Verbs*
22	C	Easy	**Standard English Conventions:** *Pronouns*
23	C	Medium	**Expression of Ideas:** *Transitions*
24	D	Hard	**Expression of Ideas:** *Transitions*
25	C	Hard	**Expression of Ideas:** *Transitions*
26	B	Medium	**Expression of Ideas:** *Rhetorical Synthesis*
27	A	Hard	**Expression of Ideas:** *Rhetorical Synthesis*

Raw Score Conversion Table

Raw Score (# of Correct Answers)	Reading and Writing Section Score	Raw Score (# of Correct Answers)	Reading and Writing Section Score
54	N/A	30	470
53	N/A	29	470
52	N/A	28	450
51	N/A	27	450
50	N/A	26	440
49	N/A	25	430
48	N/A	24	430
47	N/A	23	410
46	N/A	22	410
45	N/A	21	400
44	600	20	390
43	590	19	390
42	580	18	380
41	570	17	360
40	560	16	350
39	550	15	330
38	540	14	300
37	530	13	300
36	530	12	270
35	520	11	260
34	510	10	250
33	500	9	240
32	490	8	220
31	480	7	210

📋 Explanations

1. Words in Context: Medium

Answer: D) emphasized

Step-by-Step Explanation:

1. Let's look at what the passage is saying. The passage describes how Niels Bohr's theories are now widely recognized and taught in academic textbooks and university lectures worldwide, indicating their significant impact and importance in modern physics. However, it also notes that during his lifetime, Bohr faced skepticism and resistance from the scientific community.

2. Notice the contrast between the current widespread acceptance of Bohr's theories ("now... in academic textbooks and university lectures worldwide") and the initial resistance he faced ("his ideas were initially met with resistance"). This suggests that the word we choose should reflect the current importance and focus on Bohr's theories in education and academia.

3. The word we need should describe how Bohr's theories are now treated with great importance and focus in academic settings.

4. Ask yourself, what word best describes the act of giving something significant importance or attention? "Emphasized" is the most logical choice because it means to give special importance or prominence to something, which fits perfectly with the idea that Bohr's theories are now a key part of academic textbooks and university lectures.

Explanation of Incorrect Options:

A) rejected: This is incorrect because it means to dismiss or refuse to accept something, which contradicts the passage's description of Bohr's theories being widely recognized and taught.

B) replicated: This is incorrect because it refers to the act of copying or reproducing something, which isn't directly related to the context of the passage. The passage specifically discusses how Bohr's theories are given importance in academic textbooks and university lectures, which is also contrasted with the doubt and skepticism his ideas faced initially.

C) adjusted: This is incorrect because it means to change or modify something, which is not relevant to the passage's focus on the widespread recognition and teaching of Bohr's theories.

2. Words in Context: Easy

Answer: B) influenced by

Step-by-Step Explanation:

1. Let's deconstruct the passage together. The passage describes Pacita Abad's artwork, highlighting how it is celebrated for its bold use of color and texture. It also emphasizes that her art is deeply inspired by her travels, as well as her strong connection to Filipino culture. This indicates that her creations are closely tied to her personal experiences and cultural heritage.

2. Notice the phrases "inspired by her travels around the world" and "deep connection to Filipino culture and history." These context clues suggest that Abad's art is strongly influenced by her experiences and cultural background.

3. The word we need should reflect the idea that Abad's art is shaped or affected by her personal experiences and cultural heritage.

4. Ask yourself, what word best describes the relationship between her art and her experiences? "Influenced by" is the most logical choice because it means that her creations are shaped or guided by her experiences and cultural heritage, which fits perfectly with the context of the passage.

Explanation of Incorrect Options:

A) detached from: This is incorrect because it suggests that her art is unrelated to her experiences and cultural heritage, which contradicts the passage's emphasis on the deep connection between them.

C) revered for: This is incorrect because it means being deeply respected or admired, which is unsupported by the context of the passage. The passage focuses on the connection between her art and her heritage, not on how it is perceived by others.

D) limited to: This is incorrect because it implies that her art is restricted only to certain aspects, which does not align with the passage's description of her art being inspired by a broad range of experiences and cultural influences.

3. Words in Context: Medium

Answer: B) inconsequential

Step-by-Step Explanation:

1. Let's understand the passage together. The passage discusses a landmark study on social conformity by Solomon Asch, which revealed that individuals often conform to group opinions, even when those opinions are clearly incorrect. Initially, critics suggested an alternative explanation for the participants' conformity, but Asch's controlled experiments showed that social pressure had a significant influence on their judgments.

2. Notice the phrase "Critics, at first, suggested that the participants' conformity might simply be..." followed by "however," which introduces the contrasting findings of Asch's experiments. This indicates that the critics initially believed the conformity was of little importance or consequence, but the study revealed that it was actually significant.

3. The word we need should describe the critics' initial belief that the conformity was minor or not significant, contrasting with the actual findings that social pressure played a significant role.

4. "Inconsequential" is the most logical and precise choice because it means not significant or not important, which fits perfectly with the context of the critics initially downplaying the importance of the conformity observed in the study.

Explanation of Incorrect Options:

A) fleeting: This is incorrect because it means something that is brief or short-lived, which is not supported by the context provided in the passage. The passage focuses on the significance, not the duration, of the conformity.

C) observable: This is incorrect because it means something that can be seen or noticed, which is irrelevant to the context. The passage is discussing the significance of the conformity, not whether it was noticeable.

D) deliberate: This is incorrect because it means intentional or on purpose, which doesn't make logical sense nor precisely fit the context of Asch's experiments demonstrating that conformity was significantly influenced by certain factors.

4. Words in Context: Easy

Answer: B) proceeded

Step-by-Step Explanation:

1. The passage describes a dramatic moment in which a young man is standing before two doors, each containing a different fate: one door hides a lady, and the other hides a tiger. The princess gives him a subtle nod, and the young man, trusting her, "advanced," meaning he moved forward toward one of the doors.

2. Notice the context surrounding the word "advanced." The young man, after receiving a signal from the princess, moves forward to make his choice, showing that he continues to move toward the doors.

3. The word we need should describe the action of moving forward, especially in the context of stepping toward a potential fate.

4. "Proceeded" is the most logical choice because it means to move forward or continue with an action, which fits perfectly with the context of the young man advancing toward the doors.

Explanation of Incorrect Options:

A) surpassed: This is incorrect because it means to exceed or go beyond something, which doesn't make any logical or grammatical sense when plugged back into the original sentence.

C) hesitated: This is incorrect because it means to pause or show uncertainty, which contradicts the idea of the young man moving forward after trusting the princess's signal.

D) preceded: This is incorrect because it means to come before something else in time or order, which does not make logical sense given the passage doesn't develop the idea of a sequence of time or events.

5. Main Purpose: Easy

Answer: C) To call attention to reducing certain types of work and embracing leisurely pursuits

Logical Breakdown and Explanation:

Main purpose questions focus on the overall message or intent of the passage, capturing the central idea rather than minor details. In this case, Bertrand Russell's essay argues for the value of leisure and criticizes the overemphasis on work as a virtue.

Option C is correct because the passage primarily calls attention to reducing excessive work and embracing leisure as essential to civilization. Russell argues that society should focus on reducing work and valuing leisure for happiness and prosperity.

Option A is incorrect because the passage does not argue that hard work is essential for a life of leisure. In fact, it criticizes the belief that too much work is virtuous, which makes this option contradictory to the passage's focus.

Option B is incorrect because the passage does not praise technological advancements, although it does mention modern production methods. The focus is on reducing work, not on the benefits of technology, making this option off topic.

Option D is incorrect because the passage does not recount the societal impacts of work and leisure in a descriptive or historical sense. Instead, it argues for a shift in societal values toward leisure and away from excessive work. Because "societal impacts" are not discussed, this option is off topic and irrelevant to the main purpose.

6. Overall Structure: Hard

Answer: A) It contrasts the heart's freedom during the day with its confinement at night.

Logical Breakdown and Explanation:

The question asks you to identify the overall structure of the poem, focusing on how the heart of a woman is depicted in the two stanzas. The poem explores the heart's experiences during the day and night, highlighting a contrast between freedom and confinement.

Option A is correct because the poem contrasts the heart's freedom in the first stanza (where it "goes forth with the dawn" and "roams") with its confinement at night in the second stanza (where it "falls back with the night" and is trapped in an "alien cage"). This structural contrast between day and night highlights the heart's transition from freedom to captivity.

Option B is incorrect because the poem does not summarize a journey through various landscapes. Instead, it uses metaphorical language to describe the heart's emotional experiences, not a literal journey.

Option C is incorrect because the poem does not suggest the heart accepts reality. The heart remains confined and broken in the second stanza, without any indication of acceptance or resolution.

Option D is incorrect because, while the heart is compared to a bird, the focus of the poem is more on the contrast between freedom and confinement, rather than an extended comparison of the heart to a bird.

7. Function of the Underlined Portion: Hard

Answer: C) It underscores a significant shift in the understanding of ulcer causes.

Logical Breakdown and Explanation:

This question asks you to describe the function of the underlined portion within the overall structure of the text. The passage discusses how the discovery of *H. pylori* shifted the understanding of ulcer causes from being lifestyle-related to being bacterial in origin.

Option C is correct because the underlined portion explains that significant shift in the understanding of ulcer causes. It highlights that ulcers were not just the result of lifestyle factors like stress and spicy foods, but instead a bacterial infection that could be cured.

Option A is incorrect because, while skepticism is mentioned earlier in the passage, the underlined portion does not emphasize that skepticism. It instead focuses on the new understanding of ulcer causes.

Option B is incorrect because, while there is a comparison between old and new beliefs in the passage, the underlined portion is specifically focused on stating the new understanding of ulcer causes, not comparing the two perspectives.

Option D is incorrect because the underlined portion does not undermine treatment methods. It supports the idea that ulcers can be cured with antibiotics, rather than questioning the treatment.

8. Main Purpose: Medium

Answer: B) To demonstrate the impact of Grandma's storytelling on certain members of the family

Logical Breakdown and Explanation:

Main purpose questions ask you to identify the overall intent or message of the passage. In this text, Grandma's storytelling is highlighted, focusing on how her stories bring the children closer to a homeland they have never seen, which suggests the importance of storytelling in preserving culture and traditions.

Option B is correct because the text focuses on the impact of Grandma's storytelling on her family, specifically how her stories bring the children closer to a homeland they have never seen. It emphasizes the influence of her vivid descriptions on certain family members, particularly the children, as they imagine the landscapes of Laos through her words.

Option A is incorrect because there is no suggestion that anyone is questioning the historical accuracy of the stories.

Option C is incorrect because, although there is a nostalgic tone, the main focus is on the emotional and imaginative impact of Grandma's storytelling on her family, not just on creating nostalgia.

Option D is incorrect because it is too broad. While storytelling is important, the passage is specifically about Grandma's personal stories and how they affect her family, rather than a general reflection on the role of storytelling in maintaining traditions.

9. Main Idea: Medium

Answer: D) What activities and experiences are offered at digital detox retreats?

Logical Breakdown and Explanation:

This question asks you to determine which question the text most effectively answers, based on its focus and the details provided. The passage describes the settings, activities, and experiences offered at digital detox retreats.

Option D is correct because the text provides a detailed description of the activities and experiences at digital detox retreats, such as meditation, yoga, hikes, and communal meals. It focuses on what participants do and experience during these retreats, making it the best match for the question asking about the activities and experiences offered.

Option A is incorrect because, while the text briefly mentions settings like forests, beaches, and mountains, this is not the main focus of the passage. The primary focus is on the activities and experiences rather than the locations.

Option B is incorrect because the text does not compare digital detox retreats to typical retreats. The focus is on what happens during the retreats, not on how they are unique in comparison to others.

Option C is incorrect because, although it mentions that digital detox retreats have become popular in urban areas, the passage does not explore why they have gained popularity. It primarily describes the retreat experience, not the reasons for their rise in popularity.

10. Support a Claim: Hard

Answer: B) During periods of high humidity, the dunes produce a lower-pitched hum, while during dry conditions, they generate a higher-pitched roar.

Logical Breakdown and Explanation:

The underlined claim states that the sound produced by the Singing Sand Dunes can vary depending on factors such as humidity, temperature, and the speed at which the sand grains move. The correct answer should directly support this claim by showing a relationship between these environmental factors and the sound produced by the dunes.

Option B is correct because it directly strengthens the claim by showing how humidity affects the pitch of the sound produced by the dunes. It specifies that during high humidity, the dunes produce a lower-pitched hum, while during dry conditions, they generate a higher-pitched roar. This illustrates the claim that was made, which makes the claim more likely to be true.

Option A is incorrect because it discusses temperature changes affecting local weather patterns, but it does not relate to the sound produced by the dunes.

Option C is incorrect because it mentions the movement of the dunes during dry, windy days and their stillness at night, but it does not specifically link the speed of the sand grains to the variation in sound. Thus, the effect on the claim is unclear.

Option D is incorrect because it focuses on the composition of the sand grains (quartz) and how it might enhance sound, but it does not address how environmental factors like humidity or temperature influence the sound produced by the dunes.

11. Cite Text as Evidence: Medium

Answer: B) The Local Food Fair attracted 60,000 visitors, which is twice as many as the Historic Reenactment Fair, but it generated only half the revenue.

Logical Breakdown and Explanation:

The passage explains a general pattern: events that attract more visitors tend to generate higher revenue and cause greater increases in local business activity. However, the question asks for an example where this pattern does **not** hold true.

Option B is correct because it points out an exception to the general pattern. Although the Local Food Fair attracted **twice as many visitors** as the Historic Reenactment Fair, it **only generated half the revenue**. This breaks the expected correlation between more visitors and higher revenue, providing a clear example where the pattern doesn't apply.

Option A is incorrect because it supports the general pattern by showing that the Annual Music Festival, which attracted the most visitors, also generated the most revenue and the largest increase in business activity. It doesn't illustrate an exception.

Option C is incorrect because, although it compares the International Film Festival and the City Marathon, it follows the expected pattern of more visitors leading to higher revenue and doesn't show a case where the pattern is broken.

Option D is incorrect because it compares the Historic Reenactment Fair and the City Marathon, but the comparison doesn't break the pattern of more visitors generally leading to higher revenue or business activity; it focuses only on the percentage change in business activity without addressing a key deviation in the pattern, so it's irrelevant to the claim made in the text.

12. Cross-Text Connection: Medium

Answer: A) It exaggerates the rigidity of Egyptian social class structure and overlooks evidence of social mobility.

Logical Breakdown and Explanation:

To answer this question, you need to compare the perspectives from both texts. Text 1 presents a rigid view of ancient Egyptian social class, suggesting minimal social mobility, while Text 2, from Dr. Joyce Tyldesley, argues against this view by providing evidence of social mobility based on merit and opportunity.

Option A is correct because Dr. Tyldesley's research highlights multiple examples of individuals who rose in rank through personal achievement and royal favor, indicating that the belief in a rigid social structure, as presented in Text 1, exaggerates the lack of mobility and overlooks important evidence of social advancement.

Option B is incorrect because Dr. Tyldesley's research argues **against** the idea that social mobility was extremely limited, so he would not say that it "accurately depicts the limitations."

Option C is incorrect because Text 1 does not provide a "comprehensive" explanation of social class function, especially since it ignores the possibility of social mobility that Dr. Tyldesley emphasizes in Text 2.

Option D is incorrect because Dr. Tyldesley would not say that Text 1 acknowledges any aspects of social mobility. Text 1 presents a view that social mobility in ancient Egypt was extremely limited, without discussing any possibility of social advancement through merit or opportunity, which is the focus of Dr. Tyldesley's argument in Text 2.

13. Inference: Easy

Answer: C) a decrease in the wolf population due to a scarcity of food.

Logical Breakdown and Explanation:

The text describes how an increase in the deer population leads to an increase in the wolf population, which then causes the deer population to decline due to increased predation. The decrease in deer numbers results in a scarcity of food for wolves, and we need to choose an option that logically follows from this dynamic.

Option C is correct because the decline in the deer population, which serves as the primary food source for wolves, would logically lead to a decrease in the wolf population due to a scarcity of food. This completes the cycle described in the text and aligns with the inverse relationship between the predator (wolf) and prey (deer) populations.

Option A is incorrect because the text does not suggest that wolves expand their territory to find more deer. The focus is on the population dynamics within a given habitat, not territorial expansion, making this answer irrelevant to the information discussed.

Option B is incorrect because, although a reduction in deer might lead to increased vegetation, this idea introduces a different concept (the impact on vegetation) that is not directly related to the predator-prey relationship between wolves and deer.

Option D is incorrect because it suggests wolves would switch to hunting smaller animals, which is not mentioned or implied by the passage. The text focuses on the relationship between wolves and deer, so the idea of changing prey is out of scope.

14. Inference: Medium

Answer: B) understand that preserving cultural heritage requires attention to both the finished crafts and the methods used to create them.

Logical Breakdown and Explanation:

The passage emphasizes the importance of preserving both tangible artifacts and the creation process of traditional crafts, as some cultural expressions are best understood through their methods of creation. Therefore, the correct answer must reflect the idea that a comprehensive preservation effort should consider both the final product and the process behind it.

Option B is correct because it logically completes the argument by stating that preservation efforts should focus on both the finished crafts and the methods used to create them. This aligns with the passage's argument that some cultural expressions are best understood through their creation process.

Option A is incorrect because it introduces the idea of contemporary artistic trends, which is irrelevant to the passage's focus on preserving traditional cultural heritage.

Option C is incorrect because it suggests a commercial approach (promoting the sale of traditional crafts), which is not the focus of the passage. The passage is about preserving cultural heritage, not ensuring financial sustainability through sales.

Option D is incorrect because it contradicts the passage's main point by suggesting that preservation efforts should focus exclusively on physical artifacts, whereas the passage argues for attention to both the artifacts and the creation process.

15. Modifiers: Medium

Answer: D) they help maintain the savanna ecosystem, allowing other species to thrive

Logical Breakdown and Explanation:

The sentence begins with the modifier "By uprooting trees and trampling vegetation," which describes the actions of elephants. The subject of the independent clause that follows must be the elephants, as they are the ones performing the action described in the modifier. Therefore, the correct answer will place "elephants" (or a pronoun referring to them) as the subject of the independent clause.

Option D is correct because it starts the independent clause with "they," referring to the elephants. This structure correctly aligns the modifier with the subject of the clause, making the sentence grammatically sound: "By uprooting trees and trampling vegetation, **they** help maintain the savanna ecosystem, allowing other species to thrive."

Option A is incorrect because it introduces "other species" as the subject of the independent clause, which doesn't match the subject of the modifier. The actions of uprooting trees and trampling vegetation should be attributed to the elephants, not other species.

Option B is incorrect because the subject "the savanna ecosystem" does not match the modifier. The actions described are performed by elephants, not the ecosystem.

Option C is incorrect because it introduces "the elephants' role" as the subject, which is not appropriate given that the modifier describes the elephants' actions directly, not their role.

16. Punctuation: Easy

Answer: D) ceremonies across

Logical Breakdown and Explanation:

This question tests your understanding of when to use punctuation before a prepositional phrase. The correct answer will ensure that the prepositional phrase flows naturally with the preceding words, without unnecessary interruptions or separations. The goal is to maintain smooth and clear sentence structure while following the conventions of Standard English.

Option D is correct because it allows the phrase to flow smoothly without unnecessary punctuation. "Henna has been used for centuries in cultural ceremonies across the Middle East, South Asia, and North Africa" reads naturally since "across the Middle East..." specifies *where* the Henna was used.

Option A is incorrect because a colon is not appropriate here. Colons are used to introduce lists or explanations, but in this case, the prepositional phrase "across the Middle East..." is not a list or a clarification that needs a colon.

Option B is incorrect because the single dash unnecessarily interrupts the sentence. The prepositional phrase flows naturally with the previous words and does not require an interruption.

Option C is incorrect because a comma before "across" disrupts the natural flow of the sentence and violates a comma rule. The prepositional phrase should blend with "cultural ceremonies" without any separation.

17. Punctuation and Sentence Structure: Hard

Answer: C) globally; thanks

Logical Breakdown and Explanation:

This question is testing your understanding of how to correctly punctuate between independent clauses. The sentence before the blank mentions K-Pop's global impact, and the part after the blank explains *why* K-Pop groups have become cultural icons. Since the two parts are independent clauses, they need to be properly connected.

Option C is correct because a semicolon is used to separate two independent clauses without creating a run-on. The semicolon properly connects the first IC ("Groups like BTS and BLACKPINK have amassed millions of fans globally") and the second IC ("they have become cultural icons").

Option A is incorrect because it creates a run-on sentence by not providing the necessary punctuation between two independent clauses.

Option B is incorrect because the use of a comma creates a comma splice, which incorrectly joins two independent clauses.

Option D is incorrect because, while it uses a semicolon correctly, the additional comma after "thanks" is unnecessary and violates proper comma usage: "thanks to their catchy music" naturally blends together, so no comma should be placed between "thanks" and "to."

18. Punctuation: Medium

Answer: B) should it prioritize the safety of its passengers or pedestrians?

Logical Breakdown and Explanation:

This question tests your understanding of the difference between direct and indirect questions and the correct syntax for each. The sentence is part of a larger discussion of the ethical questions raised by the mass adoption of autonomous vehicles. The passage leads to a **direct question** about what an autonomous vehicle should do in a specific situation. Direct questions require the verb to come before the subject and are followed by a question mark.

Option B is correct because it presents a **direct question**, starting with the verb "should" and ending with a question mark: "should it prioritize the safety of its passengers or pedestrians?" This conforms to the conventions of Standard English for direct questions.

Option A is incorrect because it presents a direct question but fails to include a question mark at the end.

Option C is incorrect because it uses an indirect question structure (subject before the verb) but includes a question mark, which creates a confusing and incorrect sentence.

Option D is incorrect because it uses an indirect question structure, which is not appropriate here, as the sentence introduces a direct question. The context in the passage "The mass adoption of autonomous vehicles raises important ethical questions" indicates that we need a direct question. Using an indirect question creates an incoherent and unclear paragraph.

19. Punctuation: Easy

Answer: D) vegetables, fruits, grains, and legumes,

Logical Breakdown and Explanation:

This question tests your understanding of punctuation rules, specifically the correct way to punctuate lists within a sentence and how to handle nonessential clauses. The phrase "which emphasize..." is a nonessential clause that should be closed off correctly with a comma.

Option D is correct because it properly closes the nonessential "which" clause with a comma after "legumes." The sentence structure remains clear and grammatically correct: "Plant-based diets, which emphasize vegetables, fruits, grains, and legumes, have gained popularity in recent years."

Option A is incorrect because a colon should follow an independent clause (IC), and "Plant-based diets, which emphasize" is not an IC.

Option B is incorrect for the same reason as Option A. A single dash also requires an IC before it, and "Plant-based diets, which emphasize" does not form an IC.

Option C is incorrect because it does not include the necessary comma after "legumes" to close the nonessential "which" clause. Notice the comma before "which." There must also be a comma at the end of that clause.

20. Punctuation and Sentence Structure: Medium

Answer: C) shown

Logical Breakdown and Explanation:

This question tests your understanding of the use of "that" clauses and punctuation in sentence structure. In this case, the sentence introduces a result of research, and the correct answer should avoid unnecessary punctuation before the essential clause.

Option C is correct because it avoids unnecessary punctuation. The sentence flows naturally without needing a comma or additional punctuation: "Research has shown engaging with a good book can increase empathy, expand vocabulary, and even improve sleep quality." The word "that" is optional in this context, making both "shown that" and "shown" acceptable.

Option A is incorrect because the colon is unnecessary and would break the flow of the sentence. A colon typically follows an independent clause and introduces a list or explanation, but that is not the case here.

Option B is incorrect because the comma before "that" violates a comma rule. The "that" clause is essential, and essential clauses do not need to be set off by commas.

Option D is incorrect because the semicolon is unnecessary and incorrect in this context. Semicolons are used to separate two independent clauses, but here, "Research has shown" is not an independent clause by itself.

21. Verbs: Medium

Answer: A) is

Logical Breakdown and Explanation:

This question is testing subject-verb agreement. The subject of the sentence is "the way this theory explains the behavior of objects in gravitational fields," which is **singular**. Therefore, the verb must also be singular.

Option A ("is") is correct because "the way" is singular, and the singular present-tense verb "is" aligns with the subject. Additionally, the passage is written in the present tense (e.g., "challenges" and "is not a constant"), so it's important to maintain consistent tense throughout. Therefore, "is" keeps the sentence consistent with the other present-tense verbs in the passage: "Of great importance to physicists **is** the way this theory explains the behavior of objects in gravitational fields."

Option B ("are") is incorrect because "are" is a plural verb, but the subject ("the way") is singular.

Option C ("was") is incorrect because, although it is singular, it uses the past tense, which does not match the rest of the passage. The passage describes Einstein's theory in the present tense, and using "was" would break that consistency. In cases like this, we need to maintain the present tense to align with the surrounding verbs.

Option D ("were") is incorrect because it's both plural and in the past tense, which does not fit the singular, present-tense subject of the sentence.

22. Pronouns: Easy

Answer: C) its

Logical Breakdown and Explanation:

This question tests your understanding of possessive pronouns and subject-pronoun agreement. The sentence is referring to the invention of photography, which is singular and non-human, so the correct possessive pronoun should be singular and neutral.

Option C ("its") is correct because "its" is the singular, possessive pronoun that refers to "photography." The sentence reads: "Since **its** invention in the early 19th century, photography has dramatically evolved." This correctly shows possession (invention belonging to photography).

Option A ("it's") is incorrect because "it's" is the contraction for "it is" or "it has," not the possessive form. When plugged into the sentence, "it is invention..." or "it has invention..." makes no sense.

Option B ("their") is incorrect because "their" is plural, and "photography" is singular.

Option D ("one") is incorrect because it doesn't logically complete the sentence. The sentence is referring to photography's invention, not to "one" invention in a general sense.

23. Transitions: Medium

Answer: C) additionally,

Logical Breakdown and Explanation:

This question asks for the most logical transition to complete the sentence discussing the benefits of exercise for children. The independent clause (IC) before the blank highlights the benefits of exercise for academic performance, and the IC after the blank emphasizes an **additional benefit** of exercise—developing social skills through team sports.

Option C ("additionally") is correct because it logically transitions from the academic benefits of exercise to another benefit, highlighting that exercise **also** helps develop social skills. "Additionally" smoothly adds the next point, building on the previous information.

Option A ("therefore") is incorrect because it indicates cause and effect, which is not appropriate here. The sentence is listing benefits rather than showing a cause-effect relationship. Also, when you notice two answer choices that use transitions that are functionally identical, you can eliminate both immediately. Since A) and C) are synonyms that function in the same way (to introduce a result of the previous statement), they both can't be correct; thus, they must both be wrong.

Option B ("nevertheless") is incorrect because it signals contrast, but both ICs are positive points, so no contrast exists.

Option D ("as a result") is incorrect because it also signals cause and effect, but the second IC is not a result of the first; it is an additional benefit.

24. Transitions: Hard

Answer: D) Nevertheless,

Logical Breakdown and Explanation:

This question requires a transition that contrasts the intelligence and camouflage of cuttlefish with their short lifespan. The IC before the blank discusses the **positive traits** of cuttlefish (intelligence and camouflage), while the IC after the blank introduces a **negative aspect**—their short lifespan.

Option D ("Nevertheless") is correct because it introduces a contrast. Despite being intelligent and adept at camouflage, cuttlefish have short lifespans. "Nevertheless" introduces something unexpected (short lifespan), given the previous statement (smart creatures).

Option A ("Finally") is incorrect because it indicates the last point in a sequence, but no sequence is being established.

Option B ("Consequently") is incorrect because it indicates cause and effect, but the short lifespan is not a consequence of their intelligence or camouflage. It doesn't make logical sense to say that their intelligence is the reason they live short lives.

Option C ("For example") is incorrect because it introduces an example, which is not needed here. The sentence requires a transition that signals contrast.

25. Transitions: Hard

Answer: C) similarly,

Logical Breakdown and Explanation:

This question asks for a transition to connect deep-sea bioluminescence with terrestrial species like fireflies. The IC before the blank introduces bioluminescence in deep-sea creatures, and the IC after the blank extends the idea by mentioning that **terrestrial species** also exhibit this trait.

Option C ("similarly") is correct because it connects the idea of deep-sea bioluminescence to terrestrial bioluminescence, highlighting that fireflies exhibit a **similar** ability to produce light.

Option A ("for example") is incorrect because it introduces an example. However, fireflies are not being presented as a specific example here but as a group with **similar traits** to deep-sea creatures.

Option B ("in fact") is incorrect because it signals emphasis, but the sentence is making a comparison, not emphasizing a point.

Option D ("thus") is incorrect because it indicates a conclusion or result, which doesn't fit the context of comparing bioluminescence in different environments.

26. Rhetorical Synthesis: Medium

Answer: B) Cymatics, the study of visible sound and vibration, is used by the artist David in his installation "Resonance," where sound-induced geometric patterns are projected onto large canvases.

Logical Breakdown and Explanation:

The question asks for a definition of "cymatics" and an example of its application, so the correct answer must achieve *both* goals: a definition and an example of "cymatics."

Option B is correct because it provides a clear definition of cymatics ("the study of visible sound and vibration") and then gives a specific example by mentioning how the artist David uses cymatics in his installation "Resonance" to project sound-induced patterns. This effectively combines the definition with a practical example, meeting the student's objective.

Option A is incorrect because it provides a definition of cymatics but lacks a concrete example from the notes to illustrate the concept.

Option C is incorrect because it focuses on David's installation without explicitly defining cymatics. It provides an example but does not fulfill the requirement to define the term.

Option D is incorrect because it focuses more on the process involved in cymatics (visualizing sound waves) but doesn't clearly define the term or provide a specific example from the notes.

27. Rhetorical Synthesis: Hard

Answer: A) Maya Lin's design for the Vietnam Veterans Memorial is praised for its innovative use of reflective surfaces, which creates a personal and contemplative experience.

Logical Breakdown and Explanation:

The student wants to emphasize Maya Lin's **unique approach** to designing the Vietnam Veterans Memorial, so the correct answer should focus on her design choices that stand out as innovative or distinct.

Option A is correct because it highlights Lin's **innovative use of reflective surfaces** and describes how these surfaces create a personal and contemplative experience, emphasizing her unique approach to the memorial's design.

Option B is incorrect because, while it mentions Lin's goal of creating a space for reflection and healing, it does not focus on the **design choices** that make her approach unique.

Option C is incorrect because it emphasizes the memorial's minimalist design and black granite walls, but it does not address the **innovative elements** that make Lin's approach unique.

Option D is incorrect because it focuses more on Lin's age and background as a student rather than her **unique design approach** or innovations.

HARD: Reading and Writing

27 Questions, 32 Minutes

DIRECTIONS

The questions in this section address a number of important reading and writing skills. Each question includes one or more passages, which may include a table or graph. Read each passage and question carefully, and then choose the best answer to the question based on the passage(s).

All questions in this section are multiple-choice with four answer choices. Each question has a single best answer.

M.L. Carter and colleagues have observed that certain species of cephalopods, such as octopuses and squid, use chromatophores—specialized cells that change color—to blend in with their surroundings and avoid predators. These color changes are most <u>pronounced</u> during the mating season, when the cephalopods are actively searching to attract mates while also needing to remain hidden from predators.

1

As used in the text, what does the word "pronounced" most nearly mean?

A) Tempered
B) Ambiguous
C) Marked
D) Dormant

CONTINUE

In exploring global health issues, many researchers have concentrated solely on data from Western countries. To _____ this oversight, it's essential to conduct studies that encompass a wider array of populations. With this correction, our understanding of global health will become more comprehensive and inclusive.

Which choice completes the text with the most logical and precise word or phrase?

A) rationalize

B) exacerbate

C) sanction

D) rectify

To address the persistent problem of plastic waste, chemist Laura Green and her colleagues, in their extensive study, sought to _____ the biodegradability of newly developed biopolymers: their results showed that these biopolymers, when exposed to natural elements such as sunlight, moisture, and microorganisms, can break down completely within a few months. With this evidence, the team hopes their findings will lead to wider adoption of biodegradable materials in various industries.

Which choice completes the text with the most logical and precise word or phrase?

A) verify

B) dismiss

C) question

D) redefine

CONTINUE

The artwork of Joaquin Torres-Garcia has an important place in South American art history, partly because it was overshadowed by the works of European modernists during his time and partly because his style, which combined elements of constructivism and indigenous motifs, did not fit neatly into any one movement: his contributions are now recognized as _____ but were largely overlooked during his lifetime.

The following text is from the 1912 poem "A March Calf" by Ted Hughes, an English poet.

> With his head turned, in the sun's warmth,
> Poking out a clump of snowdrops,
> The calf looks back into the winter's night.
> Still sulking under its dirty bedding,
> Twitching its ears at a fly, dreaming.
>
> His thickened breath hangs in the clear air,
> A sign of what he suffers—patiently—
> In the soft water-colour warmth of the hill,
> While far below him the path lies, calling,
> And the grass grows on, chewing his days.

4

Which choice completes the text with the most logical and precise word or phrase?

A) regressive
B) conventional
C) pioneering
D) tenuous

5

Which choice best states the main purpose of the text?

A) To depict the calf's physical growth and development as it transitions from winter to spring
B) To explore the resilience of a calf enduring the harshness of winter and its adaptation to changing seasons
C) To describe the calf's interactions with other animals and its immediate surroundings
D) To convey the serene yet challenging life of a calf in nature by focusing on its daily routines

Practice Test 4

CONTINUE

The Waitomo Caves in New Zealand are renowned for their stunning glowworm displays. Thousands of these bioluminescent creatures light up the caves' dark interior and create an otherworldly spectacle, which attracts tourists from around the globe who are eager to witness the mesmerizing glow. Despite its allure, the cave ecosystem is delicate and threatened by human activity: pollution from nearby developments has increased by 30% over the last decade, and the constant influx of over 500,000 visitors annually can disrupt the fragile environment and harm the glowworm populations by an estimated 15%.

6

Which choice best describes the overall structure of the text?

A) It discusses the glowworms' biology, then examines the impact of tourism on their habitat.

B) It presents the positive and negative effects of tourism on the Waitomo Caves, then provides statistical evidence to support its claims.

C) It introduces the unique features of the Waitomo Caves, then presents the economic impacts of tourism on the caves.

D) It describes an uncommon phenomenon of the Waitomo Caves, then elaborates on the environmental challenges they face.

CONTINUE

Despite the common belief that expressing anger helps release pent-up emotions and reduces stress, studies by psychologist Brad Bushman reveal the opposite: <u>venting anger can actually increase feelings of aggression</u>. His research shows that individuals who engage in activities like hitting a punching bag while angry tend to feel more aggressive afterward, not less. Bushman's studies also indicate that people who vent their anger are more likely to exhibit hostile behavior towards others, including loved ones. This phenomenon, known as the "anger feedback loop," suggests that instead of finding relief, people who vent their anger may be reinforcing their aggressive tendencies.

7

Which choice best describes the function of the underlined portion in the text as a whole?

A) It provides evidence to support the claim about the negative effects of venting anger.

B) It outlines the methodology used in the research study.

C) It highlights a specific example to support the study's conclusions.

D) It clarifies a statement that was mentioned earlier in the sentence.

Turritopsis dohrnii, commonly known as the immortal jellyfish, possesses one of the most extraordinary abilities in the animal kingdom: it can reverse its aging process and effectively start its life cycle anew. When faced with injury, starvation, or the natural aging process, the immortal jellyfish reverts to its earlier polyp stage through a process called transdifferentiation, where its cells transform into different types. This unique ability allows it to bypass death, potentially making it biologically immortal. Scientists are captivated by this phenomenon, as understanding the mechanisms behind this cellular transformation could unlock new insights into aging and regenerative medicine.

8

Which choice best states the main idea of the text?

A) The immortal jellyfish possesses the unique ability to reverse its aging process, making it of great interest to scientists.

B) The immortal jellyfish, Turritopsis dohrnii, can revert to its polyp stage through a process called transdifferentiation.

C) Scientists are studying the phenomenon of transdifferentiation to unlock new insights into regenerative medicine.

D) The process of reversing to an earlier life stage to bypass death is common among various marine species.

CONTINUE

While studying law in South Africa during the 1940s, Nelson Mandela was dismayed by the pervasive racial discrimination and lack of representation for Black South Africans in political processes. According to a political historian, later in his career as a renowned anti-apartheid activist and leader, Mandela sought to address these issues, not by focusing solely on Black South Africans, but by advocating for a democratic and inclusive society where all racial groups had equal rights and representation.

9

Which finding, if true, would most directly support the historian's claim?

A) As the leader of the African National Congress, Mandela organized numerous protests and campaigns specifically aimed at highlighting the injustices faced by Black South Africans under apartheid.

B) Mandela's work in establishing the Truth and Reconciliation Commission after the end of apartheid focused on bringing together victims and perpetrators regardless of racial background to promote healing and unity.

C) Mandela's participation in the Defiance Campaign in the 1950s aimed to peacefully resist apartheid laws and involved collaboration with a diverse group of activists from various racial and ethnic backgrounds.

D) During his time as President of South Africa, Mandela prioritized economic policies aimed at reducing poverty and improving living conditions primarily in Black communities.

CONTINUE

Text 1

Conventional wisdom long held that time is an absolute, unchanging entity that flows uniformly regardless of the observer's frame of reference. This perspective, rooted in Newtonian mechanics, assumes that time is a constant backdrop against which events unfold, unaffected by motion or gravitational fields. According to this view, all observers, regardless of their state of motion, would measure the passage of time identically.

Text 2

Physicist Dr. Brian Greene, in his book "The Fabric of the Cosmos," contends that time is relative and can be influenced by factors such as velocity and gravitational fields. He demonstrates that clocks run slower in stronger gravitational fields and that time can dilate for objects moving at speeds close to the speed of light. Dr. Greene argues that time is a flexible, dynamic quantity that varies with the observer's frame of reference.

10

Based on the texts, what would Dr. Brian Greene (Text 2) most likely assert about the conventional wisdom presented in Text 1 regarding the nature of time?

A) It accurately reflects how time acts in gravitational fields but exaggerates the effects.

B) It provides a compelling argument but needs more research before it can be considered conclusive.

C) It misappropriates time as a static entity that is unaffected by external factors.

D) It misstates the idea that time varies from observer to observer based on their frame of reference.

CONTINUE

Behavioral economists who support the rational choice theory claim that people's financial decisions are always rational and based on maximizing utility. For example, when faced with a choice between two investment options—one with a higher return but higher risk and another with a lower return but lower risk—a rational individual will assess their own risk tolerance and financial goals to choose the option that provides the greatest expected utility. Examining various consumer purchasing behaviors, researchers Daniel Kahneman and Amos Tversky tested this claim by distinguishing between subjects who received a financial windfall (such as a bonus) and those who did not. Kahneman and Tversky compared the spending patterns of the groups of subjects over the following year.

Which finding from Kahneman and Tversky's study, if true, would most directly weaken the claim made by supporters of the rational choice theory?

A) Subjects' spending patterns over the year were strongly predicted by their initial financial situation, regardless of whether they received a financial windfall.

B) Subjects who did not receive a financial windfall displayed significantly more conservative spending habits over the year than they did prior to the study.

C) Subjects who received a financial windfall exhibited significantly more impulsive and varied spending patterns over the year than did subjects who did not receive a financial windfall.

D) Subjects who received a financial windfall were observed to make more calculated and long-term investment decisions than those who did not receive a windfall.

Practice Test 4

CONTINUE

Urban Green Space and Quality of Life
in Selected Cities

City	Percentage of Urban Area as Green Space	Average Quality of Life Rating (1-10)
City A	15%	7.5
City B	10%	6.7
City C	25%	8.4
City D	5%	5.8

Urban green spaces, such as parks and gardens, are often credited with improving the quality of life in cities. Proponents argue that these green spaces provide residents with recreational opportunities, reduce stress, and enhance the overall urban environment. As such, cities with a higher percentage of green space are generally believed to have higher quality of life ratings. The data collected from several cities supports this claim, indicating a direct correlation between the amount of green space and residents' quality of life.

12

Which of the following statements, if true, would most directly weaken the claim made in the passage?

A) City A, despite having a high percentage of green space, experiences severe air pollution, which negatively impacts residents' health and well-being.

B) Despite having the least green space, City D has a growing arts and culture scene that residents report has significantly enhanced their quality of life.

C) The vast majority of green spaces in City C are located on the outskirts, which make them inaccessible to most of the city's residents.

D) City C has the highest quality of life rating among the four cities, but residents report that access to green space is less important to them than other factors like job opportunities and education.

CONTINUE

Contrary to the popular belief that anime is a single-dimensional medium aimed solely at children, it is, in fact, a rich and diverse form of storytelling that appeals to all ages. While some perceive anime as simplistic cartoons, series like "Neon Genesis Evangelion" and "Akira" delve into complex themes such as existentialism and cyberpunk dystopias, engaging mature audiences with their depth. Additionally, anime spans a wide array of genres—from the whimsical fantasy of "Studio Ghibli" films to the poignant drama of "Your Lie in April"—each offering unique narratives and profound insights. As a result, this diversity _____

13

Which choice most logically completes the text?

A) reveals that anime is best suited for short-form content rather than full-length series or films.

B) has allowed anime to defy its stereotypical image and showcase its capacity for sophisticated and multifaceted storytelling.

C) indicates that anime has failed to capture the interest of audiences outside of Japan, remaining a culturally isolated phenomenon.

D) demonstrates that anime has remained largely unchanged since its inception.

CONTINUE

Located off the coast of Belize, The Great Blue Hole attracts over 200,000 visitors annually. This massive underwater cave measures over 300 meters across and 125 meters deep and offers visitors a unique opportunity to explore its crystal-clear waters and diverse marine life. Studies have shown that the Blue Hole contains ancient stalactites, which are formations that typically develop in dry, air-filled caves. These stalactites form when mineral-rich water drips from the ceiling of a cave, leaving behind deposits that accumulate over time. The presence of stalactites within the Blue Hole indicates that the cave was once above sea level and exposed to air, allowing these formations to develop. Given this evidence, researchers have concluded that _____

14

Which choice most logically completes the text?

A) the Great Blue Hole was formed during periods of significantly lower sea levels when the area was dry and exposed to the atmosphere.

B) the stalactites in the Great Blue Hole formed underwater due to marine sedimentation.

C) the Great Blue Hole is home to several unique species of marine life that have adapted to the changing environment.

D) the Great Blue Hole's formation was influenced by glacial melting events raising sea levels.

CONTINUE ➡

The tardigrade, a microscopic _____ can survive extreme conditions, is often referred to as the "water bear." These resilient organisms, which are found in a variety of environments ranging from deep oceans to mountain tops, can endure temperatures as low as -328°F and as high as 300°F.

15

Which choice completes the text so that it conforms to the conventions of Standard English?

A) creature, that

B) creature

C) creature,

D) creature that

The Moai statues, which were carved by the Rapa Nui people of Easter Island, are iconic symbols of mystery and cultural heritage. These massive stone _____ weigh over 80 tons, were transported across the island using techniques that remain a subject of debate among historians.

16

Which choice completes the text so that it conforms to the conventions of Standard English?

A) figures, some of which

B) figures, some of them

C) figures

D) figures; some of them,

The quokka, a small marsupial native to Australia, has earned the nickname "the world's happiest animal" due to its seemingly perpetual smile. Quokkas, despite _____ friendly appearance, are wild animals that should be approached with caution.

Which choice completes the text so that it conforms to the conventions of Standard English?

A) its

B) their

C) it's

D) they're

The Nobel Prize, which is awarded annually, honors individuals who have made significant contributions to various fields, including physics, chemistry, and literature. One of the most famous recipients is Marie _____ won the prize twice in different scientific disciplines.

Which choice completes the text so that it conforms to the conventions of Standard English?

A) Curie who

B) Curie, whom

C) Curie, who

D) Curie whom

CONTINUE →

The anthropologist, whom the media frequently consults, has spent years studying the cultural practices of indigenous tribes in the Amazon. Her research, which focuses on rituals and oral traditions, has provided invaluable insights into these communities. It is not clear, however, _____ her next field study will involve, as she has expressed interest in several different regions.

19

Which choice completes the text so that it conforms to the conventions of Standard English?

A) who

B) who's

C) whom

D) whose

In 1997, scientists discovered the first exoplanet orbiting a sun-like star, a finding that sparked a new era in astronomy. Today, over 5,000 exoplanets have been confirmed, with thousands more candidates awaiting verification. In the coming decades, advances in technology _____ astronomers to study these distant worlds in unprecedented detail, potentially identifying signs of extraterrestrial life.

20

Which choice completes the text so that it conforms to the conventions of Standard English?

A) allowed

B) allow

C) have allowed

D) will allow

Practice Test 4

CONTINUE ➔

During the meeting, the manager asked the team whether they had completed the project on time. She also inquired when they would submit the final report and wanted to know

_____

21

Which choice completes the text so that it conforms to the conventions of Standard English?

A) who would be responsible for presenting the results at the upcoming conference?

B) would they be responsible for presenting the results at the upcoming conference?

C) who would be responsible for presenting the results at the upcoming conference.

D) would they be responsible for presenting the results at the upcoming conference.

Known for their striking blue color, blue morpho butterflies, which are native to Central and South America, dazzle observers with their iridescent _____ through the dense rainforest, these butterflies often appear as shimmering flashes of blue, only revealing their true identity when they settle.

22

Which choice completes the text so that it conforms to the conventions of Standard English?

A) wings flying

B) wings, flying

C) wings. Flying

D) wings and fly

CONTINUE →

Catherine the Great, who ruled Russia from 1762 to 1796, was an avid patron of the arts and an enlightened ruler. She corresponded with prominent philosophers of her time, such as Voltaire, and commissioned numerous works of art to enrich the cultural landscape of her empire. Her reign, _____ was marked by significant territorial expansion, which solidified Russia's position as a major European power.

23

Which choice completes the text with the most logical transition?

A) as a result,

B) for example,

C) in fact,

D) moreover,

The architectural design of ancient Roman aqueducts, which transported water from distant sources to cities and towns, was both innovative and enduring. These structures, built using a combination of arches, tunnels, and gravity, allowed Roman civilization to thrive in regions where water was scarce. _____ some of these aqueducts are still in use today, a testament to their engineering excellence.

24

Which choice completes the text with the most logical transition?

A) Interestingly,

B) Hence,

C) Eventually,

D) In fact,

CONTINUE

The benefits of a balanced diet are well-documented. Consuming a variety of nutrient-rich foods supports overall health, helps maintain a healthy weight, and reduces the risk of chronic diseases. Regular exercise, adequate hydration, and sufficient sleep also contribute to a healthy lifestyle. _____ adopting these habits can lead to improved physical and mental well-being, increased energy levels, and a longer, healthier life.

Which choice completes the text with the most logical transition?

A) In summary,

B) Nevertheless,

C) Accordingly,

D) Additionally,

CONTINUE →

While researching a topic, a student has taken the following notes:

- In 2022, Dr. Amira El-Hassani conducted research on ancient Egyptian medical practices.
- She wanted to explore the effectiveness of ancient Egyptian medical treatments
- She analyzed papyrus scrolls dating back over 3,000 years.
- These scrolls detailed treatments for various ailments, including herbal remedies and surgical procedures.
- El-Hassani used modern chemical analysis to confirm that many of the herbal remedies mentioned in the scrolls contained active ingredients still used in medicine today.
- Her research highlighted the sophistication of ancient Egyptian medical knowledge.

26

The student wants to emphasize the findings of Dr. Amira El-Hassani's research on ancient Egyptian medicine. Which choice most effectively uses relevant information from the notes to accomplish this goal?

A) Wanting to explore the effectiveness of ancient Egyptian medical treatments, Dr. Amira El-Hassani conducted research on ancient Egyptian medical practices by analyzing papyrus scrolls from over 3,000 years ago.

B) The ancient Egyptian papyrus scrolls, analyzed by Dr. El-Hassani, detailed treatments for various ailments, including herbal remedies and surgical procedures.

C) In a 2022 study on ancient Egpytian medicine, Dr. El-Hassani analyzed papyrus scrolls using chemical analysis in order to explore the effectiveness of ancient Egyptian medical treatments.

D) After analyzing the chemicals from the herbal remedies detailed in the scrolls, Dr. El-Hassani confirmed that many of these remedies contained active ingredients still used in modern medicine.

Practice Test 4

CONTINUE

While researching a topic, a student has taken the following notes:

- Tom Cruise is an American actor and producer born in 1962.
- He has starred in a wide range of films, from action-packed blockbusters to critically acclaimed dramas.
- Cruise gained fame in the 1980s with roles in "Top Gun" (1986) and "Rain Man" (1988), which showcased his versatility as an actor.
- He has remained a major Hollywood star for over three decades, continuing to lead major film franchises like "Mission: Impossible."
- Cruise has been nominated for three Academy Awards and has won three Golden Globe Awards.
- Despite his action star persona, Cruise is known for taking on complex, dramatic roles, such as in "Born on the Fourth of July" (1989) and "Magnolia" (1999).

27

The student wants to emphasize Tom Cruise's longevity in Hollywood and the diversity of his acting roles. Which choice most effectively uses relevant information from the notes to accomplish this goal?

A) Tom Cruise starred in a wide range of films and first gained fame in the 1980s with roles in "Top Gun" and "Rain Man"

B) Despite his action star persona, Tom Cruise has starred in a wide range of films, from action-packed blockbusters like "Mission: Impossible" to critically acclaimed dramas like "Born on the Fourth of July," which highlights his versatility as an actor.

C) Over a career spanning more than three decades, Tom Cruise has starred in a wide range of films, from action-packed blockbusters like "Mission: Impossible" to complex, dramatic roles in films such as "Born on the Fourth of July" and "Magnolia."

D) Nominated for three Academy Awards and has won three Golden Globe Awards, Tom cruise's career as a major Hollywood star has spanned over three decades.

If you finish before the time is called, you may check your work on this module only.

On Test Day, you will only be able to move to the next module when time expires.

 **Answer Key**

Question Number	Correct Answer	Level of Difficulty	Question Type
1	C	Medium	**Craft and Structure:** *Interpreting Words in Context*
2	D	Hard	**Craft and Structure:** *Words in Context*
3	A	Medium	**Craft and Structure:** *Words in Context*
4	C	Hard	**Craft and Structure:** *Words in Context*
5	B	Hard	**Craft and Structure:** *Main Purpose*
6	D	Easy	**Craft and Structure:** *Overall Structure*
7	D	Medium	**Craft and Structure:** *Function of the Underlined Portion*
8	A	Medium	**Information and Ideas:** *Main Idea*
9	B	Hard	**Information and Ideas:** *Support a Claim*
10	C	Hard	**Craft and Structure:** *Cross-Text Connection*
11	C	Hard	**Information and Ideas:** *Weaken a Claim*
12	C	Hard	**Information and Ideas:** *Weaken a Claim (Infographics)*
13	B	Medium	**Information and Ideas:** *Inference (Complete the Text)*

Question Number	Correct Answer	Level of Difficulty	Question Type
14	A	Hard	**Information and Ideas:** *Inference (Complete the Text)*
15	D	Easy	**Standard English Conventions:** *Sentence Structure*
16	A	Medium	**Standard English Conventions:** *Sentence Structure*
17	B	Easy	**Standard English Conventions:** *Pronouns*
18	C	Medium	**Standard English Conventions:** *Pronouns and Sentence Structure*
19	C	Hard	**Standard English Conventions:** *Pronouns*
20	D	Medium	**Standard English Conventions:** *Verbs*
21	C	Easy	**Standard English Conventions:** *Punctuation*
22	C	Medium	**Standard English Conventions:** *Sentence Structure*
23	D	Hard	**Expression of Ideas:** *Transitions*
24	A	Hard	**Expression of Ideas:** *Transitions*
25	A	Hard	**Expression of Ideas:** *Transitions*
26	D	Medium	**Expression of Ideas:** *Rhetorical Synthesis*
27	B	Hard	**Expression of Ideas:** *Rhetorical Synthesis*

Raw Score Conversion Table

Raw Score (# of Correct Answers)	Reading and Writing Section Score	Raw Score (# of Correct Answers)	Reading and Writing Section Score
54	800	30	510
53	780	29	500
52	760	28	490
51	730	27	480
50	720	26	470
49	710	25	470
48	700	24	450
47	680	23	440
46	670	22	430
45	660	21	430
44	650	20	410
43	640	19	400
42	630	18	390
41	620		
40	610		
39	600		
38	590		
37	580		
36	570		
35	560		
34	550		
33	540		
32	530		
31	520		

 **Explanations**

1. Interpreting Words in Context: Medium

Answer: C) marked

Step-by-Step Explanation:

1. The passage describes how cephalopods like octopuses and squid use chromatophores to change color, helping them blend in with their surroundings to avoid predators. It mentions that these color changes are "most pronounced" during the mating season when the cephalopods need to attract mates while staying hidden from predators.

2. Notice the context surrounding the word "pronounced." The context clues "actively searching for mates" and "while needing to remain hidden" suggest that during the mating season, the cephalopods are under greater pressure to balance two important tasks: attracting mates and avoiding predators. As a result, their ability to change color becomes more noticeable or intense because it is crucial for both attracting a mate and staying camouflaged. This makes the color changes stand out even more during this period.

3. The word we need should describe something that is easily noticeable or evident.

4. "Marked" is the most logical choice because it means something that clearly stands out or is noticeable , which fits perfectly with the context of the color changes being particularly evident during the mating season.

Explanation of Incorrect Options:

A) tempered: This is incorrect because it means moderated or made less intense, which contradicts the idea of the color changes being more noticeable or intense during the mating season.

B) ambiguous: This is incorrect because it means unclear or open to multiple interpretations, which does not fit the context of something being distinctly noticeable.

D) dormant: This is incorrect because it means inactive or not in use, which is the opposite of the idea that the color changes are more evident or active during the mating season.

2. Words in Context: Hard

Answer: D) rectify

Step-by-Step Explanation:

1. Let's deconstruct the passage together. The passage discusses how many researchers have focused only on data from Western countries when studying global health issues. It then suggests that this focus is an "oversight" that needs to be addressed in order to achieve a more comprehensive and inclusive understanding of global health. The passage calls for studies that include a wider array of populations.

2. Notice the context clues "this oversight" and "with this correction." The phrase "this oversight" indicates that the current focus on Western countries is seen as a mistake or flaw in the research approach. The phrase "with this correction" further suggests that the passage is advocating for a change to address and fix this mistake, making the research more inclusive and accurate.

3. The word we need should describe the act of correcting or fixing this oversight to improve the understanding of global health.

4. "Rectify" is the most logical and precise choice because it means to correct or fix something, which fits perfectly with the context of addressing the oversight in global health research.

Explanation of Incorrect Options:

A) rationalize: This is incorrect because it means to justify or explain something, often to make it seem acceptable, which doesn't fit the context of correcting an oversight.

B) exacerbate: This is incorrect because it means to make a problem or situation worse, which is the opposite of what the passage suggests should be done to the oversight.

C) sanction: This is incorrect because it can mean to approve or give permission, or in some contexts, to impose a penalty, neither of which aligns with the context of correcting an oversight.

3. Words in Context: Medium

Answer: A) verify

Step-by-Step Explanation:

1. Let's understand the passage together. The passage describes how chemist Laura Green and her colleagues conducted an extensive study to address the issue of plastic waste. The study focused on the biodegradability of newly developed biopolymers, and the results showed that these biopolymers can break down completely within a few months when exposed to natural elements.

2. Notice the context clues "their results showed" and "with this evidence." These phrases indicate that the study successfully provided evidence to support the biodegradability of the biopolymers. The passage suggests that the purpose of the study was to confirm or prove the effectiveness of these biopolymers in breaking down.

3. The word we need should describe the action of confirming or proving the biodegradability of biopolymers through the study.

4. Ask yourself, what word best describes the act of confirming or proving something with evidence? "Verify" is the most logical choice because it means to confirm or validate something, which fits perfectly with the context of the study showing that the biopolymers can indeed biodegrade.

Explanation of Incorrect Options:

B) dismiss: This is incorrect because it means to reject or disregard something, which contradicts the passage's focus on proving the biodegradability of the biopolymers.

C) question: This is incorrect because it means to doubt or challenge something, which doesn't align with the study's goal of confirming the effectiveness of the biopolymers.

D) redefine: This is incorrect because it means to change the meaning or understanding of something, which is not the focus of the study described in the passage.

4. Words in Context: Hard

Answer: C) pioneering

Step-by-Step Explanation:

1. Let's look at what the passage is saying. The passage discusses the significance of Joaquin Torres-Garcia's artwork in South American art history. It mentions that his work was overshadowed by European modernists during his time and that his unique style didn't fit into any single art movement. Despite being largely overlooked during his lifetime, his contributions are now recognized for their importance.

2. Notice the context clues "his contributions are now recognized" and "were largely overlooked during his lifetime." These clues indicate that Torres-Garcia's work is now seen as valuable and significant, even though it wasn't fully appreciated when he was alive.

3. The word we need should describe Torres-Garcia's contributions as being innovative or ahead of their time, given that they are now recognized for their importance.

4. "Pioneering" is the most logical choice because it means being innovative, original, or leading the way in a particular field, which aligns with the context of his contributions being recognized as significant only later on.

Explanation of Incorrect Options:

A) regressive: This is incorrect because it means moving backward or returning to a less advanced state, which doesn't logically fit the context of Torres-Garcia's work being recognized as important.

B) conventional: This is incorrect because it means traditional or ordinary, which contradicts the passage's suggestion that Torres-Garcia's work was unique and didn't fit neatly into any one movement.

D) tenuous: This is incorrect because it means weak or insubstantial, which doesn't make logical sense given the passage's recognition of Torres-Garcia's contributions as important.

5. Main Purpose: Hard

Answer: B) To explore the resilience of a calf enduring the harshness of winter and its adaptation to changing seasons

Logical Breakdown and Explanation:

Main purpose questions require us to capture the overall essence of the passage. In this poem, the calf's endurance and quiet perseverance are central themes. The setting of winter transitioning into spring serves as the backdrop for the calf's patient suffering and adaptation to its natural environment.

Option B is correct because it captures the resilience of the calf as it faces the harshness of winter and gradually adapts to the changing seasons. The passage emphasizes the calf's endurance with phrases like "his thickened breath hangs in the clear air" and "suffers—patiently—," showing its perseverance in the cold. The shift to the "soft water-colour warmth of the hill" highlights the gradual arrival of spring, symbolizing the calf's adaptation to the environment. Additionally, the lines "the grass grows on, chewing his days" and "the path lies, calling" convey the passage of time and the calf's ongoing relationship with nature, underscoring its ability to endure and adjust to the changing seasons.

Option A is incorrect because it suggests that the passage focuses on the calf's physical growth and development. However, the poem does not mention the calf growing or changing physically, nor does it focus on its maturation over time. As there is no discussion of how the calf's body changes, this answer off topic and unsupported by the context in the poem.

Option C is incorrect because it implies that the poem centers on the calf's interactions with other animals or its surroundings. However, the poem does not include any interactions with other creatures. The focus remains on the calf's solitary existence and internal experience, making this interpretation irrelevant to the actual content of the poem.

Option D is incorrect because it emphasizes the idea of "daily routines," which are not described in the passage. While the poem does offer glimpses of the calf's life, it does so without any reference to habitual actions or a repetitive structure of daily activities. The focus is more on the calf's endurance and adaptation to its natural surroundings, making "daily routines" an unsupported interpretation of the text.

6. Overall Structure: Easy

Answer: D) It describes an uncommon phenomenon of the Waitomo Caves, then elaborates on the environmental challenges they face.

Logical Breakdown and Explanation:

To answer this question, we must determine how the passage is structured. The text starts by introducing the unique phenomenon of the glowworms in the Waitomo Caves, describing their beauty and how they attract tourists. It then shifts to discussing the environmental challenges caused by human activity, such as pollution and the high number of visitors, which threaten the cave's delicate ecosystem.

Option D is correct because the passage first describes the uncommon phenomenon of glowworms illuminating the Waitomo Caves and then moves on to explain the environmental challenges posed by pollution and tourism, including specific statistics about the negative impacts on the cave ecosystem and glowworm population.

Option A is incorrect because the passage does not delve into the biology of glowworms. Instead, it focuses on the spectacle they create in the caves and then discusses the environmental impact of tourism. There is no exploration of how glowworms function biologically.

Option B is incorrect because, while the passage does mention the allure of the glowworm display that attracts tourists, it does not discuss any positive impacts of tourism on the Waitomo Caves. The text focuses mainly on the environmental harm caused by tourism, such as pollution and the negative impact on the glowworm population, without presenting any benefits or positive effects of tourism on the caves. This makes the reference to "positive effects" unsupported by the passage.

Option C is incorrect because the passage does not discuss the economic impacts of tourism on the Waitomo Caves, such as the revenue that was generated or the jobs that were created. The focus is on the environmental effects, specifically pollution and the impact on glowworm populations.

7. Function of the Underlined Portion: Medium

Answer: D) It clarifies a statement that was mentioned earlier in the sentence.

Logical Breakdown and Explanation:

To determine the function of the underlined portion, we need to understand how it fits within the overall structure of the passage. The passage begins by challenging the common belief that venting anger reduces stress. The underlined portion presents the key finding of psychologist Brad Bushman's research, which counters that belief by stating that venting anger can actually increase aggression.

Option D is correct because the underlined portion clarifies the earlier statement by explaining that venting anger, rather than reducing stress, actually increases feelings of aggression. Additionally, it directly contradicts the common belief that expressing anger helps release pent-up emotions and reduces stress. This explanation refines the earlier claim and provides the core idea behind the passage's argument.

Option A is incorrect because the underlined portion is not serving as direct evidence or proof of the claim. It is part of the argument itself, explaining the psychological phenomenon rather than providing supporting evidence for it.

Option B is incorrect because the underlined portion does not outline the methodology of the research study. There is no description of how the research was conducted in this section.

Option C is incorrect because the underlined portion is not providing a specific example. The example comes later, where the passage describes individuals hitting a punching bag while angry.

8. Main Idea: Medium

Answer: A) The immortal jellyfish possesses the unique ability to reverse its aging process, making it of great interest to scientists.

Logical Breakdown and Explanation:

The passage primarily focuses on the unique ability of the immortal jellyfish to reverse its aging process, effectively restarting its life cycle through transdifferentiation. This ability is presented as remarkable and of significant interest to scientists due to its potential implications for understanding aging and regenerative medicine.

Option A is correct because it accurately captures the main idea by emphasizing both the jellyfish's ability to reverse its aging process and how this ability has captivated scientists. The passage highlights that the jellyfish can "bypass death" and dicusses how scientists are interested in understanding this cellular transformation for the various benefits it can provide, such as unlocking new insights into aging and regenerative medicine.

Option B is incorrect because, while it describes the process of transdifferentiation, it focuses on a minor aspect of the passage and leaves out the major idea that the jellyfish's ability to reverse its aging process is of great interest to scientists. The focus on just the biological process misses the broader, more significant context of why this ability is considered extraordinary and its potential implications for science.

Option C is incorrect because it emphasizes the scientific study of transdifferentiation, which is mentioned but not the central focus of the passage. The main idea revolves around the jellyfish's unique ability to reverse aging, with the scientific interest being a secondary point. By focusing too narrowly on the scientific research, this answer leaves out the BIG idea of the jellyfish's biological immortality.

Option D is incorrect because it introduces an idea that contradicts the passage, suggesting that reversing to an earlier life stage is common among marine species. The passage clearly states that this ability is "extraordinary" and unique to the immortal jellyfish, making this answer off-topic and unsupported by the major ideas developed in the text.

9. Support a Claim: Hard

Answer: B) Mandela's work in establishing the Truth and Reconciliation Commission after the end of apartheid focused on bringing together victims and perpetrators regardless of racial background to promote healing and unity.

Logical Breakdown and Explanation:

The historian's claim is that Mandela, in his later career, focused on advocating for an inclusive society where all racial groups had equal rights and representation, not just Black South Africans. The correct answer will strengthen this claim in a way that makes the claim more valid and likely to be true.

Option B is correct because Mandela's establishment of the Truth and Reconciliation Commission focused on promoting healing and unity among all racial groups. By bringing together victims and perpetrators regardless of racial background, this provides evidence to illustrate the historian's claim that Mandela worked toward an inclusive society where all races had equal rights and representation, thereby making the claim more likely to be true.

Option A is incorrect because it describes protests and campaigns aimed specifically at highlighting injustices faced by Black South Africans, which, while important to his early work, does not directly support the claim that Mandela later advocated for all racial groups equally. This information is only focused on one racial group, so it doesn't strengthen the claim.

Option C is incorrect because, while the Defiance Campaign involved collaboration with diverse activists, it does not explicitly focus on advocating for equal rights and representation for all racial groups, which is the main point of the historian's claim. In other words, Mandela could have worked with activists from various racial backgrounds but still only have supported one group of people. Therefore, this statement is unclear as to how it affects the claim.

Option D is incorrect because it focuses on Mandela prioritizing economic policies for Black communities during his presidency. This weakens the historian's claim by suggesting that Mandela's policies were aimed more at improving conditions primarily for Black South Africans, rather than focusing on an inclusive society for all racial groups.

10. Cross-Text Connection: Hard

Answer: C) It misappropriates time as a static entity that is unaffected by external factors.

Logical Breakdown and Explanation:

To answer this question, we need to focus on the differences between the perspectives in the two texts. Text 1 presents the conventional wisdom that time is an absolute, unchanging entity, while Text 2, through Dr. Brian Greene's argument, contends that time is relative and influenced by factors such as velocity and gravitational fields. Dr. Greene's view directly contradicts the conventional wisdom presented in Text 1.

Option C is correct because Dr. Greene in Text 2 would likely assert that the conventional wisdom in Text 1 incorrectly portrays time as a "static entity," when in fact time is "flexible" and "dynamic," influenced by external factors such as gravity and velocity. Greene's argument that "time can dilate" and "clocks run slower in stronger gravitational fields" challenges the idea that time is unaffected by motion or gravitational fields, as suggested in Text 1.

Option A is incorrect because Text 1 does not acknowledge the effects of gravitational fields on time at all, so Dr. Greene would not agree that it "accurately reflects" this aspect. He would challenge the notion that time is unaffected by external forces.

Option B is incorrect because Dr. Greene's position is presented as conclusive, based on established scientific principles like time dilation and gravitational effects. There is no indication that more research is required before Greene's ideas can be accepted.

Option D is incorrect because Text 1 does not claim that time varies from observer to observer. Instead, it asserts that time is uniform and unchanging. Therefore, Dr. Greene would not accuse it of misstating that point; he would argue that Text 1 overlooks the relativity of time altogether.

11. Weaken a Claim: Hard

Answer: C) Subjects who received a financial windfall exhibited significantly more impulsive and varied spending patterns over the year than did subjects who did not receive a financial windfall.

Logical Breakdown and Explanation:

To weaken the claim made by supporters of the rational choice theory, the correct answer must present evidence that contradicts the idea that people's financial decisions are always rational and based on maximizing utility. The rational choice theory suggests that individuals assess risk and reward to make logical decisions. Therefore, if Kahneman and Tversky's findings show behavior that deviates from this logical, utility-maximizing framework, the theory is weakened.

Option C is correct because it demonstrates that subjects who received a financial windfall exhibited "impulsive and varied spending patterns," which contradicts the idea that individuals always make rational, calculated decisions based on maximizing utility. Impulsive spending does not align with rational decision-making, making this finding directly challenge the core claim of the rational choice theory.

Option A is incorrect because it makes a statement that is largely off-topic. While the initial financial situation may predict spending patterns, this information does not directly address the rationality of decision-making based on maximizing utility. As a result, it doesn't affect the claim that people always make rational financial decisions.

Option B is incorrect because it provides information that is unclear as to how it affects the claim. Although subjects displayed more conservative spending habits, this behavior could still align with rational decision-making, depending on their financial goals. It's uncertain whether this supports or weakens the rational choice theory, making it an unclear response.

Option D is incorrect because it strengthens the claim rather than weakens it. The finding that subjects who received a financial windfall made more calculated, long-term investment decisions supports the idea that individuals act rationally and maximize utility in financial decisions, which aligns with the rational choice theory.

12. Weaken a Claim (Infographics): Hard

Answer: C) The vast majority of green spaces in City C are located on the outskirts, which make them inaccessible to most of the city's residents.

Logical Breakdown and Explanation:

The passage claims that cities with a higher percentage of green space tend to have higher quality of life ratings. Therefore, the correct answer will present information that challenges the idea that urban green space directly correlates with a better quality of life.

Option C is correct because it shows that in City C, despite having the highest percentage of green space, these areas are located on the outskirts and are inaccessible to most residents. This weakens the claim that a higher percentage of green space improves quality of life, as it suggests that simply having green spaces is not enough if they are not accessible.

Option A is incorrect because it introduces the issue of air pollution in City A, which is off topic. The passage focuses on green spaces' impact on quality of life, not environmental issues like air pollution, so this information doesn't directly address the claim about green space.

Option B is incorrect because it introduces the arts and culture scene in City D, which is irrelevant to the claim about green space. While residents report that arts and culture improve their quality of life, this does not directly challenge the idea that green spaces can improve quality of life as well.

Option D is incorrect because it makes a statement that is unclear in how it affects the claim. Although residents report that other factors, like job opportunities and education, are more important to their quality of life than green spaces, this does not directly contradict the idea that green spaces still play a role in improving quality of life.

13. Inference (Complete the Text): Medium

Answer: B) has allowed anime to defy its stereotypical image and showcase its capacity for sophisticated and multifaceted storytelling.

Logical Breakdown and Explanation:

The passage challenges the stereotype that anime is a medium solely for children and presents it as a diverse form of storytelling that engages audiences of all ages. It highlights how anime spans various genres and deals with complex themes, which appeals to mature audiences and provides unique narratives. Therefore, the logical conclusion should emphasize anime's ability to defy its stereotypical image and showcase its complexity.

Option B is correct because it directly ties into the passage's argument that anime is a multifaceted form of storytelling, appealing to various audiences. The phrase "defy its stereotypical image" matches the passage's assertion that anime is not just for children, and "showcase its capacity for sophisticated and multifaceted storytelling" logically concludes the discussion of anime's range and depth.

Option A is incorrect because it introduces the unrelated idea that anime is best suited for short-form content. The passage focuses on anime's diversity and complexity, with no mention of the format of its content, making this answer irrelevant.

Option C is incorrect because it contradicts the passage's argument. The passage does not suggest that anime has failed to capture interest outside of Japan, and this statement undermines the positive portrayal of anime's broad appeal.

Option D is incorrect because it states that anime has "remained largely unchanged," which contradicts the passage's emphasis on its diverse and evolving nature. The passage clearly presents anime as a rich and varied medium, making this answer inaccurate.

14. Inference (Complete the Text): Hard

Answer: A) the Great Blue Hole was formed during periods of significantly lower sea levels when the area was dry and exposed to the atmosphere.

Logical Breakdown and Explanation:

The passage explains that the Great Blue Hole contains stalactites, which are typically formed in dry, air-filled caves. This suggests that the cave was once above sea level, where it was exposed to air, allowing the stalactites to develop. Therefore, the logical conclusion should emphasize that the cave must have been formed when sea levels were lower, and the area was dry.

Option A is correct because it logically follows from the evidence presented. The presence of stalactites indicates that the cave was once exposed to air, which means the area was dry during a period of lower sea levels. This conclusion is directly supported by the information about how stalactites form and the cave's past environment.

Option B is incorrect because it contradicts the explanation of how stalactites form. Stalactites are created in dry, air-filled environments, not underwater due to marine sedimentation. This answer misrepresents the formation process described in the passage.

Option C is incorrect because it introduces information about marine life, which is unrelated to the formation of the cave or the stalactites. The passage focuses on geological evidence, not biological adaptations, making this option irrelevant.

Option D is incorrect because it introduces the idea of glacial melting events raising sea levels. While sea level changes are relevant, the passage focuses on how lower sea levels allowed the cave to be exposed, not how rising sea levels influenced its formation. This option contradicts the focus of the text.

15. Sentence Structure: Easy

Answer: D) creature that

Logical Breakdown and Explanation:

In this sentence, the phrase "a microscopic creature that can survive extreme conditions" is an essential clause because it provides important information about the tardigrade. According to the conventions of Standard English, no comma should be placed before an essential clause introduced by "that."

Option D is correct because it correctly uses "creature that" to introduce the essential clause without a comma. This maintains the sentence structure and conforms to the rule that no comma should be used before an essential "that" clause.

Option A is incorrect because it violates the comma rule. A comma before "that" creates a punctuation error, incorrectly separating the essential clause from the main sentence.

Option B is incorrect because it creates a sentence structure error. Without "that," the sentence reads as "The tardigrade, a microscopic creature can survive extreme conditions, is often referred to as the 'water bear.'" This results in a run-on sentence (a strange one) where "a microscopic creature can survive extreme conditions" functions as an independent clause embedded within another independent clause (The tardigrade is often referred to as the "water bear."), making the sentence grammatically incorrect.

Option C is incorrect because it also creates a run-on sentence. The sentence would read: "The tardigrade, a microscopic creature, can survive extreme conditions, is often referred to as the 'water bear.'" This answer creates a nonsensical structure where there are two main verbs ("can" and "is") that are not properly formed. If you leave out the nonessential information, the resulting sentence would be "The tardigrade *can* survive extreme conditions, *is* often referred to as the "water bear."

16. Sentence Structure: Medium

Answer: A) figures, some of which

Logical Breakdown and Explanation:

In this sentence, the correct choice must introduce the nonessential clause "some of which weigh over 80 tons" without creating a run-on or grammatical error. The clause provides additional information about the Moai statues and is appropriately separated from the main sentence with a comma.

Option A is correct because it correctly uses "some of which" to introduce the nonessential "which" clause. The dependent clause is set off by a comma, providing additional information without interrupting the sentence structure.

Option B is incorrect because it creates a run-on sentence. The sentence would read: "These massive stone figures, some of them weigh over 80 tons, were transported across the island," which contains two independent clauses ("some of them weigh over 80 tons" and "These massive stone figures were transported") improperly joined by a comma, creating a run-on sentence.

Option C is incorrect because it creates a "nonsense structure." Without additional clarification, the sentence reads: "These massive stone figures weigh over 80 tons, were transported across the island," where the verbs "weigh" and "were" are not properly connected, leading to a structurally flawed sentence with no clear relationship between the two actions.

Option D is incorrect because it violates the rule against placing a single comma between a subject and its verb. The sentence reads: "some of them, weigh over 80 tons, were transported across the island," which incorrectly creates a comma splice, separating the subject from the verb with unnecessary punctuation.

17. Pronouns: Easy

Answer: B) their

Logical Breakdown and Explanation:

This sentence requires a pronoun that correctly refers to the plural noun "quokkas." Since "quokkas" is plural, the pronoun must also be plural, and it should indicate possession because the sentence refers to the quokkas' friendly appearance.

Option B is correct because "their" is the plural possessive pronoun that correctly refers to "quokkas" and indicates ownership of the "friendly appearance."

Option A is incorrect because "its" is a singular possessive pronoun, and the subject "quokkas" is plural. Using "its" would create a pronoun-antecedent disagreement.

Option C is incorrect because "it's" is a contraction for "it is," which would not fit grammatically in this context, as the sentence requires a possessive pronoun. It would be awkward and nonsensical to say "despite *it is* (or *it has*) friendly appearance."

Option D is incorrect because "they're" is a contraction for "they are," which is not needed here. The sentence calls for a possessive pronoun, not a verb phrase. Again, it would be awkward and absurd to say "despite *they are* friendly appearance."

18. Pronouns and Sentence Structure: Medium

Answer: C) Curie, who

Logical Breakdown and Explanation:

In this sentence, the relative clause "who won the prize twice in different scientific disciplines" is nonessential in this sentence because 1) Marie Curie refers to a singular, well-identified entity, 2) the sentence naturally requires a pause, and 3) the core idea remains intact without the additional information about her winning the prize twice. Therefore, the clause should be set off with commas.

Option C is correct because it correctly uses "Curie, who" with the necessary comma to indicate that the clause is nonessential, providing extra information without altering the core meaning of the sentence. The core idea of the sentence (Marie Curie being one of the most famous Nobel Prize winners) remains intact when the nonessential information is removed (she down the prize twice in different disciplines).

Option A is incorrect because it omits the necessary comma, which makes the sentence feel rushed and improperly connects the relative clause without a clear pause.

Option B is incorrect because "whom" is used incorrectly here. "Who" is the correct relative pronoun since it functions as the subject of the clause, not the object.

Option D is incorrect because it also incorrectly uses "whom," which should not be used in this context as "who" is needed to act as the subject of the relative clause.

19. Pronouns: Hard

Answer: C) whom

Logical Breakdown and Explanation:

This sentence requires a possessive pronoun that refers to the next field study, specifically what the anthropologist's next research will involve. The correct choice must indicate possession and correctly fit within the sentence structure.

Option C is correct because "whom" is the object form of the pronoun, and in this case, it functions as the object of the relative clause. The phrase "her next field study will involve" requires an object pronoun (e.g., "whom"), as the clause is essentially saying, "her next field study will involve *whom*." If you replaced "whom" with a regular object pronoun "him" or "them," it would still be grammatical ("her next field study will involve *him*" makes sense). However, if you replaced it with a regular subject pronoun "he" or "they," the sentence wouldn't be grammatical ("her next field study will involve *he*" does not makes sense.

Option A is incorrect because "who" is a subject pronoun, and the sentence requires an object pronoun. The correct phrasing would be "whom her next field study will involve" since "whom" is the object of the verb "involve."

Option B is incorrect because "who's" is a contraction of "who is," which does not fit the context and structure of the sentence. It does not provide the object pronoun needed for the relative clause.

Option D is incorrect because "whose" is a possessive pronoun, which requires a noun to appear after it. "Whose" would create an awkward structure "*whose her*..." as we would have two possessive pronouns next to each other, which is not grammatical.

20. Verbs: Medium

Answer: D) will allow

Logical Breakdown and Explanation:

This sentence is testing verb tenses, and the key to choosing the correct tense lies in the time reference "in the coming decades," which clearly indicates a future event. The correct verb tense should reflect this future time frame.

Option D is correct because "will allow" is the future tense, aligning with the time reference "in the coming decades." The sentence is discussing technological advancements that will enable astronomers to study exoplanets in the future, making the future tense the most appropriate choice.

Option A is incorrect because "allowed" is in the past tense, which does not fit with the future time reference "in the coming decades." The sentence is discussing future technological advances, not past ones.

Option B is incorrect because "allow" is in the present tense, while the sentence refers to future developments. The phrase "in the coming decades" indicates that the action will take place in the future, not in the present.

Option C is incorrect because "have allowed" is the present perfect tense, which indicates actions that started in the past and continue to the present. This does not match the future-oriented context of the sentence.

21. Punctuation: Easy

Answer: C) who would be responsible for presenting the results at the upcoming conference.

Logical Breakdown and Explanation:

This sentence requires an indirect question structure, as the manager is asking for information in the form of a statement rather than directly posing a question. Indirect questions do not require question marks and follow regular sentence punctuation, ending with a period.

Option C is correct because it uses the appropriate structure for an indirect question, "who would be responsible for presenting the results," and ends with a period, which is proper for indirect questions. Indirect questions are statements that blend into the sentence. The sentence in the passage starts with "She also inquired..." then we see an indirect statement "when they would submit the final report" that blends into the sentence. Therefore, we need another indirect question "who would be responsible" to complete the sentence (She also inquired who would be responsible.).

Option A is incorrect because it uses a question mark, which is not appropriate for an indirect question. Since the sentence is written as a statement, it should not include a question mark.

Option B is incorrect because it not only uses a question mark but also changes the word order to that of a direct question ("would they be responsible"), which is not suitable for an indirect question in this context.

Option D is incorrect because, while it ends with a period, it still uses the word order of a direct question, "would they be responsible." Indirect questions follow statement word order, making this option grammatically incorrect.

22. Sentence Structure: Medium

Answer: C) wings. Flying

Logical Breakdown and Explanation:

This sentence structure question tests your ability to recognize run-on sentences and properly separate independent clauses. The first part of the sentence, "blue morpho butterflies dazzle observers with their iridescent wings," is an independent clause (IC 1). The second part, "these butterflies often appear as shimmering flashes of blue," is another independent clause (IC 2). Therefore, the correct choice should separate these two independent clauses properly.

Option C is correct because it uses a period to separate the two independent clauses: "wings. Flying through the dense rainforest, these butterflies often appear..." The period properly separates IC 1 ("blue morpho butterflies dazzle observers with their iridescent wings") from IC 2 ("these butterflies often appear as shimmering flashes of blue").

Option A is incorrect because it creates a run-on sentence by failing to properly separate the two independent clauses. Without punctuation, it incorrectly joins two complete thoughts into one sentence.

Option B is incorrect because, while it adds a comma, it still creates a run-on sentence. A comma alone cannot separate two independent clauses; a period or semicolon is required.

Option D is incorrect because it still creates a run-on sentence by improperly joining two independent clauses without the necessary punctuation (only a comma). The first IC would read, "blue morpho butterflies dazzle observers with their iridescent wings and fly through the dense rainforest." The second IC is "these butterflies often appear as shimmering flashes of blue."

23. Transitions: Hard

Answer: D) moreover,

Logical Breakdown and Explanation:

Transition questions test your ability to choose words or phrases that logically connect ideas within a passage, ensuring smooth flow and coherence between independent clauses (ICs). The first IC discusses Catherine the Great's role as an enlightened ruler and patron of the arts, while the second IC explains how her reign was marked by significant territorial expansion, solidifying Russia's power.

Option D ("Moreover") is correct because it introduces additional information. The second IC provides another key aspect of Catherine's reign—territorial expansion—without implying causality. "Moreover" signals a further point that complements her cultural contributions, making it the most logical transition.

Option A ("As a result") is incorrect because it suggests a cause-effect relationship, which is not present between the ICs. Cultural contributions did not cause territorial expansion.

Option B ("For example") is incorrect because the second IC does not illustrate or exemplify the first; it provides a separate but related point.

Option C ("In fact") is incorrect because it unnecessarily emphasizes the second point. In other words, IC 2 does not emphasize or confirm the validity of the first statement.

24. Transitions: Hard

Answer: A) Interestingly,

Logical Breakdown and Explanation:

Transition questions test your ability to select transitions that ensure smooth connections between independent clauses. The first IC discusses the innovative and enduring design of Roman aqueducts, while the second IC highlights that some of these aqueducts are still in use today, showcasing their engineering excellence.

Option A ("Interestingly") is correct because it introduces a surprising and notable fact about the aqueducts still being in use. This transition helps highlight the remarkable durability of these ancient structures.

Option B ("Hence") is incorrect because it implies a cause-and-effect relationship. The first IC describes how Roman aqueducts were designed, and the second IC mentions that they are still in use today. However, "hence" suggests that their continued use is the direct result of the innovative design mentioned in the first IC, which isn't clearly established in the passage. The second IC is more of an observation rather than a consequence of the first.

Option C ("Eventually") is incorrect because it implies a progression or future development. The sentence focuses on the present state of the aqueducts ("some of these aqueducts are still in use today"), so "eventually" is inappropriate, as it would suggest that the aqueducts will be in use at some later point, which contradicts the focus on their current condition.

Option D ("In fact") is incorrect because it emphasizes an idea that typically reinforces or strengthens a previously mentioned fact. While the second IC introduces new information about the aqueducts still being in use, it is not directly reinforcing the first IC but rather expanding on it with an additional detail. "In fact" would be more appropriate if the second IC were providing further evidence of the innovation already mentioned, but in this case, it is offering new insight.

25. Transitions: Hard

Answer: A) In summary,

Logical Breakdown and Explanation:

Transition questions test your ability to logically connect ideas within a passage, ensuring smooth flow between independent clauses. The first IC discusses the health benefits of balanced habits like a nutritious diet, exercise, and sleep, while the second IC explains the positive effects of adopting these habits, such as improved well-being and a longer life.

Option C ("Accordingly") is correct because it signals a logical result. The second IC explains the benefits that result from adopting the healthy habits described in the first IC, making "accordingly" the best transition.

Option A ("In summary") is incorrect because it implies that the second IC is summarizing the previous ideas. However, the second IC is not meant to be a conclusion of the entire paragraph; rather, it provides additional details about the benefits of maintaining healthy habits. "In summary" would be more appropriate at the end of a paragraph to recap multiple points, but in this case, the second IC expands on a specific aspect.

Option B ("Nevertheless") is incorrect because it introduces something unexpected or surprising, given the previous statement. "Nevertheless" would suggest that the second IC presents information that goes against the idea in the first IC, which is not the case. Both clauses are complementary, as the first IC describes the healthy habits, and the second IC describes their benefits. Using "nevertheless" here would create confusion, as there is no unexpected idea being presented.

Option D ("Additionally") is incorrect because it suggests the introduction of new information that continues the discussion of the previous topic along the same lines. While the second IC does provide further details, it is not introducing a new topic but rather elaborating on the direct effects of the habits mentioned in the first IC. "Additionally" would be better used if the second IC were adding another independent benefit or new habit, but here, it is stating the result mentioned in the first IC.

26. Rhetorical Synthesis: Medium

Answer: D) After analyzing the chemicals from the herbal remedies detailed in the scrolls, Dr. El-Hassani confirmed that many of these remedies contained active ingredients still used in modern medicine.

Logical Breakdown and Explanation:

The student wants to emphasize the findings of Dr. Amira El-Hassani's research on ancient Egyptian medicine, focusing on the outcomes and discoveries made during her analysis.

Option D is correct because it directly highlights the key finding of Dr. El-Hassani's research: that many ancient Egyptian herbal remedies contained active ingredients still used in modern medicine. This effectively emphasizes the sophistication of ancient Egyptian medical knowledge, which is the most relevant finding from her research.

Option A is incorrect because it focuses more on the process of conducting the research and the papyrus scroll analysis rather than emphasizing the findings or discoveries made as a result of the research.

Option B is incorrect because it describes the content of the scrolls without addressing the significant findings from Dr. El-Hassani's analysis, which the student wants to emphasize.

Option C is incorrect because it mainly describes the research method (chemical analysis) and objective (exploring effectiveness), but it does not emphasize the important outcome of her research: the connection between ancient remedies and modern medicine.

27. Rhetorical Synthesis: Hard

Answer: B) Despite his action star persona, Tom Cruise has starred in a wide range of films, from action-packed blockbusters like "Mission: Impossible" to critically acclaimed dramas like "Born on the Fourth of July," which highlights his versatility as an actor.

Logical Breakdown and Explanation:

The student wants to emphasize two aspects of Tom Cruise's career: his *longevity* in Hollywood, meaning how long he has remained a major star, and the *diversity* of his acting roles, which refers to his ability to perform in a wide range of film genres, from action blockbusters to deep, dramatic roles. The correct answer must effectively highlight both the duration and range of his career.

Option C is correct because it directly addresses both the longevity of Tom Cruise's career ("over a career spanning more than three decades") and the diversity of his acting roles by mentioning both action-packed blockbusters like *Mission: Impossible* and complex, dramatic roles like *Born on the Fourth of July* and *Magnolia*. This effectively fulfills the student's goal.

Option A is incorrect because it only focuses on the early stage of Cruise's career in the 1980s, mentioning *Top Gun* and *Rain Man*, but does not address his long-term success or the wide variety of roles he has played since then.

Option B is incorrect because it emphasizes Cruise's versatility by mentioning his range of roles in action and drama, but it fails to highlight his long-term success. Without referencing the longevity of his career, this answer does not fully meet the student's goal.

Option D is incorrect because it focuses on Cruise's awards and the length of his career but neglects to mention the variety of roles he has played, missing the second part of the student's goal, which is to emphasize his versatility as an actor.